Classic Edition

Sources

Psychology

Contemporary Learning Series

2460 Kerper Blvd., Dubuque, IA 52001

Visit us on the Internet
www.mhcls.com

Classic Edition

Sources

Psychology

Edited by

TERRY PETTIJOHN
Ohio State University

Contemporary Learning Series

2460 Kerper Blvd., Dubuque, IA 52001

Visit us on the Internet
www.mhcls.com

EDITORIAL STAFF

Larry Loeppke, Managing Editor
Susan Brusch, Senior Developmental Editor
Jay Oberbroeckling, Developmental Editor
Bonnie Coakley, Editorial Assistant

TECHNOLOGY STAFF

Luke David, eContent Coordinator

PERMISSIONS STAFF

Lenny J. Behnke, Permissions Coordinator
Lori Church, Permissions Coordinator
Shirley Lanners, Permissions Coordinator

MARKETING STAFF

Julie Keck, Senior Marketing Manager
Mary Klein, Marketing Communications Specialist
Alice Link, Marketing Coordinator
Tracie Kammerude, Senior Marketing Assistant

PRODUCTION STAFF

Beth Kundert, Production Manager
Trish Mish, Production Assistant
Jade Benedict, Production Assistant
Kari Voss, Lead Typesetter
Jean Smith, Typesetter
Karen Spring, Typesetter
Sandy Wille, Typesetter
Tara McDermott, Designer
Maggie Lytle, Cover Graphics

Cataloging in Publication Data
Main entry under title: Sources Psychology
1. Psychology. I. Pettijohn, Terry F., *comp.* II. Title: Sources Psychology.
ISBN-13: 978–0–07–340404–2   ISBN-10: 0–07–340404–7   150   ISSN 96–85797

© 2007 by McGraw-Hill Contemporary Learning Series, Dubuque, IA 52001, A Division of The McGraw-Hill Companies.

Fourth Edition

Cover image © Siede Preis/Getty Images

Printed in the United States of America   34567890QPDQPD987   Printed on Recycled Paper

TERRY PETTIJOHN
Ohio State University

Terry F. Pettijohn is a professor of psychology at the Ohio State University at Marion, where he has been teaching introductory psychology for over three decades. As an undergraduate, he attended Alma College and Michigan State University, where he earned his B.S. in 1970. He obtained his M.A. in 1972 and his Ph.D. in experimental psychology in 1974 from Bowling Green State University. He is the author of a number of teaching publications for the introductory psychology course, including Psychology: A ConnecText, 4th ed., published by Dushkin/McGraw-Hill in 1999, as well as the accompanying teaching and testing materials. He served as editor of MicroPsych Computer Network Newsletter, and currently serves on the Advisory Board for the McGraw-Hill's Annual Editions: Psychology. In addition to introductory psychology, he teaches social and experimental psychology, learning and memory, motivation and emotion, human adjustment, psychobiology, animal behavior, and research methods. Dr. Pettijohn has been recognized for his teaching efforts, including being a recipient of the Ohio State University Distinguished Teaching Award three times. His current research interests include the study of human emotion, memory, and animal social behavior. He is a member of the American Psychological Society, the Psychonomic Society, the Animal Behavior Society, the Society for Computers in Psychology, and the American Psychological Association, where he is affiliated with the Society for the Teaching of Psychology.

Preface

*A*lthough barely a century old as a formal discipline, the study of psychology has revolutionized how we look at ourselves and others. Psychology is the science of behavior and cognition; it is a rigorous brain science and, at the same time, it seeks to help people with adjustment problems. Psychologists study behaviors, such as eating, talking, writing, running, or fighting, precisely because they can be directly observed and recorded. But psychologists also study mental processes, such as dreaming, thinking, remembering, and problem solving, which are not directly observable and are often studied through reports provided by human research participants. Psychologists are also interested in the physiological processes that often accompany both overt behavior and cognition. Finally, some psychologists are concerned with applying psychological principles to help people become more successful in their lives.

Most introductory psychology textbooks cover the important topics in psychology, but are not able to go into the depth required for complete understanding of the discipline. Textbooks summarize results of research studies, but the richness of the original sources is not available. The selections in this book supplement the textbook by providing the original sources for some of the landmark studies in our discipline. They allow students to obtain a "behind the scenes" look at how the leaders in psychology think, feel, conduct research, and develop theories.

Many instructors want students to develop critical thinking skills in their courses. One excellent opportunity is to provide original articles and chapters written by the prominent researchers and scholars who carved out psychology as we currently know it. Some of these writers are of historical significance, while others are on the cutting edge of research and knowledge today. Through reading what these psychologists have to say, students can truly appreciate what psychology is currently and where it is going. In many ways, being able to read original selections

provides a "behind the scenes" glimpse of the making of psychology.

As a discipline, psychology has evolved its own history of ideas and thinkers, research methods, and theories. In this volume I have put into your hands directly those researchers and writers whose works are essential to the study of psychology. Classic Edition Sources—Psychology (4th ed.) brings together 50 selections of enduring intellectual value—classic articles, reviews, book chapter excerpts, and research studies—that have shaped the study of psychology and our contemporary understanding of it. The book includes carefully edited selections from the works of the most distinguished psychological researchers and practitioners, past and present, from William James, Sigmund Freud, and B.F. Skinner to Mary D.S. Ainsworth, David Buss, Martin Seligman, and Elizabeth F. Loftus. These selections allow you to obtain a behind-the-scenes look, so to speak, at psychology in the making.

This edition represents over 100 years of psychological thought and application. The actual dates of publication range from 1890 to 1995. I have made every effort to portray psychology as a dynamic and changing discipline. Obviously, new research has modified our understanding of some of the ideas covered in some of the selections; nonetheless, using these original sources will enrich your understanding of psychology and its core concepts.

Glancing over the Table of Contents should convince you that many of the people most frequently cited in psychology textbooks are included here. These widely recognized psychologists have made major contributions to the field and are well-respected researchers and writers. Care has been taken to provide something representative of each person included. Of course, not everyone who made major contributions to psychology was able to be included in the final Table of Contents. But I believe the rich diversity of psychology is captured by the final selections.

REVISION PROCEDURE

The challenge of revising this book was carefully considered. In the first edition, I paid great attention to finding those classic works that could best communicate the excitement of psychology. Readability was the top priority, and each selection was carefully edited so that the essence of the original work could be readily understood. Students were able to experience first hand many of the greatest thinkers in psychology. The descriptions in their textbook came alive through the actual writings of these highly influential people. These goals also guided the development of subsequent editions.

I wanted to ensure that the fourth edition continued to be truly representative of the breadth of psychology, both in terms of the distinguished people and of the important issues. I began by reviewing hundreds of sources that were not included in earlier editions, as well as the most historical and contemporary influential articles. Computer searches identified writings by some of the well-respected names in psychology. I asked students to provide feedback on the most effective selections as well as the ones that were not quite as informative. Unfortunately, much of the feedback I received was extremely positive on almost all of the selections, making the process of replacing selections a very difficult one. Although not everyone will agree with the final decisions on individual selections, I believe that with the advice of many people I was able to significantly strengthen the book through inclusion of some of the best work of the past century.

New to the fourth edition are 19 selections from some of the most distinguished researchers, theorists, writers, and practitioners in psychology. Care was taken to include gender and cultural diversity issues as they relate to the discipline of psychology. In many ways, the most difficult task was deleting selections, many of which are extremely interesting and important. I am confident that the final compilation of writings will challenge students to think and discuss the core issues that make up psychology today. Some of the selections provide theories that have shaped our discipline; some discuss crucial issues that have confronted psychologists during the past century; and many present the results of original research studies. Together they comprise a snapshot of psychology as it currently exists, including important landmarks in its development.

ORGANIZATION OF THE BOOK

The selections are organized topically around 15 of the major areas of study within psychology: Introduction, psychobiology, sensation and perception, sleep and consciousness, learning, human memory, cognition and intelligence, motivation, emotion, human development, personality, stress and adjustment, abnormal behavior, and social psychology. The selections are organized so as to parallel most introduction to psychology textbooks. This means that these original sources, these classic works that underlie the key psychological concepts covered in the textbooks, can be easily read along with any textbook. However, each selection is independent and can be assigned in any order that is assigned by your instructor.

Included at the front of this book is a listing of relevant Internet links that should be of interest to you as you investigate the topics presented in the selections you read. I have tried to include links that are focused and useful in helping you understand the concepts. There are many resources available on the Internet to help you learn about psychology. In addition to the specific ones included for each unit, I have also included some general psychology sites that contain information and additional links to other resources.

New to this edition is a timeline of important dates in the history of psychology. Located at the front of the book, this timeline is a valuable resource for you to put each selection within a historical context. When you read a selection, be sure to check the Internet resources and the timeline for background information and a time perspective as you study and learn.

SUGGESTIONS FOR READING EACH SELECTION

As you read these original writings, it is important to keep in mind that ideas and standards have evolved over the last century. In particular, changes in ethical concerns and in how language is used need to be mentioned here. Currently there are very strict ethical guidelines for conducting human and animal research. Today, researchers must submit proposals to committees that ensure that ethical standards are met. Some of the studies carried out in the past would not be considered ethical today. As you read these selections, consider how the research contributed to psychology and whether or not the benefits outweighed the potential harm to the individuals who participated in the actual research studies.

Each selection is representative of the time in which it was written. Just as psychologists have become more sensitive to ethical considerations over the years, so too have they become more aware of the issue of gender, particularly as regards language. Many of the older articles use the masculine pronoun he when referring to both men and women, and some of the early studies had only male participants. I recommend that you view each selection in the context of when it was written and focus on the psychological issues rather than the semantic ones. These classic studies have had a major impact on the development of psychology as a discipline and should be read from that perspective.

Each selection is preceded by an introductory headnote that establishes the relevance of the selection, provides biographical information about the author, and includes a brief background discussion of the topic. I have also provided suggestions for understanding statistical tests and thought questions designed to guide critical thinking. It is important to read the headnote before beginning the selection itself.

As you read these selections, you will experience first-hand the ideas of some of the most important and influential psychologists. Remember that in most cases they are writing not to students but to other professionals in their field. This means that some of the selections will be more challenging to read, but it also means that you will gain a rare behind the scenes experience of how psychologists think and write.

Take an active approach when reading each selection. For example, when reading an experiment, determine what the research hypothesis is, identify the independent and dependent variables, and analyze the research methodology. Does the experiment raise ethical concerns? Do the conclusions stem from the results? Are there any extraneous variables or alternative explanations for the results? When reading a theoretical or summary article, organize the main themes, identify the conclusions, evaluate the relevance of the theory, and question the applications to everyday situations.

As you read a selection, consider the setting in which it was written. Note the date of publication and the institutional location of the author. If it is a research article, note the participants who served in the research. Many of these research articles were mainly concerned with American participants. Could the results be generalized to other cultures? How might a multicultural perspective affect the study? You should refer back to your textbook to determine how the selection fits into the overall psychological literature. Was it written early or late in the author's career? Are there conflicting theories or research findings?

Let me make a couple of additional study suggestions to help you get the most out of each selection. First, be sure to read the headnote to gain background information on the topic and on the author. Recognize that some of these selections are easy to read and understand, whereas others may have more challenging language, theories, or statistical concepts. Focus on the main ideas and important concepts in each selection. Remember that journal research articles include an introduction to the problem, a description of the research methods, a presentation of the results, and a discussion of the significance of the results. Selections from book chapters often discuss and summarize research and theories, and thus are written in a more informal style. When you finish reading a selection, reread the headnote to make sure that you focused on the important concepts. Finally, take notes on the selection and reflect upon the importance of the writing to your understanding of psychology.

A WORD TO THE INSTRUCTOR

An instructor's manual with test questions (including multiple-choice and essay questions) is available for instructors using this book of readings in the classroom.

ACKNOWLEDGMENTS

I was extremely excited when I was first approached with the idea for this reader. For a long time I had wanted to be able to introduce my students to original writings in psychology. I was thrilled to be able to share with students the excitement of learning directly from some of the most influential figures in psychology.

This project is very much a joint effort. Although my name as editor is the only one on the cover, I had lots of help from many people. The McGraw-Hill editorial staff, especially Senior Developmental Editor Susan Brusch, deserve much credit in rethinking this edition. I appreciate the valuable feedback from instructors across the country who have used previous editions of the book. I thank the many students who used earlier editions of the book and took the time to provide evaluation feedback. Whenever I had a question about the readability or relevance of a selection, my students provided comments and suggestions. I especially appreciate the support of the Ohio State University in facilitating scholarship. My father, Don, provided suggestions for topics in everyday life. My late mother, Ella Jean, provided a source of motivation. My wife, Bernie, typed the materials and provided much emotional support. And my family, Terry and his wife Shelley, Karen and her husband Kenny, and Tommy, were patient as I worked on this project.

Classic Edition Sources—Psychology (4th ed.) is designed particularly to meet the needs of those instructors who want to convey to students the rich-ness of the psychological perspective through original writings. I have worked hard to produce a valuable resource, and I would very much appreciate any comments or suggestions you might have on the book. Although I feel that these selections represent some of the most significant studies in psychology, not everyone will agree with all of the particular selections. I promise to carefully consider all of your suggestions as the book goes through the revision process (my email address is Pettijohn.1@osu.edu). I hope you find this collection useful in your teaching.

Terry F. Pettijohn
Ohio State University

Contents

Sensation and Perception *31*

Sleep and Consciousness *37*

Learning 48

Human Memory 63

Cognition and Intelligence 81

8   Motivation   *92*

9   Emotion   *106*

Human Development   *120*

Personality   *137*

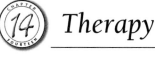

(15) *Social Psychology* 190

Internet References

General Internet Sites for Psychology

The Virtual Psychology Classroom
Allpsych Online, a Virtual Classroom is a comprehensive site with many links for psychology.
http://allpsych.com/

American Psychological Association
The APA site provides numerous resources in all areas of psychology, from careers to current applications.
http://www.apa.org

Association for Psychological Science
The APS site provides resources for teaching and research in scientific psychology.
http://www.psychologicalscience.org

Psych Web Resources
This Georgia Southern University site run by Russ Dewey provides numerous psychology resource links in all areas. A great place to start.
http://www.psywww.com

Psychology Online Resource Central
An online resource for psychology students and their professors, with numerous psychology links.
http://www.psych-central.com

Social Science, Psychology
This is a general psychology search site.
http://dir.yahoo.com/Social_Science/Psychology/

Psychology Tutorials and Demonstrations
http://psych.hanover.edu/Krantz/tutor.html
Tutorials in Psychology from Hanover College. Site is maintained by John Krantz.

Center for Psychology Resources
Centre for Psychology Resources at Athabasca University provides many links and information.
http://psych.athabascau.ca/html/aupr/psycres.shtml

Chapter 1

Divisions of the American Psychological Association
Description and information on the divisions of the American Psychological Association.
http://www.apa.org/about/division.html

Today in the History of Psychology
The APA's historical database is a collection of dates and brief descriptions
of over 3,100 events in the history of psychology, maintained by Warren Street.
http://www.cwu.edu/~warren/today.html

William James
Emory University's site on William James, with biographical information and excerpts from his writings.
http://www.emory.edu/EDUCATION/mfp/james.html

Center for Evolutionary Psychology
The Center for Evolutionary Psychology site at the University of California Santa Barbara provides information on evolutionary psychology.
http://www.psych.ucsb.edu/research/cep/

Chapter 2

Basic Neural Processes
Tutorial on neurons and brain structures developed by John Krantz of Hanover College.
http://psych.hanover.edu/Krantz/neurotut.html

Basic Neural Processes
Drugs, Brain, and Behavior, a webbook by C. Robin Timmons & Leonard W. Hamilton.
http://www.rci.rutgers.edu/~lwh/drugs/

Human Genome Project Information
Behavioral genetics information from the Human Genome Project website.
http://www.ornl.gov/sci/techresources/Human_Genome/elsi/behavior.shtml

Neurotransmitter Net
Neurotransmitter Net website provides information about neurotransmitters and various conditions.
http://www.neurotransmitter.net/

Chapter 3

Gestalt Psychology
Gestalt psychology website by George Boeree provides information on people and theories of Gestalt psychology.
http://www.ship.edu/~cgboeree/gestalt.html

Visual Perceptions
Joy of Visual Perception webbook by Peter Kaiser of York University.
http://www.yorku.ca/eye/

Illusions Gallery
A series of visual illusions created by David Landrigan, University of Massachusetts.
http://dragon.uml.edu/psych/

Eye, Brain, and Vision
Eye Brain and Vision webbook by David Hubel.
http://neuro.med.harvard.edu/site/dh/bcontex.htm

Chapter 4

Tips for Better Sleep
Resources and information on dreaming and sleep disorders.
http://www.sleepnet.com/

Basics of Sleep Behavior
Basics of sleep behavior provided by Sleep Research Society.
http://www.sleephomepages.org/sleepsyllabus/sleephome.html

Study of Dreams
International Association for the Study of Dreams website contains information and a journal on dreams.
http://www.asdreams.org/

Chapter 5

Positive Reinforcement
A positive reinforcement interactive exercise developed by Lyle Grant, Athabasca University.
http://server.bmod.athabascau.ca/html/prtut/reinpair.htm

B. F. Skinner
B. F. Skinner Foundation website provides information and resources about psychologist B. F. Skinner.
http://www.bfskinner.org/

Chapter 6

Memory Techniques and Mnemonics
Memory Techniques and Mnemonics site from Mindtools provides much information and suggested activities to improve your memory.
http://www.psychwww.com/mtsite/memory.html

Alzheimer's Association
The Alzheimer's Home Page site provides information on Alzheimer's disease.
http://www.alz.org/

Chapter 7

Human Intelligence
Human intelligence website maintained by Jonathan Plucker of Indiana University.
http://www.indiana.edu/~intell/

Sensitive Language
Sensitive Language website at Random House provides information on sexist language.
http://www.randomhouse.com/words/language/avoid_guide.html

Chapter 8

Humanistic Psychology
The Association for Humanistic Psychology website contains historical as well as contemporary humanistic psychology resources.
http://ahpweb.org/

Self Efficacy
Information on Self-Efficacy - A community of scholars website provides many resources on the topic of self-efficacy.
http://www.des.emory.edu/mfp/self-efficacy.html

Chapter 9

Facial Analysis
The Perceptual Science Laboratory at the University of California Santa Cruz, has put together this facial analysis page, which provides information and resources on researchers such as Paul Ekman.
http://mambo.ucsc.edu/psl/fanl.html

Emotion
The Emotion Home Page, maintained by Jean-Marc Fellous and Eva Hudlicka, provides information and resources on research in emotion.
http://emotion.bme.duke.edu/emotion.html

Ways to be Romantic
1001 Ways to be Romantic site by Gregory Godek provides romance tips and information.
http://www.1001waystoberomantic.com/romantic_tips.htm

Chapter 10

The Jean Piaget Archives
Jean Piaget Archives site, with biographical and scientific achievement information.
http://www.unige.ch/piaget/Presentations/presentg.html

Human Development Resources
Developmental resources, including theories of development (including Freud, Piaget, and Erikson). Site at George Mason University maintained by Adam Winsler and Susan Keegan.
http://classweb.gmu.edu/awinsler/ordp/topic.html

Attachment Theory and Research
Attachment: Theory and Research website at State University of New York Stoney Brook provides information on attachment.
http://www.psychology.sunysb.edu/attachment/

Chapter 11

The Personality Project
The Personality Project site of William Revelle, director of the Graduate Program in Personality in the Department of Psychology at Northwestern University, has research resources in personality.
http://personality-project.org/

Personality Theories
Personality Theories, a site maintained by C. George Boeree, of Shippensburg University, provides complete descriptions of many theories of personality.
http://www.ship.edu/~cgboeree/perscontents.html

Chapter 12

Hot to Master Stress

The How to Master Stress site by Mind Tools provides useful information on stress and stress management.

http://www.psychwww.com/mtsite/smpage.html

Psychology Self Help

Psych Web's psychology self-help resources on the Internet has numerous adjustment and self-help resource links.

http://www.psychwww.com/resource/selfhelp.htm

Chapter 13

Disorders

The Mental Health Infosource site provides information on a variety of psychological disorders.

http://www.mhsource.com/disorders/

Dr. John Grohol's Psych Central

Symptoms and Treatments of Mental Disorders from John Grohol's Psych Central provides a wealth of information on psychological disorders.

http://psychcentral.com/disorders/

Chapter 14

Psychotherapy

About Psychotherapy website by Bennett Pologe provides information and resources on psychotherapy.
http://www.aboutpsychotherapy.com/TMain.htm

APA Help Center

The American Psychological Association's HelpCenter site presents information on getting help with personal problems.
http://www.apahelpcenter.org/

Chapter 15

Social Psychology Network

The Social Psychology Network is maintained by Scott Plous of Wesleyan University, and provides a vast array of resources and links to information on social psychology.
http://www.socialpsychology.org/

Social Cognition

This social cognition paper archive and information center is maintained by Elliot Smith of Purdue University.
http://www.psych.purdue.edu/~esmith/scarch.html

Stanley Milgram

The Stanley Milgram Page includes information on his biography as well as his theories and research.
http://muskingum.edu/~psychology/psycweb/history/milgram.htm

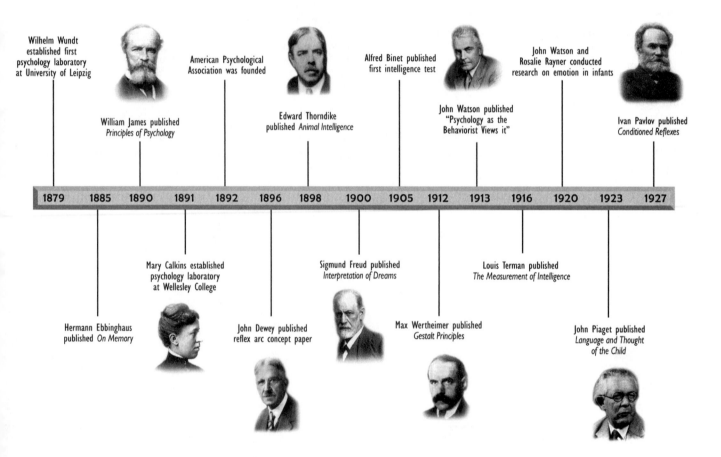

Wilhelm Wundt established first psychology laboratory at University of Leipzig

William James published *Principles of Psychology*

American Psychological Association was founded

Edward Thorndike published *Animal Intelligence*

Alfred Binet published first intelligence test

John Watson published "Psychology as the Behaviorist Views it"

John Watson and Rosalie Rayner conducted research on emotion in infants

Ivan Pavlov published *Conditioned Reflexes*

1879 1885 1890 1891 1892 1896 1898 1900 1905 1912 1913 1916 1920 1923 1927

Hermann Ebbinghaus published *On Memory*

Mary Calkins established psychology laboratory at Wellesley College

John Dewey published reflex arc concept paper

Sigmund Freud published *Interpretation of Dreams*

Max Wertheimer published *Gestalt Principles*

Louis Terman published *The Measurement of Intelligence*

John Piaget published *Language and Thought of the Child*

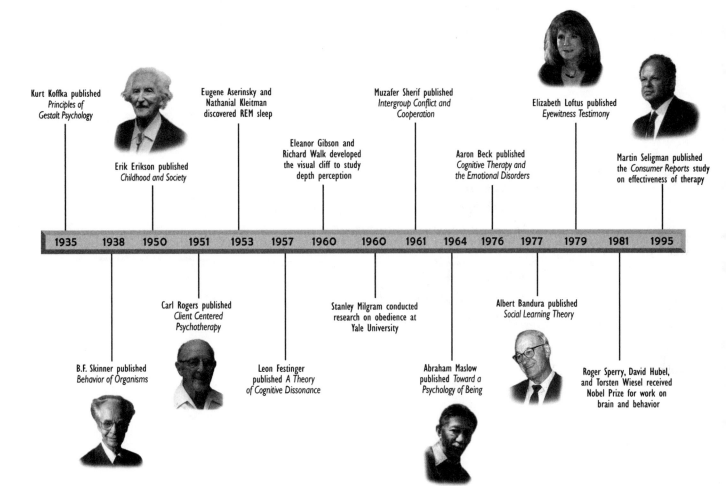

Kurt Koffka published
*Principles of
Gestalt Psychology*

Eugene Aserinsky and
Nathanial Kleitman
discovered REM sleep

Muzafer Sherif published
*Intergroup Conflict and
Cooperation*

Elizabeth Loftus published
Eyewitness Testimony

Erik Erikson published
Childhood and Society

Eleanor Gibson and
Richard Walk developed
the visual cliff to study
depth perception

Aaron Beck published
*Cognitive Therapy and
the Emotional Disorders*

Martin Seligman published
the *Consumer Reports* study
on effectiveness of therapy

1935	1938	1950	1951	1953	1957	1960	1960	1961	1964	1976	1977	1979	1981	1995

Carl Rogers published
*Client Centered
Psychotherapy*

Stanley Milgram conducted
research on obedience at
Yale University

Albert Bandura published
Social Learning Theory

B.F. Skinner published
Behavior of Organisms

Leon Festinger
published *A Theory
of Cognitive Dissonance*

Abraham Maslow
published *Toward a
Psychology of Being*

Roger Sperry, David Hubel,
and Torsten Wiesel received
Nobel Prize for work on
brain and behavior

Introducing Psychology

The Scope of Psychology

William James (1890)

The American psychologist William James's *Principles of Psychology*, published in 1890, was a major milestone in the history of psychology. In it, James asserts that psychology should focus on the functions of consciousness, an idea that helped establish the school of functionalism and that continues to be important to the study of psychology today.

James (1842–1910) obtained his M. D. from Harvard University in 1869 and accepted a teaching position in psychology there three years later. He was a popular professor at Harvard, and wrote on a variety of topics, including consciousness, emotion, personality, learning, and religion. His impact in psychology is still evident today, as students continue to learn about the topics he wrote about back at the turn of last century.

This selection is taken from James's most famous work, the two-volume *Principles of Psychology*. In it, James argues that psychology is the "science of mental life." Although he includes feelings and cognitions in his definition of psychology, he emphasizes the role of the brain in behaviors that serve the function of survival. His book formed the cornerstone of many early psychology courses, and it encouraged psychologists to take a broad view of their discipline. This book is still very much read and studied today. As you read this selection, note the changes that have occurred since James wrote about psychology.

Key Concept: an early definition of psychology

APA Citation: James, W. (1890). *Principles of psychology*. *Volume 1*. New York: Holt.

*P*sychology is the Science of Mental Life, both of its phenomena and their conditions. The phenomena are such things as we call feelings, desires, cognitions, reasonings, decisions, and the like; and, superficially considered, their variety and complexity is such as to leave a chaotic impression on the observer. ...

[R]eflection shows that phenomena [experience in the outer world] have absolutely no power to influence our ideas until they have first impressed our senses and our brain. The bare existence of a past fact is no ground for our remembering it. Unless we have seen it, or somehow *undergone* it, we shall never know of its having been. The experiences of the body are thus one of the conditions of the faculty of memory being what it is. And a very small amount of reflection on facts shows that one part of the body, namely, the brain, is the part whose experiences are directly concerned. If the nervous communication be cut off between the brain and other parts, the experiences of those other parts are non-existent for the mind. The eye is blind, the ear deaf, the hand insensible and motionless. And conversely, if the brain be injured, consciousness is abolished or altered, even although every other organ in the body be ready to play its normal part. A blow on the

head, a sudden subtraction of blood, the pressure of an apoplectic hemorrhage, may have the first effect; whilst a very few ounces of alcohol or grains of opium or hasheesh, or a whiff of chloroform or nitrous oxide gas, are sure to have the second. The delirium of fever, the altered self of insanity, are all due to foreign matters circulating through the brain, or to pathological changes in that organ's substance. The fact that the brain is the one immediate bodily condition of the mental operations is indeed so universally admitted nowadays that I need spend no more time in illustrating it, but will simply postulate it and pass on. ...

Bodily experiences, therefore, and more particularly brain-experiences, must take a place amongst those conditions of the mental life of which Psychology need take account. ...

Our first conclusion, then, is that a certain amount of brain-physiology must be presupposed or included in Psychology.

In still another way the psychologist is forced to be something of a nervephysiologist. Mental phenomena are not only conditioned ... by bodily processes; but they lead to them. ... That they lead to *acts* is of course the most familiar of truths, but I do not merely mean acts in the sense of voluntary and deliberate muscular performances. Mental states occasion also changes in the calibre of blood-vessels, or alteration in the heart-beats, or processes more subtle still, in glands and viscera. If these are taken into account, as well as acts which follow at some *remote period* because the mental state was once there, it will be safe to lay down the general law that *no mental modification ever occurs which is not accompanied or followed by a bodily change*. The ideas and feelings, *e.g.* , which these present printed characters excite in the reader's mind not only occasion movements of his eyes and nascent movements of articulation in him, but will some day make him speak, or take sides in a discussion, or give advice, or choose a book to read, differently from what would have been the case had they never impressed his retina. Our psychology must therefore take account not only of the conditions antecedent to mental states, but of their resultant consequences as well.

But actions originally prompted by conscious intelligence may grow so automatic by dint of habit as to be apparently unconsciously performed. Standing, walking, buttoning and unbuttoning, piano-playing, talking, even saying one's prayers, may be done when the mind is absorbed in other things. The performances of animal *instinct* seem semi-automatic, and the *reflex acts* of self-preservation certainly are so. Yet they resemble intelligent acts in bringing about the *same ends* at which the animals' consciousness, on other occasions, deliberately aims. Shall the study of such machine-like yet purposive acts as these be included in Psychology?

The boundary line of the mental is certainly vague. It is better not to be pedantic, but to let the science be as vague as its subject, and include such phenomena as these if by so doing we can throw any light on the main business in hand. It will ere long be seen, I trust, that we can; and that we gain much more by a broad than by a narrow conception of our subject. At a certain stage in the development of every science a degree of vagueness is what best consists with fertility. On the whole, few recent formulas have done more real service of a rough sort in psychology than the … one that the essence of mental life and of bodily life are one, namely, 'the adjustment of inner to outer relations.' Such a formula is vagueness incarnate; but because it takes into account the fact that minds inhabit environments which act on them and on which they in turn react; because, in short, it takes mind in the midst of all its concrete relations, it is immensely more fertile than the old-fashioned 'rational psychology,' which treated the soul as a detached existent, sufficient unto itself, and assumed to consider only its nature and properties. I shall therefore feel free to make any sallies into zoology or into pure nerve-physiology which may seem instructive for our purposes, but otherwise shall leave those sciences to the physiologists.

Can we state more distinctly still the manner in which the mental life seems to intervene between impressions made from without upon the body, and reactions of the body upon the outer world again? Let us look at a few facts.

If some iron filings be sprinkled on a table and a magnet brought near them, they will fly through the air for a certain distance and stick to its surface. A savage seeing the phenomenon explains it as the result of an attraction or love between the magnet and the filings. But let a card cover the poles of the magnet, and the filings will press forever against its surface without its ever occurring to them to pass around its sides and thus come into more direct contact with the object of their love. …

If now we pass from such actions as these to those of living things, we notice a striking difference. Romeo wants Juliet as the filings want the magnet; and if no obstacles intervene he moves towards her by as straight a line as they. But Romeo and Juliet, if a wall be built between them, do not remain idiotically pressing their faces against its opposite sides like the magnet and the filings with the card. Romeo soon finds a circuitous way, by scaling the wall or otherwise, of touching Juliet's lips directly. With the filings the path is fixed; whether it reaches the end depends on accidents. With the lover it is the end which is fixed, the path may be modified indefinitely.

Such contrasts between living and inanimate performances end by leading men to deny that in the physical world final purposes exist at all. Loves and desires are today no longer imputed to particles of iron or of air. No one supposes now that the end of any activity which they may display is an ideal purpose presiding over the activity from its outset. … The end, on the contrary, is deemed a mere passive result, … having had, so to speak, no voice in its own production. Alter the pre-existing conditions, and with inorganic materials you bring forth each time a different apparent end. But with intelligent agents, altering the conditions changes the activity displayed, but not the end reached; for here the idea of the yet unrealized end co-operates with the conditions to determine what the activities shall be.

The pursuance of future ends and the choice of means for their attainment are thus the mark and criterion of the presence of mentality in a phenomenon. We all use this test to discriminate between an intelligent and a mechanical performance. We impute no mentality to sticks and stones, because they never seem to move for *the sake of* anything, but always when pushed, and then indifferently and with no sign of choice. So we unhesitatingly call them senseless.

Just so we form our decision upon the deepest of all philosophic problems: Is the [C]osmos [the universe] an expression of intelligence rational in its inward nature, or a brute external fact pure and simple? If we find ourselves, in contemplating it, unable to banish the impression that it is a realm of final purposes, that it exists for the sake of something, we place intelligence at the heart of it and have a religion. If, on the contrary, in surveying its irremediable flux, we can think of the present only as so much mere mechanical sprouting from the past, occurring with no reference to the future, we are atheists and materialists.

Psychology as the Behaviorist Views It

John B. Watson (1913)

From the 1920s through the 1960s the field of psychology was largely dominated by behaviorists, who focused on the objective measurement of behavior. The founder of the school of behaviorism was John B. Watson, whose view of psychology as a "purely objective experimental branch of natural science" had a major influence on early psychologists. Watson's belief that psychology should be the science of overt behavior, modeled after the natural sciences, is expressed in this selection.

Watson (1878–1958) earned his Ph.D. in experimental psychology from the University of Chicago in 1903. He began teaching at the John Hopkins University in 1908 and stayed there until a divorce forced him to resign in 1920. Although he left academic psychology after only 12 years for a career in advertising, his influence is still felt in the discipline today.

This selection is from "Psychology as the Behaviorist Views It," published in *Psychological Review* in 1913. This article marked the introduction of the school of behaviorism. In it, Watson discards the subject of consciousness and the method of introspection from psychology and argues for an objective study of the behavior of both people and animals. His goal is to help psychology become more applicable in other areas (such as education, law, and business) as it is develops into an experimental natural science.

Key Concept: school of behaviorism

APA Citation: Watson, J. B. (1913). Psychology as the behaviorist views it. *Psychological Review, 20,* 158–177.

*P*sychology as the behaviorist views it is a purely objective experimental branch of natural science. Its theoretical goal is the prediction and control of behavior. Introspection forms no essential part of its methods, nor is the scientific value of its data dependent upon the readiness with which they lend themselves to interpretation in terms of consciousness. The behaviorist, in his efforts to get a unitary scheme of animal response, recognizes no dividing line between man and brute. The behavior of man, with all of its refinement and complexity, forms only a part of the behaviorist's total scheme of investigation. …

The time seems to have come when psychology must discard all reference to consciousness; when it need no longer delude itself into thinking that it is making mental states the object of observation. We have become so enmeshed in speculative questions concerning the elements of mind, the nature of conscious content (for example, imageless thought, attitudes, … etc.) that I, as an experimental student, feel that something is wrong with our premises and the types of problems which develop from them. There is no longer any guarantee that we all mean the same thing when we use the terms now current in psychology. Take the case of sensation. A sensation is defined in terms of its attributes. One psychologist will state with readiness that the attributes of a visual sensation are *quality, extension, duration,* and *intensity.* Another will add *clearness.* Still another that of *order.* I doubt if any one psychologist can draw up a set of statements describing what he means by sensation which will be agreed to by three other psychologists of different training. Turn for a moment to the question of the number of isolable sensations. Is there an extremely large number of color sensations— or only four, red, green, yellow and blue? Again, yellow, while psychologically simple, can be obtained by superimposing red and green spectral rays upon the same diffusing surface! If, on the other hand, we say that every just noticeable difference in the spectrum is a simple sensation, and that every just noticeable increase in the white value of a given color gives simple sensations, we are forced to admit that the number is so large and the conditions for obtaining them so complex that the concept of sensation is unusable, either for the purpose of analysis or that of synthesis. Titchener, who has fought the most valiant fight in this country for a psychology based upon introspection, feels that these differences of opinion as to the number of sensations and their attributes; as to whether there are relations (in the sense of elements) and on the many others which seem to be fundamental in every attempt at analysis, are perfectly natural in the present undeveloped state of psychology. While it is admitted that every growing science is full of unanswered questions, surely only those who are wedded to the system as we now have it, who have fought and suffered for it, can confidently believe that there will ever be any greater uniformity than there is now in the answers we have to such questions. I firmly believe that two hundred years from now, unless the introspective method is discarded, psychology will still be divided on the question as to whether auditory sensations have the quality of 'extension,' whether intensity is an attribute which can be applied to color, whether there is a difference in 'texture' between image and sensation and upon many hundreds of others of like character. ...

I was greatly surprised some time ago when I opened Pillsbury's book and saw psychology defined as the 'science of behavior.' A still more recent text states that psychology is the 'science of mental behavior.' When I saw these promising statements I thought, now surely we will have texts based upon different lines. After a few pages the science of behavior is dropped and one finds the conventional treatment of sensation, perception, imagery, etc., along with certain shifts in emphasis and additional facts which serve to give the author's personal imprint. ...

This leads me to the point where I should like to make the argument constructive. I believe we can write a psychology, define it as Pillsbury, and never go back upon our definition: never use the terms consciousness, mental states, mind, content, introspectively verifiable, imagery, and the like. ... It can be done in terms of stimulus and response, in terms of habit formation, habit integrations and the like. Furthermore, I believe that it is really worthwhile to make this attempt now.

The psychology which I should attempt to build up would take as a starting point, first, the observable fact that organisms, man and animal alike, do adjust themselves to their environment by means of hereditary and habit equipments. These adjustments may be very adequate or they may be so inadequate that the organism barely maintains its existence; secondly, that certain stimuli lead the organisms to make the responses. In a system of psychology completely worked out, given the response the stimuli can be predicted; given the stimuli the response can be predicted. Such a set of statements is crass and raw in the extreme, as all such generalizations must be. Yet they are hardly more raw and less realizable than the ones which appear in the psychology texts of the day. I possibly might illustrate my point better by choosing an everyday problem which anyone is likely to meet in the course of his work. Some time ago I was called upon to make a study of certain species of birds. Until I went to Tortugas I had never seen these birds alive. When I reached there I found the animals doing certain things:

some of the acts seemed to work peculiarly well in such an environment, while others seemed to be unsuited to their type of life. I first studied the responses of the group as a whole and later those of individuals. In order to understand more thoroughly the relation between what was habit and what was hereditary in these responses, I took the young birds and reared them. In this way I was able to study the order of appearance of hereditary adjustments and their complexity, and later the beginnings of habit formation. My efforts in determining the stimuli which called forth such adjustments were crude indeed. Consequently my attempts to control behavior and to produce responses at will did not meet with much success. Their food and water, sex and other social relations, light and temperature conditions were all beyond control in a field study. I did find it possible to control their reactions in a measure by using the nest and egg (or young) as stimuli. It is not necessary in this paper to develop further how such a study should be carried out and how work of this kind must be supplemented by carefully controlled laboratory experiments. ... In the main, my desire in all such work is to gain an accurate knowledge of adjustments and the stimuli calling them forth. My final reason for this is to learn general and particular methods by which I may control behavior. ... If psychology would follow the plan I suggest, the educator, the physician, the jurist and the business man could utilize our data in a practical way, as soon as we are able, experimentally, to obtain them. Those who have occasion to apply psychological principles practically would find no need to complain as they do at the present time. Ask any physician or jurist today whether scientific psychology plays a practical part in his daily routine and you will hear him deny that the psychology of the laboratories finds a place in his scheme of work. I think the criticism is extremely just. One of the earliest conditions which made me dissatisfied with psychology was the feeling that there was no realm of application for the principles which were being worked out in content terms.

What gives me hope that the behaviorist's position is a defensible one is the fact that those branches of psychology which have already partially withdrawn from the parent, experimental psychology, and which are consequently less dependent upon introspection are today in a most flourishing condition. Experimental pedagogy, the psychology of drugs, the psychology of advertising, legal psychology, the psychology of tests, and psychopathology are all vigorous growths. These are sometimes wrongly called "practical" or "applied" psychology. Surely there was never a worse misnomer. In the future there may grow up vocational bureaus which really apply psychology. At present these fields are truly scientific and are in search of broad generalizations which will lead to the control of human behavior. For example, we find out by experimentation whether a series of stanzas may be acquired more readily if the whole is learned at once, or whether it is more advantageous to learn each stanza separately and then pass to the succeeding. We do not attempt to apply our findings. The application of this principle is purely voluntary on the part of the teachers. In the psychology of drugs we may show the effect upon behavior of certain doses of caffeine. We may reach the conclusion that caffeine has a good effect upon the speed and accuracy of work. But these are general principles. We leave it to the individual as to whether the results of our tests shall be applied or not. Again, in legal testimony, we test the effects of recency upon the reliability of a witness's report. We test the accuracy of the report with respect to moving objects, stationary objects, color, etc. It depends upon the judicial machinery of the country to decide whether these facts are ever to be applied. For a 'pure' psychologist to say that he is not interested in the questions raised in these divisions of the science because they relate indirectly to the application of psychology shows, in the first place, that he fails to understand the scientific aim in such problems, and secondly, that he is not interested in a psychology which concerns itself with human life. The only fault I have to find with these disciplines is that much of their material is stated in terms of introspection, whereas a statement of terms of objective results would be far more valuable. ...

In concluding, I suppose I must confess to a deep bias on these questions. I have devoted nearly twelve years to experimentation on animals. It is natural that such a one should drift into a theoretical position which is in harmony with his experimental work. Possibly I have put up a straw man and have been fighting that. ... Certainly the position I advocate is weak enough at present and can be attacked from many standpoints. Yet when all this is admitted I still feel that the considerations which I have urged should have a wide influence upon the type of psychology which is to be developed in the future. What we need to do is to start work upon psychology, making *behavior*, not *consciousness*, the objective point of our attack. Certainly there are enough problems in the control of behavior to keep us all working many lifetimes without ever allowing us time to think of consciousness. ... Once launched in the undertaking, we will find ourselves in a short time as far divorced from an introspective psychology as the psychology of the present time is divorced from faculty psychology.

Experimental Psychology at Wellesley College

Mary Whiton Calkins (1892)

Most people have learned about the discipline of psychology through taking academic courses in college. Mary Whiton Calkins was a pioneer in the field. She not only taught but also was active in psychological research and leadership in the American Psychological Association.

Calkins (1863–1930) studied under American psychologist and philosopher William James at Harvard, but it seems she was refused her Ph.D. simply because she was a woman. She accepted a position at Wellesley College, where she conducted research on memory, perception, personality, emotion, and dreaming. Calkins was elected as the first woman president of the American Psychological Association in 1905 and worked to reconcile the structural and functional schools of psychology.

In the following selection, "Experimental Psychology at Wellesley College, " published in 1892 in the *American Journal of Psychology*, Calkins provides a glimpse into her psychology classroom. She carefully describes the details of her experimental psychology class, along with some student experiences and her own insights into the teaching presentations. As you read this selection, imagine what a psychology course was like at the time that Calkin's work was published. How has psychology changed during the past century?

Key Concept: teaching psychology, history

APA Citation: Calkins, M. W. (1892). Experimental psychology at Wellesley College. *American Journal of Psychology, 5*, 464–471.

After the discussion of the relative merits of experimental as compared with merely introspective psychology, a practical question suggests itself concerning the introduction of experimental psychology into the regular college curriculum. This is a complicated problem of expediency, the question of the equipment of the laboratory, of the relative amount of laboratory work, of the proper direction of students' experiments. Such questions are especially prominent in cases in which psychology is a required subject, and in which our course is a general one and must be adapted to students without especial scientific training or without particular interest in experimental work. In such a course, it is sometimes urged, the introduction of experimental methods burdens the general student with details valuable only to the specialist, substitutes technical minutiae for psychological principle and tends to confuse psychology with the other sciences.

This paper is an attempt to meet with difficulties of this sort by the record of a year's experience with a general course in psychology, making extensive use of experi-

mental methods. In the fall of 1892 a course in "Psychology, including Experimental Psychology," was offered at Wellesley College as one of the alternative senior requirements in psychology. The course was taken by fifty-four students, of whom all but one or two had had no previous training in the subject. All of these had taken a year's course, including laboratory work, in chemistry, and only three had failed to follow a similar course in physics. Most had no training in physiology, and many of them had a more or less pronounced distaste for laboratory work. The aim throughout was to supplement, and in no sense to supersede, introspection; to lead students to observe in detail and to verify facts of their ordinary experience; to familiarize them with the results of modern investigation and with the usual experimental methods, and to introduce them to the important works of psychological literature.

The first month was devoted to a study of cerebral physiology. Ladd's "Elements of Psychology" was used in this early part of the course as a text-book. The class work included recitations, informal lectures and some written work on the part of the students. One of these papers, for example, required an enumeration, accompanying a rough diagram, of the parts of the human brain, as developed from the dorsal and ventral sides respectively of the three "primary bulbs." The study of the brain by text-book, by plates, and especially by models, preceded the dissection by each student of a lamb's brain. The brains had been preserved according to Dr. James's directions.[1] (Wide-mouthed candy jars, fitted with rubbers to prevent evaporation, proved an inexpensive substitute for the regular Whitehall and Taitum jars.) The dissection was under the general direction of the instructor. The students were provided with simple directions and were required to identify the most important parts of the brain. The results of this work were very satisfactory. The students, even those who had dreaded the dissection, were practically unanimous in regard to its value, as clearing up the difficult points in cerebral anatomy. In the class room, during this week, in which the dissection was going on, the principal theories of cerebral localization were discussed.

The next six weeks were spent in experimental study of sensation. About seventy experiments were performed by the students on sensations of contact, of pressure, of temperature, of taste, of hearing and of sight. The experiments, almost without exception, were selected from those suggested by Dr. E. C. Sanford in his "Laboratory Course in Psychology,"[2] but re-arranged with reference to the plan of the lectures and of the class discussion. Papyrographed descriptions of the experiments were distributed to the students and commented on in class before the experiments were undertaken. The instructor kept daily laboratory hours in order to answer questions and to offer assistance. Each student was responsible for the record of her own experiments.

In class, reports were made on the results of experiments, and recitations were conducted on the physiology of the different senses. The bearing of the different experiments on the theory of perception was carefully discussed. Special effort was made to free the word "sensation" from the vague, dualistic meaning which it often carries with it; sensation was treated as essentially "the first thing in the way of consciousness." The three theories of perception, Associationist, Intellectualist and Physiological-psychological, were carefully studied, and in this connection parts of Dr. James's chapters on "The Mind-Stuff Theory," "Sensations" and "Perception" were assigned for reading. Of course, in so elementary a course no new experimental results were gained. All the more important experiments usually performed were repeated. The taste experiments were so unpopular that I should never repeat them in a general class of students who are not specializing in the subject. I should also omit most experiments involving exact measurement. For instance, I should do no more than familiarize the class with the use of the Galton bar and of the perimeter.

Some of the students were genuinely interested in the experiments, carried them further than required and made independent observations; a large number, on the other hand, performed them conscientiously, but without especial enthusiasm; some cordially detested them from beginning to end; but almost all recognized their value as a stimulus to observation and as a basis for psychological theory.

The following questions, asked at an informal, forty-five minute examination, suggest the character of the experimental work:—

I. Describe fully the following experiments. State the theories on which they bear and the conclusions which you draw from them:—
a. The "colored shadows" experiment.
b. Scheiner's experiment.
II. What are the dermal senses?
III. What is the (so-called) joint sense? Describe an experiment proving its existence.

In the study of association, the old distinction between association "by contiguity" and that "by similarity" was replaced by one between "desistent association," in which no part of the earlier object of consciousness persists in consciousness and "persistent association," in which all or part of it persists.[3] Dr. James's quantitative distinctions, corresponding with the terms "total," "partial" and "focalized," were also made. Students were referred to Hobbes, to Hartley, to Bain and to Dr. James, and were required to illustrate, by original examples or by quotation, the different sorts of association. This work proved very interesting and was valuable in co-ordinating psychological with literary study. The experimental work accompanying this study illustrated the value of association in shortening intellectual processes, and consisted simply in comparing the slower reading of one hundred unconnected monosyllables with the reading of one hundred connected words. Reading of passages of one hundred words in different languages was also carefully timed and compared.

A more extended experiment in association was later carried out. Each student wrote a list of thirty words, so associated that each suggested the next. The starting point was the word "book," suggested in writing, but not read until the time of the experiment. Each list was studied by its writer, who marked with a V the names of objects or events which were visualized; indicated with a C those connected with childhood life; classified the association, as desistent or as persistent (of quality or of object); and indicated, in each case, the so-called secondary law of the association (recency, frequency or vividness). Of course each list was written when the subject was alone and undisturbed. ...

The subject of attention was discussed on the basis of Dr. James's admirable chapter. The experimental work was in divided attention, the performance and accurate timing of two intellectual processes, first separately and then in combination.

A brief study of consciousness in its "identifying" and "discriminating" aspects was followed by a six-weeks' study of space-perception. Lectures were offered on the three chief theories, the Empiricist, and Nativist-Kantian and the Nativist-Sensational. The required reading included references to Berkeley, to Mill, to Spencer, to D.A. Spalding (MacMillan, February, 1873), to Preyer (Appendix C of Vol. II., The Mind of The Child) [4] to James (parts of the Space-Chapter), to Kant (Aesthetic, "Metaphysical Deduction").

The experiments, of which there were more than thirty, illustrated the methods of gaining, or at least of developing, the space-consciousness. The theories of single vision were carefully studied and were illustrated by diagrams and by "Cyclopean eye" experiments. The study of the perception of depth included an adaptation from Hering's experiment, in which the subject, looking through a tube, finds that he can correctly distinguish, within very small distances, whether a shot is dropped before or behind a black string, stretched before a white background. The fact and the laws of convergence were studied with the aid of a Wheatstone stereoscope.

There followed a consideration of illusions of space; and of Unvisual space, including the experiments suggested by Dr. James on so-called tympanum spatial-sensations, and others, with a telegraph-snapper, on the location of sounds. ...

In the study of memory and of the imagination, the only experiments were a few on "The Mental Span." Students were referred to James, to Burnham, to Lewes, to Ruskin and to Everett. Paramnesia was of course discussed.

Abnormal psychology received, throughout the course, comparatively little attention, because it seemed so evident that a careful study of the facts of normal consciousness must precede any scholarly consideration of the abnormal; because, also, there seemed special need of combating the popular notion which apparently regards psychology as a synonym for hypnotism and telepathy. The abnormal was therefore treated throughout from the point of view of the ordinary consciousness and its phenomena were discussed as exaggerated manifestations of the phases of all consciousness. The subject was naturally introduced by a study of dreams; hypnotism was the only other topic considered.

The study of the emotions and of the will was accompanied by no experimental work. Chapters of Höffding, of James, of Mill, of Spencer and of Darwin formed the required reading; James's theory of the emotions was discussed; a classification of the feelings, adapted from Mercier[5], but rejecting his physiological principle of division, was the starting-point of a somewhat practical discussion.

The last week of the course was occupied with reaction-time experiments, which had been postponed to this time, only through necessary delay in procuring the apparatus; the work should properly have been scattered through the year. There was time for little more than an illustration of method and an approximate verification of the more important results in reactions to sound and in more complicated reactions, involving association, discrimination and choice. Averages of simple reaction-times, with and then without signal, showing a general increase in the time of the latter, were made by several students and included in essays on attention. Students were required to read Jastrow's "Time-Relations of Mental Phenomena."

The study of volition led to several days' discussion of the problems of determinism and indeterminism. This was undertaken with the express remark that the subject is metaphysical and not psychological. The favorable result of this study confirms my opinion of the value of an occasional consideration of so-called metaphysical problems in a general course of psychology, with students who are neither studying philosophy nor specializing in psychology. ...

In place of a final examination, a psychological essay was required. The subjects assigned were very general and were intended as subjects for study rather than as definite essay-headings. The immediate topic of the paper was to be decided after the study and not before. Such subjects as "Association," "Attention," "Memory," "Imagination," "The Psychology of Language," "The Psychology of Childhood," "The Psychology of Blindness," "Aphasia," "Animal Psychology," were chosen in this way.

Notes

1. Since published in the Briefer Course in Psychology, pp. 81–90.
2. American Journal of Psychology.
3. Cf. an article in the Philosophical Review, July, 1892.
4. Inquiries into Human Faculty, pp. 191–203.
5. Mind, Vol. IX.

Human Nature, Individual Differences, and the Importance of Context

Perspectives from Evolutionary Psychology

W. Todd DeKay and David M. Buss (1992)

Trying to understand why people do the things they do has long been a goal of psychologists. One of the newest theoretical approaches to understanding human nature, evolutionary psychology, revives an old biological theme. Because psychology focuses on mental and personality traits rather than physical ones, understanding the role of evolution in the development of psychological mechanisms is a difficult concept for many people to understand.

Todd DeKay was in graduate school at the University of Michigan when he completed his Ph.D. in 1997 under David Buss. Since graduation, he taught at Albright College, and recently was appointed Associate Dean at Franklin and Marshall College. David M. Buss (b. 1953) received his Ph.D. from the University of California in 1981. He joined the faculty of the University of Michigan in 1985, where he was a professor of psychology until he moved to the University of Texas at Austin in 1996. His evolutionary theory of human mate selection is detailed in his book, *The Evolution of Desire: Strategies of Human Mating* (Basic Books, 1994).

This selection, from "Human Nature, Individual Differences and the Importance of Context: Perspectives from Evolutionary Psychology," was published in *Current Directions in Psychology* in 1992. In it, DeKay and Buss present an overview of evolutionary psychology theory and how it is impacting psychology in many areas. As you read this selection, consider the functions of the psychological mechanisms that make each of us unique. One area of controversy is predicting sex differences. What alternative explanations exist for the findings of evolutionary psychologists?

Key Concept: evolutionary psychology

APA Citation: DeKay, W. T., & Buss, D. M. (1992). Human nature, individual differences and the importance of context: Perspectives from evolutionary psychology. *Current Directions in Psychological Science, 1,* 184–189.

Evolutionary psychology is emerging as an important theoretical perspective in many branches of psychology: cognition,[1] perception, psycholinguistics,[2] social psychology,[3] developmental psychology,[4] clinical psychology, and personality psychology.[5] Its promise lies not in supplanting other psychological perspectives or research programs, but rather in adding additional layers of analysis and understanding to human psychological phenomena. Evolutionary psychology starts by posing three important questions that have been relatively neglected over the past century: What are the origins of human psychological mechanisms? What adaptive problems selected for their existence? What functions were they designed to serve?

Most psychologists are Darwinian in the sense that they believe that evolutionary processes are responsible for human origins.[6] The crucial issues are which evolutionary processes have shaped human psychological mechanisms and how these mechanisms have been shaped. Among the major evolutionary processes—mutation, inheritance, drift, isolation, and selection—it is generally recognized that natural selection, or the differential reproduction of genetic variants by virtue of differences in design, is the principal guiding force in the creation of complex, functional mechanisms known as adaptations.

The focus on selection as the key causal process has some heuristic value, but by itself does not get us very far.

Evolutionary theory at this general level of abstraction offers only a few predictions (e.g., that adaptations cannot exist exclusively for the benefit of another species or conspecific competitors) and only the crudest heuristic value (e.g., events surrounding survival and reproduction take on special importance). Evolutionary psychology, in contrast, combines the principles of natural selection with (a) specific evolutionary subtheories, such as the theory of parental investment and sexual selection; (b) an analysis of the specific adaptive problems humans have faced over evolutionary history; and (c) specific models of psychological mechanisms and behavioral strategies that may have evolved as solutions to those adaptive problems. Evolutionary psychology acquires the heuristic and predictive value we associate with powerful scientific theories when these conceptual elements are combined.

Evolved Psychological Mechanisms

Since the cognitive revolution, psychologists have become increasingly aware of the need to understand decision-making rules and other information processing devices in the head. But although most psychologists have jettisoned behaviorism's unworkable antimentalism, many have retained the behavioristic assumption of equipotentiality and assumed that cognitive mechanisms are general-purpose, free of content-specialized procedures.[6] Because psychological mechanisms are often presumed to operate in the same manner regardless of content, the selection of stimuli used in cognitive experiments has often been arbitrary, stripped of context, content, and meaning to the organism—nonsense syllables provide a prototypical exemplar.

Evolutionary psychologists, in contrast, argue that evolved psychological mechanisms cannot be solely general-purpose, are highly likely to be saturated with content, and operate differently in response to external input about different adaptive problems.[7] Just as the body contains a large number of specific and dedicated physiological mechanisms (taste buds, sweat glands, lungs, heart, kidneys, larynx, pituitary gland), so, according to evolutionary psychologists, the mind contains a large number of specialized psychological mechanisms, each "designed"[8] to solve particular adaptive problems. Because what constitutes a "successful solution" to adaptive problems differs across domains (e.g., criteria for food selection differ from criteria for mate selection), the requisite psychological solution mechanisms are likely to be special-purpose and domain tailored.

Some psychologists do not realize that manifest behavior depends on psychological mechanisms plus inputs into those mechanisms, both environmental and interoceptive. Environmental inputs alone cannot cause behavior in the absence of psychological mechanisms designed to process input. If a human, a chimp, and a dog react differently to identical environmental cues, it is because there is something different about the psychological mechanisms of the human, the chimp, and the dog. The central goal of evolutionary psychology is to identify these evolved psychological mechanisms and to understand their functions.

The Centrality of Context in Evolutionary Psychology

A common misconception about evolutionary approaches is that they postulate "instincts"—rigid, genetically inflexible behavior patterns that are invariantly expressed and unmodifiable by the environment. Although this view may have characterized some previous evolutionary perspectives, nothing could be farther from the current views in evolutionary psychology.

Contextual evolutionary analysis takes place at several levels in the causal sequence leading to manifest human behavior. One is the *historical context*—the selection pressures that humans and their ancestors have faced over thousands of generations. Because we share part of our evolutionary history with other species (e.g., humans and chimps share common ancestors), we share some mechanisms with those species (e.g., mechanisms of vision). But because human evolutionary history differs from that of all other species and the selection pressures we experienced were different in many ways (e.g., importance of long-term reciprocity, degree of group-on-group warfare, magnitude of male parental investment), many of our evolved psychological mechanisms are unique to us (e.g., those underlying complex toolmaking and tool use, language, culture, and consciousness). Evolutionary psychology requires an analysis of both these shared and unique features of our historical context.

A second level of contextual analysis in evolutionary psychology is *ontogenetic*. Evolutionary analyses of ontogenetic context have taken two forms. First, experiences during development can dispose individuals toward different strategies.[5] There is some evidence, for example, that absence of the father during childhood shunts individuals toward a more promiscuous mating strategy, whereas the presence of an investing father during childhood shunts individuals toward a more monogamous mating strategy.[4] Clearly, more research is needed to verify this finding. Second, developmental experiences may set different thresholds on species-typical psychological mechanisms. The threshold for responding to a threat with extreme violence is apparently low in some cultures, such as among the Yanomamo Indians of Brazil, and is high in others, such as among the !Kung San of Botswana. Ontogenetic contexts include, of course, sex-differentiated socialization as well as culturally variable input.[7]

The third level of contextual analysis entails description of the *immediate situational inputs* that activate particular psychological mechanisms, just as callous-producing mechanisms are activated only if a person experiences repeated friction to the skin, so psychological mechanisms such as those responsible for sexual jealousy,[9] detection of cheaters,[1] or discriminative parental solicitude[10] are activated only by particular contextual input such as cues to infidelity, cues to nonreciprocation, or the simultaneous presence of genetically related children and stepchildren, respectively.

A central goal of evolutionary psychology is to explicate historical, ontogenetic, and situational forms of contextual input.

Human Nature and Cultural Variation

A long-standing dogma in this century's social science has been that the nature of humans is that they have no nature, except perhaps a few highly domain-general learning mechanisms. Evidence that such a view is empirically untenable has been accumulating over the past decade.[11] Conceptual analyses by scientists in artificial intelligence, psycholinguistics, cognitive psychology, and evolutionary psychology are showing why such a view is untenable even in principle.[7] Humans could not possibly perform the numerous complex, situationally contingent tasks that they do routinely without considerable intricate and domain-dedicated psychological machinery. These psychological mechanisms, coupled with the social, cultural, and ecological inputs that reliably activate them, and linked to the adaptive problems they were "designed" to solve, provide a starting point for a description of human nature. Although exactly which couplings are part of human nature must be determined empirically, possible candidates include childhood fears of loud noises, darkness, snakes, spiders, and strangers; characteristic emotions such as anger, envy, passion, and love; characteristic facial expressions such as those showing happiness and disgust; competition for limited resources; specific mate preferences; classification of kin; love of kin; preferential altruism directed toward kin; socialization from senior kin; play; deceit; concepts of property; enduring reciprocal alliances or friendships; retaliation and revenge; sanctions for crimes against the group; rites of passage; concepts of self; concepts of intentions, beliefs, and desires as part of a theory of mind; status differentiation; status seeking; prestige criteria; humor; gender terminology; sexual attraction; sexual attractiveness; sexual jealousy; sexual modesty; toolmaking; tool use; tools for toolmaking; weapon making; weapon use; coalitions that use weapons for war; collective identities; cooking; coyness; crying; and probably hundreds more (see Brown[11] for an extended list of possibilities).

Hearing references to concepts like human nature, evolved mechanisms, and evolutionary biology, people tend to think the reference is to robotlike automatons, rigidly programmed by genes to carry out activities that are inflexible and impermeable to environmental, social, and cultural influences. Even the most casual observation

shows that people are not like this. We respond with enormous flexibility and variability to even the slightest shifts in context. This observation, reasonably enough, causes most scientists to reject notions of instinctual rigidity, programmed inflexibility, and environmental unmodifiability.

A central message of evolutionary psychology is that the enormous flexibility and context contingency of human behavior *requires* a highly articulated, extremely complex architecture of dedicated, species-typical psychological mechanisms. Without those mechanisms to guide action, the islands of adaptive solutions could never be discovered amid the expansive oceans of maladaptive possibilities.

Sex Differences

Evolutionary psychology provides a powerful framework for predicting when we should and should not expect sex differences. Men and women are expected to differ only in the delimited domains where they have faced different adaptive problems over the course of human evolutionary history. In domains where the sexes have faced the same adaptive problems, no sex differences are expected.

Historically, men and women have faced many adaptive problems that are highly similar. Both sexes needed to maintain body temperature (adaptive problem of thermal regulation), so both sexes have sweat glands and shivering mechanisms. Repeated friction to certain areas of the skin was damaging to both sexes in ancestral environments, so both sexes have callous-producing mechanisms. Analogously, both sexes needed to solve the adaptive problem of identifying a good cooperator when seeking a long-term partner, and this may be one reason why both sexes, across all cultures whose partner preferences have been studied, value kindness in a partner so highly.[12]

In several domains, however, the sexes have faced different adaptive problems. For 99% of human evolutionary history, men faced the adaptive problem of hunting and women of gathering, possible selective reasons for greater male upper body strength and spatial rotation ability and for greater female spatial location memory.[13] Internal fertilization and gestation produced an adaptive problem for men, but not for women, of uncertainty of parenthood. Cryptic or concealed ovulation may have created the adaptive problem for men of knowing when a female was ovulating. The dual male mating strategy, seeking (a) short-term sex partners with little investment and (b) long-term marriage partners with high investment, created for women an adaptive problem of having to discern whether particular men saw them as temporary sex partners or as potential spouses.[14] Sex differences in mate preferences,[12,15] courting strategies,[14] and sexual fantasies[16] correspond remarkably well to these sex-linked adaptive problems. Evolutionary psychology offers the promise of providing a powerful and coherent theory of sexual differences as well as sexual similarities.

Individual Differences

Evolutionary psychology aspires to understand not just our species-typical, sex-differentiated, and culturally differentiated nature, but also the ways in which individuals differ within species, within sex, and within cultures. Several promising avenues of investigation are being pursued. One approach attempts to understand individual differences resulting from different experiences during development. The father-absence versus father-presence theory of individual differences in mating strategies developed by Draper and Belsky[4] represents a fascinating example of the developmental evolutionary psychological approach.

A second approach examines individual differences as a function of different environments that are currently inhabited. People married to partners who are perceived by others as relatively desirable, for example, may be reliably prone to jealousy over time, not because they are inherently "jealous people," but because they inhabit an enduring environment that recurrently activates jealousy mechanisms.

A third approach examines what may be termed "reactive individual differences." Individuals who are mesomorphic are better able to carry out an aggressive strategy, whereas those who are ectomorphic may perforce cultivate diplomatic skills.[17] In this example, it is not the case that some individuals are innately more aggressive or agreeable, but rather that all people have the potential for both characteristics, and the strategy that gets adopted is contingent on species-typical decision rules that evaluate anatomical input and strategic success.

A fourth evolutionary approach to individual differences develops models of frequency-dependent selection that predict genetic differences among members of the same sex. Gangestad and Simpson.[18] for example, have explored individual differences in "sociosexual orientation," the degree to which individuals seek sex with many partners with low investment in each versus with few partners with high investment in each. They present evidence that these individual differences may be heritable, may be bimodally distributed, and may covary with other personality characteristics in ways that support a conception of evolved strategy differences.

Because the analysis of individual differences represents the most recent and least explored avenue of inquiry within evolutionary psychology, it is not clear which among these four approaches (or alternative approaches) will prove most useful. Indeed, some represent competing approaches to the same set of phenomena. Draper and Belsky,[4] for example, propose that differences in mating strategy stem from critical events during development, whereas Gangestad and Simpson[18] propose that they stem from heritable differences caused ultimately by frequency-dependent selection. Both approaches, however, represent improvements over prior evolutionary approaches that examined sex differences in mating strategies but ignored individual differences within sex in the strategies adopted.

Notes

1. L. Cosmides, The logic of social exchange: Has natural selection shaped how humans reason? Studies With the Watson selection task, *Cognition, 31,* 187–276 (1989).
2. S. Pinker and P. Bloom, Natural language and natural selection, *Behavioral and Brain Sciences, 13,* 707–784 (1990).
3. R.E. Nisbett, Evolutionary psychology, biology, and cultural evolution, *Motivation and Emotion, 14,* 255–265 (1991).
4. J. Belsky, L. Steinberg, and P. Draper, Childhood experience, interpersonal development, and reproductive strategy: An evolutionary theory of socialization. *Child Development, 62,* 647–670 (1991).
5. D.M. Buss, Evolutionary personality psychology. *Annual Review of Psychology, 42,* 459 491 (1991).
6. D. Symons, If we're all Darwinians, what's the fuss about? in *Sociobiology and Psychology,* C.B. Crawford, M.F. Smith, and D.L. Krebs, Eds. (Erlbaum, Hillsdale, NJ, 1987).
7. J. Tooby and L. Cosmidos, Psychological foundations of culture, in *The Adapted Mind: Evolutionary Psychology and the Generation of Culture,* J. Barkow, L. Cosmides, and J. Tooby, Eds. (Oxford University Press, New York, 1992).
8. We are not implying that evolution is purposeful or forward-looking; rather, this phrase is shorthand to refer to the adaptive product of the evolutionary process.
9. D.M. Buss, R.J. Larsen, D. Westen, and J. Semmeiroth, Sex differences in jealousy. Evolution, physiology, and psychology. *Psychological Science, 3,* 231–255 (1992).
10. M. Daly and M. Wilson, *Homicide* (Aldine, New York, 1988).
11. D. Brown, *Human Universals* (Temple University Press, Philadelphia, 1991).
12. D.M. Buss, Sex differences in human mate preferences: Evolutionary hypotheses tested in 37 cultures, *Behavioral and Brain Sciences, 12,* 1–49 (1989).
13. I. Silverman and M. Eals, Sex differences in spatial abilities: Evolutionary theory and data, in *The Adapted Mind: Evolutionary Psychology and the Generation of Culture,* J. Barkow, L. Cosmides, and J. Tooby, Eds. (Oxford University Press, New York, 1992).
14. D.M. Buss and D.P. Schmitt, Sexual strategies theory: A contextual evolutionary analysis of human mating. *Psychological Review* (in press).
15. D.T. Kenrick and R.C. Keefe, Age preferences in mates reflect sex differences in reproductive strategies. *Behavioral and Brain Sciences* (in press).
16. B.J. Ellis and D. Symons, Sex differences in sexual fantasy: An evolutionary psychological approach. *The Journal of Sex Research, 27,* 527–555 (1990).
17. J. Tooby and L. Cosmides, On the universality of human nature and the uniqueness of the individual: The role of genetics and adaptation, *Journal of Personality, 58,* 17–67 (1990).
18. J.W. Gangestad and J.A. Simpson, Toward an evolutionary history of female sociosexual variation, *Journal of Personality, 58,* 69–96 (1990).

Psychobiology

SELECTION 5

Hemisphere Deconnection and Unity in Conscious Awareness

Roger W. Sperry (1968)

The fact that the human brain is divided into two cerebral hemispheres has always intrigued scientists. In the 1950s, neurosurgeon Philip Vogel developed the technique of cutting the corpus callosum (the neural bundle connecting the two cerebral hemispheres) to reduce the severity of seizures in epileptic patients. This allowed researchers, particularly Roger W. Sperry, to study the conscious behavior of so-called split-brain patients.

Sperry (1913–1994) received his Ph.D. from the University of Chicago in 1941. He became a professor of psychobiology at the California Institute of Technology in 1954. Sperry initially studied cerebral hemisphere disconnection in cats and then moved on to study humans who underwent split-brain surgery. In 1981, Sperry received a Nobel Prize in physiology and medicine for his research on the brain.

This selection from "Hemisphere Deconnection and Unity in Conscious Awareness," which was published in 1968 in *American Psychologist,* describes some of the research conducted by Sperry and his colleagues. Through his research, Sperry discovered that the two cerebral hemispheres have distinct functions—the left side is involved in reasoning, language, and writing, whereas the right side is involved in nonverbal processes, such as art, music, and creativity. This selection conveys the excitement of discovering how human consciousness functions and the intricacies of the human brain.

Key Concept: split-brain research

APA Citation: Sperry, R. W. (1968). Hemisphere deconnection and unity in conscious awareness. *American Psychologist, 23,* 723–733.

The following article is a result of studies my colleagues and I have been conducting with some neurosurgical patients of Philip J. Vogel of Los Angeles. These patients were all advanced epileptics in whom an extensive midline section of the cerebral commissures had been carried out in an effort to contain severe epileptic convulsions not controlled by medication. In all these people the surgical sections included division of the corpus callosum in its entirety, plus division also of the smaller anterior and hippocampal commissures, plus in some instances the massa intermedia. So far as I know, this is the most radical disconnection of the cerebral hemispheres attempted thus far in human surgery. The full array of sections was carried out in a single operation.

No major collapse of mentality or personality was anticipated as a result of this extreme surgery: earlier clinical observations on surgical section of the corpus callosum in man, as well as the results from dozens of monkeys on which I had carried out this exact same surgery, suggested that the functional deficits might very likely be less damaging than some of the more common forms of cerebral surgery, such as frontal lobotomy, or even some of the unilateral lobotomies performed more routinely for epilepsy.

The first patient on whom this surgery was tried had been having seizures for more than 10 years with generalized convulsions that continued to worsen despite treatment that had included a sojourn in Bethesda at the National Institutes of Health. At the time of the surgery, he had been averaging two major attacks per week, each of which left him debilitated for another day or so. Episodes of *status epilepticus* (recurring seizures that fail to stop and represent a medical emergency with a fairly high mortality risk) had also begun to occur at 2- to 3-month intervals. Since leaving the hospital following his surgery over 5½ years ago, this man has not had, according to last reports,

14

a single generalized convulsion. It has further been possible to reduce the level of medication and to obtain an overall improvement in his behavior and well being (see Bogen & Vogel, 1962).

The second patient, a housewife and mother in her 30s, also has been seizure-free since recovering from her surgery, which was more than 4 years ago (Bogen, Fisher, & Vogel, 1965). Bogen related that even the EEG has regained a normal pattern in this patient. The excellent outcome in the initial, apparently hopeless, last-resort cases led to further application of the surgery to some nine more individuals to date, the majority of whom are too recent for therapeutic evaluation. Although the alleviation of the epilepsy has not held up 100% throughout the series (two patients are still having seizures, although their convulsions are much reduced in severity and frequency and tend to be confined to one side), the results on the whole continue to be predominantly beneficial, and the overall outlook at this time remains promising for selected severe cases.

The therapeutic success, however, and all other medical aspects are matters for our medical colleagues, Philip J. Vogel and Joseph E. Bogen. Our own work has been confined entirely to an examination of the functional outcome, that is, the behavioral, neurological, and psychological effects of this surgical disruption of all direct cross-talk between the hemispheres. Initially we were concerned as to whether we would be able to find in these patients any of the numerous symptoms of hemisphere deconnection that had been demonstrated in the so-called "split-brain" animal studies of the 1950s (Myers, 1961; Sperry, 1967a, 1967b). The outcome in man remained an open question in view of the historic Akelaitis (1944) studies that had set the prevailing doctrine of the 1940s and 1950s. This doctrine maintained that no important functional symptoms are found in man following even complete surgical section of the corpus callosum and anterior commissure, provided that other brain damage is excluded.

These earlier observations on the absence of behavioral symptoms in man have been confirmed in a general way to the extent that it remains fair to say today that the most remarkable effect of sectioning the neocortical commissures is the apparent lack of effect so far as ordinary behavior is concerned. This has been true in our animal studies throughout, and it seems now to be true for man also, with certain qualifications that we will come to later. At the same time, however—and this is in contradiction to the earlier doctrine set by the Akelaitis studies—we know today that with appropriate tests one can indeed demonstrate a large number of behavioral symptoms that correlate directly with the loss of the neocortical commissures in man as well as in animals (Gazzaniga, 1967; Sperry, 1967a, 1967b; Sperry, Gazzaniga, & Bogen, 1968). Taken collectively, these symptoms may be referred to as the syndrome of the neocortical commissures or the syndrome of the forebrain commissures or, less specifically, as the syndrome of hemisphere deconnection.

One of the more general and also more interesting and striking features of this syndrome may be summarized as an apparent doubling in most of the realms of conscious awareness. Instead of the normally unified single stream of consciousness, these patients behave in many ways as if they have two independent streams of conscious awareness, one in each hemisphere, each of which is cut off from and out of contact with the mental experiences of the other. In other words, each hemisphere seems to have its own separate and private sensations; its own perceptions; its own concepts; and its own impulses to act, with related volitional, cognitive, and learning experiences. Following the surgery, each hemisphere also has thereafter its own separate chain of memories that are rendered inaccessible to the recall processes of the other.

This presence of two minds in one body, as it were, is manifested in a large number and variety of test responses which, for the present purposes, I will try to review very briefly and in a somewhat streamlined and simplified form. First, however, let me take time to emphasize that the work reported here has been very much a team project. The surgery was performed by Vogel at the White Memorial Medical Center in Los Angeles. He has been assisted in the surgery and in the medical treatment throughout by Joseph Bogen. Bogen has also been collaborating in our behavioral testing program, along with a number of graduate students and postdoctoral fellows, among whom M. S. Gazzaniga, in particular, worked closely with us during the first several years and managed much of the testing during that period. The patients and their families have been most cooperative, and the whole project gets its primary funding from the National Institute of Mental Health.

Most of the main symptoms seen after hemisphere deconnection can be described for convenience with reference to a single testing setup—shown in Figure 1 (omitted). Principally, it allows for the lateralized testing of the right and left halves of the visual field, separately or together, and the right and left hands and legs with vision excluded. The tests can be arranged in different combinations and in association with visual, auditory, and other input, with provisions for eliminating unwanted stimuli. In testing vision, the subject with one eye covered centers his gaze on a designated fixation point on the upright translucent screen. The visual stimuli on 35-millimeter transparencies are arranged in a standard projector equipped with a shutter and are then back-projected at 1/10 of a second or less—too fast for eye movements to get the material into the wrong half of the visual field. Figure 2 (omitted) is merely a reminder that everything seen to the left of the vertical meridian through either eye is projected to the right hemisphere and vice versa. The midline division along the vertical meridian is found to be quite precise without significant gap or overlap (Sperry, 1968).

When the visual perception of these patients is tested under these conditions the results indicate that these people have not one inner visual world any longer, but rather two separate visual inner worlds, one serving the right half of the field of vision and the other the left half—each, of course, in its respective hemisphere. This doubling in the visual sphere shows up in many ways: For example, after a projected picture of an object has been identified and responded to in one half field, we find that it is recognized again only if it reappears in the same half of the field of vision. If the given visual stimulus reappears in the opposite half of the visual field, the subject responds as if he had no recollection of the previous exposure. In other words, things seen through the right half of the visual field (i.e., through the left hemisphere) are registered in mental experience and remembered quite separately from things seen in the other half of the field. Each half of the field of vision in the commissurotomized patient has its own train of visual images and memories.

This separate existence of two visual inner worlds is further illustrated in reference to speech and writing, the cortical mechanisms for which are centered in the dominant hemisphere. Visual material projected to the right half of the field—left-hemisphere system of the typical right-handed patient—can be described in speech and writing in an essentially normal manner. However, when the same visual material is projected into the left half of the field, and hence to the right hemisphere, the subject consistently insists that he did not see anything or that there was only a flash of light on the left side. The subject acts as if he were blind or agnostic for the left half of the visual field. If, however, instead of asking the subject to tell you what he saw, you instruct him to use his left hand to point to a matching picture or object presented among a collection of other pictures or objects, the subject has no trouble as a rule in pointing out consistently the very item that he has just insisted he did not see.

We do not think the subjects are trying to be difficult or to dupe the examiner in such tests. Everything indicates that the hemisphere that is talking to the examiner did in fact not see the left-field stimulus and truly had no experience with, nor recollection of, the given stimulus. The other, the right or nonlingual hemisphere, however, did see the projected stimulus in this situation and is able to remember and recognize the object and can demonstrate this by pointing out selectively the corresponding or matching item. This other hemisphere, like a deaf mute or like some aphasics, cannot talk about the perceived object and, worse still, cannot write about it either.

If two different figures are flashed simultaneously to the right and left visual fields, as for example a "dollar sign" on the left and a "question mark" on the right and the subject is asked to draw what he saw using the left hand out of sight, he regularly reproduces the figure seen on the left half of the field, that is, the dollar sign. If we now ask him what he has just drawn, he tells us without hesitation that the figure he drew was the question mark, or whatever appeared in the right half of the field. In other words, the one hemisphere does not know what the other hemisphere has been doing. The left and the right

halves of the visual field seem to be perceived quite separately in each hemisphere with little or no cross-influence.

When words are flashed partly in the left field and partly in the right, the letters on each side of the midline are perceived and responded to separately. In the "key case" example shown in Figure 2 (omitted) the subject might first reach for and select with the left hand a key from among a collection of objects indicating perception through the minor hemisphere. With the right hand he might then spell out the word "case" or he might speak the word if verbal response is in order. When asked what kind of "case" he was thinking of here, the answer coming from the left hemisphere might be something like "in *case* of fire" or "the *case* of the missing corpse" or "a *case* of beer," etc., depending upon the particular mental set of the left hemisphere at the moment. Any reference to "key case" under these conditions would be purely fortuitous, assuming that visual, auditory, and other cues have been properly controlled.

A similar separation in mental awareness is evident in tests that deal with stereognostic [involving tactile recognition] or other somesthetic [related to bodily sensations] discriminations made by the right and left hands, which are projected separately to the left and right hemispheres, respectively. Objects put in the right hand for identification by touch are readily described or named in speech or writing, whereas, if the same objects are placed in the left hand, the subject can only make wild guesses and may often seem unaware that anything at all is present. As with vision in the left field, however, good perception, comprehension, and memory can be demonstrated for these objects in the left hand when the tests are so designed that the subject can express himself through nonverbal responses. For example, if one of these objects which the subject tells you he cannot feel or does not recognize is taken from the left hand and placed in a grab bag or scrambled among a dozen other test items, the subject is then able to search out and retrieve the initial object even after a delay of several minutes is deliberately interposed. Unlike the normal subject, however, these people are obliged to retrieve such an object with the same hand with which it was initially identified. They fail at cross-retrieval. That is, they cannot recognize with one hand something identified only moments before with the other hand. Again, the second hemisphere does not know what the first hemisphere has been doing.

When the subjects are first asked to use the left hand for these stereognostic tests they commonly complain that they cannot "work with that hand," that the hand "is numb," they "just can't feel anything or can't do anything with it," or that they "don't get the message from that hand." If the subjects perform a series of successful trials and correctly retrieve a group of objects which they previously stated they could not feel, and if this contradiction is then pointed out to them, we get comments like "Well, I was just guessing," or "Well, I must have done it unconsciously." . . .

Much of the foregoing is summarized schematically in Figure 3 (omitted). The left hemisphere in the right-handed patients is equipped with the expressive mechanisms for speech and writing and with the main centers for the comprehension and organization of language. This "major" hemisphere can communicate its experiences verbally and in an essentially normal manner. It can communicate, that is, about the visual experiences of the right half of the optic field and about the somesthetic and volitional experiences of the right hand and leg and right half of the body generally. In addition, and not indicated in the figure, the major hemisphere also communicates, of course, about all of the more general, less lateralized cerebral activity that is bilaterally represented and common to both hemispheres. On the other side we have the mute aphasic and a graphic right hemisphere, which cannot express itself verbally, but which through the use of nonverbal responses can show that it is not agnostic; that mental processes are indeed present centered around the left visual field, left hand, left leg, and left half of the body; along with the auditory, vestibular, axial somatic, and all other cerebral activities that are less lateralized and for which the mental experiences of the right and left hemispheres may be characterized as being similar but separate.

It may be noted that nearly all of the symptoms of cross-integrational impairment that I have been describing are easily hidden or compensated under the conditions of ordinary behavior. For example, the visual material has to be flashed at 1/10 of a second or less to one half of the field in order to prevent compensation by eye movements. The defects in manual stereognosis are not apparent unless vision is excluded; nor is doubling in olfactory perception evident without sequential occlusion of right and left nostril and elimination of visual cues. In many tests the major hemisphere must be prevented from talking to the minor hemisphere and thus giving away the answer through auditory channels. And, similarly, the minor hemisphere must be prevented from giving nonverbal signals of various sorts to the major hemisphere. There is a great diversity of indirect strategies and response signals, implicit as well as overt, by which the informed hemisphere can be used to cue-in the uninformed hemisphere (Levy-Agresti, 1968).

Normal behavior under ordinary conditions is favored also by many other unifying factors. Some of these are very obvious, like the fact that these two separate mental spheres have only one body, so they always get dragged to the same places, meet the same people, and see and do the same things all the time and thus are bound to have a great overlap of common, almost identical, experience. Just the unity of the optic image—and even after chiasm section in animal experiments, the conjugate movements of the eyes—means that both hemispheres automatically center on, focus on, and hence probably attend to, the same items in the visual field all the time. Through sen-

sory feedback a unifying body schema is imposed in each hemisphere with common components that similarly condition in parallel many processes of perception and motor action onto a common base. To get different activities going and different experiences and different memory chains built up in the separated hemispheres of the bisected mammalian brain, as we do in the animal work, requires a considerable amount of experimental planning and effort. . . .

Let me emphasize again in closing that the foregoing represents a somewhat abbreviated and streamlined account of the syndrome of hemisphere deconnection as we understand it at the present time. The more we see of these patients and the more of these patients we see, the more we become impressed with their individual differences, and with the consequent qualifications that must be taken into account. Although the general picture has continued to hold up in the main as described, it is important to note that, with respect to many of the deconnection symptoms mentioned, striking modifications and even outright exceptions can be found among the small group of patients examined to date. Where the accumulating evidence will settle out with respect to the extreme limits of such individual variations and with respect to a possible average "type" syndrome remains to be seen.

REFERENCES

Akelaitis, A. J. A study of gnosis, praxis, and language following section of the corpus callosum and anterior commissure. *Journal of Neurosurgery,* 1944, 1, 94–102.

Bogen, J. E., Fisher, E. D., & Vogel, P. J. Cerebral commissurotomy: A second case report. *Journal of the American Medical Association,* 1965, 194, 1328–1329.

Bogen, J. E., & Vogel, P. J. Cerebral commissurotomy: A case report. *Bulletin of the Los Angeles Neurological Society,* 1962, 27, 169.

Gazzaniga, M. S. The split brain in man. *Scientific American,* 1967, 217, 24–29.

Levy-Agresti, J. Ipsilateral projection systems and minor hemisphere function in man after neocommissurotomy. *Anatomical Record,* 1968, 160, 384.

Myers, R. E. Corpus callosum and visual gnosis. In J. F. Delafresnaye (Ed.), *Brain mechanisms and learning.* Oxford: Blackwell, 1961.

Sperry, R. W. Mental unity following surgical disconnection of the hemispheres. *The Harvey lectures.* Series 62. New York: Academic Press, 1967. (a)

Sperry, R.W. Split-brain approach to learning problems. In G. C. Quarton, T. Melnechuk, & F. O. Schmitt (Eds.), *The neurosciences: A study program.* New York: Rockefeller University Press, 1967. (b)

Sperry, R. W. Apposition of visual half-fields after section of neocortical commissures. *Anatomical Record,* 1968, 160, 498–499.

Sperry, R.W., Gazzaniga, M. S., & Bogen, J. E. Function of neocortical commissures: Syndrome of hemisphere deconnection. In P. J. Vinken & G.W. Bruyn (Eds.), *Handbook of neurology.* Amsterdam: North Holland, 1968, in press.

SELECTION 6

The Central Nervous System and the Reinforcement of Behavior

James Olds (1969)

James Old's discovery of pleasure centers in the brain in the early 1950s demonstrated that reinforcement of behavior has a physiological basis. The early work in electrical brain stimulation performed by Olds and his colleagues has been followed by increasingly more sophisticated techniques designed to unravel the mysteries of the brain.

Olds (1922–1976) received his Ph.D. from Harvard University in 1952. He taught at the University of Michigan until 1969, when he moved to the California Institute of Technology in Pasadena. Through his research, he discovered much about the regions of the brain that are responsible for the effects of reinforcement and punishment. Olds described his research in his book *Drives and Reinforcements: Behavioral Studies of Hypothalamic Functions* (Raven Press, 1977).

This selection, "The Central Nervous System and the Reinforcement of Behavior," published in *American Psychologist* in 1969, summarizes much of the brain research conducted by Olds and his colleagues and shows how the brain is involved in our daily experiences. The detailed description of the function of the hypothalamus and its various pathways illustrates how reinforcement is related to motivation. Notice how the entire research program developed from a fortuitous chance event to a systematic program involving the investigation of various brain sites.

Key Concept: reinforcement through brain stimulation

APA Citation: Olds, J. (1969). The central nervous system and the reinforcement of behavior. *American Psychologist, 24*, 114–118, 120, 131–132.

*R*eward and drive processes are intricately related to those of learning. Therefore brain studies of reward can be expected to provide a basis or at least an introduction to the study of physiological mechanisms underlying learning. Rewards and drives have been studied with lesions and electric stimulations which usually affected many hundreds of neurons at a time. While the grossness of these methods was not a clearly insuperable obstacle in the study of motivational processes, the methods have not yet proved fruitful in the study of the more detailed aspects of learning. It is possible to suppose that the root of the difficulty lies in our inability, with these methods, to study neurons one at a time or in very small families. Newer single unit studies are therefore currently pursued with the hope of finding by their use a key to the mnemonic aspects of brain function. However, in view of the large number of neurons and areas that might be sampled, it has seemed that certain guidelines might be provided if we organized the newer pursuits on the basis of the more solid generalizations distilled from the data obtained with the older methods.

A long and reasonably happy research program was launched in 1953 when a rat fortuitously evidenced a neuronal rewarding effect by returning to the place on a table top where it had been when an electrical stimulus was applied to the brain via chronically implanted electrodes (Olds, 1955). The ensuing studies provided not only a neural substrate as a focal point for further study of a key psychological concept, namely the law of effect, but also a stable method for studying many brain behavior relationships. On the basis of accomplishments to date, the method bodes well in its own way to prove as fruitful as other well-known landmarks in the behavioral sciences such as Skinner's method for studying operant behavior or Lashley's method for studying discrimination and choice on a jumping stand.

The initial observation led to studies which showed that electrical excitation in a restricted region of the central nervous system caused rats to work steadily at arbitrarily assigned tasks in order to obtain the electric stimulus (Olds & Milner, 1954). The behavior was easily

18

reproducible from animal to animal, it was sustained during extended periods of testing, and it was not accompanied by any other obvious pathological signs. It seemed, therefore, possible to view this self-stimulation behavior as evidence of an artificial activation of the brain's normal positive reinforcement mechanism. This discovery has led to much research in our laboratory and has instigated parallel investigations in many other laboratories. At first much of this work was related to the question of whether we were being fooled by the data. Was this a psychologically valid reward or merely a sham having the appearance but not the substance of a positive emotional effect? Experiments showed that animals would improve performance in a maze, running faster and eliminating errors from trial to trial, in order to arrive at the goal point where stimulation was administered (Olds, 1956). Twenty-three hours after a previous brain stimulation they would run purposefully through the maze without errors and without dalliance. In an obstruction box animals repeatedly crossed an electrified grid which applied aversive shock to the feet in order to obtain brain rewards (Olds, 1961). In performance tests when a choice between food and brain stimulation rewards was presented to hungry rats, they often chose brain rewards and underwent the danger of starvation (Routtenberg & Lindy, 1965). In a Skinner box animals would press one bar 50 or even 100 times in order to gain access to a second bar with which they could stimulate their brains (Pliskoff, Wright, & Hawkins, 1965). In extinction experiments animals which had learned to press one of two pedals for brain rewards continued to press that pedal in preference to the other for days after the brain rewards were discontinued (Koenig, 1967). All of these tests fostered a positive answer to the question of whether this was a psychologically valid reward.

The anatomical study of brain rewards showed a relatively unified system to be involved (see Figure 1), consisting of the "old" olfactory cortex, nearby nuclear masses, and the hypothalamus which is a descending extension of this system connecting it to parts of the midbrain (Olds & Olds, 1963). The upper or cortical parts of this system had previously been correlated by neurological evidence and speculation with "emotional experience" (Papez, 1937). The lower part, that is, the hypothalamus, had been connected by experimental work with the control of consummatory responses and basic drives related to food, water, sex, temperature, and so forth (Miller, 1958; Stellar, 1954).

The main two pathways connecting this relatively unified system together are the medial forebrain bundle (Kappers, Huber, & Crosby, 1936) and the fornix (Nauta, 1956). In the hypothalamus the medial forebrain bundle, which is the main one of the two, forms a relatively compact lateral hypothalamic bundle but in anterior parts it fans out to the various olfactory cortical centers. In it, messages from the paleocortex seem to converge upon hypothalamus and messages from hypothalamus diverge to cortex. After rewarding effects were obtained by stimulating in the paleocortical

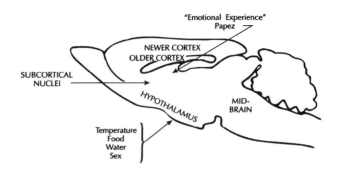

Figure 1 Brain map with arrows indicating the parts of the brain involved in reward and titles indicating other functions ascribed to these areas.

emotional system and in the hypothalamic drive system which were connected by the medial forebrain bundle, it was not surprising to obtain the same effects by stimulating some parts of the anatomically related reticular system which had been previously shown to be involved in awakening and arousing the animal (Moruzzi & Magoun, 1949). But it was paradoxical to obtain these positive effects by stimulating some of the same areas which had previously been shown to be involved in neurally stimulated aversive behavior (Delgado, Roberts, & Miller, 1954). The rewarding effects were not very stable or intense when evoked from the mixed positive and negative areas, and they were often similarly mild or variable when evoked in paleocortex. They were stable and intense when evoked from the lateral hypothalamic bundle, that is, the compact part of the medial forebrain bundle. These are some of the same arenas which have been called drive centers on the basis of other investigations. Therefore, we have thought that the hypothalamic drive centers are the main focus of the brain-stimulated reward effect.

The relations between brain-stimulated positive reinforcement and similarly stimulated negative reinforcement or pain behavior were clarified to some degree in a series of experiments.

In one hypothalamic center with three connecting pathways, stimulation of the first yielded positive reinforcement, stimulation of the second yielded negative reinforcement, and stimulation of the third yielded positive reinforcement again (Olds & Olds, 1963; Roberts, 1958). Stimulation of the center itself yielded mixed positive-negative effects. It was appealing to suppose that such a center receiving both plus and minus emotional inputs might give rise to a set of output messages which would reflect the integrated sum of the organism's emotional state at a given time and which would be effective in determining later behavior.

In keeping with the theory that interaction occurred, we found that stimulation of reward pathway number one inhibited behavior driven by escape pathway number two (Routtenberg & Olds, 1963). Stimulation of escape pathway number two inhibited behavior induced by stimulating reward pathway three (Olds & Olds, 1962). Stimulation at number three did not inhibit anything, but lesions here impaired both self-stimulation and escape behavior so we supposed that this might be the common pathway between reward and punishment (Olds & Olds, 1964). Because stimulation in this pathway itself yielded self-stimulation, we concluded that reward was an active excitatory or incremental process in these neurons, and negative reinforcement might be a negative inhibitory process in the same group.

Because of time limitations, I will bypass details and go on to a discussion of the second important series of interaction studies, namely, those relating neural rewards to the basic drives. In midline hypothalamic centers, lesions have been found by previous investigators to cause overeating and obesity (Brobeck, 1946). Here also, electric stimulation caused cessation of eating (Wyrwicka & Dobrzecka, 1960). Because this stimulus terminated feeding it seemed that it might be drive reducing and rewarding. In fact, there were only aversive effects of stimulating this part of the hypothalamus (Krasne, 1962). In a more lateral area, lesions caused starvation (Anand & Brobeck, 1951) and electric stimulation caused animals to work for food and to eat even when satiated (Miller, 1960). Because this seemed to be a drive-inducing stimulus it was expected to have aversive properties. The finding again was quite the opposite. Stimulating at these feeding center points was often rewarding (Margules & Olds, 1962). Our first interpretation of this was to guess that the stimulation induced not a drive but a consummatory response and therefore might well be rewarding. However, stimulation here caused not only eating of food when food was available but also working for food when food was absent (Miller, 1960). This belied the supposition that these were mere consummatory centers and suggested that there was the induction by stimulation at these points of something very much like the hunger drive itself. The association of neural reward in its strongest form with brain points where basic drives were also induced was later confirmed by other experiments which found drinking and self-stimulation to be induced by stimulation in some nearby brain areas (Mogenson & Stevenson, 1966) and sexual responding and self-stimulation in others (Caggiula & Hoebel, 1966; Herberg, 1963). Thus, the common denominator between many drive-inducing points was the fact that their stimulation was quite often rewarding to the animal.

In trying to make sense out of the feeding data, it was easy to imagine that medial hypothalamic satiety caused an aversive condition of the organism which brought eating to a halt. While this reversed a priori notions about relations between satiety and reward, it was not out of harmony with everyday experience which indicates that eating ceases to be rewarding and even becomes aversive

when the animal eats too much. Second, during a meal or between meals there might be a middle condition in which eating would induce rewarding effects and these might induce further eating. This also might be out of harmony with the a priori notions about connections between hunger and negative factors, but it was in harmony with experience which shows that food often is positively reinforcing and simultaneously induces further hunger. What was missing was a center representing the other extreme from satiety, namely starvation. It seemed that we should find somewhere in the hypothalamus an area where stimulation would be aversive but would also induce eating. In recent research we believe we have found this center in the dorsal part of the medial hypothalamic area. Here, not too far from the lateral hypothalamic feeding center, instrumental and consummatory feeding responses were induced by electric stimulation together with aversive behavior. In another dorsal area, not too far from this, stimulation induced eating with no reinforcing side effects at all. We have thought that both satiety and starvation centers might inhibit a lateral hypothalamic food-reward center. And both the lateral hypothalamic food-reward center and the starvation center might excite a dorsal drive center.

Hypothalamic reward centers related to other drives such as sex or temperature regulation might have equally complex relations but they would not need to be parallel to these. Each drive must have its own problems.

References

Anand, B., & Brobeck, J. R. Hypothalamic control of food intake in rats and cats. *Yale Journal of Biology and Medicine*, 1951, **24**, 123–140.

Broceck J. R. Mechanisms of the development of obesity in animals with hypothalamic lesions. *Physiological Review*, 1946, **26**, 541–559.

Caggiula, A. R., & Hoebel, B. G. "Copulation-reward site" in the posterior hypothalamus. *Science*, 1966, **153**, 1284–1285.

Delgado, J. M. R., Roberts, W. W., & Miller, N. E. Learning motivated by electrical stimulation of the brain. *American Journal of Physiology*, 1954, **179**, 587–593.

Herberg, L. J. Seminal ejaculation following positively reinforcing electrical stimulation of the rat hypothalamus. *Journal of Comparative and Physiological Psychology*, 1963, **56**, 679–685.

Kappers, C. U. A., Huber, G. C, & Crosby, E. C. *The comparative anatomy of the nervous system of vertebrates.* New York: Macmillan, 1936.

Koenig, I. D. V. The reinforcement value of intracranial stimulation and its interaction with arousal level. Cited in D. E. Berlyne, Arousal and reinforcement, *Nebraska Symposium of Motivation*, 1967, **15**, 1–110.

Krasne, F. B. General disruption resulting from electrical stimulus of ventro-medial hypothalamus. *Science*, 1962, 138, 822–823.

Margules, D. L., & Olds, J. Identical "feeding" and "rewarding" systems in the lateral hypothalamus of rats. *Science*, 1962, **135**, 374–375.

Miller, N. E. Central stimulation and other new approaches to motivation and reward. *American Psychologist*, 1958, **13**, 100–108.

Miller, N. E. Motivational effects of brain stimulation and drugs. *Federation Proceedings*, 1960, **19,** 846–854.

Mogenson, G. J., & Stevenson, J. A. F. Drinking and self-stimulation with electrical stimulation of the lateral hypothalamus. *Physiology And Behavior*, 1966, **1,** 251–254.

Moruzzi, G., & Magoun, H. W. Brain stem reticular formation and activation of the EEC. *Electroencephalography and Clinical Neurophysiology*, 1949, **1,** 455–473.

Nauta, W. J. H. An experimental study of the fornix system in the rat. *Journal of Comparative Neurology*, 1956, **104,** 247–271.

Olds, J. Physiological mechanisms of reward. *Nebraska Symposium on Motivation*, 1955, **3,** 73–138.

Olds J. Runway and maze behavior controlled by basomedial forebrain stimulation in the rat. *Journal of Comparative and Physiological Psychology*, 1956, **49,** 507–512.

Olds, J. Differential effects of drives and drugs on self-stimulation at different brain sites. In D. E. Sheer (Ed.), *Electrical stimulation of the brain*. Austin: University of Texas Press, 1961.

Olds, J., & Milner, P. Positive reinforcement produced by electrical stimulation of septal area and other regions of rat brain. *Journal of Comparative and Physiological Psychology*, 1954, **47,** 419–427.

Olds, J., & Olds, M. E. The mechanisms of voluntary behavior. In R. G. Heath (Ed.), *The role of pleasure in behavior*. New York: Hoeber Medical Division, Harper & Row, 1964.

Olds, M. E., & Olds, J. Approach-escape interactions in rat brain. *American Journal of Physiology*, 1962, **203,** 803–810.

Olds, M. E., & Olds, J. Approach-avoidance analysis of rat diencephalon. *Journal of Comparative Neurology*, 1963, **120,** 259–295.

Papez, J. W. A proposed mechanism of emotion. *Archives of Neurology and Psychiatry*, 1937, **38,** 725–743.

Persson, N. Self-stimulation in the goat. *Acta Physiologica Scandinavica*, 1962, **55,** 276–285.

Pliskoff, S. S., Wright, J. E., & Hawkins, D. T. Brain stimulation as a reinforcer: Intermittent schedules. *Journal of the Experimental Analyses of Behavior*, 1965, **8,** 75–88.

Roberts, W. W. Both rewarding and punishing effects from stimulation of posterior hypothalamus of cat with same electrode at same intensity. *Journal of Comparative and Physiological Psychology*, 1958, **51,** 400–407.

Routtenberg, A., & Lindy, J. Effects of the availability of rewarding septal and hyppothalamic stimulation on bar-pressing for food under conditions of deprivation. *Journal of Comparative and Physiological Psychology*, 1965, **60,** 158–161.

Routtenberg, A., & Olds, J. The attenuation of response to an aversive brain stimulus by concurrent rewarding septal stimulation, *Federation Proceedings*, 1963, **22** (No. 2, Part I), 515. (Abstract)

Stellar, E. The physiology of motivation. *Psychological Review*, 1954, **61,** 5–22.

Wyrwicka, W., & Dobrzecka, C. Relationship between feeding and satiation centers of the hypothalamus. *Science*, 1960, **132,** 805–806.

Serotonin, Motor Activity and Depression-Related Disorders

Barry L. Jacobs (1994)

Recently, a great deal of attention has been devoted to the study of how brain chemicals called neurotransmitters can affect people's behavior and moods. Of particular interest are drugs such as Prozac, which alter neurotransmitters, because they appear to have great abilities to treat psychological disorders. How does the brain chemical serotonin affect behavior and mood? Psychologist Barry L. Jacobs and his colleagues are trying to find out.

Jacobs is currently a professor of psychology and director of the neuroscience program at Princeton University in Princeton, New Jersey. His research on serotonin makes him one of the leading authorities in this field.

This selection from "Serotonin, Motor Activity and Depression-Related Disorders," which was published in American Scientist in 1994, provides an exciting look into the chemical processes affecting depression. Especially intriguing is the finding that motor activity could be important in treating depression and obsessive-compulsive disorder. The technical details of this selection may be challenging, but it is more important to focus on the implications for better understanding everyday emotion. Does exercise improve your mood? How might an exercise program be developed to help people who feel depressed?

Key Concept: neurotransmitters and behavior

APA Citation: Jacobs, B. L. (1994). Serotonin, motor activity and depression-related disorders. *American Scientist, 82,* 456–463.

Prozac, Zoloft and Paxil are drugs that have been widely celebrated for their effectiveness in the treatment of depression and obsessive-compulsive disorders. The popular press has also made much of Prozac's ability to alleviate minor personality disorders such as shyness or lack of popularity. The glamorous success of these drugs has even inspired some writers to propose that we are at the threshold of a new era reminiscent of Aldous Huxley's *Brave New World,* in which one's day-to-day emotions can be fine-tuned by simply taking a pill. Yet for all the public attention that has been focused on the apparent benefits of Prozac-like drugs, the fundamental players in this story—the cells and the chemicals in the brain modified by these drugs—have been largely ignored.

This is partly a consequence of the complexity of the nervous system and the fact that so little is known about *how* the activity of cells in the brain translates into mood or behavior. We know that Prozac-like drugs work by altering the function of neurons that release the signaling chemical (neurotransmitter) serotonin. Serotonin has been implicated in a broad range of behavioral disorders involving the sleep cycle, eating, the sex drive and mood. Prozac-like drugs prevent a neuron from taking serotonin back into the cell. Hence Prozac and related drugs are collectively known as selective serotonin reuptake inhibitors, or SSRIs. In principle, blocking the reuptake of serotonin should result in a higher level of activity in any part of the nervous system that uses serotonin as a chemical signal between cells. The long-term effects of these drugs on the function of a serotonin-based network of neurons, however, are simply not known.

My colleagues and I have attempted to understand the role of serotonin in animal physiology and behavior by looking at the activity of the serotonin neurons themselves. For more than 10 years at Princeton University, Casimir Fornal and I have been studying the factors that control the activity of serotonin neurons in the brain. I believe these studies provide the linchpin for understanding depression and obsessive-compulsive disorders and their treatment with therapeutic drugs. Our work provides some unique and unexpected perspectives on these illnesses and will serve, we hope, to open new avenues of clinical research.

SEROTONIN, DRUGS AND DEPRESSION

Communication between neurons is mediated by the release of small packets of chemicals into the tiny gap, the synapse, that separates one neuron from another. The brain uses a surprisingly large number of these chemical neurotransmitters, perhaps as many as 100. However, the preponderance of the work is done by four chemicals that act in a simple and rapid manner: glutamate and aspartate (both of which excite neurons) and gamma-aminobutyric acid (GABA) and glycine (both of which inhibit neurons). Other neurotransmitters, such as serotonin, norepinephrine and dopamine are somewhat different. They can produce excitation *or* inhibition, often act over a longer time scale, and tend to work in concert with one of the four chemical workhorses in the brain. Hence they are also referred to as neuromodulators.

Even though serotonin, norepinephrine and dopamine may be considered to be comparatively minor players in the overall function of the brain, they appear to be major culprits in some of the most common brain disorders: schizophrenia, depression and Parkinson's disease. It is interesting to observe that glutamate, aspartate, GABA and glycine are generally not centrally involved in psychiatric or neurological illnesses. It may be the case that a primary dysfunction of these systems is incompatible with sustaining life.

Serotonin's chemical name is 5-hydroxytryptamine, which derives from the fact that it is synthesized from the amino acid *L*-tryptophan. After a meal, foods are broken down into their constituent amino acids, including tryptophan, and then transported throughout the body by the circulatory system. Once tryptophan is carried into the brain and into certain neurons, it is converted into serotonin by two enzymatic steps.

Serotonin's actions in the synapse are terminated primarily by its being taken back into the neuron that released it. From that point, it is either recycled for reuse as a neurotransmitter or broken down into its metabolic by-products and transported out of the brain. With this basic understanding of serotonin neurotransmission, we can begin to understand the mechanisms of action of antidepressant drugs.

One of the earliest antidepressant drugs, iproniazid, elevates the level of a number of brain chemicals by inhibiting the action of an enzyme, monoamine oxidase, involved in their catabolism. For example, monoamine oxidase inhibitors (MAOIs) block the catabolism of serotonin into its metabolite, 5- hydroxyindole acetic acid (5-HIAA), leading to a buildup of serotonin in the brain. Unfortunately, because monoamine oxidase catabolizes a number of brain chemicals (including norepinephrine and dopamine), there are a number of side-effects associated with these drugs. Some interactive toxicity of MAOIs is also a major drawback for their use in the treatment of depression.

Tricyclic antidepressants (so named because of their three-ringed chemical structure), do not share the interactive toxicity of MAOIs. Tricyclics such as imipramine act to block the reuptake of serotonin from the synapse back into the neuron that released it. In a sense, this floods the synapse with serotonin. These drugs are quite effective in treating depression, but they also induce some unpleasant side-effects, such as constipation, headache and dry mouth. This may be due to the fact that tricyclic antidepressants not only block the reuptake of serotonin, but also exert similar effects on norepinephrine and dopamine.

The obvious benefit of the selective serotonin reuptake inhibitors is that their action is effectively limited to the reuptake of serotonin. This probably accounts for the fewer side-effects experienced by people taking SSRIs. Like other antidepressant drugs, the SSRIs have a therapeutic lag. They typically require 4 to 6 weeks to exert their full effects. Claude DeTontigny and his colleagues at McGill University have suggested that one of the consequences of increasing the levels of serotonin in the brain is a compensatory feedback inhibition that decreases the discharge of brain serotonergic neurons. This results in a "zero sum game" in which there is no net increase in functional serotonin. However, with continuous exposure to serotonin, the receptors mediating this feedback inhibition (the 5-HT$_{1A}$ receptor) become desensitized. It is hypothesized that after several weeks this results in progressively less feedback, increased serotonergic neurotransmission and clinical improvement.

BEHAVIOR OF SEROTONIN NEURONS

Essentially all of the serotonin-based activity in the brain arises from neurons that are located within cell clusters known as the raphe nuclei. These clusters of serotonin neurons are located in the brainstem, the most primitive part of the brain. It is not surprising, then, that serotonin appears to be involved in some fundamental aspects of physiology and behavior, ranging from the control of body temperature, cardiovascular activity and respiration to involvement in such behaviors as aggression, eating and sleeping.

The broad range of physiology and behavior associated with serotonin's actions is at least partly attributable to the widespread distribution of serotonin-containing nerve-fiber terminals that arise from the raphe nuclei. Indeed, the branching of the serotonin network comprises the most expansive neurochemical system in the brain. Serotonin neurons project fibers to virtually all parts of the central nervous system, from the various layers of the cerebral cortex down to the tip of the spinal cord. . . .

Serotonin neurons have a characteristic discharge pattern that distinguishes them from most other cells in the brain. They are relatively regular, exhibiting a slow and steady generation of spikes. Serotonin neurons retain this rhythmic pattern even if they are removed from the brain and isolated in a dish, suggesting that their clocklike regularity is intrinsic to the individual neurons.

One of the first significant discoveries about the behavior of serotonin neurons in the brain was that the rate of these discharges was dramatically altered during different levels of behavioral arousal. When an animal is quiet but awake, the typical serotonin neuron discharges at about 3 spikes per second. As the animal becomes drowsy and enters a phase known as slow-wave sleep, the number of spikes gradually declines. During rapid-eye movement (REM) sleep, which is associated with dreaming in human beings, the serotonin neurons fall completely silent. In anticipation of waking, however, the neuronal activity returns to its basal level of 3 spikes per second. When an animal is aroused or in an active waking state, the discharge rate may increase to 4 or 5 spikes per second. . . .

Interestingly, some serotonin neurons tend to become active just *before* a movement begins. Their activity may also occasionally synchronize with a specific phase of the movement—discharging most, for example, during a particular aspect of the quadrupedal stepping cycle. Moreover, the rate of the spike discharge often increases linearly with increases in the rate or strength of a movement, such as an increase in running speed or the depth of respiration.

One final observation provides a noteworthy clue to the function of serotonin neurons. When an animal is presented with a strong or novel stimulus, such as a sudden loud noise, it often suppresses all ongoing behavior, such as walking or grooming, and turns toward the stimulus. This orienting is essentially a "what is it?" response. In such instances serotonin neurons fall completely silent for several seconds, and then resume their normal activity.

Anatomical evidence supports these observations about the activity of serotonin neurons. For one thing, serotonin neurons preferentially make contacts with neurons that are involved in tonic and gross motor functions, such as those that control the torso and limbs. Reciprocally, serotonin neurons tend not to make connections with neurons that carry out episodic behavior and fine movements, such as those neurons that control the eyes or the fingers.

Our observations of the activity of serotonin neurons during different aspects of an animal's behavior lead us to conclude that the primary function of the brain serotonin system is to prime and facilitate gross motor output in both tonic and repetitive modes. At the same time, the system acts to inhibit sensory-information processing while coordinating autonomic and neuroendocrine functions with the specific demands of the motor activity. When the serotonin system is not active (for example, during an orientation response), the relations are reversed: Motor output is disfacilitated, and sensory-information processing is disinhibited.

BRAIN CELLS AND MENTAL DISORDERS

Although we are far from understanding the precise neural mechanisms involved in the manifestation of any mental illness, a number of studies have linked serotonin to depression. One of the most notable findings is that the major metabolite of serotonin (5-HIAA) appears to be significantly reduced in the cerebrospinal fluid of suicidally depressed patients. Our own studies suggest that serotonin neurons may be centrally involved in the physiological abnormality that underlies depression-related disorders. Recall that serotonin neurons appear to play crucial roles in facilitating tonic motor actions and inhibiting sensory-information processing. If an animal's serotonin neurons are responding abnormally, such that the rate or pattern of their activity is modified, then one might expect that both motor functions and sensory-information processing would be impaired.

Depression is frequently associated with motor retardation and cognitive impairment. If serotonin neurons are not facilitating tonic motor activity, then it should not be surprising that depressed patients feel listless and often appear to require enormous effort merely to raise themselves out of bed. Inappropriate activity during sensory-information processing might also account for the lapses of memory and the general lack of interest in the environment experienced by depressed patients. It might also be worth noting here that the well-known efficacy of REM-sleep deprivation for treating depression is at least partly dependent on serotonin. Since serotonin neurons are usually silent during REM sleep, depriving an animal of REM sleep maintains a generally higher level of activity in the system. Preliminary research in my laboratory suggests that the deprivation of REM sleep also increases the activity of serotonin neurons when the animal is in the awake state.

The activity of serotonin neurons may also be central to the manifestation of obsessive-compulsive disorders. Since our results show that repetitive motor acts increase serotonin neuronal activity, patients with this disorder may be engaging in repetitive rituals such as hand washing or pacing as a means of self-medication. In other words, they have learned to activate their brain serotonin system in order to derive some benefit or rewarding effect, perhaps the reduction of anxiety. Since the compulsive acts tend to be repeated, often to the point of becoming continuous, such activity may provide an almost limitless supply of serotonin to the brain. (The same may also be true for repetitive obsessional thoughts, but this is obviously difficult to test in animals.) Treating obsessive-compulsive disorders with a selective serotonin reuptake inhibitor ultimately accomplishes the same neurochemical endpoint, thus allowing these people to disengage from time-consuming, socially unacceptable and often physically harmful behavior.

Our studies suggest that regular motor activity may be important in the treatment of affective disorders. For example, if there is a deficiency of serotonin in some forms of depression, then an increase in tonic motor activity or some form of repetitive motor task, such as riding a bicycle or jogging, may help to relieve the depression. Indeed, there are various reports that jogging and other forms of exercise have salutary effects for depressed patients. This does not mean that exercise is a panacea for depressive disorders. Since the long-term effects of exercise on brain serotonin levels are not known, the benefits may prove to be transient. On the other hand, exercise may be an important adjunct to drug treatments, and may permit a reduction in the required drug dosage. . . .

CONCLUSION

Our research raises the issue of why the manipulation of a system that is primarily a modulator of motor activity has profound effects on mood. Aside from recognizing that the raphe nuclei are connected to regions of the brain that are known to be involved in the emotions (such as the limbic system), it is worth noting that a common organizational plan underlies the distribution of serotonin cell bodies and fiber terminals in essentially all vertebrate brains. This implies that the system has been conserved through evolution, and suggests that there may be some adaptive significance to linking mood and motor activity.

Consider the following possibility. We know that emotions play a role in allowing an animal to withdraw from an ongoing sequence of activities to consider alternative paths. When something bad (perhaps even life-threatening) transpires, it seems reasonable to suppress motor activity and to contemplate the available options. To put it another way: If something negative has happened in one's world, it might be counterproductive, or even dangerous, to explore and engage the environment. The most adaptive response is to withdraw and ruminate. In this light, emotions act at a higher level of complexity in the service of effective motor behavior. When one's mood is bright and expansive, on the other hand, it may be profitable to explore new options. Wide mood swings may allow an exploration of a broader spectrum of perspectives and thus may be related to the well-documented relationship between mood disorders and creativity in artists, writers and composers.

As a final note, the brain serotonin system may be involved in some nonclinical aspects of human behavior. Why do some people endlessly engage in rhythmic leg bouncing? What is rewarding about chewing gum? What underlies the therapeutic or reinforcing effects of breathing exercises, and the twirling or dancing movements employed by various cults and religious groups? The reader can probably think of other behaviors that increase serotonin release in his or her brain.

SELECTION 8

Environment and Genes: Determinants of Behavior

Robert Plomin (1989)

The importance of nature (genetics) and nurture (environment) on behavioral development has been debated for centuries. Only in the past few decades, however, have psychologists begun to discover the specific mechanisms by which heredity influences cognition and behavior. At the same time, psychologists have found that behavior is also influenced by one's environment and that, in fact, all behavior is the result of the interaction of heredity and·the environment. Behavior geneticist Robert Plomin has been studying this interaction.

Plomin (b. 1948) earned his Ph.D. in biological psychology from the University of Texas at Austin in 1974. He worked at the University of Colorado and Pennsylvania State University before accepting his current position at the University of London Psychiatry Research Center. He has been actively involved in behavioral genetic research, and he is coauthor of the textbook *Behavioral Genetics: A Primer,* 3rd ed. (Worth, 2001).

This selection is from "Environment and Genes: Determinants of Behavior," which was published in *American Psychologist* in 1989. In it, Plomin reviews some of the research findings in the field of behavior genetics that came to light during the 1980s. The field of behavior genetics is important because it helps us understand ourselves and those around us. Today, reports are being made regularly on how specific genes influence intelligence, personality, and psychopathology, as well as other bodily processes. As you read this selection, notice Plomin's emphasis on how both heredity and environment influence human behavior.

Key Concept: Behavior genetics

APA Citation: Plomin, R. (1989). Environment and genes: Determinants of behavior. *American Psychologist, 44,* 105–111.

ABSTRACT: *Recent behavioral genetic research has demonstrated that genetic influence on individual differences in behavioral development is usually significant and often substantial and, paradoxically, also supports the important role of the environment. This article reviews research on the heritability of intellectual factors, personality factors, and psychopathology. It discusses the importance of investigating within-family environmental differences in order to understand the environmental origins of individual differences in development.*

Increasing acceptance of hereditary influence on individual differences in development represents one of the most remarkable changes in the field of psychology that has occurred during the decade since the 1979 special issue of the *American Psychologist* on children. Even for IQ scores, traditionally one of the most controversial areas, a recent survey of over 1,000 scientists and educators indicates that most now believe that individual differences in IQ scores are at least partially inherited (Snyderman & Rothman, 1987). Recent behavioral genetic research providing the empirical basis for this trend is reviewed in the first half of this article.

The wave of acceptance of genetic influence on behavior is growing into a tidal wave that threatens to engulf the second message of this research: These same data provide the best available evidence for the importance of environmental influence. Variability in complex behaviors of interest to psychologists and to society is due at least as much to environmental influences as it is to genetic influences. Because its methods recognize both environmental and genetic influences on behavior, behavioral genetic research has made some novel advances in understanding the environment. . . .

Although the brevity of this article precludes a discussion of the theory and methods of behavioral genetics, the two major methods are the twin design, in which identical twin resemblance is compared with fraternal twin resemblance, and the adoption design, in which genetically related individuals reared apart and genetically unrelated individuals reared together are studied. These methods are used to assess heritability, a statistic that describes the proportion of observed variance for a behavior that can be ascribed to genetic differences among individuals in a particular population. . . .

Two conceptual issues about the field of behavioral genetics need to be mentioned. First, behavioral genetic theory and methods address the genetic and environmental sources of differences among individuals. Behavioral genetics has little to say about universals of development (e.g., why the human species uses language) or about average differences between groups (e.g., why girls perform better than boys on verbal tests). This critical issue, the cause of much misunderstanding, is discussed at length elsewhere (Plomin, DeFries, & Fulker, 1988). Second, when genetic differences among children are found to relate to differences in their behavior, this is a probabilistic relationship in much the same way as finding associations between environmental factors and children's development. . . .[G]enetic influences on behavior are multifactorial—that is, they involve many genes, each with small effects—as well as environmental influences. In other words, genetic influences on the complex behaviors of interest to psychologists do not fit the deterministic model of a single-gene effect—like Mendel's pea-plant characteristics or like some genetic diseases such as sickle-cell anemia—which operates independently of other genes or of environmental influences. . . .

HIGHLIGHTS OF RECENT BEHAVIORAL GENETIC RESEARCH

This section provides a brief overview of recent human behavioral genetic research indicating that behavior can no longer be considered innocent of genetic influence until proven guilty. The litany includes intellectual factors, including IQ, specific cognitive abilities, academic achievement, reading disability . . . ; personality factors, including extraversion and neuroticism, temperament in childhood, and attitudes and beliefs; and psychopathology, including schizophrenia, affective disorders, delinquent and criminal behavior, and alcoholism.

Intellectual Factors

IQ. More behavioral genetic data have been obtained for IQ than for any other trait. A summary of dozens of studies prior to 1980 includes nearly 100,000 twins and biological and adoptive relatives and makes it difficult to escape the conclusion that heredity importantly influences individual differences in IQ scores (Bouchard & McGue, 1981). For example, genetically related individuals adopted apart show

significant resemblance, and identical twins are substantially more similar than fraternal twins. An interesting twist is that, for reasons as yet unknown, studies in the 1970s yielded lower estimates of heritability (about 50%) than older studies (about 70%; Plomin & DeFries, 1980; cf. Loehlin, Willerman, & Horn, 1988).

Recent studies include two ongoing studies of twins reared apart that will triple the number of identical twins reared apart who have been studied for IQ and will also, for the first time, add hundreds of pairs of the equally important group of fraternal twins reared apart. Preliminary reports from these two studies indicate that their results are in line with the rest of the behavioral genetics literature in implicating substantial genetic influence on IQ scores (Bouchard, 1984; Pedersen, McClearn, Plomin, & Friberg, 1985). . . .

Specific cognitive abilities. Although there is some evidence that verbal and spatial abilities show greater genetic influence than do perceptual speed tests and memory tests, the general message is that diverse cognitive tests show significant and often substantial (almost as much as for IQ) genetic influence throughout the life span (Plomin, 1988). In 10 twin studies, tests of creativity show less genetic influence than any other dimension within the cognitive domain, especially when IQ is controlled (R. C. Nichols, 1978).

Research on specific cognitive abilities during the past decade includes a study of over 6,000 individuals in nearly 2,000 families, three twin studies in childhood and one in adulthood, and several parent–offspring adoption studies in addition to the two studies of twins reared apart mentioned in relation to IQ (Plomin, 1986).

Academic achievement. Although no new behavioral genetic research on school-relevant behavior has been reported during the past decade, genetic influence is pervasive here as well. Twin studies of academic-achievement test scores show substantial genetic influence, about the same as for specific cognitive abilities. Even report-card grades and years of schooling show substantial genetic influence. Vocational interests are also substantially influenced by genetic factors, as shown in twin and adoption studies. (For references, see Plomin, 1986.)

Reading disability. Reading disability shows considerable familial resemblance (DeFries, Vogler, & LaBuda, 1985). One recent twin study found evidence for a genetic basis for this familial resemblance (DeFries, Fulker, & LaBuda, 1987); another twin study found genetic influence on spelling disability but not on other aspects of reading disability (Stevenson, Graham, Fredman, & McLoughlin, 1987). A single-gene effect has been proposed for spelling disability (Smith, Kimberling, Pennington, & Lubs, 1983), although subsequent analyses have not confirmed the linkage (Kimberling, Fain, Ing, Smith, & Pennington, 1985; McGuffin, 1987). . . .

Personality Factors

Extraversion and neuroticism. One focus of recent research on personality involves two "super factors" of personality: extraversion and neuroticism. A review of research involving over 25,000 pairs of twins yielded heritability estimates of about 50% for these two traits (Henderson, 1982). This review also pointed out that extraversion and other personality traits often show evidence for nonadditive genetic variance. Nonadditive effects of genes involve unique combinations of genes that contribute to the similarity of identical twins but not to the resemblance of first-degree relatives. These conclusions are supported by a recent large-scale twin study in Australia (N. G. Martin & Jardine, 1986) and by two studies of twins reared apart (Pedersen, Plomin, McClearn, & Friberg, 1988; Tellegen et al., 1988). The presence of nonadditive genetic variance may be responsible for the lower estimates of heritability from adoption studies of first-degree relatives (Loehlin, Willerman, & Horn, 1982, 1985; Scarr, Webber, Weinberg, & Wittig, 1981).

Emotionality, activity, and sociability (EAS). Extraversion and neuroticism are global traits that encompass many dimensions of personality. The core of extraversion, however, is sociability, and the key component of neuroticism is emotionality. From infancy to adulthood, these two traits and activity level have been proposed as the most heritable components of personality, a theory referred to with the acronym EAS (Buss & Plomin, 1984). A review of behavioral genetic data for these three traits in infancy, childhood, adolescence, and adulthood lends support to the EAS theory (Plomin, 1986). However, note that many personality traits display genetic influence, and it is difficult to prove that some traits are more heritable than others, perhaps because of the pervasive genetic influence of extraversion and neuroticism (Loehlin, 1982). . . .

Attitudes and beliefs. Surprisingly, some attitudes and beliefs show almost as much genetic influence as do other behavioral traits. One focus of recent interest is traditionalism, the tendency to follow rules and authority and to endorse high moral standards and strict discipline. For example, a large twin study estimated that half of the variance on this measure is due to genetic influence (N. G. Martin et al., 1986), and a report of twins reared apart has also found substantial genetic influence for traditionalism (Tellegen et al., 1988). Religiosity and certain political beliefs, however, show no genetic influence.

Psychopathology

Behavioral genetic research on psychopathology in children and adults is especially active (Loehlin et al., 1988; Vandenberg, Singer, & Pauls, 1986). This section provides a brief overview of recent research in schizophrenia, affective disorders, delinquent and criminal behavior, alcoholism, and other psychopathology.

Schizophrenia. In 14 older studies involving over 18,000 first-degree relatives of schizophrenics, the risk for first-degree relatives was about 8%, eight times greater than the risk for individuals chosen randomly from the population (Gottesman & Shields, 1982). Recent family studies continue to yield similar results.

Twin studies suggest that this familial resemblance is due to heredity. The most recent twin study involved all male twins who were veterans of World War II (Kendler & Robinette, 1983). Twin concordances were 30.9% for 164 pairs of identical twins and 6.5% for 268 pairs of fraternal twins. Adoption studies of schizophrenia support the twin findings of genetic influence on schizophrenia. . . .

Affective disorders. Although twin results for affective disorders suggest even greater genetic influence than for schizophrenia, adoption studies indicate less genetic influence (Loehlin et al., 1988). In one recent adoption study, affective disorders were diagnosed in only 5.2% of biological relatives of affectively-ill adoptees, although this risk is greater than the risk of 2.3% found in the biological relatives of control adoptees (Wender et al., 1986). The biological relatives of affected adoptees also showed greater rates of alcoholism (5.4% vs. 2.0%) and attempted or actual suicide (7.3% vs. 1.5%). . . .

Delinquent and criminal behavior. The spotlight on controversies concerning genetic influence on IQ has switched to criminal behavior with the publication of a recent book (Wilson & Herrnstein, 1985) claiming that biology affects such behaviors. Six twin studies of juvenile delinquency yielded 87% concordance for identical twins and 72% concordance for fraternal twins, suggesting slight genetic influence and substantial environmental sources of resemblance (Gottesman, Carey, & Hanson, 1983). A recent quantitative study of delinquent acts indicated greater genetic influence than did earlier studies that attempted to diagnose delinquency (Rowe, 1983b).

It has been suggested that juvenile delinquents who go on to become adult criminals may have a genetic liability (Wilson & Herrnstein, 1985). Eight older twin studies of adult criminality yielded identical and fraternal twin concordances of 69% and 33%, respectively. Adoption studies are consistent with the hypothesis of some genetic influence on adult criminality, although the evidence is not as striking as in the twin studies (Mednick, Gabrielli, & Hutchings, 1984).

Alcoholism. Alcoholism runs in families. Alcoholism in a first-degree relative is by far the single best predictor of alcoholism (Mednick, Moffitt, & Stack, 1987). About 25% of the male relatives of alcoholics are themselves alcoholics, as compared with fewer than 5% of the males in the general population. Although twin studies of normal drinkers show substantial genetic influence (for example, Pedersen, Friberg, Floderus-Myrhed, McClearn, & Plomin, 1984), no twin studies have focused on alcoholism per se. A Swedish adoption study provides the best evidence for genetic influence on alcoholism, at least in males (Bohman, Cloninger, Sigvardsson, & von Knorring, 1987;

cf. Peele, 1986). Twenty-two percent of the adopted-away sons of biological fathers who abused alcohol were alcoholic, suggesting substantial genetic influence.

Other psychopathology. Although most research on psychopathology has focused on psychoses, criminality, and alcoholism, attention has begun to turn to other disorders. Areas of recent research include a family study of anxiety neurosis sometimes known as panic disorder, twin and family studies of anorexia nervosa, and family and adoption studies of somatization disorder that involves multiple and chronic physical complaints of unknown origin (Loehlin et al., 1988).

Summary

The first message of behavioral genetic research is that genetic influence on individual differences in behavioral development is usually significant and often substantial. Genetic influence is so ubiquitous and pervasive in behavior that a shift in emphasis is warranted: Ask not what is heritable, ask what is not heritable.

The second message is just as important: These same data provide the best available evidence of the importance of the environment. The data reviewed in this section suggest pandemic genetic influence, but they also indicate that nongenetic factors are responsible for more than half of the variance for most complex behaviors. For example, identical twins show concordance of less than 40% for schizophrenia. Because identical twins are genetically identical, most of the reason one person is diagnosed as schizophrenic and another is not has to do with environmental rather than genetic reasons. The phrase "behavioral genetics" is in a sense a misnomer because it is as much the study of nurture as nature. In addition to documenting the importance of environmental variation, it provides a novel perspective for viewing environmental influences, especially the family environment, in the context of heredity. . . .

The move away from a rigid adherence to environmental explanations of behavioral development to a more balanced perspective that recognizes genetic as well as environmental sources of individual differences must be viewed as healthy for the social and behavioral sciences. The danger now, however, is that the swing from environmentalism will go too far. During the 1970s, I found I had to speak gingerly about genetic influence, gently suggesting heredity might be important in behavior. Now, however, I more often have to say, "Yes, genetic influences are significant and substantial, but environmental influences are just as important." This seems to be happening most clearly in the field of psychopathology, where evidence of significant genetic influence has led to a search for single genes and simple neurochemical triggers at the expense of research on its psychosocial origins. It would be wonderful if some simple, and presumably inexpensive, biochemical cure could be found for schizophrenia. However, this happy outcome seems highly un-

likely given that schizophrenia is as much influenced by environmental factors as it is by heredity.

Furthermore, as mentioned earlier, genetic effects on behavior are polygenic and probabilistic, not single gene and deterministic. The characteristics in the pea plant that Mendel studied and a few diseases such as Huntington's disease and sickle-cell anemia are due to single genes that have their effects regardless of the environment or the genetic background of the individual. The complexity of behaviors studied by psychologists makes it unlikely that such a deterministic model and the reductionistic approach that it suggests will pay off. There is as yet no firm evidence for a single-gene effect that accounts for a detectable amount of variation for any complex behavior. . . .

As the pendulum swings from environmentalism, it is important that the pendulum be caught midswing before its momentum carries it to biological determinism. Behavioral genetic research clearly demonstrates that both nature and nurture are important in human development.

REFERENCES

Bohman, M., Cloninger, R., Sigvardsson, S., & von Knorring, A. L. (1987). The genetics of alcoholisms and related disorders. *Journal of Psychiatric Research, 21,* 447–452.

Bouchard, T. J. (1984). Twins reared together and apart: What they tell us about human diversity. In S.W. Fox (Ed.), *Individuality and determinism* (pp. 147–178). New York: Plenum Press.

Bouchard, T. J., Jr., & McGue, M. (1981). Familial studies of intelligence: A review. *Science, 212,* 1055–1059.

Buss, A. H., & Plomin, R. (1984). *Temperament: Early developing personality traits.* Hillsdale, NJ: Erlbaum.

DeFries, J. C., Fulker, D. W., & LaBuda, M. C. (1987). Evidence for a genetic etiology in reading disability in twins. *Nature, 329,* 537–539.

DeFries, J. C., Vogler, G. P., & LaBuda, M. C. (1985). Colorado Family Reading Study: An overview. In J. L. Fuller & E. C. Simmel (Eds.), *Behavior genetics: Principles and applications II.* (pp.357–368). Hillsdale, NJ: Erlbaum.

Donis-Keller, H., Green, P., Helms, C., Cartinhour, S., & Weiffenbach, B. (1987). A human gene map. *Cell, 51,* 319–337.

Egeland, J. A., Gerhard, D. S., Pauls, D. L., Sussex, J. N., & Kidd, K. K. (1987). Bipolar affective disorders linked to DNA markers on chromosome 11. *Nature, 325,* 783–787.

Gottesman, I. I., Carey, G., & Hanson, D. R. (1983). Pearls and perils in epigenetic psychopathology. In S. B. Guze, E. J. Earls, & J. E. Barrett (Eds.), *Childhood psychopathology and development* (pp. 287–300). New York: Raven Press.

Gottesman, I. I., & Shield, J. (1982). *Schizophrenia: The epigenetic puzzle.* Cambridge, England: Cambridge University Press.

Gusella, J. F., Wexler, N. S., Conneally, P. M., Naylor, S. L., Anderson, M. A., Tanzi, R. E., Watkins, P. C., & Ottina, K. (1983). A polymorphic DNA marker genetically linked to Huntington's disease. *Nature, 306,* 234–238.

Henderson, N. D. (1982). Human behavior genetics. *Annual Review of Psychology, 33,* 403–440.

Kendler, K. S., & Robinette, C. D. (1983). Schizophrenia in the National Academy of Sciences–National Research Council twin registry: A 16-year update. *American Journal of Psychiatry, 140,* 1551–1563.

Kimberling, W. J., Fain, P. R., Ing, P. S., Smith, S. D., & Pennington, B. F. (1985). Linkage analysis of reading disability with chromosome 15. *Behavior Genetics, 15,* 597–598.

Loehlin, J. C. (1982). Are personality traits differentially heritable? *Behavior Genetics, 12,* 417–428.

Loehlin, J. C., Willerman, L., & Horn, J. M. (1982). Personality resemblances between unwed mothers and their adopted-away offspring. *Journal of Personality and Social Psychology, 42,* 1089–1099.

Loehlin, J. C., Willerman, L., & Horn, J. M. (1985). Personality resemblance in adoptive families when the children are late adolescents and adults. *Journal of Personality and Social Psychology, 48,* 376–392.

Loehlin, J. C., Willerman, L., & Horn, J. M. (1988). Human behavior genetics, *Annual Review of Psychology, 38,* 101–133.

Martin, J. B. (1987). Molecular genetics: Applications to the clinical neurosciences. *Science, 238,* 765–772.

Martin, N. G., Eaves, L. J., Heath, A. C., Jardine, R., Feingold, L. M., & Eysenck, H. J. (1986). Transmission of social attitudes. *Proceedings of the National Academy of Sciences, USA, 83,* 4364–4368.

Martin, N. G., & Jardine, R. (1986). Eysenck's contributions to behaviour genetics. In S. Modgil & C. Modgil (Eds.), *Hans Eysenck: Consensus and controversy* (pp. 13–27). Philadelphia: Falmer.

McGuffin, P. (1987). The new genetics and childhood psychiatric disorder. *Journal of Child Psychology and Psychiatry, 28,* 215–222.

Mednick, S. A., Gabrielli, W. F., Jr., & Hutchings, B. (1984). Genetic influences in criminal convictions: Evidence from an adoption cohort. *Science, 224,* 891–894.

Mednick, S. A., Moffitt, T. E., & Stack, S. (1987). *The causes of crime: New biological approaches.* New York: Cambridge University Press.

Nichols, R. C. (1978). Twin studies of ability, personality, and interests. *Homo, 29,* 158–173.

Pedersen, N. L., Friberg, L., Floderus-Myrhed, B., McClearn, G. E., & Plomin, R. (1984). Swedish early separated twins: Identification and characterization. *Acta Geneticae Medicae et Gemellologiae, 33,* 243–250.

Pedersen, N. L., McClearn, G. E., Plomin, R., & Friberg, L. (1985). Separated fraternal twins: Resemblance for cognitive abilities. *Behavior Genetics, 15,* 407–419.

Pedersen, N. L., Plomin, R., McClearn, G. E., & Friberg, L. (1988). Neuroticism, extraversion, and related traits in adult twins reared apart and reared together. *Journal of Personality and Social Psychology, 55,* 950–957.

Peele, S. (1986). The implications and limitations of genetic models of alcoholism and other addictions. *Journal of Studies on Alcohol, 47,* 63–73.

Plomin, R. (1986). *Development, genetics, and psychology.* Hillsdale, NJ: Erlbaum.

Plomin, R. (1988). The nature and nurture of cognitive abilities. In R. J. Sternberg (Ed.), *Advances in the psychology of human intelligence* (Vol. 4, pp. 1–33). Hillsdale, NJ: Erlbaum.

Plomin, R., & DeFries, J. C. (1980). Genetics and intelligence: Recent data. *Intelligence, 4,* 15–24.

Plomin, R., DeFries, J. C., & Fulker D. W. (1988). *Nature and nurture during infancy and early childhood.* New York: Cambridge University Press.

Roew, D. C. (1983b). Biometrical genetic models of self-reported delinquent behavior: Twin study. *Behavior Genetics, 13,* 473–489.

Scarr, S., Webber, P. I., Weinberg, R. A., & Wittig, M. A. (1981). Personality resemblance among adolescents and their parents in biologically related and adoptive families. *Journal of Personality and Social Psychology, 40,* 885–898.

Smith, S. D., Kimberling, W. J., Pennington, B. F., & Lubs, H. A. (1983). Specific reading disability: Identification of an inherited form through linkage analysis. *Science, 219,* 1345–1347.

Snyderman, M., & Rothman, S. (1987). Survey of expert opinion on intelligence and aptitude testing. *American Psychologist, 42,* 137–144.

Stevenson, J., Graham, P., Fredman, G., & McLoughlin, V. (1987). A twin study of genetic influences on reading and spelling ability and disability. *Journal of Child Psychology and Psychiatry, 28,* 229–247.

Tellegen, A., Lykken, D. T., Bouchard, T. J., Wilcox, K., Segal, N., & Rich, S. (1988). Personality similarity in twins reared apart and together. *Journal of Social and Personality Psychology, 54,* 1031–1039.

Vandenberg, S. G., Singer, S. M., & Pauls, D. L. (1986). *The heredity of behavior disorders in adults and children.* New York: Plenum.

Wender, P. H., Kety, S. S., Rosenthal, D., Schulsinger, F., Ortmann, J., & Lunde, I. (1986). Psychiatric disorders in the biological and adoptive families of adopted individuals with affective disorders. *Archives of General Psychiatry, 43,* 923–929.

Wilson, J. Q., & Herrnstein, R. J. (1985). *Crime and human nature.* New York: Simon & Schuster.

Wyman, A. R., & White, R. L. (1980). A highly polymorphic locus in human DNA. *Proceedings of the National Academy of Sciences, 77,* 6754–6758.

Preparation of this article was supported in part by grants from the National Science Foundation (BNS-8643938) and the National Institute of Aging (AG-04563).

Sensation and Perception

Perception: An Introduction to the Gestalt-Theorie

Kurt Koffka (1922)

Perception has always been a core topic in psychology. Today, scientists' understanding of perceptual principles is strongly influenced by the German Gestalt psychologists, Max Wertheimer, Wolfgang Köhler, and Kurt Koffka.

Koffka (1886–1941) earned his Ph.D. from the University of Berlin in 1909, and then went to the University of Frankfurt, where he met the other Gestalt founders in 1910. He taught at the University of Giessen from 1911 to 1924, when he came to the United States. In 1927 he was appointed as a professor of psychology at Smith College, where he stayed until his death. Koffka was especially interested in studying the laws that govern our perceptions of the environment. Among his publications was the influential book, *Principles of Gestalt Psychology* (1935).

This selection is from "Perception: An Introduction to Gestalt-theorie," which was published in *Psychological Bulletin* in 1922. The article was an attempt by the German psychologist to encourage American psychologists to support the Gestalt viewpoint. In it, Koffka discusses the relevance of sensation, association, and attention to psychology. Notice his reference to the American psychology of behaviorism. Although this paper was written over 80 years ago, it touches on many of the same issues that are important to cognitive psychologists today. How important are association and attention to perception? Why do you think Koffka argued that Gestalt theory is more than a theory of perception?

Key Concept: Gestalt theory of perception

APA Citation: Koffka, K. (1922). Perception: An introduction to the Gestalt-theorie. *Psychological Bulletin, 19*, 531–585.

When it was suggested to me that I should write a general critical review of the work recently carried on in the field of perception, I saw an opportunity of introducing to American readers a movement in psychological thought which has developed in Germany during the last ten years. In 1912 Wertheimer stated for the first time the principles of a *Gestalt-Theorie* which has served as the starting point of a small number of German psychologists. Wherever this new method of thinking and working has come in touch with concrete problems, it has not only showed its efficiency, but has also brought to light startling and important facts, which, without the guidance of this theory, could not so easily have been discovered.

The *Gestalt-Theorie* is more than a theory of perception: it is even more than a mere psychological theory. Yet it originated in a study of perception, and the investigation of this topic has furnished the better part of the experimental work which has been done. Consequently, an introduction to this new theory can best be gained, perhaps, by a consideration of the facts of perception.

Since the new point of view has not yet won its way in Germany, it is but fair to state at the outset that the majority of German psychologists still stands aloof. However, much of the work done by other investigators contains results that find a place within the scope of our theory. Accordingly I shall refer to these results as well as to those secured by the *Gestalt*-psychologists proper; for I wish to demonstrate the comprehensiveness of our theory by showing how readily it embraces a number of facts hitherto but imperfectly explained. For the same reason I shall occasionally go farther back and refer to older investigations. On the other hand, I cannot hope to give a complete survey of the work on perception, and I shall therefore select my facts with reference to my primary purpose. ...

When I speak of perception in the following essay, I do not mean a specific psychical function; all I wish to denote by this term is the realm of experiences which are not merely "imagined," "represented," or "thought of." Thus, I would call the desk at which I am now writing a perception, likewise the flavor of the tobacco I am now inhaling from my pipe, or the noise of the traffic in the street below my window. That is to say, I wish to use the term perception in a way that will exclude all theoretical prejudice; for it is my aim to propose a theory of these everyday perceptions which has been developed in Germany during the last ten years, and to contrast this theory with the traditional views of psychology. With this purpose in mind, I need a term that is quite neutral. In the current textbooks of psychology the term perception is used in a more specific sense, being opposed to sensation, as a more complex process. Here, indeed, is the clue to all the existing theories of perception which I shall consider in this introductory section, together with a glance at the fundamental principles of traditional psychology. Thus I find three concepts, involving three principles of psychological theory, in every current psychological system. In some systems these are the only fundamental concepts, while in others they are supplemented by additional conceptions; but for a long time the adequacy of these three has been beyond dispute. The three concepts to which I refer are those of *sensation, association,* and *attention.* I shall formulate the theoretical principles based upon these concepts and indicate their import in a radical manner so as to lay bare the methods of thinking which have been employed in their use. I am fully aware, of course, that most, if not all, the writers on this subject have tried to modify the assertions which I am about to make; but I maintain, nevertheless, that in working out concrete problems these principles have been employed in the manner in which I shall state them.

1. Sensation: All present or existential consciousness consists of a finite number of real, separable (though not necessarily separate) elements, each element corresponding to a definite stimulus or to a special memory-residuum. Since a conscious unit is thus taken to be a bundle of such elements, Wertheimer, in a recent paper on the foundations of our new theory, has introduced the name "bundle-hypothesis" for this conception[7]. These elements, or rather, some of them, are the sensations, and it is the first task of psychology to find out their number and their properties.

The elements, once aroused in the form of sensations, may also be experienced in the form of images. The images are also accepted as elements or atoms of psychological textures and are distinguishable from sensations by certain characteristic properties. They are, however, very largely a dependent class, since every image presupposes a corresponding sensation. Thus the concept of image though not identical with that of sensation, rests upon the same principle, namely, the bundle-hypothesis.

In accordance with the method by which sensations have been investigated, it has been necessary to refer to the stimulus-side in defining the principle which underlies this concept. More explicitly, this relation of the sensation to its stimulus is expressed by a generally accepted rule, termed by Köhler the "constancy-hypothesis"[4]; that the sensation is a direct and definite function of the stimulus. Given a certain stimulus and a normal sense-organ, we know what sensation the subject must have, or rather, we know its intensity and quality, while its "clearness" or its "degree of consciousness" is dependent upon still another factor, namely, *attention.*

What the stimulus is to the sensation, the residuum is to the image. Since each separate sensation-element leaves behind it a separate residuum, we have a vast number of these residua in our memory, each of which may be separately aroused, thus providing a certain independence of the original arrangement in which the sensations were experienced. This leads to the theory of the "association mixtures" *(associative Mischwirkungen)* propounded by G. E. Müller[5] and carried to the extreme in a paper by Henning[2].

2. Association: Even under our first heading we have met with the concept of memory. According to current teaching, the chief working principle of memory is association, although the purest of associationists recognize that it is not the only principle. It may suffice to point out in this connection that Rosa Heine[1] concludes from experiments performed in G. E. Müller's laboratory, that recognition is not based upon association; for she failed to detect in recognition any trace of that retroactive inhibition which is so powerful a factor in all associative learning. Likewise, Müller himself, relying upon experiments by L. Schlüter[6] acknowledges the possibility of reproduction by similarity. Yet, despite all this, association holds its position as the primary factor governing the coming and the going of our ideas, and the law of association is based upon the sensation-image concept. Our train of thought having been broken up into separate elements, the question is asked by what law does one element cause the appearance of another, and the answer is, association, the tie that forms between each element and all those other elements with which it has ever been in contiguity. As Wertheimer[7] again has pointed out, the core of this theory is this, that the necessary and sufficient cause for the formation and operation of an association is an original existential connection—the mere coexistence of *a* and *b* gives to each a tendency to reproduce the other. Meaning, far from being regarded as one of the conditions of association, is explained by the working of associations, which in themselves are meaningless.

Another feature of this theory is its statistical nature. At every moment, endless associations are working, reinforcing and inhibiting each other. Since we can never have a complete survey of all the effective forces, it is impossible in any single case to make accurate prediction. As the special laws of association can be discovered by statistical methods only, so our predictions can be only statistical.

3. Attention: It is a recognized fact, that, clear and simple as association and sensation appear to be, there is a

good deal of obscurity about the concept of attention. And yet, wherever there is an effect that cannot be explained by sensation or association, there attention appears upon the stage. In more complex systems attention is the makeshift, or the scapegoat, if you will, which always interferes with the working out of these other principles. If the expected sensation does not follow when its appropriate stimulus is applied, attention to other contents must have caused it to pass unnoticed, or if a sensation does not properly correspond to the stimulus applied, the attention must have been inadequate, thus leading us to make a false judgment. We meet with like instances over and over again which justify the following general statement, that attention must be added as a separate factor which not only influences the texture and the course of our conscious processes, but is also likely to be influenced by them.

Modern psychology has endeavored to give a physiological foundation to its psychological conceptions. Let us therefore glance at the physiological side of these three principles. The substratum of sensation (and image) is supposed to be the arousal of a separate circumscribed area of the cortex, while the substratum for association is the neural connection established between such areas. Again attention holds an ambiguous position, for some see its essence as a facilitation and some as an inhibition of the nervous processes. Without going more into detail, let us examine the nature of this psycho-physical correspondence. Methodologically the physiological and the psychological aspects of these three principles are in perfect harmony; the cortex has been divided into areas, the immediate experience has been analyzed into elements, and connections are assumed to exist between brain areas as between the elements of consciousness. Furthermore, the nervous processes may be altered functionally and their corresponding psychological elements are subject to the functional factor of attention. Evidently the psychological and the physiological are interdependent, and are not sensation, association, and attention, factual? Do not cortical areas exist, and likewise nervous tracts, and the facilitation and inhibition of excitations? Certainly facts exist which have been interpreted in these ways, but we believe it can be proved that this interpretation is insuffi-cient in the face of other and more comprehensive facts. Furthermore, we maintain that the insufficiency of the older theory cannot be remedied by supplementing the three principles, but that these must be sacrificed and replaced by other principles....

Just a line at this point upon certain recent tendencies in American psychology. Behaviorism, excluding as it does all forms of consciousness from its realm, strictly speaking denies the use of these three principles altogether. Therefore we do not find the terms attention and sensation in the behaviorist's writings, and even association has disappeared from the explanation in the sense of a tie that can be formed as an original act. And yet, as I have shown in a paper which discusses the fundamental differences between Wertheimer's theory and that of Meinong and Benussi[3], despite the restriction in his use of terms, the outfit of the Behaviorist is essentially the same as that of the traditional psychologist. He says "reaction" where the latter said "sensation," and in so doing includes the effector side of the process, but apart from this he builds his system in exactly the same manner, joining reflex arcs to reflex arcs entirely in accordance with the method of the "bundle-hypothesis."

References

1. Heine, R. Über Wiederkennen und rückwirkende Hemmung. *Zeits. f. Psychol.*, 1914, **68,** 161–236.
2. Henning, H. Experimentelle Untersuchungen zur Denkpsychologie. 1. Die assoziative Mischwirkung, das Vorstellen von noch nie Wahrgenommenem und deren Grenzen. *Zeits. f. Psychol.*, 1919, **81,** 1–96.
3. Koffka, K. The same. III. Zur Grundlegung der Wahrnehmungspsychologie. Eine Auseinandersetzung mit V. Benussi, von *K. Koffka. Zeits. f. Psychol.*, 1915, **73,** 11–90
4. Köhler, W. Über unbemerkte Empfindungen und Urteilstiuschungen. *Zeits. f. Psychol.*, 1913, **66,** 51–80.
5. Müller, G.E. und Pilzecker, A. Experimenelle Beiträge zur Lehre vom Gedächtnis. *Erg. Bd.* **I,** *d. Zeits. f. Psychol.* Leipzig: Barth, 1900, pp. xiv+300.
6. Schlüter, L. Experimentelle Beiträge zur Prüfung der Auschauungs und der Übersetzungsmethode bei der Einführung in einen fremdsprachlichen Wortschatz. *Zeits. f. Psychol.*, 1914, **68,** 1–114.
7. Wertheimer, M. Untersuchungen zur Lehre von der Gestalt. I. Prinzipielle Bemerkungen. *Psychol. Forsch.*, 1922, **1,** 47–58.

Pattern Vision in Newborn Infants

Robert L. Fantz (1963)

For many years, psychologists believed that the senses in newborn infants did not function well, partly because they found it impossible to properly test newborns to determine what they could perceive. Over the years, new techniques have been developed to measure the sensory capabilities of infants. A pioneer in the field, Robert L. Fantz, developed a technique for studying pattern vision in newborn infants.

Fantz (b. 1925) was a psychology professor at Western Reserve University in Cleveland during the 1960s when he studied perception in infants. This selection, "Pattern Vision in Newborn Infants" was published in *Science* in 1963. The "chamber" (its full name is "looking chamber") Fantz refers to in the selection is his own invention. During experimentation with the chamber, visual targets are shown on the ceiling of the chamber, and the eye movements and fixation points of the subject (infant), who is inside the chamber, can be observed through a peephole. Because Fantz had developed a simple design for research, his techniques became useful for other psychologists to learn about visual preference in newborn infants. Since the early studies by Fantz, much more sophisticated procedures have been developed to study infants. As you read this selection, consider the implications of providing a stimulating visual environment for newborn infants. Also, why is it important to understand the sensory capabilities of infants?

Key Concept: vision in newborn infants

APA Citation: Fantz, R. L. (1963). Pattern vision in newborn infants. *Science, 140,* 296-297.

*A*bstract. *Human infants under 5 days of age consistently looked more at black-and-white patterns than at plain colored surfaces, which indicates the innate ability to perceive form.*

It is usually stated or implied that the infant has little or no pattern vision during the early weeks or even months, because of the need for visual learning or because of the immature state of the eye and brain, or for both reasons[2]. This viewpoint has been challenged by the direct evidence of differential attention given to visual stimuli varying in form or pattern[2]. This evidence has shown that during the early months of life, infants: (i) have fairly acute pattern vision (resolving $\frac{1}{8}$-inch stripes at a 10-inch distance; (ii) show greater visual interest in patterns than in plain colors; (iii) differentiate among patterns of similar complexity; and (iv) show visual interest in a pattern similar to that of a human face.

The purpose of the present study was to determine whether it was possible to obtain similar data on newborn infants and thus further exclude visual learning or postnatal maturation as requirements for pattern vision. It is a repetition of a study of older infants which compared the visual responsiveness to patterned and to plainly colored surfaces[3]. The results of the earlier study were essentially duplicated, giving further support for the above conclusions.

The subjects were 18 infants ranging from 10 hours to 5 days old. They were selected from a much larger number on the basis of their eyes remaining open long enough to be exposed to a series of six targets at least twice. The length of gaze at each target was observed through a tiny hole in the ceiling of the chamber and recorded on a timer. The fixation time started as soon as one or both eyes of the infant were directed towards the target, using as criterion the superposition over the pupil of a tiny corneal reflection of the target; it ended when the eyes turned away or closed. The six targets were presented in random order for each infant, with the sequence repeated up to eight times when possible. Only completed sequences were included in calculating the percentage of total fixation time for each target.

The targets were circular, 6 inches in diameter, and had nonglossy surfaces. Three contained black-and-white patterns—a schematic face, concentric circles, and a section of

TABLE 1

Relative Duration of Initial Gaze of Infants at Six Stimulus Objects in Successive and Repeated Presentations

Age group	N	Mean Percentage of Fixation Time						
		Face	Circles	News	White	Yellow	Red	P*
Under 48 hours	8	29.5	23.5	13.1	12.3	11.5	10.1	.005
2 to 5 days	10	29.5	24.3	17.5	9.9	12.1	6.7	.001
2 to 6 months†	25	34.3	18.4	19.9	8.9	8.2	10.1	.001

*Significance level.

†From an earlier study (2).

newspaper containing print $\frac{1}{16}$ to $\frac{1}{4}$ inch high. The other three were unpatterned—white, fluorescent yellow, and dark red. The relative luminous reflectance was, in decreasing order: yellow, white, newsprint, face and circles, red. Squares containing the patterns or colors were placed in a flat holder which slid horizontally into a slightly recessed portion of the chamber ceiling to expose the pattern or color to the infant through a circular hole in the holder. The chamber and underside of the holder were lined with blue felt to provide a contrasting background for the stimuli, and to diffuse the illumination (between 10 and 15 ft-ca) from lights on either side of the infant's head. The subject was in a small hammock crib with head facing up directly under the targets, 1 foot away.

The results in Table 1 show about twice as much visual attention to patterns as to plainly colored surfaces. Differences in response to the six stimulus objects are significant for the infants both under and over 2 days of age; results from these groups do not differ reliably from each other, and are similar to earlier results from much older infants. The selectivity of the visual responses is brought out still more strikingly by tabulating the longest-fixated target for each newborn infant: 11 for face, 5 for concentric circles, 2 for newsprint, and 0 for white, yellow, and red. For comparison, the first choices of infants 2 to 6 months were distributed as follows: 16, 4, 5, 0, 0, 0.

Three infants under 24 hours could be tested sufficiently to indicate the individual consistency of response. Two of these showed a significant (.005 and .05) difference among the targets in successive sets of exposures, one looking longest at the face pattern in 7 of 8 exposures, the other looking longest at the "bull's-eye" in 3 of 6 exposures. The third infant 10 hours after birth looked longest at the face in 3 of 8 exposures.

It is clear that the selective visual responses were related to pattern rather than hue or reflectance, although the latter two variables are often thought to be primary visual stimuli. . . . The results do not imply "instinctive recognition" of a face or other unique significance of this pattern; it is likely there are other patterns which would elicit equal or greater attention. Longer fixation of the face suggests only that a pattern with certain similarities to social objects also has stimulus characteristics with considerable intrinsic interest or stimulating value; whatever the mechanism underlying this interest, it should facilitate the development of social responsiveness, since what is responded to must first be attended to.

Substantiation for the visual selection of patterned over unpatterned objects is given in an independent study of newborn infants in which more visual attention was given to a colored card with a simple figure, when held close to the infant, than to a plain card of either color[6].

The results of Table 1 demonstrate that pattern vision can be tested in newborn infants by recording differential visual attention; these and other results call for a revision of traditional views that the visual world of the infant is initially formless or chaotic and that we must learn to see configurations.

REFERENCES AND NOTES

1. See, for example, Evelyn Dewey, *Behavior Development in Infants* (Columbia Univ. Press. New York, 1935).

2. R. L. Fantz, J. M. Ordy, M. S. Udelf, *J. Comp. Physiol Psychol* **55**, 907 (1962); R. L. Fantz, *Psychol Rec. 8*, 43 (1958).

3. R. L. Fantz, *Sci. Am.* **204,** No. 5, 66 (1961).

4. F. Stirnimann, *Ann. Paediat.* **163,** 1 (1944).

Sleep and Consciousness

The Dream as a Wish-Fulfilment

Sigmund Freud (1900)

If you sleep eight hours per night, you spend approximately two of those hours dreaming. People have always been fascinated with dreams, and many have proposed theories to explain the functions and meaning of dreams. The most popular and well-known dream theory was proposed by Sigmund Freud in 1900. Freud believed that dreams were the road to the elusive unconscious mind. His theory of dreams as wish fulfillments, which is examined in this selection, has sparked a great deal of controversy over the years.

Freud (1856–1939), a neurologist, received his M.D. in 1881 from Vienna University. He spent most of his life in Vienna, Austria, practicing medicine and studying mental disorders through clinical observation. As father of psychoanalysis, Freud significantly influenced many areas of psychology, including personality, development, and clinical psychology.

In Freud's book, *The Interpretation of Dreams* (1900), he presents his theory of the meaning of dreams. This selection is from chapter 3, "The Dream as a Wish-Fulfillment," of that book and it illustrates one of the main points of Freud's dream theory. This selection allows you to see how Freud conceptualized dream interpretation as well as psychoanalysis. As you read this selection, think about how you interpret your own dreams. How could you test Freud's theory of dream interpretation?

Key Concept: Freud's theory of dreaming

APA Citation: Freud, S. (1900). *The interpretation of dreams.* New York: Random House.

When, after passing through a narrow defile, one suddenly reaches a height beyond which the ways part and a rich prospect lies outspread in different directions, it is well to stop for a moment and consider whither one shall turn next. We are in somewhat the same position after we have mastered this first interpretation of a dream. We find ourselves standing in the light of a sudden discovery. The dream is not comparable to the irregular sounds of a musical instrument, which, instead of being played by the hand of a musician, is struck by some external force; the dream is not meaningless, not absurd, does not presuppose that one part of our store of ideas is dormant while another part begins to awake. It is a perfectly valid psychic phenomenon, actually a wish-fulfilment; it may be enrolled in the continuity of the intelligible psychic activities of the waking state; it is built up by a highly complicated intellectual activity. But at the very moment when we are about to rejoice in this discovery a host of problems besets us. If the dream, as this theory defines it, represents a fulfilled wish, what is the cause of the striking and unfamiliar manner in which this fulfilment is expressed? What transformation has occurred in our dream-thoughts before the manifest dream, as we remember it on waking, shapes itself out of them? How has this transformation taken place? Whence comes the material that is worked up into the dream? What causes many of the peculiarities which are to be observed in our dream-thoughts; for example, how is it that they are able to contradict one another? … Is the dream capable of teaching us something new concerning our internal psychic processes, and can its content correct opinions which we have held during the day? I suggest that for the present all these problems be laid aside, and that a single path be pursued. We have found that the dream represents a wish as fulfilled. Our next purpose should be to ascertain whether this is a general characteristic of dreams, or whether it is only the accidental content of [a] particular dream … ; for even if we conclude that every dream has a meaning and psychic value, we must nevertheless allow for the possibility that this meaning may not be the same in every dream. The first dream … [may be] the fulfilment of a wish; another may turn out to be the realization of an apprehension; a third may have a reflection as its content; a fourth may simply reproduce a reminiscence. Are there, then, dreams other than wish-dreams; or are there none but wish-dreams?

It is easy to show that the wish-fulfilment in dreams is often undisguised and easy to recognize, so that one may wonder why the language of dreams has not long since been understood. There is, for example, a dream which I can evoke as often as I please, experimentally, as it were. If, in the evening, I eat anchovies, olives, or other strongly salted foods, I am thirsty at night, and therefore I wake. The waking, however, is preceded by a dream, which has always the same content, namely, that I am drinking. I am drinking long draughts of water; it tastes as delicious as only a cool drink can taste when one's throat is parched; and then I wake, and find that I have an actual desire to drink. The cause of this dream is thirst, which I perceive when I wake. From this sensation arises the wish to drink, and the dream shows me this wish as fulfilled. It hereby serves a function, the nature of which I soon surmise. I sleep well, and am not accustomed to being waked by a bodily need. If I succeed in appeasing my thirst by means of the dream that I am drinking, I need not wake up in order to satisfy that thirst. It is thus a *dream of convenience*. The dream takes the place of action, as elsewhere in life. Unfortunately, the need of water to quench the thirst cannot be satisfied by a dream, as can my thirst for revenge upon [some adversary], but the intention is the same. Not long ago I had the same dream in a somewhat modified form. On this occasion I felt thirsty before going to bed, and emptied the glass of water which stood on the little chest beside my bed. Some hours later, during the night, my thirst returned, with the consequent discomfort. In order to obtain water, I should have had to get up and fetch the glass which stood on my wife's bed-table. I thus quite appropriately dreamt that my wife was giving me a drink from a vase; this vase was an Etruscan cinerary urn, which I had brought home from Italy, and had since given away. But the water in it tasted so salty (apparently on account of the ashes) that I was forced to wake. It may be observed how conveniently the dream is capable of arranging matters. Since the fulfilment of a wish is its only purpose, it may be perfectly egoistic. Love of comfort is really not compatible with consideration for others. The introduction of the cinerary urn is probably once again the fulfilment of a wish; I regret that I no longer possess this vase; it, like the glass of water at my wife's side, is inaccessible to me. The cinerary urn is appropriate also in connection with the sensation of an increasingly salty taste, which I know will compel me to wake.

Such convenience-dreams came very frequently to me in my youth. Accustomed as I had always been to working until late at night, early waking was always a matter of difficulty. I used then to dream that I was out of bed and standing at the washstand. After a while I could no longer shut out the knowledge that I was not yet up; but in the meantime I had continued to sleep. The same sort of lethargy-dream was dreamed by a young colleague of mine, who appears to share my propensity for sleep. With him it assumed a particularly amusing form. The landlady with whom he was lodging in the neighbourhood of

the hospital had strict orders to wake him every morning at a given hour, but she found it by no means easy to carry out his orders. One morning sleep was especially sweet to him. The woman called into his room: "Herr Pepi, get up; you've got to go to the hospital." Whereupon the sleeper dreamt of a room in the hospital, of a bed in which he was lying, and of a chart pinned over his head, which read as follows: "Pepi M., medical student, 22 years of age." He told himself in the dream: "If I am already at the hospital, I don't have to go there," turned over, and slept on. He had thus frankly admitted to himself his motive for dreaming.

Here is yet another dream of which the stimulus was active during sleep: One of my women patients, who had been obliged to undergo an unsuccessful operation on the jaw, was instructed by her physicians to wear by day and night a cooling apparatus on the affected cheek; but she was in the habit of throwing it off as soon as she had fallen asleep. One day I was asked to reprove her from doing so; she had again thrown the apparatus on the floor. The patient defended herself as follows: "This time I really couldn't help it; it was the result of a dream which I had during the night. In the dream I was in a box at the opera, and was taking a lively interest in the performance. But Herr Karl Meyer was lying in the sanatorium and complaining pitifully on account of pains in his jaw. I said to myself, 'Since I haven't the pains, I don't need the apparatus either'; that's why I threw it away." The dream of this poor sufferer reminds me of an expression which comes to our lips when we are in a disagreeable situation: "Well, I can imagine more amusing things!" The dream presents these "more amusing things!" Herr Karl Meyer, to whom the dreamer attributed her pains, was the most casual acquaintance of whom she could think.

It is quite as simple a matter to discover the wish-fulfilment in several other dreams which I have collected from healthy persons. A friend who was acquainted with my theory of dreams, and had explained it to his wife, said to me one day: "My wife asked me to tell you that she dreamt yesterday that she was having her menses. You will know what that means." Of course I know: if the young wife dreams that she is having her menses, the menses have stopped. I can well imagine that she would have liked to enjoy her freedom a little longer, before the discomforts of maternity began. It was a clever way of giving notice of her first pregnancy. Another friend writes that his wife had dreamt not long ago that she noticed milk-stains on the front of her blouse. This also is an indication of pregnancy, but not of the first one; the young mother hoped she would have more nourishment for the second child than she had for the first.

A young woman who for weeks had been cut off from all society because she was nursing a child who was suffering from an infectious disease dreamt, after the child had recovered, of a company of people in which Alphonse Daudet, Paul Bourget, Marcel Prévost and others were present; they were all very pleasant to her and amused her enormously. In her dream these different authors had the features which their portraits give them. M. Prévost, with whose portrait she is not familiar, looked like the man who had disinfected the sickroom the day before, the first outsider to enter it for a long time. Obviously the dream is to be translated thus: "It is about time now for something more entertaining than this eternal nursing."

Perhaps this collection will suffice to prove that frequently, and under the most complex conditions, dreams may be noted which can be understood only as wish-fulfilments, and which present their content without concealment. In most cases these are short and simple dreams, and they stand in pleasant contrast to the confused and overloaded dream-compositions which have almost exclusively attracted the attention of the writers on the subject. But it will repay us if we give some time to the examination of these simple dreams. The simplest dreams of all are, I suppose, to be expected in the case of children whose psychic activities are certainly less complicated than those of adults. Child psychology, in my opinion, is destined to render the same services to the psychology of adults as a study of the structure or development of the lower animals renders to the investigation of the structure of the higher orders of animals. Hitherto but few deliberate efforts have been made to make use of the psychology of the child for such a purpose.

The dreams of little children are often simple fulfilments of wishes, and for this reason are, as compared with the dreams of adults, by no means interesting. They present no problem to be solved, but they are invaluable as affording proof that the dream, in its inmost essence, is the fulfilment of a wish. I have been able to collect several examples of such dreams from the material furnished by my own children.

For two dreams, one that of a daughter of mine, at that time eight and a half years of age, and the other that of a boy of five and a quarter, I am indebted to an excursion to Hallstatt, in the summer of 1896. I must first explain that we were living that summer on a hill near Aussee, from which, when the weather was fine, we enjoyed a splendid view of the Dachstein. With a telescope we could easily distinguish the Simony hut. The children often tried to see it through the telescope—I do not know with what success. Before the excursion I had told the children that Hallstatt lay at the foot of the Dachstein. They looked forward to the outing with the greatest delight. From Hallstatt we entered the valley of Eschern, which enchanted the children with its constantly changing scenery. One of them, however, the boy of five, gradually became discontented. As often as a mountain came into view, he would ask: "Is that the Dachstein?" whereupon I had to reply: "No, only a foot-hill." After this question had been repeated several times he fell quite silent, and did not wish to accompany us up the steps leading to the waterfall. I thought he was tired. But the next morning he came to me, perfectly happy, and said: "Last night I dreamt that we went to the Simony hut."

I understood him now; he had expected, when I spoke of the Dachstein, that on our excursion to Hallstatt he would climb the mountain, and would see at close quarters the hut which had been so often mentioned when the telescope was used. When he learned that he was expected to content himself with foot-hills and a waterfall he was disappointed, and became discontented. But the dream compensated him for all this. I tried to learn some details of the dream; they were scanty. "You go up steps for six hours," as he had been told.

On this excursion the girl of eight and a half had likewise cherished wishes which had to be satisfied by a dream. We had taken with us to Hallstatt our neighbour's twelve-year-old boy; quite a polished little gentleman, who, it seemed to me, had already won the little woman's sympathies. Next morning she related the following dream: "Just think, I dreamt that Emil was one of the family, that he said 'papa' and 'mamma' to you, and slept at our house, in the big room, like one of the boys. Then mamma came into the room and threw a handful of big bars of chocolate, wrapped in blue and green paper, under our beds." The girl's brothers, who evidently had not inherited an understanding of dream-interpretation, declared … : "That dream is nonsense." The girl defended at least one part of the dream, and from the standpoint of the theory of the neuroses it is interesting to learn which part it was that she defended: "That Emil was one of the family was nonsense, but that part about the bars of chocolate wasn't." It was just this latter part that was obscure to me, until my wife furnished the explanation. On the way home from the railway-station the children had stopped in front of a slot-machine, and had wanted exactly such bars of chocolate, wrapped in paper with a metallic lustre, such as the machine, in their experience, provided. But the mother thought, and rightly so, that the day had brought them enough wish-fulfilments, and therefore left this wish to be satisfied in the dream. This little scene had escaped me. That portion of the dream which had been condemned by my daughter I understood without any difficulty. I myself had heard the well-behaved little guest enjoining the children, as they were walking ahead of us, to wait until 'papa' or 'mamma' had come up. For the little girl the dream turned this temporary relationship into a permanent adoption. Her affection could not as yet conceive of any other way of enjoying her friend's company permanently than the adoption pictured in her dream, which was suggested by her brothers. Why the bars of chocolate were thrown under the bed could not, of course, be explained without questioning the child.

From a friend I have learned of a dream very much like that of my little boy. It was dreamed by a little girl of eight. Her father, accompanied by several children, had started on a walk to Dornbach, with the intention of visiting the Rohrer hut, but had turned back, as it was growing late, promising the children to take them some other time. On the way back they passed a signpost which pointed to the Hameau. The children now asked him to take them to the Hameau, but once more, and for the same reason, they had to be content with the promise that they should go there some other day. Next morning the little girl went to her father and told him, with a satisfied air: "Papa, I dreamed last night that you were with us at the Rohrer hut, and on the Hameau." Thus, in the dream her impatience had anticipated the fulfilment of the promise made by her father.

Another dream, with which the picturesque beauty of the Aussee inspired my daughter, at that time three and a quarter years of age, is equally straightforward. The little girl had crossed the lake for the first time, and the trip has passed too quickly for her. She did not want to leave the boat at the landing, and cried bitterly. The next morning she told us: "Last night I was sailing on the lake." Let us hope that the duration of this dream-voyage was more satisfactory to her.

My eldest boy, at that time eight years of age, was already dreaming of the realization of his fancies. He had ridden in a chariot with Achilles, with Diomedes as charioteer. On the previous day he had shown a lively interest in a book on the myths of Greece which had been given to his elder sister.

If it can be admitted that the talking of children in their sleep belongs to the sphere of dreams, I can relate the following as one of the earliest dreams in my collection: My youngest daughter, at that time nineteen months old, vomited one morning, and was therefore kept without food all day. During the night she was heard to call excitedly in her sleep: "Anna F(r)eud, *st'awbewy, wild st'awbewy, om'lette, pap!*" She used her name in this way in order to express the act of appropriation; the menu presumably included everything that would seem to her a desirable meal; the fact that two varieties of strawberry appeared in it was a demonstration against the sanitary regulations of the household, and was based on the circumstance, which she had by no means overlooked, that the nurse had ascribed her indisposition to an over-plen-

tiful consumption of strawberries; so in her dream she avenged herself for this opinion which met with her disapproval.

When we call childhood happy because it does not yet know sexual desire, we must not forget what a fruitful source of disappointment and renunciation, and therefore of dream-stimulation, the other great vital impulse may be for the child. Here is a second example. My nephew, twenty-two months of age, had been instructed to congratulate me on my birthday, and to give me a present of a small basket of cherries, which at that time of the year were scarce, being hardly in season. He seemed to find the task a difficult one, for he repeated again and again: "Cherries in it," and could not be induced to let the little basket go out of his hands. But he knew how to indemnify himself. He had, until then, been in the habit of telling his mother every morning that he had dreamt of the "white soldier," an officer of the guard in a white cloak, whom he had once admired in the street. On the day after the sacrifice on my birthday he woke up joyfully with the announcement, which could have referred only to a dream: "*He[r] man eaten all the cherries!*"

What animals dream of I do not know. A proverb for which I am indebted to one of my pupils professes to tell us, for it asks the question: "What does the goose dream of?" and answers: "Of maize." The whole theory that the dream is the fulfilment of a wish is contained in these two sentences.

We now perceive that we should have reached our theory of the hidden meaning of dreams by the shortest route had we merely consulted the vernacular. Proverbial wisdom, it is true, often speaks contemptuously enough of dreams—it apparently seeks to justify the scientists when it says that "dreams are bubbles"; but in colloquial language the dream is predominantly the gracious fulfiller of wishes. "I should never have imagined that in my wildest dreams," we exclaim in delight if we find that the reality surpasses our expectations.

Regularly Occurring Periods of Eye Motility, and Concomitant Phenomena, During Sleep[1]

Eugene Aserinsky[2] *and Nathaniel Kleitman*

The understanding of sleep changed drastically in 1953, the year when Eugene Aserinsky, working with Nathaniel Kleitman in a sleep laboratory, first observed rapid eye movements (REM) during sleep. We now know that restful sleep is interrupted periodically with brain activity similar to what is observed when we are awake. One sign of REM sleep is the rapid movement of the eyes as they dart back and forth, up and down. Dreaming is believed to take place largely during REM sleep.

Aserinsky (1921–1998) was a graduate student at University of Chicago in 1953 when he discovered REM sleep in his eight year old son. He earned his Ph.D. from the University of Chicago, and taught at Jefferson Medical College and Marshall University. Kleitman (1895–1999) earned his PhD in 1923 from the University of Chicago, where he had a long career in sleep research until his retirement in 1960. Among his books is *Sleep and Wakefulness* (2nd ed.), published by the University of Chicago Press in 1963. Together Aserinsky and Kleitman pioneered techniques of studying eye movements that have become standard in sleep research, and hence they are considered founders of modern sleep research.

In this selection, from "Regularly Occurring Periods of Eye Mobility and Concomitant Phenomena, During Sleep," Aserinsky and Kleitman describe the important finding of rapid eye movements (REM) in sleep. Before this discovery, it was believed that sleep was a passive state of consciousness. Although a little technical in places, you can easily see that REM is found in all people, and that other bodily processes such as heart rate and respiration are also different during REM sleep. Why do you think it took so long before scientists noticed REM sleep? Why is it important to understand REM sleep?

Key Concept: REM sleep

APA Citation: Aserinsky, E., & Kleitman, N. (1953). Regularly occurring periods of eye mobility and concomitant phenomena, during sleep. *Science, 118*, 273-274.

Department of Physiology, University of Chicago, Chicago, Illinois

Slow, rolling or pendular eye movements such as have been observed in sleeping children or adults by Pietrusky *(1)*, De Toni *(2)*, Fuchs and Wu (3), and Andreev (4), anid in sleep and anesthesia by Burford (5) have also been noted by us. However, this report deals with a different type of eye movement—rapid, jerky, and binocularly symmetrical—which was briefly described elsewhere *(6)*.

The eye movements were recorded quantitatively as electrooculograms by employing one pair of leads on the superior and inferior orbital ridges of one eye to detect changes of the corneo—retinal potential in a vertical plane, and another pair of leads on the internal and external canthi of the same eye to pick up mainly the horizontal component of eye movement. The potentials were led into a Grass Electroencephalograph with the EOG[3] channels set at the longest time constant. The criterion for identification of eye movement was confirmed by direct observation of several subjects under both weak and gradually intensified illumination. Under the latter condition, motion pictures were taken of 2 subjects without awakening them, thereby further confirming the validity of our recording method and also the synchronicity of eye movements.

Twenty normal adult subjects were employed in several series of experiments although not all the subjects were involved in each series. To confirm the conjecture that this particular eye activity was associated with dreaming, 10 sleeping individuals in 14 experiments were awakened and interrogated during the occurrence of this eye motility and also after a period of at least 30 min to 3 hr of ocular quiescence. The period of ocular inactivity was selected on the basis of the EEG pattern to represent, as closely as possible, a depth of sleep comparable to that present during ocular motility. Of 27 interrogations during ocular motility, 20 revealed detailed dreams usually involving visual imagery; the replies to the remaining 7 queries included complete failure of recall, or else, "the feeling of having dreamed," but with inability to recollect any detail of the dream. Of 23 interrogations during ocular inactivity, 19 disclosed complete failure of recall, while the remaining 4 were evenly divided into the other 2 categories. Recognizing the inadequacies of employing a x^2 test for the independence of the 2 groups of interrogations, the probability nevertheless on a x^2 basis is that the ability to recall dreams is significantly associated with the presence of the eye movements noted, with a p value of less than 0.01.

Eleven subjects in one series of 16 experiments were permitted to sleep uninterruptedly throughout the night. The mean duration of sleep was 7 hr. The first appearance of a pattern of rapid, jerky eye movements was from 1 hr 40 min to 4 hr 50 min (3 hr 14 min, mean) after going to bed. This pattern of eye motility was of variable duration and frequently disappeared for a fraction of a minute or for several minutes only to reappear and disappear a number of times. The period from the onset of the first recognizable pattern to the disappearance of the last pattern was from 6 to 53 min with a mean of 20 min. A second period of eye movement patterns appeared from 1 hr 10 min to 3 hr 50 min (2 hr 16 min, mean) after the onset of the first eye motility period. With lengthier sleep there occurred a third and, rarely, a fourth such period. The electrooculogram disclosed vivid potentials with amplitudes as high as 300-400 μv, each potential lasting about 1 sec. This was further striking in comparison with simultaneously recorded monopolar EEG's, from the frontal and occipital areas, which were invariably of low amplitude (5-30 μv) and irregular frequency (15-20/sec and 5-8/sec predominating).

In another series of experiments involving 14 subjects, the respiratory rate was calculated for a minimum of ½ min during eye motility and compared with the rate for a similar duration 15 min before and after an eye motility period. The respiratory rate had a mean of 16.9/min during eye motility in contrast with 13.4/min during ocular quiescence. By using Fisher's t method, the difference in rates was found to be statistically significant with a probability of less than 0.001. Experiments now in progress suggest that heart rate also is probably higher in the presence of these eye movements. Body motility records were secured in 6 experiments by attaching a sensitive crystal to the bed spring and leading the output through a resistance to a Grass preamplifier. In every case the eye motility periods were associated with peaks of overt bodily activity although the latter were frequently present in the absence of eye movements.

Data obtained from the 2 female subjects used in these experiments were at least qualitatively similar to that obtained from males.

The fact that these eye movements, EEG pattern, and autonomic nervous system activity are significantly related and do not occur randomly suggests that these physiological phenomena, and probably dreaming, are very likely all manifestations of a particular level of cortical activity which is encountered normally during sleep. An eye movement period first appears about 3 hr after going to sleep, recurs 2 hr later, and then emerges at somewhat closer intervals a third or fourth time shortly prior to awakening. This method furnishes the means of determining the incidence and duration of periods of dreaming.

Notes

1. Aided by a grant from the Wallace C. and Clara A. Abbott Memorial Fund of the University of Chicago.
2. Public Health Service Research Fellow of the National Institute of Mental Health.
3. Electrooculogram.

References

1. PIETRUSKY, F. *Klin. Monatsbl. f. Augenheilk.,* **63,** 355 (1922).
2. DE TONI, G. *Pediatria,* **41,** 489 (1933).
3. FUCHS, A., and WU, F. C. *Am. J. Ophthalmol.,* **31,** 717 (1948).
4. ANDREEV, B. V. *Fiziol. Zhur. SSSR,* **36,** 429 (1950).
5. BURFORD, G. E. *Anesth. & Analgesia,* 20, 191 (1941).
6. ASERINSKY, E., and KLEITMAN, N. *Federation Proc.,* **12,** 6 (1953).

The Brain as a Dream State Generator

An Activation-Synthesis Hypothesis of the Dream Process

Hobson, J. A., & McCarley, R. W. (1977)

Poets and philosophers, psychologists and biologists have all pondered the meaning of dreams. Many of us wonder what our dreams mean. The popular wish-fulfillment theory of Freud has been around for a hundred years. More recently, theories suggest dreaming may allow us to consolidate the information we learn during the day. A different approach, however, was taken by researchers J. Allan Hobson and Robert W. McCarley, when they proposed their activation-synthesis theory.

Hobson (b. 1933) received his M.D. from Harvard Medical School in 1959, where he is currently a professor of psychiatry. His books include *The Dreaming Brain* (Basic Books, 1988), and *Sleep* (Scientific American Library, 1989). McCarley received his M.D. from Harvard Medical School in 1964. He is currently a professor of psychiatry at Boston VA Medical Center. Hobson and McCarley are best known for their work on sleep and dreaming, including the activation-synthesis hypothesis of dreaming.

In the current selection, from "The Brain as a Dream State Generator: An Activation-Synthesis Hypothesis of the Dream Process," which was published in *American Journal of Psychiatry* in 1977, the authors review Freud's theory of dreaming and then propose a new theory based on modern knowledge of the brain. Basically, they state that the brain generates its own electrical activity, which it then tries to synthesis into some meaningful experience for the dreamer. This interesting proposal has generated a good deal of discussion among dream researchers, but no solid consensus has yet been reached. As you read this selection, consider your own dreams. What do you dream about? Is your dreaming organized and relevant, or does it seem that you are just trying to make sense out of physiological processes which are occurring?

Key Concept: dreaming

APA Citation: Hobson, J. A., & McCarley, R. W. (1977). The brain as a dream state generator: An activation-synthesis hypothesis of the dream process. *American Journal of Psychiatry, 134,* 1335–1348.

Since the turn of the century, dream theory has been dominated by the psychoanalytic hypothesis that dreaming is a reactive process designed to protect consciousness and sleep from the disruptive effect of unconscious wishes that are released in sleep (1). Thus dreaming has been viewed as a psychodynamically determined state, and the distinctive formal features of dream content have been interpreted as manifestations of a defensive transformation of the unconscious wishes found unacceptable to consciousness by a hypothetical censor. A critical tenet of this wish fulfillment-disguise theory is that the transformation of the unconscious wish by the censor disguises or degrades the ideational information in forming the dream imagery. We were surprised to discover the origins of the major tenets of psychoanalytic dream theory in the neurophysicology of 1890 and

have specified the transformations made by Freud in an earlier, related article (2). In detailing the neurophysiological origins of psychoanalytic dream theory, the concept of mind-body isomorphism, denoting similarity of form between psychological and physiological events, was seen as an explicit premise of Freud's thought.

Sharing Freud's conviction that mind-body isomorphism is a valid approach, we will now review modern neurophysiological evidence that we believe permits and necessitates important revisions in psychoanalytic dream theory. The activation-synthesis hypothesis that we will begin to develop in this paper asserts that many formal aspects of the dream experience may be the obligatory and relatively undistorted psychological concomitant of the regularly recurring and physiologically determined brain state called "dreaming sleep." It ascribes particular formal features of the dream experience to the particular organizational features of the brain during that state of sleep. More specifically, the theory details the mechanisms by which the brain becomes periodically activated during sleep and specifies the means by which both sensory input and motor output are simultaneously blocked, so as to account for the maintenance of sleep in the face of strong central activation of the brain. The occurrence and character of dreaming are seen as both determined and shaped by these physiological processes.

The most important tenet of the activation-synthesis hypothesis is that during dreaming the activated brain generates its own information by a pontine brain stem neuronal mechanism, which will be described in detail. We hypothesize that this internally generated sensorimotor information, which is partially random and partially specific, is then compared with stored sensorimotor data in the synthesis of dream content. The functional significance of the brain activation and the synthesis of endogenous information in dreaming sleep is not known, but we suggest that state-dependent learning is at least as likely a result of dreaming as is tension reduction or sleep maintenance.

While we believe that the two processes emphasized in this paper—activation and synthesis—are major and important advance in dream theory, we wish to state explicitly and comment on some of the things that our theory does not attempt to do. The activation-synthesis hypothesis does not exclude possible defensive distortions of the value-free sensorimotor dream stimuli, but it does deny the primacy of any such process in attempting to explain *formal* aspects of dream content or the fundamental impetus to dreaming itself. The idea that dreams reveal wishes is also beyond the direct reach of our new theory, but some specific alternatives to this interpretation of several classic dream situations can be advanced.

The new theory cannot yet account for the emotional aspects of the dream experience, but we assume that they are produced by the activation of brain regions subserving affect in parallel with the activation of the better known sensorimotor pathways. Finally, the new theory does not deny meaning to dreams, but it does suggest 1) a more direct route to their acquisition than anamnesis via free association, since dream origins are in basic physiological processes and not in disguised wishes, 2) a less complex approach to their interpretation than conversion from manifest to latent content, since unusual aspects of dreams are not seen as disguises but as results of the way the brain and mind function during sleep, and 3) a broader view of their use in therapy than that provided by the transference frame of reference, since dreams are not to be interpreted as the product of disguised unconscious (transference) wishes. Dreams offer a royal road to the mind and brain in a behavioral state, with different operating rules and principles than during waking and with the possibility of clinically useful insights from the product of these differences.

What Is a Dream?

A dream may be defined as a mental experience, occurring in sleep, which is characterized by hallucinoid imagery, predominantly visual and often vivid; by bizarre elements due to such spatiotemporal distortions as condensation, discontinuity, and acceleration; and by a delusional acceptance of these phenomena as "real" at the time that they occur. Strong emotion may or may not be associated with these distinctive formal properties of the dream, and subsequent recall of these mental events is almost invariable poor unless an immediate arousal from sleep occurs.

That this technical jargon describes a universal human experience seems certain, since the five key points in this definition are easily elicited from both naïve and sophisticated individuals when they are asked to characterized their dreams. We leave aside the question of whether other less vivid and nonperceptual forms of mental activity during sleep should also be called "dreams" and confine ourselves here to the psychophysiology of the hallucinoid type of dream. In doing so, we not only simplify the immediate task at hand but may also gain insight into the mechanisms underlying the most florid symptoms of psychopathology. We mean, of course, the hallucinations and delusions of the psychotic experience, which have so often invited comparison with the dream as we have defined it here.

What Is the State of the Brain During Dreaming Sleep?

The physiological substrate of the dream experience is the CNS in one of its three principal operating states: waking (W), synchronized (S), and desynchronized sleep (D). these states can be reliably and objectively differentiated by recording the EEG, the electromyogram (EMG), and the electrooculogram. Hallucinoid dreaming in man occurs predominantly during the periodically recurrent phase of sleep characterized by EEG desynchronization, EMG suppression, and REMs (3). We call this kind of sleep "D" (meaning desynchronized, but also conveniently denoting dreaming).

In the systems analysis terms used in figure 1, this D brain state is characterized by the following "sensorimotor" properties: activation of the brain; relative exclusion of external input; generation of some internal input, which the activated forebrain then processes as information; and blocking of motor output, except for the oculomotor pathway. In this model the substrate of emotion is considered to be a part of the forebrain; it will not be further distinguished here because we have no specific physiological evidence as to how this part of the system might work in any brain state. Memory is not shown but is considered to be a differentiated function of the brain that operates during the D state, such that output from long-term storage is blocked. A highly specific hypothesis about dream amne-

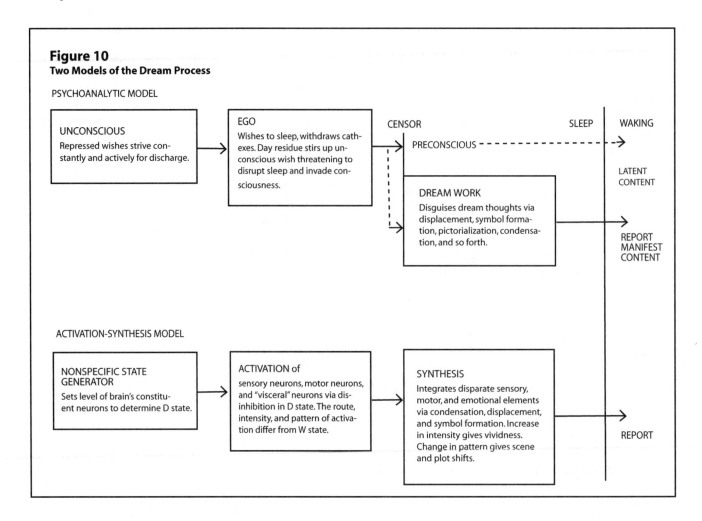

Figure 10
Two Models of the Dream Process

PSYCHOANALYTIC MODEL

| UNCONSCIOUS
Repressed wishes strive constantly and actively for discharge. | EGO
Wishes to sleep, withdraws cathexes. Day residue stirs up unconscious wish threatening to disrupt sleep and invade consciousness. | CENSOR | SLEEP | WAKING |

PRECONSCIOUS

LATENT CONTENT

DREAM WORK
Disguises dream thoughts via displacement, symbol formation, pictorialization, condensation, and so forth.

REPORT MANIFEST CONTENT

ACTIVATION-SYNTHESIS MODEL

NONSPECIFIC STATE GENERATOR
Sets level of brain's constituent neurons to determine D state.

ACTIVATION of
sensory neurons, motor neurons, and "visceral" neurons via disinhibition in D state. The route, intensity, and pattern of activation differ from W state.

SYNTHESIS
Integrates disparate sensory, motor, and emotional elements via condensation, displacement, and symbol formation. Increase in intensity gives vividness. Change in pattern gives scene and plot shifts.

REPORT

---

sia has previously been derived from the same evidence that we will now review in our attempt to account for the general sensorimotor aspects of the dream process.

Electrophysiology of the Brain During the Dream State

The three major electrographic features of the D state are of obvious relevance to our attempt to answer the following three questions about the organization of the brain in the dream state.

How is the forebrain activated in the D state? Physiological evidence clearly shows that the profound EMG suppression of D sleep is a consequence of the direct inhibition of spinal cord motoneurons (5). As a consequence, any organized motor patterns that might be generated during the intense brain activation of D sleep cannot be expressed.

That organized movement patterns are in fact generated, but not expressed, in normal D sleep is dramatically demonstrated by cats with lesions of the anterodorsal pontine brain stem (6). The animals show all of the major manifestations of D sleep except the atonia; instead of the fine twitches of the digits and the limb jerks that are normally present in D, these cats display complex motor be-

haviors including repetitive paw movements and well-coordinated attack and defense sequences that have no apparent relationship to the environment.

How is sensory imagery generated in the D state? In waking, a corollary discharge of the oculomotor system has been shown to suppress visual transmission during saccadic eye movement, possibly contributing to the stability of the visual field during that state (7). The same mechanisms might underlie the hallucinoid dream imagery by inhibiting and exciting neurons of the lateral geniculate body and the visual cortex during D sleep, when retinal input is reduced and unformed.

Psychological Implications of the Cellular Neurophysiology of Dream Sleep Generation

Hallucinoid dreaming is regarded as the psychological concomitant of D sleep. Brain activity in the D state has been analyzed to account for activation of the forebrain, occlusion of sensory input, blockade of motor output at the spinal cord level, and the generation of information within the system. The evidence that the pontine brain stem contains a clock-trigger mechanism that contributes to activation of the forebrain, occlusion of sensory input, and the generation of internal information has been reviewed. The periodicity of the triggering mechanism is hypothesized to be a function of reciprocal interaction of reciprocally connected, chemically coded cell groups in the pontine brain stem.

The psychological implications of this model, which we call the activation-synthesis hypothesis of the dream process (schematically represented in figure 10) contrast sharply with many tenets of the dream theory provided by psychoanalysis (also represented in figure 10) in the following ways:

1. *The primary motivating force for dreaming* is not psychological but physiological since the time of occurrence and duration of dreaming sleep are quite constant, suggesting a preprogrammed, neurally determined genesis. In fact, the neural mechanisms involved can now be precisely specified. This conclusion does not, of course, mean that dreams are not also psychological events; nor does it imply that they are without psychological meaning or function. But it does imply that the process is much more basic than the psychodynamically determined, evanescent, "guardian of sleep" process that Freud had imagined it to be; and it casts serious doubt upon the exclusively psychological significance attached to both the occurrence and quality of dreams.

2. *Specific stimuli for the dream imagery* appear to arise intracerebrally but from the pontine brain stem and not in cognitive areas of the cerebrum. These stimuli, whose generation appears to depend upon a largely random or reflex process, may provide spatially specific information which can be used in constructing dream imagery; but the unusual intensity, intermittency, and velocity of the eye movements may also contribute to features of the dream experience which are formally bizarre and have been interpreted as defensive by psychoanalysis. Thus such features as scene shifts, time compression, personal condensations, splitting, and symbol formation may be directly isomorphic with the state of the nervous system during dreaming sleep. In other words, the forebrain may be making the best of a bad job in producing even partially coherent dream imagery from the relatively noisy signals sent up to it from the brain stem.

The dream process is thus seen as having its origin in sensorimotor systems, with little or no primary ideational, volitional, or emotional content. This concept is markedly different from that of the "dream thoughts" or wishes seen by Freud as the primary stimulus for the dream. The sensorimotor stimuli are viewed as possibly providing a frame into which ideational, volitional, or emotional content may be projected to form the integrated dream image, but this frame is itself conflict free. Thus both the major energetic drive for the dream process and the specific primary stimulus of the dream content are genotypically determined and therefore conflict free in the specifically psychodynamic sense of the term.

3. *The elaboration of the brain stem stimulus* by the perceptual, conceptual, and emotional structures of the forebrain is viewed as primarily a synthetic constructive process, rather than a distorting one as Freud presumed. Best fits to the relative inchoate and incomplete data provided by the primary stimuli are called up from memory, the access to which is facilitated during dreaming sleep. The brain, in the dreaming sleep state, is thus likened to a computer searching its addresses for key words. Rather than indicating a need for disguise, this fitting of phenotypic experiential data to genotypic stimuli is seen as the major basis of the "bizarre" formal qualities of dream mentation. There is, therefore, no need to postulate either a censor or an information degrading process working at the censor's behest. The dream content elaborated by the forebrain may include conflictually charged memories, but even this aspect of dream construction is seen as synthetic and transparent rather than degradative and opaque.

4. *With respect to the forgetting of dreams*, the normally poor recall is seen principally to reflect a state-dependent amnesia, since a carefully effected state change, to waking, may produce abundant recall even of highly charged dream material. There is thus no need to invoke repression to account for the forgetting of dreams. This hypothesis is appealingly economical, and in the light of the reciprocal interaction hypothesis is appealingly economical, and in the light of the reciprocal interaction hypothesis dream amnesia can now be modeled in a testable way as the result of a different balance between cholinergic and aminergic neuropal activity and the resulting effects on second messengers and macromelecules. Among its other surprising gifts to psychophysiology, dreaming sleep may thus also provide a biological model for the study of memory, and a functional role for dreaming sleep in promoting some aspect of the learning process is suggested.

References

1. Freud S: The interpretation of dreams (1900), in The Complete Psychological Works, standard ed, vols 4 and 5. Translated and edited by Strachey J. London, Hagarth Press, 1966
2. McCarley RW, Hobson JA: The neurobiological origins of psychoanalytic dream theory. AM J Psychiatry 134:1211–1221, 1977
3. Dement W, Kleitman N: The relation of eye movements during sleep to dream activity: an objective method for the study of dreaming. J Exp Psychol 53:89–97, 1957
4. Pompeiano O: The neurophysiological mechanisms of the postural and motor events during desynchronized sleep. Res Publ Assoc Res Nerv Ment Dis 45:351–423, 1967
5. Volkman F: Vision during voluntary saccadic eye movements. J Opt Soc Am 52:571–578, 1962
6. Bizzi E: Discharge pattern of single geniculate neurons during the rapid eye movements of sleep. J Neurophysiol 29:1087–1095, 1966
7. Evarts EV: Activity of individual cerebral neurons during sleep and arousal. Res Publ Assoc Res Nerv Ment Dis 45:319–337, 1967

Learning

Selection 14
I.P. PAVLOV, from Conditioned Reflexes: An Investigation of the Physiological Activity of the Cerebral/Cortex, trans. and edited G.V. Anrer

Selection 15
JOHN B. WATSON and ROSALIE RAYNER, from "Conditioned Emotional Reactions," Journal of Economic Perspectives

Selection 16
B. F. SKINNER, from "Shaping and Maintaining Operant Behavior," Science and Human Behavior

Conditioned Reflexes: An Investigation of the Physiological Activity of the Cerebral Cortex

Ivan P. Pavlov (1927)

Learning has been a topic of great interest to psychologists during most of psychology's history. Indeed, it could be argued that learning is involved in everything we do. One of the most significant research programs was conducted not by a psychologist, but rather a medical physiologist living in Russia, Ivan P. Pavlov.

Pavlov (1849–1936) earned a medical degree from the Imperial Medicosurgical Academy in 1879 and studied physiology in Germany before accepting a position as professor of pharmacology at the St. Petersburg Institute of Experimental Medicine in 1890. Pavlov won a Nobel Prize in 1904 for his research on the physiology of digestion in dogs.

The selection that follows is from chapter 2, "Lecture II," of Pavlov's book, *Conditioned Reflexes: An Investigation of the Physiological Activity of the Cerebral Cortex*, published in 1927 by Oxford University Press. Pavlov designed the laboratory where he studied conditioned reflexes in dogs. He presents the basic terminology of classical conditioning and discusses some of the factors that influence learning. Pavlov uses a lecture format and includes demonstrations of the actual research experiments.

Key Concept: Classical conditioning

APA Citation: Pavlov, I. P. (1927). *Conditioned reflexes: An investigation of the physiological activity of the cerebral cortex*. London: Oxford University Press.

To come to the general technique of the [salivary secretion] experiments, it is important to remember that our research deals with the highly specialized activity of the cerebral cortex, a signalizing apparatus of tremendous complexity and of most exquisite sensitivity, through which the animal is influenced by countless stimuli from the outside world. Every one of these stimuli produces a certain effect upon the animal, and all of them taken together may clash and interfere with, or else reinforce, one another. Unless we are careful to take special precautions the success of the whole investigation may be jeopardized, and we should get hopelessly lost as soon as we began to seek for cause and effect among so many and various influences, so intertwined and entangled as to form a veritable chaos. It was evident that the experimental conditions had to be simplified, and that this simplification must consist in eliminating as far as possible any stimuli outside our control which might fall upon the animal, admitting only such stimuli as could be entirely controlled by the experimenter. It was thought at the beginning of our research that it would be sufficient simply to isolate the experimenter in the research chamber with the dog on its stand, and to refuse admission to anyone else during the course of an experiment. But this precaution was found to be wholly inadequate, since the experimenter, however still he might try to be, was himself a constant source of a large number of stimuli. His slightest movements—blinking of the eyelids or movement of the eyes, posture, respiration and so on—all acted as stimuli which, falling upon the dog, were sufficient to vitiate the experiments by making exact interpretation of the results extremely difficult. In order to exclude this undue influence on the part of the experimenter as far as possible, he had to be stationed outside the room in which the dog was placed, and even this precaution proved unsuccessful in laboratories not specially designed for the study of these particular reflexes. The environment of the animal, even when shut up by itself in a room, is perpetually changing. Footfalls of a passer-by, chance conversations in neighbouring rooms, slamming of a door or vibration from a passing van, street-cries, even shadows cast through the windows into the room, any of these casual uncontrolled stimuli falling upon the receptors of the dog set up a disturbance in the cerebral hemispheres and vitiate the experiments. To get over all these disturbing factors a special laboratory was built at the Institute of Experimental Medicine in Petrograd, the funds being provided by a keen and public-spirited Moscow business man. The primary task was the protection of the dogs from uncontrolled extraneous stimuli, and this was effected by surrounding the building with an isolating trench and employing other special structural devices. Inside the building all the research rooms (four to each floor) were isolated from one another by a cross-shaped corridor; the top and ground floors, where these rooms were situated, were separated by an intermediate floor. Each research room was carefully partitioned by the use of sound-proof materials into two compartments—one for the animal, the other for the experimenter. For stimulating the animal, and for registering the corresponding reflex response, electrical methods or pneumatic transmission were used. By means of these arrangements it was possible to get something of that stability of environmental conditions so essential to the carrying out of a successful experiment. …

The foregoing remarks give an idea of our general aim and of the technical side of our methods. I propose to introduce you to the first and most elementary principles of the subject matter of our research by means of a few demonstrations:

DEMONSTRATION.—The dog used in the following experiment has been operated upon [so that the opening of the salivary duct is transplanted to the outside skin in order to more easily measure secretory activity of the gland]. It can be seen that so long as no special stimulus is applied the salivary glands remain quite inactive. But when the sounds from a beating metronome are allowed to fall upon the ear, a salivary secretion begins after 9 seconds, and in the course of 45 seconds eleven drops have been secreted. The activity of the salivary gland has thus been called into play by impulses of sound—a stimulus quite alien to food. This activity of the salivary gland cannot be regarded as anything else than a component of the alimentary reflex. Besides the secretory, the motor component of the food reflex is also very apparent in experiments of this kind. In this very experiment the dog turns in the direction from which it has been customary to present the food and begins to lick its lips vigorously.

This experiment is an example of a central nervous activity depending on the integrity of the hemispheres. A decerebrate dog would never have responded by salivary secretion to any stimulus of the kind. It is obvious also

that the underlying principle of this activity is signalization. The sound of the metronome is the signal for food, and the animal reacts to the signal in the same way as if it were food; no distinction can be observed between the effects produced on the animal by the sounds of the beating metronome and showing it real food.

DEMONSTRATION.—Food is shown to the animal. The salivary secretion begins after 5 seconds, and six drops are collected in the course of 15 seconds. The effect is the same as that observed with the sounds of the metronome. It is again a case of signalization, and is due to the activity of the hemispheres.

That the effect of sight and smell of food is not due to an inborn reflex, but to a reflex which has been acquired in the course of the animal's own individual existence, was shown by experiments carried out by Dr. Zitovich in the laboratory of the late Prof. Vartanov. Dr. Zitovich took several young puppies away from their mother and fed them for a considerable time only on milk. When the puppies were a few months old he established fistulae of their salivary ducts, and was thus able to measure accurately the secretory activity of the glands. He now showed these puppies some solid food—bread or meat—but no secretion of saliva was evoked. It is evident, therefore, that the sight of food does not in itself act as a direct stimulus to salivary secretion. Only after the puppies have been allowed to eat bread and meat on several occasions does the sight or smell of these foodstuffs evoke the secretion.

The following experiment serves to illustrate the activity of the salivary gland as an inborn reflex in contrast to signalization:

DEMONSTRATION.—Food is suddenly introduced into the dog's mouth; secretion begins in 1 to 2 seconds. The secretion is brought about by the physical and chemical properties of the food itself acting upon receptors in the mucous membrane of the mouth and tongue. It is purely reflex.

This comparatively simple experiment explains how a decerebrate dog can die of starvation in the midst of plenty, for it will only start eating if food chances to come into contact with its mouth or tongue. Moreover, the elementary nature of the inborn reflexes, with their limitations and inadequacy, are clearly brought out in these experiments, and we are now able to appreciate the fundamental importance of those stimuli which have the character of *signals*.

Our next step will be to consider the question of the nature of signalization and of its mechanism from a purely physiological point of view. … [A] reflex is an inevitable reaction of the organism to an external stimulus, brought about along a definite path in the nervous system. Now it is quite evident that in signalization all the properties of a reflex are present. In the first place an external stimulus is required. This was given in our first experiment by the sounds of a metronome. These sounds falling on the auditory receptor of the dog caused the propagation of an impulse along the auditory nerve. In the brain the impulse was transmitted to the secretory nerves of the salivary glands, and passed thence to the glands, exciting them to active secretion. It is true that in the experiment with the metronome an interval of several seconds elapsed between the beginning of the stimulus and the beginning of the salivary secretion, whereas the time interval for the inborn reflex secretion was only 1 to 2 seconds. The longer latent period was, however, due to some special conditions of the experiment, as will come out more clearly as we proceed. But generally speaking the reaction to signals under natural conditions is as speedy as are the inborn reflexes. . . .

In our general survey we characterized a reflex as a necessary reaction following upon a strictly definite stimulus under strictly defined conditions. Such a definition holds perfectly true also for signalization; the only difference is that the type of the effective reaction to signals depends upon a greater number of conditions. But this does not make signalization differ fundamentally from the better known reflexes in any respect, since in the latter, variations in character or force, inhibition and absence of reflexes, can also be traced to some definite change in the conditions of the experiment.

Thorough investigation of the subject shows that accident plays no part whatever in the signalizing activity of the hemispheres, and all experiments proceed strictly according to plan. In the special laboratory I have described, the animal can frequently be kept under rigid experimental observation for 1 to 2 hours without a single drop of saliva being secreted independently of stimuli applied by the observer, although in the ordinary type of physiological laboratory experiments are very often distorted by the interference of extraneous and uncontrolled stimuli.

All these conditions leave no grounds for regarding the phenomena which we have termed "signalization" as being anything else than reflex. There is, however, another aspect of the question which at a first glance seems to point to an essential difference between the better known reflexes and signalization. Food, through its chemical and physical properties, evokes the salivary reflex in every dog right from birth, whereas this new type claimed as reflex—"the signal reflex"—is built up gradually in the course of the animal's own individual existence. But can this be considered as a fundamental point of difference, and can it hold as a valid argument against employing the term "reflex" for this new group of phenomena? It is certainly a sufficient argument for making a definite distinction between the two types of reflex and for considering the signal reflex in a group distinct from the inborn reflex. But this does not invalidate in any way our right logically to term both "reflex," since the point of distinction does not concern the character of the response on the part of the organism, but only the mode of formation of the reflex mechanism. We may take the telephonic

installation as an illustration. Communication can be effected in two ways. My residence may be connected directly with the laboratory by a private line, and I may call up the laboratory whenever it pleases me to do so; or on the other hand, a connection may have to be made through the central exchange. But the result in both cases is the same. The only point of distinction between the methods is that the private line provides a permanent and readily available cable, while the other line necessitates a preliminary central connection being established. In the one case the communicating wire is always complete, in the other case a small addition must be made to the wire at the central exchange. We have a similar state of affairs in reflex action. The path of the inborn reflex is already completed at birth; but the path of the signalizing reflex has still to be completed in the higher nervous centres. We are thus brought to consider the mode of formation of new reflex mechanisms. A new reflex is formed inevitably under a given set of physiological conditions, and with the greatest ease, so that there is no need to take the subjective states of the dog into consideration. With a complete understanding of all the factors involved, the new signalizing reflexes are under the absolute control of the experimenter; they proceed according to as rigid laws as do any other physiological processes, and must be regarded as being in every sense a part of the physiological activity of living beings. I have termed this new group of reflexes conditioned reflexes to distinguish them from the inborn or unconditioned reflexes. The term "conditioned" is becoming more and more generally employed, and I think its use is fully justified in that, compared with the inborn reflexes, these new reflexes actually do depend on very many conditions, both in their formation and in the maintenance of their physiological activity. Of course the terms "conditioned" and "unconditioned" could be replaced by others of arguably equal merit. Thus, for example, we might retain the term "inborn reflexes," and call the new type "acquired reflexes"; or call the former "species reflexes" since they are characteristic of the species, and the latter "individual reflexes" since they vary from animal to animal in a species, and even in the same animal at different times and under different conditions. Or again we might call the former "conduction reflexes" and the latter "connection reflexes."

There should be no theoretical objection to the hypothesis of the formation of new physiological paths and new connections within the cerebral hemispheres. Since the especial function of the central nervous system is to establish most complicated and delicate correspondences between the organism and its environment we may not unnaturally expect to find there, on the analogy of the methods used by the technician in everyday experience, a highly developed connector system superimposed on a conductor system. The physiologist certainly should not object to this conception seeing that he has been used to employing the German conception of "Bahnung," which means a laying down of fresh physiological paths in the centres. Conditioned reflexes are phenomena of common and widespread occurrence: their establishment is an integral function in everyday life. We recognize them in ourselves and in other people or animals under such names as "education," "habits," and "training;" and all of these are really nothing more than the results of an establishment of new nervous connections during the post-natal existence of the organism. They are, in actual fact, links connecting definite extraneous stimuli with their definite responsive reactions. I believe that the recognition and the study of the conditioned reflex will throw open the door to a true physiological investigation probably of all the highest nervous activities of the cerebral hemispheres, and the purpose of the present lectures is to give some account of what we have already accomplished in this direction.

We come now to consider the precise conditions under which new conditioned reflexes or new connections of nervous paths are established. The fundamental requisite is that any external stimulus which is to become the signal in a conditioned reflex must overlap in point of time with the action of an unconditioned stimulus. In the experiment which I chose as my example the unconditioned stimulus was food. Now if the intake of food by the animal takes place simultaneously with the action of a neutral stimulus which has been hitherto in no way related to food, the neutral stimulus readily acquires the property of eliciting the same reaction in the animal as would food itself. This was the case with the dog employed in our experiment with the metronome. On several occasions this animal had been stimulated by the sound of the metronome and immediately presented with food—*i.e.* a stimulus which was neutral of itself had been superimposed upon the action of the inborn alimentary reflex. We observed that, after several repetitions of the combined stimulation, the sounds from the metronome had acquired the property of stimulating salivary secretion and of evoking the motor reactions characteristic of the alimentary reflex. The first demonstration was nothing but an example of such a conditioned stimulus in action. Precisely the same occurs with the mild defence reflex to rejectable substances. Introduction into the dog's mouth of a little of an acid solution brings about a quite definite responsive reaction. The animal sets about getting rid of the acid, shaking its head violently, opening its mouth and making movements with its tongue. At the same time it produces a copious salivary secretion. The same reaction will infallibly be obtained from any stimulus which has previously been applied a sufficient number of times while acid was being introduced into the dog's mouth. Hence a first and most essential requisite for the formation of a new conditioned reflex lies in a coincidence in time of the action of any previously neutral stimulus with some definite unconditioned stimulus. Further, it is not enough that there should be overlapping between the two stimuli; it is also and equally necessary that the conditioned stimulus should begin to operate before the unconditioned stimulus comes into action.

If this order is reversed, the unconditioned stimulus being applied first and the neutral stimulus second, the conditioned reflex cannot be established at all. Dr. Krestovnikov performed these experiments with many different modifications and controls, but the effect was always the same. The following are some of his results:

In one case 427 applications were made in succession of the odour of vanillin together with the introduction of acid into the dog's mouth, but the acid was always made to precede the vanillin by some 5 to 10 seconds. Vanillin failed to acquire the properties of a conditioned stimulus. However, in the succeeding experiment, in which the order of stimuli was reversed, the odour, this time of amyl acetate, became an effective conditioned stimulus after only 20 combinations. With another dog the loud buzzing of an electric bell set going 5 to 10 seconds after administration of food failed to establish a conditioned alimentary reflex even after 374 combinations, whereas the regular rotation of an object in front of the eyes of the animal, the rotation beginning before the administration of food, acquired the properties of a conditioned stimulus after only 5 combinations. The electric buzzer set going before the administration of food established a conditioned alimentary reflex after only a single combination.

Dr. Krestovnikov's experiments were carried out on five dogs, and the result was always negative when the neutral stimulus was applied, whether 10 seconds, 5 seconds or only a single second after the beginning of the unconditioned stimulus. During all these experiments not only the secretory reflex but also the motor reaction of the animal was carefully observed, and these observations always corroborated one another. We thus see that the first set of conditions required for the formation of a new conditioned reflex encompasses the time relation between the presentation of the unconditioned stimulus and the presentation of that agent which has to acquire the properties of a conditioned stimulus.

As regards the condition of the hemispheres themselves, an alert state of the nervous system is absolutely essential for the formation of a new conditioned reflex. If the dog is mostly drowsy during the experiments, the establishment of a conditioned reflex becomes a long and tedious process, and in extreme cases is impossible to accomplish. The hemispheres must, however, be free from any other nervous activity, and therefore in building up a new conditioned reflex it is important to avoid foreign stimuli which, falling upon the animal, would cause other reactions of their own. If this is not attended to, the establishment of a conditioned reflex is very difficult, if not impossible. Thus, for example, if the dog has been so fastened up that anything causes severe irritation, it does not matter how many times the combination of stimuli is repeated, we shall not be able to obtain a conditioned reflex. A somewhat similar case was described [elsewhere] —that of the dog which exhibited the *freedom reflex* in an exaggerated degree. It can also be stated as a rule that the establishment of the first conditioned reflex in an animal is usually more difficult than the establishment of succeeding ones. It is obvious that this must be so, when we consider that even in the most favourable circumstances the experimental conditions themselves will be sure to provoke numerous different reflexes—*i.e.* will give rise to one or other disturbing activity of the hemispheres. But this statement must be qualified by remarking that in cases where the cause of these uncontrolled reflexes is not found out, so that we are not able to get rid of them, the hemispheres themselves will help us. For if the environment of the animal during the experiment does not contain any powerful disturbing elements, then practically always the extraneous reflexes will with time gradually and spontaneously weaken in strength.

The third factor determining the facility with which new conditioned reflexes can be established is the health of the animal. A good state of health will ensure the normal functioning of the cerebral hemispheres, and we shall not have to bother with the effects of any internal pathological stimuli.

The fourth, and last, group of conditions has to do with the properties of the stimulus which is to become conditioned, and also with the properties of the unconditioned stimulus which is selected. Conditioned reflexes are quite readily formed to stimuli to which the animal is more or less indifferent at the outset, though strictly speaking no stimulus within the animal's range of perception exists to which it would be absolutely indifferent. In a normal animal the slightest alteration in the environment—even the very slightest sound or faintest odour, or the smallest change in intensity of illumination—immediately evokes the reflex which I refer ... to ... as the investigatory reflex—"What is it?"—manifested by a very definite motor reaction. However, if these neutral stimuli keep recurring, they spontaneously and rapidly weaken in their effect upon the hemispheres, thus bringing about bit by bit the removal of this obstacle to the establishment of a conditioned reflex. But if the extraneous stimuli are strong or unusual, the formation of a conditioned reflex will be difficult, and in extreme cases impossible.

Conditioned Emotional Reactions

John B. Watson and Rosalie Rayner (1920)

The desire of early researchers to apply the techniques of classical and operant conditioning—two forms of behavior learning involving stimulus association and reinforcement—to understand practical problems led to John B. Watson's well-known Little Albert experiment, which is discussed in this selection. The classic experiment of how Albert learned to fear a white rat—and other furry or rat-like stimuli—has been a favorite of students and instructors alike.

Watson (1878–1958), the founder of the school of behaviorism, received his Ph.D. from the University of Chicago in 1903, where he taught until 1908. He then taught at Johns Hopkins University until 1920. Among his influential books is his 1919 *Psychology from the Standpoint of a Behaviorist.* Rosalie Rayner (1899–1936) was an assistant in the psychology laboratory during the Little Albert experiment. Rayner and Watson were married in 1920.

This selection is from "Conditioned Emotional Reactions," which was published in *Journal of Experimental Psychology* in 1920. Although the Little Albert experiment was originally intended as a pilot study and had some methodological flaws, it serves as an example of how conditioning can modify behavior. Watson and Rayner describe explicitly the procedures they used and the results they obtained. Unfortunately, Albert's mother moved immediately after the experiment was conducted; hence the experimenters could not develop a technique to remove the conditioned fear reaction from him. As you read this selection, try to remember how you learned to fear certain events as you were growing up.

Key Concept: conditioned emotional reactions in infants

APA Citation: Watson, J. B., & Rayner, R. (1920). Conditioned emotional reactions. *Journal of Experimental Psychology, 3,* 1–14.

*I*n recent literature various speculations have been entered into concerning the possibility of conditioning various types of emotional response, but direct experimental evidence in support of such a view has been lacking. If the theory advanced by Watson and Morgan to the effect that in infancy the original emotional reaction patterns are few, consisting so far as observed of fear, rage and love, then there must be some simple method by means of which the range of stimuli which can call out these emotions and their compounds is greatly increased. Otherwise, complexity in adult response could not be accounted for. These authors without adequate experimental evidence advanced the view that this range was increased by means of conditioned reflex factors. It was suggested there that the early home life of the child furnishes a laboratory situation for establishing conditioned emotional responses. The present authors have recently put the whole matter to an experimental test.

Experimental work has been done so far on only one child, Albert B. This infant was reared almost from birth in a hospital environment; his mother was a wet nurse in the Harriet Lane Home for Invalid Children. Albert's life was normal: he was healthy from birth and one of the best developed youngsters ever brought to the hospital, weighing twenty-one pounds at nine months of age. He was on the whole stolid and unemotional. His stability was one of the principal reasons for using him as a subject in this test. We felt that we could do him relatively little harm by carrying out such experiments as those outlined below.

At approximately nine months of age we ran him through the emotional tests that have become a part of our regular routine in determining whether fear reactions can be called out by other stimuli than sharp noises and the sudden removal of support. … In brief, the infant was confronted suddenly and for the first time successively with a white rat, a rabbit, a dog, a monkey, with masks with and without hair, cotton wool, burning newspapers, etc. A permanent record of Albert's reactions to these objects and situations has been preserved in a motion picture study. Manipulation was the most usual reaction called out. *At no time did this infant ever show fear in any sit-*

uation. These experimental records were confirmed by the casual observations of the mother and hospital attendants. No one had ever seen him in a state of fear and rage. The infant practically never cried.

Up to approximately nine months of age we had not tested him with loud sounds. The test to determine whether a fear reaction could be called out by a loud sound was made when he was eight months, twenty-six days of age. The sound was that made by striking a hammer upon a suspended steel bar four feet in length and three-fourths of an inch in diameter. The laboratory notes are as follows:

> One of the two experimenters caused the child to turn its head and fixate her moving hand; the other, stationed back of the child, struck the steel bar a sharp blow. The child started violently, his breathing was checked and the arms were raised in a characteristic manner. On the second stimulation the same thing occurred, and in addition the lips began to pucker and tremble. On the third stimulation the child broke into a sudden crying fit. This is the first time an emotional situation in the laboratory has produced any fear or even crying in Albert.

We had expected just these results on account of our work with other infants brought up under similar conditions. It is worth while to call attention to the fact that removal of support (dropping and jerking the blanket upon which the infant was lying) was tried exhaustively upon this infant on the same occasion. It was not effective in producing the fear response. This stimulus is effective in younger children. At what age such stimuli lose their potency in producing fear is not known. Nor is it known whether less placid children ever lose their fear of them. This probably depends upon the training the child gets. It is well known that children eagerly run to be tossed into the air and caught. On the other hand it is equally well known that in the adult fear responses are called out quite clearly by the sudden removal of support, if the individual is walking across a bridge, walking out upon a beam, etc. There is a wide field of study here which is aside from our present point.

The sound stimulus, thus, at nine months of age, gives us the means of testing several important factors. I. Can we condition fear of an animal, *e.g.*, a white rat, by visually presenting it and simultaneously striking a steel bar? II. If such a conditioned emotional response can be established, will there be a transfer to other animals or other objects? …

I. The establishment of conditioned emotional responses. At first there was considerable hesitation upon our part in making the attempt to set up fear reactions experimentally. A certain responsibility attaches to such a procedure. We decided finally to make the attempt, comforting ourselves by the reflection that such attachments would arise anyway as soon as the child left the sheltered environment of the nursery for the rough and tumble of the home. We did not begin this work until Albert was eleven months, three days of age. Before attempting to set up a conditioned response we, as before, put him through all of the regular emotional tests. *Not the slightest sign of a fear response was obtained in any situation.*

The steps taken to condition emotional responses are shown in our laboratory notes.

11 Months 3 Days

1. White rat suddenly taken from the basket and presented to Albert. He began to reach for rat with left hand. Just as his hand touched the animal the bar was struck immediately behind his head. The infant jumped violently and fell forward, burying his face in the mattress. He did not cry, however.
2. Just as the right hand touched the rat the bar was again struck. Again the infant jumped violently, fell forward and began to whimper.

In order not to disturb the child too seriously no further tests were given for one week.

11 Months 10 Days

1. Rat presented suddenly without sound. There was steady fixation but no tendency at first to reach for it. The rat was then placed nearer, whereupon tentative reaching movements began with the right hand. When the rat nosed the infant's left hand, the hand was immediately withdrawn. He started to reach for the head of the animal with the forefinger of the left hand, but withdrew it suddenly before contact. It is thus seen that the two joint stimulations given the previous week were not without effect. He was tested with his blocks immediately afterwards to see if they shared in the process of conditioning. He began immediately to pick them up, dropping them, pounding them, etc. In the remainder of the tests the blocks were given frequently to quiet him and to test his general emotional state. They were always removed from sight when the process of conditioning was under way.
2. Joint stimulation with rat and sound. Started, then fell over immediately to right side. No crying.
3. Joint stimulation. Fell to right side and rested upon hands, with head turned away from rat. No crying.
4. Joint stimulation. Same reaction.
5. Rat suddenly presented alone. Puckered face, whimpered and withdrew body sharply to the left.
6. Joint stimulation. Fell over immediately to right side and began to whimper.
7. Joint stimulation. Started violently and cried, but did not fall over.
8. Rat alone. *The instant the rat was shown the baby began to cry. Almost instantly he turned sharply to the left, fell over on left side, raised himself on all fours and began to crawl away so rapidly that he was caught with difficulty before reaching the edge of the table.*

This was as convincing a case of a completely conditioned fear response as could have been theoretically pictured. In all seven joint stimulations were given to bring about the complete reaction. It is not unlikely had the sound been of greater intensity or of a more complex clang character that the number of joint stimulations might have been materially reduced. Experiments designed to define the nature of the sounds that will serve best as emotional stimuli are under way.

II. When a conditioned emotional response has been established for one object, is there a transfer? Five days later Albert was again brought back into the laboratory and tested as follows:

11 Months 15 Days

1. Tested first with blocks. He reached readily for them, playing with them as usual. This shows that there has been no general transfer to the room, table, blocks, etc.

2. Rat alone. Whimpered immediately, withdrew right hand and turned head and trunk away.

3. Blocks again offered. Played readily with them, smiling and gurgling.

4. Rat alone. Leaned over to the left side as far away from the rat as possible, then fell over, getting up on all fours and scurrying away as rapidly as possible.

5. Blocks again offered. Reached immediately for them, smiling and laughing as before. The above preliminary test shows that the conditioned response to the rat had carried over completely for the five days in which no tests were given. The question as to whether or not there is a transfer was next taken up.

6. Rabbit alone. The rabbit was suddenly placed on the mattress in front of him. The reaction was pronounced. Negative responses began at once. He leaned as far away from the animal as possible, whimpered, then burst into tears. When the rabbit was placed in contact with him he buried his face in the mattress, then got up on all fours and crawled away, crying as he went. This was a most convincing test.

7. The blocks were next given him, after an interval. He played with them as before. It was observed by four people that he played far more energetically with them than ever before. The blocks were raised high over his head and slammed down with a great deal of force.

8. Dog alone. The dog did not produce as violent a reaction as the rabbit. The moment fixation occurred the child shrank back and as the animal came nearer he attempted to get on all fours but did not cry at first. As soon as the dog passed out of his range of vision he became quiet. The dog was then made to approach the infant's head (he was lying down at the moment). Albert straightened up immediately, fell over to the opposite side and turned his head away. He then began to cry.

9. The blocks were again presented. He began immediately to play with them.

10. Fur coat (seal).Withdrew immediately to the left side and began to fret. Coat put close to him on the left side, he turned immediately, began to cry and tried to crawl away on all fours.

11. Cotton wool. The wool was presented in a paper package. At the end the cotton was not covered by the paper. It was placed first on his feet. He kicked it away but did not touch it with his hands. When his hand was laid on the wool he immediately withdrew it but did not show the shock that the animals or fur coat produced in him. He then began to play with the paper, avoiding contact with the wool itself. He finally, under the impulse of the manipulative instinct, lost some of his negativism to the wool.

12. Just in play W. put his head down to see if Albert would play with his hair. Albert was completely negative. Two other observers did the same thing. He began immediately to play with their hair. W. then brought the Santa Claus mask and presented it to Albert. He was again pronouncedly negative. …

From the above results it would seem that emotional transfers do take place. Furthermore it would seem that the number of transfers resulting from an experimentally produced conditioned emotional reaction may be very large. In our observations we had no means of testing the complete number of transfers which may have resulted. …

Incidental Observations

(a) Thumb sucking as a compensatory device for blocking fear and noxious stimuli. During the course of these experiments, … it was noticed that whenever Albert was on the verge of tears or emotionally upset generally he would continually thrust his thumb into his mouth. The moment the hand reached the mouth he became impervious to the stimuli producing fear. Again and again while the motion pictures were being made at the end of the thirty-day rest period, we had to remove the thumb from his mouth before the conditioned response could be obtained. This method of blocking noxious and emotional stimuli (fear and rage) through erogenous stimulation seems to persist from birth onward. …

(b) Equal primacy of fear, love and possibly rage. While in general the results of our experiment offer no particular points of conflict with Freudian concepts, one fact out of harmony with them should be emphasized. According to proper Freudians sex (or in our terminology, love) is the principal emotion in which conditioned responses arise which later limit and distort personality. We wish to take sharp issue with this view on the basis of the experimental evidence we have gathered. Fear is as primal a factor as love in influencing personality. Fear does not gather its potency in any derived manner from love. It belongs to the original and inherited nature of man. Probably the same may be true of rage although at present we are not so sure of this. ...

It is probable that many of the phobias in psychopathology are true conditioned emotional reactions either of the direct or the transferred type. One may possibly have to believe that such persistence of early conditioned responses will be found only in persons who are constitutionally inferior. Our argument is meant to be constructive. Emotional disturbances in adults cannot be traced back to sex alone. They must be retraced along at least three collateral lines—to conditioned and transferred responses set up in infancy and early youth in all three of the fundamental human emotions.

SELECTION 16

Shaping and Maintaining Operant Behavior

B. F. Skinner (1953)

Reinforcement—an event that increases the probability that the behavior preceding it will be repeated—can have a profound effect on behavior, and we typically do things that lead to reinforcement. Much of what scientists originally discovered about the effects of reinforcement on animals has been applied to human behavior. The study of how reinforcement changes behavior is known as operant conditioning.

B. F. Skinner (1904–1990) was a pioneer in the study of operant conditioning. Skinner earned a B.A. in English from Hamilton College in 1926, but he decided he did not have anything important to say, so he went back to school and earned a Ph.D. in psychology from Harvard University in 1931. Indeed, he did have much to say, and he wrote numerous books, including *The Behavior of Organisms* (1938) and the fictional *Walden Two* (1948), in which Skinner describes a utopian society run in accordance with operant principles. In *Beyond Freedom and Dignity* (Alfred A. Knopf, 1971), he explains why it is important to understand how we control behavior in our day-to-day lives.

This selection is from chapter 6, "Shaping and Maintaining Operant Behavior," of Skinner's *Science and Human Behavior* (Macmillan, 1953). Although Skinner's favorite subject for study was the pigeon, as illustrated in this selection, he believed that the laws of behavior apply to all organisms. Note how Skinner neatly applies the results of his animal research to human beings, as well as how clearly he defines the four intermittent schedules of reinforcement.

Key Concept: operant conditioning

APA Citation: Skinner, B. F. (1953). *Science and human behavior.* New York: Macmillan.

THE CONTINUITY OF BEHAVIOR

Operant conditioning [a process in which reinforcement changes the frequency of a behavior] shapes behavior as a sculptor shapes a lump of clay. Although at some point the sculptor seems to have produced an entirely novel object, we can always follow the process back to the original undifferentiated lump, and we can make the successive stages by which we return to this condition as small as we wish. At no point does anything emerge which is very different from what preceded it. The final product seems to have a special unity or integrity of design, but we cannot find a point at which this suddenly appears. In the same sense, an operant [behavior generated by reinforcement consequences] is not something which appears full grown in the behavior of the organism. It is the result of a continuous shaping process.

The pigeon experiment demonstrates this clearly. "Raising the head" is not a discrete unit of behavior. It does not come, so to speak, in a separate package. We reinforce only slightly exceptional values of the behavior observed while the pigeon is standing or moving about. We succeed in shifting the whole range of heights at which the head is held, but there is nothing which can be accurately described as a new "response." A response such as turning the latch in a problem box appears to be a more discrete unit, but only because the continuity with other behavior is more difficult to observe. In the pigeon, the response of pecking at a spot on the wall of the experimental box seems to differ from stretching the neck because no other behavior of the pigeon resembles it. If in reinforcing such a response we simply wait for it to occur—and we may have to wait many hours or days or weeks—the whole unit appears to emerge in its final form and to be strengthened as such. There may be no appreciable behavior which we could describe as "almost pecking the spot."

The continuous connection between such an operant and the general behavior of the bird can nevertheless easily be demonstrated. It is the basis of a practical procedure for setting up a complex response. To get the pigeon to peck the spot as quickly as possible we proceed as follows: We first give the bird food when it turns slightly in the direction of the spot from any part of the cage. This increases the frequency of such behavior. We then withhold reinforcement until a slight movement is made toward the spot. This again alters the general distribution of behavior without producing a new unit. We continue by reinforcing positions successively closer to the spot, then by reinforcing only when the head is moved slightly forward, and finally only when the beak actually makes contact with the spot. We may reach this final response in a remarkably short time. A hungry bird, well adapted to the situation and to the food tray, can usually be brought to respond in this way in two or three minutes.

The original probability of the response in its final form is very low; in some cases it may even be zero. In this way we can build complicated operants which would never appear in the repertoire of the organism otherwise. By reinforcing a series of successive approximations, we bring a rare response to a very high probability in a short time. This is an effective procedure because it recognizes and utilizes the continuous nature of a complex act. The total act of turning toward the spot from any point in the box, walking toward it, raising the head, and striking the spot may seem to be a functionally coherent unit of behavior; but it is constructed by a continual process of differential reinforcement from undifferentiated behavior, just as the sculptor shapes his figure from a lump of clay. When we wait for a single complete instance, we reinforce a similar sequence but far less effectively because the earlier steps are not optimally strengthened.

This account is inaccurate in one respect. We may detect a discontinuity between bringing the head close to the spot and pecking. The pecking movement usually emerges as an obviously preformed unit. There are two possible explanations. A mature pigeon will already have developed a well-defined pecking response which may emerge upon the present occasion. The history of this response might show a similar continuity if we could follow it. It is possible, however, that there is a genetic discontinuity, and that in a bird such as the pigeon the pecking response has a special strength and a special coherence as a form of species behavior. Vomiting and sneezing are human responses which probably have a similar genetic unity. Continuity with other behavior must be sought in the evolutionary process. But these genetic units are rare, at least in the vertebrates. The behavior with which we are usually concerned, from either a theoretical or practical point of view, is continuously modified from a basic material which is largely undifferentiated.

Through the reinforcement of slightly exceptional instances of his behavior, a child learns to raise himself, to stand, to walk, to grasp objects, and to move them about. Later on, through the same process, he learns to talk, to sing, to dance, to play games—in short, to exhibit the enormous repertoire characteristic of the normal adult. When we survey behavior in these later stages, we find it convenient to distinguish between various operants which differ from each other in topography and produce different consequences. In this way behavior is broken into parts to facilitate analysis. These parts are the units which we count and whose frequencies play an important role in arriving at laws of behavior. They are the "acts" into which, in the vocabulary of the layman, behavior is divided. But if we are to account for many of its quantitative properties, the ultimately continuous nature of behavior must not be forgotten. …

THE MAINTENANCE OF BEHAVIOR

One reason the term "learning" is not equivalent to "operant conditioning" is that traditionally it has been confined to the process of learning *how to do something*. In trial-and-error learning, for example, the organism learns how to get out of a box or how to find its way through a maze. It is easy to see why the acquisition of behavior should be emphasized. Early devices for the study of learning did not reveal the basic process directly. The effect of operant reinforcement is most conspicuous when there is a gross change in behavior. Such a chance occurs when an organism learns how to make a response which it did not or could not make before. A more sensitive measure, however, enables us to deal with cases in which the acquisition of behavior is of minor importance.

Operant conditioning continues to be effective even when there is no further change which can be spoken of as acquisition or even as improvement in skill. Behavior continues to have consequences and these continue to be important. If consequences are not forthcoming, extinction occurs. When we come to consider the behavior of the organism in all the complexity of its everyday life, we need to be constantly alert to the prevailing reinforcements, which maintain its behavior. We may, indeed, have little interest in how that behavior was first acquired. Our concern is only with its present probability of occurrence, which can be understood only through an examination of current contingencies of reinforcement. This is an aspect of reinforcement which is scarcely ever dealt with in classical treatments of learning.

INTERMITTENT REINFORCEMENT

In general, behavior which acts upon the immediate physical environment is consistently reinforced. We orient ourselves toward objects and approach, reach for, and seize them with a stable repertoire of responses which have uniform consequences arising from the optical and mechanical properties of nature. It is possible, of course, to disturb the uniformity. In a "house of mirrors" in an amusement park, or in a room designed to supply misleading cues to the vertical, well-established responses may fail to have their usual effects. But the fact that such conditions are so unusual as to have commercial value testifies to the stability of the everyday world.

A large part of behavior, however, is reinforced only intermittently. A given consequence may depend upon a series of events which are not easily predicted. We do not always win at cards or dice, because the contingencies are so remotely determined that we call them "chance." We do not always find good ice or snow when we go skating or skiing. Contingencies which require the participation of people are especially likely to be uncertain. We do not always get a good meal in a particular restaurant because cooks are not always predictable. We do not always get an answer when we telephone a friend because the friend is not always at home. We do not always get a pen by reaching into our pocket because we have not always put it there. The reinforcements characteristic of industry and education are almost always intermittent because it is not feasible to control behavior by reinforcing every response.

As might be expected, behavior which is reinforced only intermittently often shows an intermediate frequency of occurrence, but laboratory studies of various schedules have revealed some surprising complexities. Usually such behavior is remarkably stable and shows great resistance to extinction.* An experiment has already been mentioned in which more than 10,000 responses appeared in the extinction curve of a pigeon which had been reinforced on a special schedule. Nothing of the sort is ever obtained after continuous reinforcement. Since this is a technique for "getting more responses out of an organism" in return for a given number of reinforcements, it is widely used. Wages are paid in special ways and betting and gambling devices are designed to "pay off" on special schedules because of the relatively large return on the reinforcement in such a case. Approval, affection, and other personal favors are frequently intermittent, not only because the person supplying the reinforcement may behave in different ways at different times, but precisely because he may have found that such a schedule yields a more stable, persistent, and profitable return.

It is important to distinguish between schedules which are arranged by a system outside the organism and those which are controlled by the behavior itself. An example of the first is a schedule of reinforcement which is determined by a clock—as when we reinforce a pigeon every five minutes, allowing all intervening responses to go unreinforced. An example of the second is a schedule in which a response is reinforced after a certain number of responses have been emitted—as when we reinforce every fiftieth response the pigeon makes. The cases are similar in the sense that we reinforce intermittently in both, but subtle differences in the contingencies lead to very different results, often of great practical significance.

---

*[Extinction is a decline in behavior frequency due to the withholding of reinforcement.—Ed.]

Interval Reinforcement

If we reinforce behavior at regular intervals, an organism such as a rat or pigeon will adjust with a nearly constant rate of responding, determined by the frequency of reinforcement. If we reinforce it every minute, the animal responds rapidly; if every five minutes, much more slowly. A similar effect upon probability of response is characteristic of human behavior. How often we call a given number on the telephone will depend, other things being equal, upon how often we get an answer. If two agencies supply the same service, we are more likely to call the one which answers more often. We are less likely to see friends or acquaintances with whom we only occasionally have a good time, and we are less likely to write to a correspondent who seldom answers. The experimental results are precise enough to suggest that in general the organism gives back a certain number of responses for each response reinforced. We shall see, however, that the results of schedules of reinforcement are not always reducible to a simple equating of input with output.

Since behavior which appears under interval reinforcement is especially stable, it is useful in studying other variables and conditions. The size or amount of each reinforcement affects the rate—more responses appearing in return for a larger reinforcement. Different kinds of reinforcers also yield different rates, and these may be used to rank reinforcers in the order of their effectiveness. The rate varies with the immediacy of the reinforcement: a slight delay between response and the receipt of the reinforcer means a lower over-all rate. Other variables which have been studied under interval reinforcement will be discussed in later chapters. They include the degree of deprivation and the presence or absence of certain emotional circumstances.

Optimal schedules of reinforcement are often of great practical importance. They are often discussed in connection with other variables which affect the rate. Reinforcing a man with fifty dollars at one time may not be so effective as reinforcing him with five dollars at ten different times during the same period. This is especially the case with primitive people where conditioned reinforcers have not been established to bridge the temporal span between a response and its ultimate consequence. There are also many subtle interactions between schedules of reinforcement and levels of motivation, immediacy of reinforcement, and so on.

If behavior continues to be reinforced at fixed intervals, another process intervenes. Since responses are never reinforced just after reinforcement, a change … eventually takes place in which the rate of responding is low for a short time after each reinforcement. The rate rises again when an interval of time has elapsed which the organism presumably cannot distinguish from the interval at which it is reinforced. These changes in rate are not characteristic of the effect of wages in industry, which would otherwise appear to be an example of a fixed-interval schedule. The discrepancy is explained by the fact that other reinforcing systems are used to maintain a given level of work. . . . Docking a man for time absent guarantees his presence each day by establishing a timecard entry as a conditioned reinforcer. The aversive reinforcement supplied by a supervisor or boss is, however, the principal supplement to a fixed-interval wage.

A low probability of response just after reinforcement is eliminated with what is called *variable-interval* reinforcement. Instead of reinforcing a response every five minutes, for example, we reinforce every five minutes *on the average*, where the intervening interval may be as short as a few seconds or as long as, say, ten minutes. Reinforcement occasionally occurs just after the organism has been reinforced, and the organism therefore continues to respond at that time. Its performance under such a schedule is remarkably stable and uniform. Pigeons reinforced with food with a variable interval averaging five minutes between reinforcements have been observed to respond for as long as fifteen hours at a rate of from two to three responses per second without pausing longer than fifteen or twenty seconds during the whole period. It is usually very difficult to extinguish a response after such a schedule. Many sorts of social or personal reinforcement are supplied on what is essentially a variable-interval basis, and extraordinarily persistent behavior is sometimes set up.

Ratio Reinforcement

An entirely different result is obtained when the schedule of reinforcement depends upon the behavior of the organism itself—when, for example, we reinforce every fiftieth response. This is reinforcement at a "fixed ratio"—the ratio of reinforced to unreinforced responses. It is a common schedule in education, where the student is reinforced for completing a project or a paper or some other specific amount of work. It is essentially the basis of professional pay and of selling on commission. In industry it is known as piecework pay. It is a system of reinforcement which naturally recommends itself to employers because the cost of the labor required to produce a given result can be calculated in advance.

Fixed-ratio reinforcement generates a very high rate of response provided the ratio is not too high. This should follow from the input-output relation alone. Any slight increase in rate increases the frequency of reinforcement with the result that the rate should rise still further. If no other factor intervened, the rate should reach the highest possible value. A limiting factor, which makes itself felt in industry, is simple fatigue. The high rate of responding and the long hours of work generated by this schedule can be dangerous to health. This is the main reason why piecework pay is usually strenuously opposed by organized labor.

Another objection to this type of schedule is based upon the possibility that as the rate rises, the reinforcing agency will move to a larger ratio. In the laboratory, after

first reinforcing every tenth response and then every fiftieth, we may find it possible to reinforce only every hundredth, although we could not have used this ratio in the beginning. In industry, the employee whose productivity has increased as the result of a piecework schedule may receive so large a weekly wage that the employer feels justified in increasing the number of units of work required for a given unit of pay.

Under ratios of reinforcement which can be sustained, the behavior eventually shows a very low probability just after reinforcement, as it does in the case of fixed-interval reinforcement. The effect is marked under high fixed ratios because the organism always has "a long way to go" before the next reinforcement. Wherever a piecework schedule is used—in industry, education, salesmanship, or the professions—low morale or low interest is most often observed just after a unit of work has been completed. When responding begins, the situation is improved by each response and the more the organism responds, the better the chances of reinforcement become. The result is a smooth gradient of acceleration as the organism responds more and more rapidly. The condition eventually prevailing under high fixed-ratio reinforcement is not an efficient over-all mode of responding. It makes relatively poor use of the available time, and the higher rates of responding may be especially fatiguing.

The laboratory study of ratio reinforcement has shown that for a given organism and a given measure of reinforcement there is a limiting ratio beyond which behavior cannot be sustained. The result of exceeding this ratio is an extreme degree of extinction of the sort which we call abulia. Long periods of inactivity begin to appear between separate ratio runs. This is not physical fatigue, as we may easily show by shifting to another schedule. It is often called "mental" fatigue, but this designation adds nothing to the observed fact that beyond a certain high ratio of reinforcement the organism simply has no behavior available. In both the laboratory study of ratio reinforcement and its practical application in everyday life, the first signs of strain imposed by too high a ratio are seen in these breaks. Before a pigeon stops altogether—in complete "abulia"—it will often not respond for a long time after reinforcement. In the same way, the student who has finished a term paper, perhaps in a burst of speed at the end of the gradient, finds it difficult to start work on a new assignment.

Exhaustion can occur under ratio reinforcement because there is no self-regulating mechanism. In interval reinforcement, on the other hand, any tendency toward extinction is opposed by the fact that when the rate declines, the next reinforcement is received in return for fewer responses. The variable interval schedule is also self-protecting: an organism will stabilize its behavior at a given rate under any length of interval.

We get rid of the pauses after reinforcement on a fixed-ratio schedule by adopting essentially the same practice as in variable-interval reinforcement: we simply vary the ratios over a considerable range around some mean value. Successive responses may be reinforced or many hundreds of unreinforced responses may intervene. The probability of reinforcement at any moment remains essentially constant and the organism adjusts by holding to a constant rate. This "variable-ratio reinforcement" is much more powerful than a fixed ratio schedule with the same mean number of responses. A pigeon may respond as rapidly as five times per second and maintain this rate for many hours.

The efficacy of such schedules in generating high rates has long been known to the proprietors of gambling establishments. Slot machines, roulette wheels, dice cages, horse races, and so on pay off on a schedule of variable ratio reinforcement. Each device has its own auxiliary reinforcements, but the schedule is the important characteristic. Winning depends upon placing a bet and in the long run upon the number of bets placed, but no particular payoff can be predicted. The ratio is varied by any one of several "random" systems. The pathological gambler exemplifies the result. Like the pigeon with its five responses per second for many hours, he is the victim of an unpredictable contingency of reinforcement. The long-term net gain or loss is almost irrelevant in accounting for the effectiveness of this schedule.

Human Memory

Storage and Retrieval Processes in Long-Term Memory

Richard M. Shiffrin and Richard C. Atkinson (1969)

People have always been fascinated with how human memory works. For most of the past four decades, the dominant model of human memory has been the three-memory store theory described by Richard M. Shiffrin and Richard C. Atkinson. According to this theory, information is processed in the sensory register, short-term store, and then long-term store.

Shiffrin received his Ph.D. from Stanford University in 1968, and then joined the faculty of Indiana University, where he currently is professor of psychology and director of the cognitive science program. He was awarded a Guggenheim fellowship in 1975. Atkinson (b. 1929) earned his Ph.D. in 1955 from Indiana University. He served as professor of psychology at Stanford University from 1956 until 1975, when he became director of the National Science Foundation. He served as president of the University of California from 1995 to 2003, when he retired.

The selection that follows, from "Storage and Retrieval Processes in Long-Term Memory," was published in *Psychological Review* in 1969. The authors suggest that memory is transferred from the sensory register to the short-term store and then to the long-term store, where it is permanently housed. They theorize that if one is unable to retrieve a memory, it is because other information is interfering with it. As you read this selection, think of applications for improving your memory based on this model.

Key Concept: model of memory

APA Citation: Shiffrin, R. M., & Atkinson, R. C. (1969). Storage and retrieval processes in long-term memory. *Psychological Review, 76,* 179-193.

We begin by describing the overall conception of the memory system. The system follows that described in Atkinson and Shiffrin (1965, 1968a), and is similar to those proposed by Feigenbaum (1966) and Norman (1968). The major components of the system are diagrammed in Figure 1: the sensory register, the short-term store (STS) and the long-term store (LTS). The solid arrows in the diagram represent directions in which information is transferred from one part of the system to another. Note that transfer is not meant to imply the removal of information from one store and the placing of it in the next; rather, transfer is an operation in which information in one store is "copied" into the next without affecting its status in the original store. It should be emphasized that our hypotheses about the various memory stores do not require any assumptions regarding the physiological locus of these stores; the system is equally consistent with the view that the stores are separate physiological structures as

with the view that the short-term store is simply a temporary activation of information permanently stored in the long-term store. The control processes listed in Figure 1 are a sample of those which the subject (S) can call into play at his discretion, depending upon such factors as the task and the instructions. Control processes govern informational flow, rehearsal, memory search, output of responses, and so forth.

The sensory register is a very short-lived memory store which temporarily holds incoming sensory information while it is being initially processed and transferred to the short-term store. In the visual modality, for example, information will decay from the sensory register in a period of several hundred milliseconds (Sperling, 1960). Information in the short-term store, if not attended to by S, will decay and be lost in a period of about 30 seconds or less, but control processes such as rehearsal can maintain information in STS for as long as S desires (the buffer process in Figure 1 is

FIGURE 1

A Flow Chart of the Memory System.

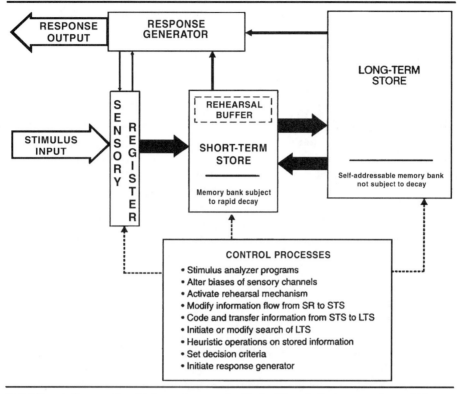

(Solid lines indicate paths of information transfer. Dashed lines indicate connections which permit comparison of information arrays residing in different parts of the system; they also indicate paths along which control signals may be sent which activate information transfer, rehearsal mechanisms, etc.)

one highly organized rehearsal scheme). While information resides in STS, portions of it are transferred to LTS. The long-term store is assumed to be a permanent repository of information; we realize that factors such as traumatic brain damage, lesions, and deterioration with extreme age must lead to memory loss, but such effects should be negligible in the types of experiments considered in this paper. Thus it is hypothesized that information, once stored in LTS, is never thereafter destroyed or eliminated. Nevertheless, the ability to retrieve information from LTS varies considerably with time and interfering material.

The short-term store serves a number of useful functions. On the one hand it decouples the memory system from the external environment and relieves the system from the responsibility of moment-to-moment attention to environmental changes. On the other hand, STS provides a working memory in which manipulations of information may take place on a temporary basis. Because STS is a memory store in which information can be maintained if desired, it is often used as the primary memory device in certain types of tasks; in these tasks the information presented for retention is maintained in STS until the moment of test and then emitted. Tasks in which STS is utilized for this purpose, and the mechanisms and control

processes that may come into play, have been examined extensively in Atkinson and Shiffrin (1968a). In this report we are primarily interested in STS as a temporary store in which information is manipulated for the purposes of storage and retrieval from LTS, rather than as a store in which information is maintained until test. In the remainder of this paper, discussion is limited to that component of memory performance which involves LTS retrieval, and the components arising from STS and the sensory register will not be considered.

LONG-TERM STORE

In describing the structure of LTS, an analogy with computer memories is helpful. The usual computer memory is "location addressable"; if the system is given a certain location it will return with the contents of that location. When given the contents of a word (a "word" refers to a single computer memory location), such a system must be programmed to examine each location in turn in order to find the possible locations of these contents in the memory. It seems untenable that an exhaustive serial search is made of all of LTS whenever retrieval is desired. An alternative type of memory may be termed "content addressable"; if the system is given the contents of a word it will return with the locations in memory containing those contents. One way in which such a memory may be constructed utilizes a parallel search through all memory locations; the system then returns with the locations of all matches. If this view is adopted, however, an additional process is needed to select the desired location from among the many returned by the parallel search. Thus, if we feed the system the word "red," it would not be useful for the system to return with all references or locations of "red"; there are simply too many and the original retrieval problem would not be significantly reduced in scale. There is, however, an alternative method for forming a content-addressable memory; in this method, the contents to be located themselves contain the information necessary to specify the storage location(s). This can occur if the information is originally stored in locations specified by some master plan dependent upon the contents of the information. Such a system will be termed "self-addressing." A self-addressing memory may be compared with a library shelving system which is based upon the contents of the books. For example, a book on "caulking methods used for 12th century Egyptian rivercraft" will be placed in a specific library location (in the Egyptian room, etc.). If a user desires this book it may be located by following the same shelving plan used to store it in the first place. We propose that LTS is to a large degree just such a self-addressable memory. An ensemble of information presented to the memory system will define a number of memory areas in which that information is likely to be stored; the memory search will therefore have certain natural starting points. The system is assumed to be only partially self-addressing in that the degree to which the storage locations are specified will vary from one ensemble to the next and one moment to the next, in much the way as proposed in stimulus sampling theory (Estes, 1959). Thus it may be necessary to embark upon a memory search within the specified locations, a search which may proceed serially from one location to the next. This conception of LTS leads to a number of predictions. For example, a recognition test of memory will not proceed via exhaustive scanning of all stored codes, nor will a recognition test eliminate in all cases the necessity for an LTS search. If information is presented and S must indicate whether this information has been presented previously, then the likely storage location(s) is queried. To the degree that the information has highly salient characteristics which precisely identify the storage location, the extent of the LTS search will be reduced. Thus, for items with highly salient characteristics, S should be able to identify quickly and accurately whether the item was presented previously, and the identification might not require a memory search which interrogates more than a single storage location. The less well-specified the storage location, the greater the memory search needed to make an accurate recognition response....

The term "location" is used in relation to the organizational schema; an LTS location is defined by the place in the organizational structure occupied by an information ensemble. The location will be defined in terms of the modality of the information (e.g., visual versus auditory), the level of analysis, (e.g., spelling versus syntactic structure), and all other dimensions of organization that may be relevant. Two locations will be said to be "close" if the information in them tends to be retrieved together. In particular, we shall refer to a *code*, or an *image*, as an ensemble of information that is closely related and very likely to be retrieved together. We do not wish to imply that there is some unitary atom of storage called a code or an image. The information making up a code in one task may be considered to be several codes in a different task. For example, an entire sentence may be considered a code if we are comparing the meaning of that sentence with others; however, the same sentence might be considered to be made up of a series of codes if we are comparing it with sentences of the same meaning but different grammatical form. Nevertheless, for most tasks the concept of a code or image as representing a cohesive array of information in a single storage location proves useful....

STORAGE AND RETRIEVAL

Since LTS is self-addressing, storage and retrieval have many features in common, one process mirroring the other. Storage is assumed to consist of three primary mechanisms: *transfer, placement,* and *image-production*. The transfer mechanism includes those control processes by which S decides what to store, when to store, and how to store information in LTS. The placement mechanism determines the locations in which the ensemble of information under consideration will be stored. To a large degree, the components of the ensemble itself will determine the location of storage. That is, in the action of encoding the desired information for storage, S may supplement the information currently in STS with pertinent information retrieved from LTS; the resultant ensemble in STS determines the storage location. The image production mechanism determines what proportion of the current ensemble of information in STS will be placed in the designated LTS location(s). The proportion stored should be a function of the duration of the period that the ensemble is maintained in STS. Retrieval, like storage, is assumed to consist of three primary mechanisms: *search, recovery,* and *response generation*. The search process is a recursive loop in which locations or images are successively selected for examination. As each image is examined, the recovery process determines how much information will be recovered from the image and placed in STS. The response generation process then examines the recovered information and decides whether to continue the search or terminate and emit a response. If the search does not terminate, the selection of the next location or image for examination may depend upon information already uncovered during the search.

Although storage and retrieval are treated separately in this paper, we do not wish to imply that these processes are separated in time, one following the other. Rather, long-term storage is continually occurring for the information residing in short-term store. In addition, retrieval is continually occurring during storage attempts by S; for example, S may try to store a paired-associate by searching LTS for prominent associations to the stimulus, associations which could then be used as mediators....

APPLICATIONS OF THE SYSTEM

Forgetting

Decrements in performance occur in the system as a result of the input of additional information to LTS. These decrements result from three related mechanisms. First is a mechanical effect; information sufficient to respond correctly at one point in time may prove inadequate after additional information has been added. For example, a paired-associate GAX-4 may be stored as G**-4, and this code will be sufficient for correct responding (if recovered) when GAX is tested. Suppose, however, that GEK-3 is now presented and stored as G**-3. When either of these stimuli is tested later, both codes may be retrieved from LTS and therefore S will have to guess whether the correct response is 3 or 4.

The second cause of forgetting arises from a breakdown in the directed component of the search mechanism. That is, correct retrieval requires that the same memory area be searched at test as was used for storage during study. This may not occur, however, if only a portion of the input information is used to direct storage during study, for a different portion might be utilized to locate the storage area during retrieval. This process could be viewed within the framework of stimulus sampling theory (Estes, 1959) if the stimulus elements are taken to represent dimensions of organization. For clarity, let us denote the image which encodes the correct response for the current test as a "c code," and denote the other codes as "i codes." Thus the i codes are irrelevant codes which should lead to intrusion errors, whereas the c code, if examined, should lead to a correct response. Then the directed component of search can be characterized by the probability that the c code is in the examination subset, called p_c. In experiments in which clues are available to denote the organizational dimensions to be searched, p_c may be close to 1.0. In other situations, such as continuous tasks with randomly chosen stimuli and responses, p_c will be lower and dependent upon such factors as the amount of information in the c code and its age (where "age" denotes the position of the code on the temporal dimension). Although the breakdown in the directed component can provide a reasonable degree of forgetting, we shall focus primarily upon the third mechanism of forgetting: the increasing size of the examination subset.

When searching the examination subset, there are a number of possible results. The c code may be examined and give rise to a correct response, one of the i codes may be examined and produce an intrusion response, or none of the codes may give rise to a response and the search terminates. If the search through the examination subset is at least partially random, then the following conclusions may be reached. When the size of the subset is increased (i.e., the number of i codes is increased), then the probability of giving an intrusion will increase, the average time until the c code is examined will increase, and the probability of giving a correct response will decrease. When we say that the order of search is *partially* random, we mean to imply that the order in which codes in the examination subset are selected for consideration may depend upon both the amount of information in the code and the age of the code. Clearly, as the amount of information in a code tends toward zero, or as the age of a code increases, the probability of examining that code early in the search should decrease....

Interference

Various interference phenomena are readily predicted by the system. Although in general the order of search through the examination subset will depend upon the age and amount of information in the codes, suppose for simplicity that the search order is entirely random. Then both nonspecific proactive and retroactive interference effects are predicted, and in a sense are predicted to be equal. That is, extra i codes in the examination subset added either temporally before or after the c code will cause the correct retrieval probability to drop; in the case of a random search the probability decrease will be the same whether caused by an i code preceding or following the c code. The drop occurs because the extra codes increase the amount of time required to find the c code. Therefore, if the size of the examination subset is increased, it is more likely that either response time will run out or an intrusion response will occur. Obviously the greater the degree to which the search is ordered temporally backwards from the most recent item, the less the proactive, and the greater the retroactive interference effect. Thus if codes are examined strictly in temporal order, the average amount of time until the c code is examined will be independent of the number of codes which are older than the c code and hence no proactive effect will be expected. One of the best places to examine nonspecific proactive and retroactive interference effects is in the study of free-verbal recall as a function of list length (Murdock, 1962). In this task a list of words is read to S, who attempts to recall as many of them as possible following their presentation. The data are usually graphed as a serial-position curve which gives the probability of correct recall as a function of the presentation position (and hence as a function of the number of preceding and succeeding items in the list). As the list length is varied, the number of preceding and succeeding items is systematically varied and it is possible to apply the theory to the resultant data. The application of the theory is made particularly easy in this case because *S* is trying to recall all of the list, and hence the examination subset can be assumed to consist of all codes that have been stored. In fact, a model derived from the theory has been applied to free-verbal recall data as a function of list length and has proved remarkably successful (Atkinson & Shiffrin, 1965, 1968a). The model assumes that performance decreases with list length because more codes are missed in the memory search at longer list lengths. This model also predicts that some of the missed codes should be retrieved if a second recall test is given following the first. Just such an effect was found by Tulving (1967), and its magnitude is predicted accurately by the model. Three successive recall tests were given following a single list presentation and only 50% of the items recalled were recalled on all three tests, even though the actual number recalled remained constant over the three tests.

Item-specific interference is also readily predicted via the search mechanism. Item interference refers to that condition arising when a stimulus originally paired with one response is later paired with a second, different response. In this case two different codes with the same stimulus may be placed in LTS. Thus, the amount of proactive or retroactive interference will depend upon the number of times the wrong code is examined and accepted prior to the correct code. In particular, the degree of temporal ordering in the search will affect the relative amounts of proactive and retroactive effects. That is, the greater the degree that the search is ordered temporally backwards from the most recent item, the less proactive and the greater retroactive effect is predicted. The reasoning is similar to that in the previous paragraph for nonspecific effects. This rather simple view of interference is complicated by at least two factors. First, if *S* is aware that he will eventually be tested for both responses, he may link them in nearby codes, or in a single code, and thereby reduce interference effects (Dallet & D'Andrea, 1965). Second, when the first response is changed, *S* may tag the first code with the information that the response is now wrong. If the first code is later recovered during search, then this information will enable him to inhibit an intrusion and continue the search; an effect like this was found by Shiffrin (1968)....

Intrusions

Another useful feature of the model is its natural prediction of intrusions, and of variations in intrusion rates over differing conditions. In a paired associate task, an intrusion occurs when the response contained in an *i* code is recovered and emitted. Actually, the intrusion process has not yet been specified clearly, since both the probability of being in the examination subset and the probability of accepting the recovered response will be smaller for an *i* code than a *c* code containing an equal amount of information. It may be assumed that the likelihood of an *i* code being in the examination subset will be a function of its similarity to the test stimulus, since storage is carried out primarily on the basis of stimulus information. The probability of accepting an *i* code as being correct will similarly depend upon the generalization from the test stimulus to the stimulus information encoded in the *i* code. Given that the *i* code is examined and accepted, however, the probability that a response will be recovered and emitted should depend directly upon the response information encoded, just as for a *c* code....

Another phenomenon predicted by the theory is that of second-guessing, where second-guessing refers to the giving of a second response after *S* has been told that his first response is incorrect. A variety of assumptions can be made about this process, the simplest of which postulates that *S* continues his search of the examination subset from the point where the intrusion occurred. This assumption predicts that the level of second-guessing will be above chance, an effect found by Binford and Gettys (1965). If the search is temporally ordered to any degree, then strong predictions can be made concerning the second guessing rate depending upon whether the response given in error was paired in the sequence with a stimulus occurring before or after the tested stimulus (assuming that the task utilizes a set of unique responses). In fact, examination of this effect is one method of determining the temporal characteristics of the search.

Latency of Responses

Another variable which may be predicted from the theory in a straightforward way is the latency of responses. The basic assumption requires latency to be a monotonic increasing function of the number of images examined before a response is emitted. Among the implications of this assumption are the following. Latencies of correct responses should increase with increases in the number of intervening items. This prediction holds whenever there is some temporal component to the search, or whenever the number of items preceding the tested item is large. If the reasonable assumption is made that codes containing more information are examined earlier in the search, then a decrease in correct response latency is expected as the number of reinforcements increase, since the item will gain stored information over reinforcements and therefore tend to be examined earlier in the search. This effect has been found by Rumelhart (1967) and Shiffrin (1968) in a continuous paired-associate task. In general, any manipulation designed to vary the number of codes examined, whether by instructions, by organization of the presented material, or by other means should affect the response latencies in a specifiable way.

Recognition and Recall

In terms of the present system the search proceeds in a similar manner whether recognition or recall is the mode of test; the difference lies in the size of the examination subset in the two cases. Once information is recovered from LTS, however, the decision process involved in response generation may be somewhat different for recognition and recall. In a paired-associate design, the search will begin with an attempted recognition of the stimulus, with the decision whether to continue the search dependent upon a positive stimulus recognition (Martin, 1967). Hypotheses which ascribe different retrieval mechanisms for recognition and recall are not necessary. In both recognition and recall the presented stimulus will be sorted into an LTS area, and a search initiated there. In the case of recognition, this search can be quite limited, perhaps consisting of an examination of a single image. In the case of recall, the stimulus may be recognized with little search needed, but the necessity for recovering the response may entail a larger search, although "larger" might imply only examination of two to five additional items (Shiffrin, 1968).

References

Atkinson, R. C., & Shiffrin, R. M. Human memory: A proposed system and its control processes. In K. W. Spence & J. T. Spence (Eds.), *The psychology of learning and motivation: Advances in research and theory*, Vol. 2. New York: Academic Press, 1968. (a)

Atkinson, R. C., & Shiffrin, R. M. Mathematical models for memory and learning. Technical Report 79, Institute for Mathematical Studies in the Social Sciences, Stanford University, 1965. (Republished: D. P. Kimble (Ed.), *Proceedings of the third conference on learning, remembering and forgetting.* New York: New York Academy of Science, in press.)

Binford, J. R., & Gettys, C. Nonstationarity in paired-associate learning as indicated by a second guess procedure. *Journal of Mathematical Psychology*, 1965, **2**, 190–195.

Dallet, K. M., & D'Andrea, L. Mediation instructions versus unlearning instructions in the A-B, A-C paradigm. *Journal of Experimental Psychology*, 1965, **69**, 460–466.

Estes, W. K. The statistical approach to learning theory. In S. Koch (Ed.), *Psychology: A study of a science.* Vol. 2. New York: McGraw-Hill, 1959.

Feigenbaum, E. A. Information processing and memory. In *Proceedings of the fifth Berkeley symposium on mathematical statistics and probability, 1966.* Vol. IV. Berkeley: University of California Press, 1966.

Martin, E. Stimulus recognition in aural paired-associate learning. *Journal of Verbal Learning and Verbal Behavior, 1967,* **6**, 272–276.

Murdock, B. B., JR. The serial position effect of free recall. *Journal of Experimental Psychology*, 1962, **64**, 482–488.

Norman, D. A. Toward a theory of memory and attention. *Psychological Review*, 1968, **75**, 522–536.

Rumelhart, D. E. The effects of interpresentation intervals in a continuous paired-associate task. Technical Report 116, Institute for Mathematical Studies in the Social Sciences, Stanford University, 1967.

Shiffrin, R. M. Search and retrieval processes in long-term memory. Technical Report 137, Institute for Mathematical Studies in the Social Sciences, Stanford University, 1968.

Sperling, G. The information available in brief visual presentations. *Psychological Monographs*, 1960, **74**(11, Whole No. 498).

Tulving, E. The effects of presentation and recall of material in free-recall learning. *Journal of Verbal Learning and Verbal Behavior*, 1967, **6**, 175–184.

Short-Term Retention of Individual Verbal Items

Lloyd R. Peterson and Margaret Jean Peterson (1959)

Memory involves mentally storing information that we learn so we can retrieve and use it at a later time. Short-term memory is the store where we hold the information we are aware of at any particular moment. Because people tend to rehearse information in short-term memory (for example, repeating a phone number until the number is dialed), psychologists found it difficult to accurately determine how long a person could keep information in short-term memory; that is, until Lloyd R. Peterson and Margaret Jean Peterson developed the procedure described in this selection.

Lloyd R. Peterson (b. 1922) earned his Ph.D. from the University of Minnesota in 1954. He then taught at Indiana University, until 1987, when he retired. Margaret Jean Intons-Peterson (b. 1930) earned her Ph.D. from the University of Minnesota in 1955, and is currently a professor emeritus of psychology at Indiana University.

This selection, "Short-Term Retention of Individual Verbal Items," was published in the *Journal of Experimental Psychology* in 1959, and it provides an excellent opportunity to read original research in the area of memory. Experiment 1 (Experiment 2 is not included here) presents a useful technique for measuring the duration of a verbal stimulus in short-term memory. Keep in mind that statistical tests determine if we can conclude that real differences occur between experimental conditions. Also note that statistical significance (a real difference) is obtained when the probability (p) is less than .05. As you read this article, consider how quickly information fades from your short-term memory.

Key Concept: short-term memory

APA Citation: Peterson, L. R., & Peterson, M. J. (1959). Short-term retention of individual verbal items. *Journal of Experimental Psychology, 58*, 193–198.

It is apparent that the acquisition of verbal habits depends on the effects of a given occasion being carried over into later repetitions of the situation. Nevertheless, textbooks separate acquisition and retention into distinct categories. The limitation of discussions of retention to long-term characteristics is necessary in large part by the scarcity of data on the course of retention over intervals of the order of magnitude of the time elapsing between successive repetitions in an acquisition study. The presence of a retentive function within the acquisition process was postulated by Hull (1940) in his use of the stimulus trace to explain serial phenomena. Again, Underwood (1949) has suggested that forgetting occurs during the acquisition process. But these theoretical considerations have not led to empirical investigation....

Two studies have shown that the effects of verbal stimulation can decrease over intervals measured in seconds. Pills-

bury and Sylvester (1940) found marked decrement with a list of items tested for recall 10 sec. after a single presentation. However, it seems unlikely that this traditional presentation of a list and later testing for recall of the list will be useful in studying intervals near or shorter than the time necessary to present the list. Of more interest is a recent study by Brown (1958) in which among other conditions a single pair of consonants was tested after a 5-sec. interval. Decrement was found at the one recall interval, but no systematic study of the course of retention over a variety of intervals was attempted.

Experiment I

The present investigation tests recall for individual items after several short intervals. An item is presented and tested without related items intervening. The initial study examines the course of retention after one brief presentation of the item.

Method

Subjects.—The Ss [subjects] were 24 students from introductory psychology courses at Indiana University. Participation in experiments was a course requirement.

Materials.—The verbal items tested for recall were 48 consonant syllables with Witmer association value no greater than 33%* (Hilgard, 1951). Other materials were 48 three-digit numbers obtained from a table of random numbers. One of these was given to S after each presentation under instructions to count backward from the number. It was considered that continuous verbal activity during the time between presentation and signal for recall was desirable in order to minimize rehearsal behavior. The materials were selected to be categorically dissimilar and hence involve a minimum of interference.

Procedure.—The S was seated at a table with E [experimenter] seated facing in the same direction on S's right. A black plywood screen shielded E from S. On the table in front of S were two small lights mounted on a black box. The general procedure was for E to spell a consonant syllable and immediately speak a three-digit number. The S then counted backward by three or four from this number. On flashing of a signal light S attempted to recall the consonant syllable. The E spoke in rhythm with a metronome clicking twice per second and S was instructed to do likewise. As E spoke the third digit, he pressed a button activating a Hunter interval timer. At the end of a preset interval the timer activated a red light and an electric clock. The light was the signal for recall. The clock ran until E heard S speak three letters, when E stopped the clock by depressing a key. This time between onset of the light and completion of a response will be referred to as a latency. It is to be distinguished from the interval from completion of the syllable by E to onset of the light, which will be referred to as the recall interval.

The instructions read to S were as follows: "Please sit against the back of your chair so that you are comfortable. You will not be shocked during this experiment. In front of you is a little black box. The top or green light is on now. This green light means that we are ready to begin a trial. I will speak some letters and then a number. You are to repeat the number immediately after I say it and begin counting backwards by 3's (4's) from that number in time with the ticking that you hear. I might say, ABC 309. Then you say, 309, 306, 303, etc., until the bottom or red light comes on. When you see this red light come on, stop counting immediately and say the letters that were given at the beginning of the trial. Remember to keep your eyes on the black box at all times. There will be a short rest period and then the green light will come on again and we will start a new trial." The E summarized what he had already said and then gave S two practice trials. During this practice S was corrected if he hesitated before starting to count, or if he failed to stop counting on signal, or if he in any other way deviated from the instructions.

*[A low Witmer association value means that the consonant syllables used by the experimenters to test the subjects were nonsensical. It is a measure of the syllables' lack of meaning.—Ed.]

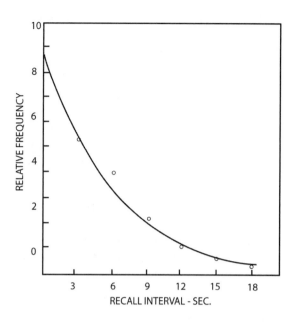

Figure 1   Correct recalls with latencies below 2.83 sec. as a function of recall interval

Each S was tested eight times at each of the recall intervals, 3, 6, 9, 12, 15, and 18 sec. A given consonant syllable was used only once with each S. Each syllable occurred equally often over the group at each recall interval. A specific recall interval was represented once in each successive block of six presentations. The S counted backward by three on half of the trials and by four on the remaining trials. No two successive items contained letters in common. The time between signal for recall and the start of the next presentation was 15 sec.

Results and Discussion

Responses occurring any time during the 15-sec. interval following signal for recall were recorded....

The feasibility of an interpretation by a statistical model was explored by fitting to the data the exponential curve of Fig. 1. The empirical points plotted here are proportions of correct responses with latencies shorter than 2.83 sec. Partition of the correct responses on the basis of latency is required by considerations developed in detail by Estes (1950). A given probability of response applies to an interval of time equal in length to the average time required for the response under consideration to occur. The mean latency of correct responses in the present experiment was 2.83 sec. Differences among the proportions of correct responses with latencies shorter than 2.83 sec. were evaluated by sign tests. The difference between the 3- and 18-sec. conditions was found to be significant at the .01 level. All differences among the 3-, 6-, 9-, 12-, and 48-sec. conditions were significant at the .05 level.

The general equation of which the expression for the curve of Figure 1 is a specific instance is derived from the stimulus fluctuation model developed by Estes (1955). In applying the model to the present experiment it is assumed that the verbal stimulus produces a response in S which is conditioned to a set of elements contiguous with the response. The elements thus conditioned are a sample of a larger population of elements into which the conditioned elements disperse as time passes. The proportion of conditioned elements in the sample determining *S's* behavior thus decreases and with it the probability of the response. Since the fitted curve appears to do justice to the data, the observed decrement could arise from stimulus fluctuation.

The independence of successive presentations might be questioned in the light of findings that performance deteriorates as a function of previous learning (Underwood, 1957). The presence of proactive interference was tested by noting the correct responses within each successive block of 12 presentations. The short recall intervals were analyzed separately from the long recall intervals in view of the possibility that facilitation might occur with the one and interference with the other. The proportions of correct responses for the combined 3- and 6-sec. recall intervals were in order of occurrence .57, .66, .70, and .74. A sign test [statistical test] showed the difference between the first and last blocks to be significant at the .02 level. The proportions correct for the 15- and 18-sec. recall intervals were .08, .15, .09, and .12. The gain from first to last blocks is not significant in this case.

There is no evidence for proactive interference. There is an indication of improvement with practice....

Summary

The investigation differed from traditional verbal retention studies in concerning itself with individual items instead of lists. Forgetting over intervals measured in seconds was found. The course of retention after a single presentation was related to a statistical model.... It was concluded that short-term retention is an important, though neglected, aspect of the acquisition process.

References

Brown, J. Some tests of the decay theory of immediate memory. *Quart. J. exp. Psychol.,* 1958, 10, 12–21.

Estes, W. K. Toward a statistical theory of learning. *Psychol. Rev.* 1950, 57, 94–107.

Estes, W. K. Statistical theory of spontaneous recovery and regression. *Psychol. Rev.,* 1955, 62, 145–154.

Hilgard, E. R. Methods and procedures in the study of learning. In S.S. Stevens (Ed.), *Handbook of experimental psychology.* New York: Wiley, 1951.

Hull, C.L., Hovland, C.I., Ross, R. T., Hall, M, Perkins, D. T., & Fitch, F. B. *Mathematico-deductive theory of rote learning: A study in scientific methodology.* New Haven: Yale Univer. Press, 1940.

Pillsbury, W.B., & Sylvester, A. Retroactive and proactive inhibition in immediate memory. *J. exp. Psychol.,* 1940, 27, 532–545.

Underwood, B. J. *Experimental psychology,* New York: Appleton-Century-Crofts, 1949.

Underwood, B. J. Interference and forgetting. *Psychol. Rev.,* 1957, 64, 49–60.

What Is Episodic Memory?

Endel Tulving (1993)

Ultimately what we learn must enter our long-term memory, which appears to have an unlimited capacity and is relatively permanent. In the past few decades, psychologists have debated the structure of long-term memory, with respect to the number of memory systems that exist. One theory comes from psychologist Endel Tulving, who supports a classification scheme that consists of three memory systems: procedural, semantic, and episodic.

Tulving (b. 1927) received his B.A. from the University of Toronto in 1953 and his Ph.D. in experimental psychology from Harvard University in 1957. He taught at Yale University before going to the University of Toronto in 1974, where he is currently professor emeritus of psychology. He also serves as Tanenbaum Chair in Cognitive Neuroscience at Rotman Research Institute of Baycrest Centre in Toronto and as a visiting scholar at Washington University in St. Louis. Tulving, a leader in the area of long-term memory, has many publications, including *Elements of Episodic Memory* (Oxford University Press, 1983).

This selection is from "What is Episodic Memory?" which was published in the American Psychological Society's journal *Current Directions in Psychological Science* in 1993. In it, Tulving clarifies the distinction between episodic and semantic memory, and discusses the characteristics of each. He points out that episodic memory is unique in that it requires the person to be aware of the past event that is remembered (he uses the term *autonoetic awareness*). As you read this selection, try to think of situations in which you have experienced episodic memory as distinct from semantic memory.

Key Concept: Long-term memory

APA Citation: Tulving, E. (1993). What is episodic memory? *Current Directions in Psychological Science, 2,* 67–70.

Few problems in science are as difficult as those of working out the precise relation between two complex concepts that are deceptively similar. The relation between episodic and semantic memory belongs in this category. Intuition and rational thought reveal many similarities between these two kinds of memory and tempt us to think of the two as one. Yet, closer scrutiny reveals a number of fundamental differences. In this article, I discuss one such difference, namely, the nature of conscious awareness that characterizes retrieval of episodic and semantic information....

Episodic and Semantic Memory Systems

In a nutshell, the theory [of episodic memory] holds that episodic and semantic memory are two of the five major human memory systems for which reasonably adequate evidence is now available. The other three systems are procedural, perceptual representation, and short-term memory.[1] Although each system serves particular func-

tions that other systems cannot serve (the so-called criterion of functional incompatibility[2]), several systems usually interact in the performance of tasks in everyday life as well as in the memory laboratory.

Semantic memory registers and stores knowledge about the world in the broadest sense and makes it available for retrieval. If a person knows something that is in principle describable in the propositional form, that something belongs to the domain of semantic memory. Semantic memory enables individuals to represent and mentally operate on situations, objects, and relations in the world that are not present to the senses: The owner of a semantic memory system can think about things that are not here now.

Episodic memory enables a person to remember personally experienced events as such. That is, it makes it possible for a person to be consciously aware of an earlier experience in a certain situation at a certain time. Thus, the information of episodic memory could be said to concern the self's experiences in subjective space and time. In contrast, the information of semantic memory processes concerns objects and their relations in the world at large. The owner of an episodic memory system is not only capable of remembering the temporal organization of otherwise unrelated events, but is also capable of mental time travel: Such a person can transport at will into the personal past, as well as into the future, a feat not possible for other kinds of memory.

The relation between episodic and semantic memory is hierarchical: Episodic memory has evolved out of, but many of its operations have remained dependent on, semantic memory. A corollary is that semantic memory can operate (store and retrieve information) independently of episodic memory, but not vice versa. Episodic memory is not necessary for encoding and storing of information into semantic memory, although it may modulate such encoding and storage. Semantic memory develops earlier in childhood than episodic memory: Children are capable of learning facts of the world before they remember their own past experiences. Finally, whereas medial temporal lobe and diencephalic structures, among others, play a critical role in semantic memory, frontal lobe structures seem to be involved in subserving episodic memory.[3]

Conscious Awareness in Remembering

One idea that was not clearly articulated in the *Elements of Episodic Memory* concerned the nature of conscious awareness that accompanies the act of retrieval of information from the two systems. At that time, there was little objective evidence relevant to that problem. Some progress on this front has now been made, and I summarize some of it here.

The working hypothesis is that episodic and semantic memory differ fundamentally with respect to the nature of conscious awareness that accompanies retrieval of information. The act of remembering a personally experienced event, that is, consciously recollecting it, is characterized by a distinctive, unique awareness of reexperiencing here and now something that happened before, at another time and in another place. The awareness and its feeling-tone are intimately familiar to every normal human being. One seldom mistakes remembering for any other kind of experience—perceiving, imagining, dreaming, daydreaming, or just thinking about things one knows about the world.

I refer to the kind of conscious awareness that characterizes remembering one's past as *autonoetic* awareness, contrasting it with *noetic* awareness, which characterizes retrieval of information from semantic memory, and *anoetic* awareness, which accompanies expression of procedural knowledge.[4] ...

"Remember" and "Know" Judgments

If amnesics can learn new facts and subsequently know them, in the absence of any autonoetic recollection of the sources of the facts, is it possible that normal people, too, know facts without remembering where or how they acquired them? Of course, it happens all the time. Every person knows hundreds and thousands of facts, without remembering the circumstances of their acquisition. This *source amnesia* that characterizes the learning in hypnotized people and amnesics, as well as older people, is well known to all of us. The phenomenon is simply more extreme in some of these special cases than in normal adults.

Gardiner and his collaborators have reported a number of studies on remembering versus knowing newly learned information in normal people.[5] The interesting feature of these studies is that the information in question is something that is usually associated with episodic memory, namely, occurrence of familiar words in a to-be-remembered list tested by recognition. In a typical experiment, subjects see a list of unrelated words, presented one at a time, on a single study trial, and then take a two-step test. In the test, they are shown both studied and nonstudied words and are asked to make a judgment about each word's presence in or absence from the study list and to indicate the basis of each positive recognition judgment.

Subjects are instructed that there are two ways in which they can tell that a word was in the study list: They either "remember" the event of the word's presentation in the study list or simply "know" on some basis that the item had appeared in the list, without remembering its occurrence.

In one experiment, for example, subjects studied a list of words under the conditions of either full or divided attention and were then tested as described. Division of attention reduced the proportion of "remembered" words (.50 vs. .38) but did not affect the proportion of words "known" to have been in the list (.21 vs. .20). Other experiments have examined the effect of other variables, such as levels of processing, generating versus reading the word at study, retention interval, word frequency, and age of subjects. These too have produced dissociations between the "remember" and "know" components of recognition memory. Yet other studies—done on brain-damaged subjects, or using psychoactive drugs, or recording event-related potentials—have begun to identify some of the neural correlates of "remember" and "know" judgments.[6]

There are other approaches to the study of awareness of source of information,[7] and correspondingly different ways of interpreting these experiments and their results. I prefer the hypothesis that "remember" judgments, based on autonoetic awareness, reflect the operation of the episodic system, whereas "know" judgments, based on noetic awareness, reflect the operation of the semantic system.

Thus, subjects have two sources of information concerning the membership of words in a study list—episodic and semantic memory. When they retrieve this information from semantic memory, they appear to suffer source amnesia: They do not remember the particular event of encountering the word. In amnesic patients . . . , the source amnesia is more extensive, covering not just encounters with individual words, but personal encounters of all kinds.

Conclusion

Episodic memory is a neurocognitive memory system that enables people to remember past happenings. The *remembering* in this proposition is not a generic term designating all kinds of retrieval of stored information, but rather a specific concept that designates retrieval from episodic memory. For a rememberer to remember something means that he or she is autonoetically aware of a past happening in which he or she has participated. For an experimenter or theorist to study episodic memory means to study autonoetic awareness of past experiences, separately from noetic retrieval of the semantic contents of the remembered episodes.

Notes

1. E. Tulving, Concepts of human memory, in *Memory; Organization and Locus of Change*, L. R. Squire, N. M. Weinberger, G. Lynch, and J. L. McGaugh, Eds. (Oxford University Press, New York, 1991).

2. D. F. Sherry and D. L. Schacter, The evolution of multiple memory systems, *Psychological Review, 94,* 439–454 (1987).

3. E. Tulving, Memory: Performance, knowledge, and experience, *European Journal of Cognitive Psychology, 1,* 3–26 (1989); A. P. Shimamura, J. J. Janowsky, and L. R. Squire, Memory for the temporal order of events in patients with frontal lobe lesions and amnesic patients, *Neuropsychologia, 28,* 803–813 (1990).

4. E. Tulving, Varieties of consciousness and levels of awareness in memory, in *Attention: Selection, Awareness and Control: A Tribute to Donald Broadbent*, A. Baddeley and L. Weiskrantz, Eds. (Oxford University Press, London, in press).

5. J. M. Gardiner and R. I. Java, Recognizing and remembering, in *Theories of Memory*, A. Collins, M. Conway, S. Gathercole, and P. Morris, Eds. (Erlbaum, Hillsdale, NJ, in press).

6. H. V. Curran, J. M. Gardiner, R. I. Java, and D. Allen, Effects of lorazepam upon recollective experience in recognition memory, *Psychopharmacology, 110,* 374–378 (1993); M. E. Smith, Neurophysiological manifestations of recollective experience during recognition memory judgments, *Journal of Cognitive Neuroscience, 5,* 1–13 (1993); T. A. Blaxton, *The role of temporal lobes in remembering visuospatial materials: Remembering and knowing,* manuscript submitted for publication (1993).

7. G. Mandler, P. Graf, and D. Kraft, Activation and elaboration effects in recognition and word priming, *The Quarterly Journal of Experimental Psychology, 38A,* 645–662 (1986); L. L. Jacoby, A process dissociation framework: Separating automatic from intentional uses of memory, *Journal of Memory and Language, 30,* 513–541 (1991); M. K. Johnson and W. Hirst, MEM: Memory subsystems as processes, in *Theories of Memory*, A. Collins, M. Conway, S. Gathercole, and P. Morris, Eds. (Erlbaum, Hillsdale, NJ, in press).

Leading Questions and the Eyewitness Report

Elizabeth F. Loftus (1975)

Most people want to believe that they have a perfect memory. Psychologists have discovered, however, that memory is subject to a wide variety of distortions. Elizabeth F. Loftus, for example, has studied how asking certain questions of eyewitnesses to an event affects their later recall of the incident. One of her famous studies includes the "car accident" study, which illustrated the misinformation effect.

Loftus (b. 1944) earned her Ph.D. in psychology from Stanford University in 1970, and then served as a professor of psychology and an adjunct professor of law at the University of Washington from 1973 to 2002. She is currently a professor of psychology at the University of California, Irvine. Loftus is one of the leading legal consultants in the in the area of eyewitness testimony in trials. She served as president of the American Psychological Society in 1998. She has written many books, including *Eyewitness Testimony* (Harvard University Press, 1979) and, with Katherine Ketcham, *The Myth of Repressed Memory* (St. Martin's Press, 1994).

This selection from "Leading Questions and the Eyewitness Report," which was published in *Cognitive Psychology* in 1975, clearly demonstrates how easy it is to modify eyewitness memory. This selection consists of several different but related experiments, and that for each one, the methods, the results, and a discussion section are provided. The chi square (χ^2) and the *t*-test are statistical tests used to determine significance (differences between conditions). A probability (*p*) less than .05 is significant. As you read this selection, consider the implications that Loftus's research has for everyday situations.

Key Concept: eyewitness memory

APA Citation: Loftus, E. F. (1975). Leading questions and the eyewitness report. *Cognitive Psychology, 7,* 560–572.

A total of 490 subjects, in four experiments, saw films of complex, fast-moving events, such as automobile accidents or classroom disruptions. The purpose of these experiments was to investigate how the wording of questions asked immediately after an event may influence responses to questions asked considerably later. It is shown that when the initial question contains either either true presuppositions (e.g., it postulates the existence of an object that did exist in the scene) or false presuppositions (e.g., postulates the existence of an object that did not exist), the likelihood is increased that subjects will later report having seen the presupposed object. The results suggest that questions asked immediately after an event can introduce new—not necessarily correct—information, which is then added to the memorial representation of the event, thereby causing its reconstruction or alteration.

Although current theories of memory are derived largely from experiments involving lists of words or sentences, many memories occurring in everyday life involve complex, largely visual, and often fast-moving events. Of course, we are rarely required to provide precise recall of such experiences—though as we age, we often volunteer them—but on occasion such recall is demanded, as when we have witnessed a crime or an accident. Our theories should be able to encompass such socially important forms of memory. It is clearly of concern to the law, to police and insurance investigators, and to others to know something about the completeness, accuracy, and malleability of such memories.

When one has witnessed an important event, one is sometimes asked a series of questions about it. Do these questions, if asked immediately after the event, influence the memory of it that then develops? This paper first summarizes research suggesting that the wording of such initial questions can have a substantial effect on the answers given, and then reports four new studies showing that the wording of these initial questions can also influence the answers to different questions asked at some later time. The discussion of these findings develops the thesis that questions asked about an event shortly after it occurs may distort the witness' memory for that event.

Answers Depend on the Wording of Questions

An example of how the wording of a question can affect a person's answer to it has been reported by Harris (1973). His subjects were told that "the experiment was a study in the accuracy of guessing measurements, and that they should make as intelligent a numerical guess as possible to each question" (p. 399). They were then asked either of two questions such as, "How tall was the basketball player?", or, "How short was the basketball player?" Presumably the former form of the question presupposes nothing about the height of the player, whereas the latter form involves a presupposition that the player is short. On the average, subjects guessed about 79 and 69 in. (190 and 175 mm), respectively. Similar results appeared with other pairs of questions. For example, "How long was the movie?", led to an average estimate of 130 min, whereas, "How short was the movie?" led to 100 min. While it was not Harris' central concern, his study clearly demonstrates that the wording of a question may affect the answer.

Past Personal Experiences

In one study (Loftus, unpublished), 40 people were interviewed about their headaches and about headache products under the belief that they were participating in market research on these products. Two of the questions were crucial to the experiment. One asked about products other than that currently being used, in one of two wordings:

(1a) In terms of the total number of products, how many other products have you tried? 1? 2? 3?

(1b) In terms of the total number of products, how many other products have you tried? 1? 5? 10?

The 1/2/3 subjects claimed to have tried an average of 3.3 other products, whereas the 1/5/10 subjects claimed an average of 5.2; $t(38) = 3.14$, s = .61, $p < .01$.

The second key question asked about frequency of headaches in one of two ways:

(2a) Do you get headaches frequently, and, if so, how often?

(2b) Do you get headaches occasionally, and, if so, how often?

The "frequently" subjects reported an average of 2.2 headaches/wk, whereas the "occasionally" group reported only 0.7/wk; $t(38) = 3.19$, s = .47, $p < .01$.

Recently Witnessed Events

Two examples from the published literature also indicate that the wording of a question put to a person about a recently-witnessed event can affect a person's answer to that question. In one study (Loftus, 1974; Loftus & Zanni, 1975), 100 students viewed a short file segment depicting a multiple-car accident. Immediately afterward, they filled out a 22-item questionnaire which contained six critical questions. Three of these asked about items that had appeared in the film whereas the other three asked about items not present in the film. For half the subjects, all the critical questions began with the words, "Did you see a… " as in, "Did you see a broken headlight?" For the remaining half, the critical questions began with the words, "Did you see the …" as in, "Did you see the broken headlight?"

Thus, the questions differed only in the form of the article, *the* or *a*. One uses "the" when one assumes the object referred to exists and may be familiar to the listener. An investigator who asks, "Did you see the broken headlight?" essentially says, "There was a broken headlight. Did you happen to see it?" His assumption may influence a witness' report. By contrast, the article "a" does not necessarily convey the implication of existence.

The results showed that witnesses who were asked "the" questions were more likely to report having seen something, whether or not it had really appeared in the film, than those who were asked "a" questions. Even this very subtle change in wording influences a witness' report.

In another study (Loftus & Palmer, 1974), subjects saw films of automobile accidents and then answered questions about the accidents. The wording of a question was shown to affect a numerical estimate. In particular, the question, "About how fast were the cars going when they smashed into each other?" consistently elicited a higher estimate of speed than when "smashed" was replaced by "collided," "bumped," "contacted," or "hit."

We may conclude that in a variety of situations the wording of a question about an event can influence the answer that is given. This effect has been observed when a person reports about his own experiences, about events he has recently witnessed, and when answering a general question (e.g., "How short was the movie?") not based on any specific witnessed incident.

Question Wording and Answers to Subsequent Questions

Our concern in this paper is not on the effect of the wording of a question on its answer, but rather on the answers to other questions asked some time afterward. We will interpret the evidence to be presented as suggesting a memorial phenomenon of some importance.

In the present experiments, a key [set of] initial questions contains a *presupposition,* which is simply a condition that must hold in order for the question to be contextually appropriate. For example, the question, "How fast was the car going when it ran the stop sign?" presupposes that there was a stop sign. If a stop sign actually did exist, then in answering this question a subject might review, strengthen, or make more available certain memory representations corresponding to the stop sign. This being the case, the initial question might be expected to influence the answer to a subsequent question about the stop sign, such as the question, "Did you see the stop sign?" A simple extension of the argument of Clark and Haviland (in press) can be made here: When confronted with the initial question, "How fast was the car going when it ran the stop sign?", the subject might treat the presupposed information as if it were an address, a pointer, or an instruction specifying where information related to that presupposition may be found (as well as where new information is to be integrated into the previous knowledge). In the process the presupposed information may be strengthened.

What if the presupposition is false? In that case it will not correspond to any existing representation, and the subject may treat it as new information and enter it into his memory. Subsequently, the new "false" information may appear in verbal reports solicited from the subject.

To explore these ideas, subjects viewed films of complex, fast-moving events. Viewing of the film was followed by initial questions which contained presuppositions that were either true (Experiment 1) or false (Experiments 2–4). In Experiment 1, the initial questions either did or did not mention an object that was in fact present in the film. A subsequent question, asked a few minutes later, inquired as to whether the subject has seen the existing object. In Experiments 2–4, the initial questions were again asked immediately after the film, whereas the subsequent questions were asked after a lapse of 1 wk.

Experiment 1

Method

One hundred and fifty University of Washington students, in groups of various sizes, were shown a film of a multiple-car accident in which one car, after failing to stop at a stop sign, makes a right-hand turn into the main stream of traffic. In an attempt to avoid a collision, the cars in the oncoming traffic stop suddenly and a five-car, bumper-to-bumper collision results. The film lasts less than 1 min, and the accident occurs within a 4-sec period.

At the end of the film, a 10-item questionnaire was administered. A diagram of the situation labeled the car that ran the stop sign as "A," and the cars involved in the collision as "B" through "F." The first question asked about the speed of Car A in one of two ways:

(1) How fast was Car A going when it ran the stop sign?

(2) How fast was Car A going when it turned right? Seventy-five subjects received the "stop sign" question and 75 received the "turned right" question. The last

question was identical for all subjects: "Did you see a stop sign for Car A?" Subjects responded by circling "yes" or "no" on their questionnaires.

Results and Discussion

Fifty-three percent of the subjects in the "stop sign" group responded "yes" to the question, "Did you see a stop sign for Car A?", whereas only 35% in the "turn right" group claimed to have seen the stop sign; $x^2(1) = 4.98$, $p < .05$. The wording of a presupposition into a question about an event, asked immediately after that event has taken place, can influence the answer to a subsequent question concerning the presupposition itself, asked a very short time later, in the direction of conforming with the supplied information.

There are at least two possible explanations of this effect. The first is that when a subject answers the initial stop sign question, he somehow reviews, or strengthens, or in some sense makes more available certain memory representations corresponding to the stop sign. Later, when asked, "Did you see a stop sign … ?", he responds on the basis of the strengthened memorial representation.

A second possibility may be called the "construction hypothesis." In answering the initial stop sign question, the subject may "visualize" or "reconstruct " in his mind that portion of the incident needed to answer the question, and so, if he accepts the presupposition, he introduces a stop sign into his visualization whether or not it was in memory. When interrogated later about the existence of the stop sign, he responds on the basis of his earlier supplementation of the actual incident. In other words, the subject may "see" the stop sign that he has himself constructed. This would not tend to happen when the initial question refers only to the right turn.

The construction hypothesis has an important consequence. If a piece of true information supplied to the subject after the accident augments his memory, then, in a similar way, it should be possible to introduce into memory something that was not in fact in the scene, by supplying a piece of false information. For example, Loftus and Palmer (1974, Expt. 2) showed subjects a film of an automobile accident and followed it by questions about events that occurred in the film. Some subjects were asked "About how fast were the cars going when they smashed into each other?", whereas others were asked the same question with "hit" substituted for "smashed." On a retest 1 wk later, those questioned with "smashed" were more likely than those questioned with "hit" to agree that they had seen broken glass in the scene, even though none was present in the film. In the present framework, we assume that the initial representation of the accident the subject has witnessed is modified toward greater severity when the experimenter uses the term "smashed" because the question supplies a piece of new information, namely, that the cars did indeed *smash* into each other. On hearing the "smashed" question, some subjects may reconstruct the accident, integrating the new information into the existing representation. If so, the result is a representation of an accident in memory that is more severe than, in fact, it actually was. In particular, the more severe accident is more likely to include broken glass.

The presupposition that the cars smashed into each other may be additional information, but it can hardly be said to be false information. It is important to determine whether it is also true that false presuppositions can affect a witness' answer to a later question about that presupposition. Such a finding would imply that a false presupposition can be accepted by a witness, that the hypothesis of a strengthening of an existing memorial representation is untenable (since there should be no representation corresponding to nonexistent objects), and that the construction hypothesis discussed above is supported. Experiment 2 was designed to check this idea.

Experiment 2

Method

Forty undergraduate students at the University of Washington, again in groups of various sizes, were shown a 3-min videotape taken from the film *Diary of a Student Revolution.* The sequence depicted the disruption of a class by eight demonstrators; the confrontation, which was relatively noisy, resulted in the demonstrators leaving the classroom.

At the end of the videotape, the subjects received one of two questionnaires containing one key and nineteen filler questions. Half of the subjects were asked, "Was the leader of the four demonstrators who entered the classroom a male?", whereas the other half were asked, "Was the leader of the twelve demonstrators who entered the classroom a male?" The subjects responded by circling "yes" or "no."

One week later, all subjects returned and, without reviewing the videotape, answered a series of 20 new questions about the disruption. The subjects were urged to answer the questions from memory and not to make inference. The critical question here was, "How many demonstrators did you see entering the classroom?"

Results and Discussion

Subjects who had previously been asked the "12" question reported having seen an average 8.85 people 1 wk earlier, whereas those asked the "4" question recalled 6.40 people, $t(38) = 2.50$, s = .98 $p < .01$. The actual number was, it will be recalled, eight. One possibility is that some fraction of the subjects remembered the number 12 or the number 4 from the prior questionnaire and were responding to the later question with that number, whereas the remainder had the correct number. An analysis of the actual responses given reveals that 10% of the people who had been interrogated with "12" actually responded "12,"

and that 10% of those interrogated with "4" actually responded with "4." A recalculation of the means, excluding those subjects in the "12" condition who responded "12" and those in the "4" condition who responded "4," still resulted in a significant difference between the two conditions (8.50 versus 6.67), $t(34) = 1.70$, $p < .05$. This analysis demonstrates that recall of the specific number given in the initial questionnaire is not an adequate alternative explanation of the present results.

The result shows that a question containing a false numerical presupposition can, on the average, affect a witness' answer to a subsequent question about that quantitative fact. The next experiment was designed to test whether the same is true for the existence of objects when the false presupposition concerns one that did not actually exist.

Experiment 3

Method

One hundred and fifty students at the University of Washington, in groups of various sizes, viewed a brief videotape of an automobile accident and then answered ten questions about the accident. The critical one concerned the speed of a white sports car. Half of the subjects were asked, "How fast was the white sports car going when it passed the barn while traveling along the country road?", and half were asked, "How fast was the white sports car going while traveling along the country road?" In fact, no barn appeared in the scene.

All of the subjects returned 1 wk later and, without reviewing the videotape, answered ten new questions about the accident. The final one was, "Did you see a barn?" The subjects responded by circling "yes" or "no" on their questionnaires.

Results and Discussion

Of the subjects earlier exposed to the question containing the false presupposition of a barn, 17.3% responded "yes" when later asked, "Did you see a barn?", whereas only 2.7% of the remaining subjects claimed to have seen it; $x^2(1) = 8.96$, $p < .01$. An initial question containing a false presupposition can, it appears, influence a witness' later tendency to report the presence of the nonexistent object corresponding to the presupposition.

The last experiment not only extends this finding beyond the single example, but asks whether or not the effect is wholly due to the word "barn" having occurred or not occurred in the earlier session. Suppose an initial question merely asks about, instead of presupposing, a nonexistent object; for example, "Did you see a barn?," when no barn existed. Presumably subjects will mostly respond negatively to such questions. But, what if that same question is asked again some time later? It is possible that a subject will reflect to himself, "I remember something about a barn, so I guess I must have seen one." If this were the case, then merely asking about a nonexistent object could increase the tendency to report the existence of that object at some later time, thereby accounting for the results of Expt III.

Experiment 4

Method

One hundred and fifty subjects from the University of Washington, run in groups of various sizes, viewed a 3-min 8 mm film clip taken from inside of an automobile which eventually collides with a baby carriage being pushed by a man. Following presentation of the film, each subject received one of three types of booklets corresponding to the experimental conditions. One hundred subjects received booklets containing five key and 40 filler questions. In the "direct" version, the key questions asked, in a fairly direct manner, about items that were not present in the film. One example was, "Did you see a school bus in the film?" In the "False presupposition" version, the key questions contained false presuppositions referring to an item that did not occur in the film. The corresponding example was, "Did you see the children getting on the school bus?" The third group of 50 subjects received only the 40 filler questions and no key questions. The goal of using so many filler items was to minimize the possibility that subjects would notice the false presuppositions.

All subjects returned 1 wk later and, without reviewing the film clip, answered 20 new questions about the incident. Five of these questions were critical: They were direct questions that had been asked a wk earlier in identical form, of only one of the three groups of subjects. The subjects responded to all questions by circling "yes" or "no" on their questionnaires.

Results and Discussion

. . . Overall, of those who had been exposed to questions including a false presupposition, 29.2% said "yes" to the key nonexistent items; of those who had been exposed to the direct questions, 15.6% said "yes" and of those in the control group, 8.4% said "yes."

For each question individually, the type of prior experience significantly influenced the percentage of "yes" responses, with all chi-square values having $p < .05$. Additional chi-square tests were performed to test for the significance of the differences between the pairs of groups. For each of the five questions, the differences were all significant between the control group and the group exposed to false presuppositions, all chi-square values having $p < .025$. Summing over all five questions, a highly significant chi-square resulted, $x^2(5) = 40.79$, $p < .001$. Similarly, over all five questions, the difference between the group exposed to direct questions and the group exposed to false presuppositions was significant, $x^2(5) = 14.73$, $p < .025$. The difference between the control group and the group exposed to direct questions failed to reach significance, $x^2(5) = 9.24$, $p > .05$.

References

Clark, H. H., & Haviland, S. E. Psychological processes as linguistic explanation. In D. Cohen (Ed.), *The nature of explanation in linguistics.* Milwaukee: University of Wisconsin Press, in press.

Harris, R. J. Answering questions containing marked and unmarked adjectives and adverbs. *Journal of Experimental Psychology*, 1973, 97, 399–401.

Loftus, E. F. Reconstructing memory. The incredible eyewitness. *Psychology Today*, 1974, 8, 116–119.

Loftus, E. F., & Palmer, J. C. Reconstruction of automobile destruction: An example of the interaction between language and memory. *Journal of Verbal Learning and Verbal Behavior*, 1974, 13, 585–589.

Loftus, E. F., & Zanni, G. Eyewitness testimony: The influence of the wording of a question. *Bulletin of the Psychonomic Society*, 1975, 5, 86–88.

Cognition and Intelligence

The Binet-Simon Scale for Measuring Intelligence

Lewis M. Terman, Ph.D. (1911)

The past century has seen a tremendous interest in the academic study of intelligence. The original scale first published by Alfred Binet in France was investigated by Stanford University psychologist Lewis M. Terman in a series of research studies that helped to shape mental testing in the United States for many years. Various instruments were tried, but none were as successful as identifying children who performed above, at, or below their age level as the Stanford-Binet Scale of Intelligence. This test of intelligence continues to be widely used today.

Lewis Madison Terman (1877–1956) earned his Ph.D. from Clark University in 1905. He was a professor at Stanford University from 1910 until his death in 1956. His translation and revision of Alfred Binet's Binet-Simon IQ test became one of the most widely used intelligence scales, the Stanford-Binet Scale of Intelligence. He was particularly interested in helping to classify children to help them get on the most appropriate job track. He is also well-known for his research on children who were considered to be geniuses. Among his books was *Measurement of Intelligence*, published in 1916.

This selection, from "The Binet-Simon Scale for Measuring Intelligence: Impressions Gained by its Application Upon Four Hundred Non-Selected Children," was published in *The Psychological Clinic* in 1911. In it, Terman describes the different tests included in the IQ scale, and discusses some of the drawbacks and implications for education and society. Based on the results from the children he tested, he continued to revise the tests until he was able to publish the completed Stanford-Binet Scale of Intelligence in 1916. As you read this selection, think about why Terman was so enthusiastic about mental testing.

Key Concept: intelligence testing

APA Citation: Terman, L. M. (1911). The Binet-Simon Scale for Measuring Intelligence: Impressions gained by its application upon four hundred non-selected children. *The Psychological Clinic, 5,* 199–206.

Through the assistance of Mr. H. G. Childs, a graduate student in the Department of Education, Stanford University, the Binet-Simon scale was tried last year upon about four hundred children in the vicinity of Stanford University. The complete account of this work will not appear until a little later (a series of articles by Terman and Childs) but on invitation of the editor of *The Clinic* I am glad to contribute to this symposium a few impressions gained from the work, and to add some criticisms of the scale.

For the authors of the study by far the most important result was a decided conviction that measuring scales of this general type are feasible, and that when corrected, extended and multiplied, they will prove of great practical and theoretical value. This outcome was not fully anticipated. I had myself previously spent nearly two years in the use of various "tests of intelligence," from which work, in spite of many items of interest, I could hardly count value received. My present belief is that the field is one that will richly repay any careful and well-directed effort.

It is something of a mystery why the scale method in the application of mental tests should not have come into general use long ago. For twenty years numerous experimenters applied tests covering almost every type of mental function. Certain correlations were crudely attempted. Interesting suggestions were made. A few age and grade tendencies were roughly ascertained. But all will admit that, for the most part, the tests were fruitless. They were either too limited in scope, or failed to utilize non-selected subjects, or else were made under conditions impossible to duplicate. Most fatal of all, the experimentation, instead of being guided by some directing idea like that of definitely establishing age or grade standards, was usually of haphazard nature. Then came Binet with his simple device of arranging the tests in a series of groups, according to their difficulty as determined by age differences in performance. His data were of very limited extent, and rather carelessly elaborated, but the advantages of this procedure are every day becoming more apparent, and are rapidly making possible a clinical child psychology. At the same time it must be admitted that the scale is far too limited in extent, that it is very far from accurate (at least for average American children), and that it is improvable at many points.

The children tested in our experiment ranged from four to thirteen years of age. The tests were uniformly given, and with careful attention to thoroughness. Without entering here into details, it may be said that the results warrant a far more radical revision of the scale than any one else has hitherto recommended. The scale originally offered by Binet is in general far too easy at the lower end, while in the upper range it is too difficult. *In fact, the range of nine years in the actual ages of our subjects was condensed into a range of only five years of test ages.* Besides the frequent displacement up or down the scale, some of the tests are objectionable or unsatisfactory for other reasons. This is particularly true of the thirteen-year group. On the other hand, such tests as the "description of pictures," "omissions from pictures," "aesthetic judgment," drawing, "questions of comprehension," memory, reasoning ability, vocabulary and association gave specially satisfactory results.

In addition to the trial given to Binet's tests, an attempt was made to extend the scale by securing age standards of performance in four other lines. The latter included, first, a "generalization test" (interpretation of fables); second, a graded "completion test"; third, a vocabulary test of 100 words; and fourth, a test of "practical judgment" (involving the hunting of a lost ball in a circular field). The authors devised new methods of grading performance for the fable and completion tests which they believe will add much to the serviceableness of both. The vocabulary test is based upon Laird and Lee's "Vest Pocket Dictionary," and is, therefore, designed to test the child's acquaintance with the most common concepts of everyday usage, and thus to display grade of intelligence rather than accidents of technical education. It is believed that all of the above four tests will prove usable additions to the scale.

The authors have also devised a method for calculating "test age" which they believe is a decided improvement over that used by Binet, a method which gives exactly equal value to all the tests of any year group. The tests of a year group are given a combined value of 1, and the "unit value" of each question in a group is determined by dividing 1 by the number of tests in that group. It is thus possible to retain an unequal number of tests in the different groups without giving undue weight to any one test in the estimation of test age.

I believe that tests of intelligence stand in serious need of further attention before we undertake to determine standards of performance in the different branches of the curriculum. Everything else is relative to intelligence. For clinical purposes, at least, it will be of relatively little value to ascertain where a pupil stands in geography or history or arithmetic in comparison with other children, unless we also know such pupil's intellectual status. All the numerous previously made correlations which have been based upon estimates of intelligence made by the teacher or inferred from school progress are unreliable. Lacking suitable scales for measuring intelligence (and there should be at least three or four such scales instead of one), we shall never be able to determine satisfactorily any of the following matters:

1. The effects of adenoids, bad teeth, malnutrition, partial deafness, nervous inco-ordination, or any other physical defect, alone or in combination with others, upon mental progress.
2. The relation between mental progress and physiological age (An important matter sadly in need of investigation.)
3. The relation between intellectual growth and pedagogical progress.
4. The relation between incorrigibility and intellectual retardation. The degree to which morality depends upon the powers of abstraction, or generalization. (Thought to be important according to some data now in press.)
5. Hereditary influences in the field of intelligence.
6. The influences of prolonged unfavorable social conditions, chronic insufficiency of food, sleep, etc.

The reader can extend this list indefinitely. It is readily seen how fundamentally important it is to have some means available for measuring the intelligence of school children. Intellectual status is concerned in almost every problem of pedagogy or of child hygiene. Without a scale to measure mentality we are almost blocked in the further study of retardation and its causes, nor can we successfully prosecute researches with feeble-minded or supernormal children. At the present time the scale does not seem to be improving in proportion either to the rapidly increasing interest in it or to the demands upon it. An illustration is the recent New Jersey law requiring tests of intelligence to be applied in the case of all public school children retarded three years or more.

However, in spite of the many imperfections and inadequacies of the revised scale I believe that by its use it is possible for the psychologist to submit, after a forty-minute diagnostication, a more reliable and more enlightening estimate of the child's intelligence than most teachers can offer after a year of daily contact in the schoolroom. Since all human estimations are relative to some standard, the teacher has no means of discovering whether her class on the whole is above or below the normal for the corresponding age. Her standard may be too high or too low, too vague, too mechanical or fragmentary. Before many years it will probably become a matter of course to apply serial mental tests in the public schools to all pupils who are retarded or about to become retarded, or who give indication of unusual ability. The scientific management of special classes for atypical children in the public schools will be impossible until similar series of tests are multiplied indefinitely.

To ascertain the full extent and true nature of a case of mental retardation, together with its causes, is, it must be confessed, extremely difficult. In fact, with existent methods it is hardly possible at all. Our treatment of such cases hardly transcends guess-work. May we not hope that several such scales will soon "be devised, each more perfect than the revision here offered, which collectively will enable the clinical psychologist in a few days to lay bare the "natural history" of a child's development; tests which will explore every line of efficiency, intellectual, volitional, motor, personal, social, linguistic, etc., which will relate all these at every point to individual peculiarities of instincts and interests and to all significant accidents of experience.

In order to make the tests of the greatest practical use it will be necessary to apply along with such measuring scales the newly-developed tests of *physiological age*. Unless this is done many children are certain to be grossly misjudged as to native ability, a mistake which in individual cases may be fraught with the most serious consequences. In justice to the child, the normality of whose intelligence has been questioned, tests for physiological age should always be applied before institutional treatment is recommended, and perhaps occasionally after commitment.

Now that the individual treatment of pupils in the schools has begun, there is no stopping short of this ideal. Tests must be developed which will enable us to differentiate all degrees of intellectual ability and all kinds of intellective unevenness; others which will mark for special educational effort the pupil whose emotional equipment and volitional tendencies threaten the onset of criminality, insanity, hysteria, neurasthenia, or other of the neuroses. With the accumulation of positive experimental data on so many aspects of individual mentality John Stuart Mill's suggestion looking toward a science of human character, *ethology*, as he called it, would gradually become possible. The modern studies in the psychology of testimony, suggestibility, measurements of mental growth, super and sub-normality, submerged complexes, emotivity, psycho-analysis and association reactions offer a fascinating field for the genetic study of personality.

A word may be added respecting recent criticisms which have been offered to the effect that so-called mental tests being measures of a product, not of a mental process, are hence valueless for psychology. This, of course, is the extreme point of view of the uncompromising structural psychologist who limits by definition the legitimate scope of the science to the study of the content of consciousness. In the light of the recent developments in dynamic psychology mentioned in the last paragraph, all of which (together with certain others) have emphasized anew and more forcibly than ever before the importance for human behavior of the subconscious, instinctive and submerged elements of mental life, such a limitation of the scope of psychology becomes an anachronism. In so far as these structural elements shed light upon function they are significant, but they can no more usurp the entire domain of psychology than the chemistry of the bones and muscles can swallow up or displace the science of physiology. As a man's efficiency in the material sense is measured by the quantity and quality of the work turned out in a given time, with method occupying a secondary place, so in the mental realm, the accomplishments of mental activity are the thing of most vital concern; the structural elements are simply a means to the end. Furthermore, in child psychology, as in animal psychology, it is impossible to get at the structural elements. We can only measure the performance in terms of objective results. It appears no more unreasonable to state a child's mental ability in terms of performance than it is for the historian to assign Napoleon his place in history from a consideration of his life activities. It would, of course, be interesting to know Napoleon's type of imagery, the structural accompaniments of his reaction time to various kinds of sense stimuli, even the chemical formulas for all parts of his material body,—but it is not clear how much this would add to our understanding of Napoleon as an historical figure.

Teachers' Expectancies: Determinants of Pupils' IQ Gains

Robert Rosenthal and Lenore Jacobson (1968)

Psychological research is sometimes difficult to correctly interpret, in part because people can unintentionally bring bias into the research setting. Without being aware of it, our expectations can alter our perception and behavior. The pioneering work of Robert Rosenthal and Lenore Jacobson helped psychologists become more aware of the potential for bias in research studies. Rosenthal (b. 1933) earned his Ph.D. in psychology in 1956 from the University of California, Los Angeles. In 1962 he began a career at Harvard University, where he stayed until he retired and accepted his current position as professor of psychology at University of California at Riverside. Jacobson was with the South San Francisco Unified School District at the time of their research. Rosenthal and Jacobson co-authored a book on expectancy effect entitled, *Pygmalion in the Classroom: Teacher Expectations and Pupils' Intellectual Development* (Holt, Rinehart & Winston, 1968).

This selection, from "Teacher's Expectancies: Determinants of Pupils' IQ Gains," was published in *Psychological Reports* in 1966. It demonstrated how teacher expectancy (in this study, expectancy that certain students would "intellectually bloom" during a school year) had a significant effect on student behavior (the randomly selected students increased their IQ scores). As you read this selection, think about your elementary school years. Did you do best in classes in which your teachers expected high performance? How does expectancy play a role in our everyday lives? How could we design research studies to minimize the effects of expectancy?

Key Concept: Bias in psychological research

APA Citation: Rosenthal, R., & Jacobson, L. (1968). Teachers' expectancies: Determinants of pupils' I.Q. gains. *Psychological Reports, 19*, 115–118.

Experiments have shown that in behavioral research employing human or animal Ss, E's expectancy can be a significant determinant of S's response (Rosenthal, 1964, in press). In studies employing animals, for example, Es led to believe that their rat Ss has been bred for superior learning ability obtained performance superior to that obtained by Es led to believe that their rats had been bred for inferior learning ability (Rosenthal & Fode, 1963; Rosenthal & Lawson, 1964). The present study was designed to extend the generality of this finding from Es to teachers and from animal Ss to school children.

Flanagan (1960) has developed a nonverbal intelligence test (*Tests of General Ability* or *TOGA*) which is not explicitly dependent on such school-learned skills as reading, writing, and arithmetic. The test is composed of two types of items, "verbal" and "reasoning." The "verbal" items measure the child's level of information, vocabulary, and concepts. The "reasoning" items measure the child's concept formation ability by employing abstract line drawings. Flanagan's purpose in developing the TOGA was "to provide a relatively fair measure of intelligence for all individuals, even those who have had atypical opportunities to learn" (1960, p. 6).

Flanagan's test was administered to all children in an elementary school, disguised as a test designed to predict academic "blooming" or intellectual gain. Within each of the six grades in the school were three classrooms, one each of children performing at above average, average, and below average levels of scholastic achievement. In each of the 18 classes an average of 20% of the children were assigned to the experimental condition. The names of these children were given to each teacher who was told that their scores on the "test for intellectual blooming" indicated that they

"his" may be gender-neutral in a grammatical sense, it is not gender neutral in a psychological sense. Even when the rest of the sentence explicitly provides a gender-neutral context, subjects more often think of a male when the pronoun is "his." …

In theoretical accounts and empirical investigations of gender-role development, the roles of imitation and reinforcements (Bandura & Walters, 1963; Mischel, 1966) and level of cognitive development (Kohlberg, 1966) have received great attention. In contrast, the role of language in gender-role development has been virtually ignored. The foregoing studies of adults raise some important questions for the developmental psychologist. How do children process sexist language, specifically gender-neutral "he?" Does their processing change with age, and does it differ from adults' processing? Is language a contributor to gender-role development, and can it be integrated into theories of gender-role development? …

A more complete statement of the cognitive approach is Bem's Gender Schema Theory (1981; see also Martin & Halverson, 1981). Bem argued that children learn a gender schema, a set of associations linked with maleness and femaleness in our society. This schema in turn organizes perception and affects the processing of information. Sex typing occurs because the self-concept becomes assimilated to the gender schema. Her studies with college students provided evidence consistent with the processing of information according to a gender schema, based on measures of clustering in free-recall and reaction times. Although she provided no data for children, she cited two studies, the results of which are consistent with the existence of gender-schematic processing in children as early as 6 years of age (Kail & Levine, 1976; Liben & Signorella, 1980). Martin and Halverson (1983) have also demonstrated, with 5- and 6-year-olds, that children distort information in sex-inconsistent pictures to make them sex consistent, a result that is congruent with the Gender Schema Theory. According to Bem, there are numerous inputs into the formation of the gender schema, and one of these is language, although she did not pursue this point empirically.

Two lines of thought, then—concern over sexist language as a social issue and a concern for a theoretical understanding of inputs into gender-role development—combine to raise a number of questions. How do children, compared with adults, process sexist language, specifically gender-neutral "he?" What is the effect on children of the use of gender-neutral "he"—does it contribute to the sex-typing process? Does it contribute to stereotyping, for example, stereotyping of occupations? Does it affect the formation of the gender schema? If so, what specific aspects of the gender schema might be affected—stereotyping of occupations, or perhaps more diffuse aspects, such as the relative status attached to the male and female roles, or the relative status of the self as a male or female?

The purpose of Experiment 1 was to replicate the Moulton et al. study with college students, and to extend it to first, third, and fifth graders, to assess age differences in responses to gender-neutral "he." Several other tasks were included in order to gain a more complete understanding of the nature of the responses. A fill-in task was used, and subjects were questioned for their understanding of the grammatical rule underlying the use of gender-neutral "he."

Experiment 1

Method

Subjects A total of 310 subjects participated: 60 first graders (23 boys, 37 girls, 5–8* to 7–8, M = 6–7), 67 third graders (34 boys, 33 girls, 7–8 to 10–2, M = 8–11), 59 fifth graders (26 boys, 33 girls, 9–8 to 12–0, M = 10–10), and 124 college students (57 men, 67 women, 17–11 to 21–9, M = 19–3). College students participated in order to fulfill the requirements for introductory psychology. The parents of all elementary subjects had returned signed consent forms for their children to participate. The elementary school children were drawn from three elementary schools, two middle-class, the other working-class to lower class.

Procedure All elementary school children were interviewed individually, half by a male interviewer, half by a female.

Stories. After a brief warm up, the interviewer said "I'm going to tell you a little bit about a kid, and then I want you to make up a story about that child and tell and tell it to me, and I'll write it down. When a kid goes to school, ____ often feels excited on the first day." One third of the subjects received "he" for the blank, one third "they" and one third "he or she." The cue sentence was designed as an age-appropriate parallel to the neutral sentence used by Moulton et al. The interviewers recorded the basic content of the story, including the character's name. Later in the interview (at the end of the correct-sentences task), subjects were explicitly asked "Is (name of their character) a boy or a girl? Why did you make up your story about a ____?"

Fill-in sentences. Next, children were questioned in several ways to determine their understanding of gender-neutral masculine pronoun use. First they were asked to complete a fill-in-the-blank task. In each case, the interviewer read the following sentences (or allowed the child to read it if he or she wanted to and was able):

1. If a kid likes candy, ____ might eat too much.
2. Most parents want ____ kids to get good grades.
3. When a kid plays football, ____ likes to play with friends.
4. When a kid learns to read, ____ can do more at school.

*[Age 5–8 means 5 years, 8 months.—Ed.]

Correct sentences. Children were then asked to correct sentences with pronouns. They were told, "Now I'm going to read you some sentences and I want you to tell me if they're right or wrong, and if they're wrong, what's wrong with them. For example, if I say 'he goed to the store' would that be right or wrong? Why?"

1. When a baby starts to walk ____ often falls down. Right or wrong? Why?
2. Usually a kid wants to be just like ____ own parents. Right or wrong? Why?
3. The average kid learns to read before ____ can write. Right or wrong? Why?
4. The average kid likes to play football with ____ friends. Right or wrong? Why?

Each child randomly received one of the following four pronouns replacing the blank: his (or he), they (or their), he or she (or his or her), or her (she).

Rule knowledge. Subjects were asked "When you use 'he' in a sentence, does it always mean it's a boy? For example, when I say 'When a kid goes to school, he often feels excited on the first day,' does that mean the kid is a boy?" If the child answered no, then he or she was asked what it did mean.

College students. College students were tested in groups using a printed form. The form said:

> Your task is to make up a story creating a fictional character who fits the following theme. Please do not write about yourself.
>
> In a large coeducational institution the average student will feel isolated in ____ introductory courses.

One third received "his" for the blank, one third "his or her," and one third "their."

When subjects had completed the task, they were told to turn the papers over and answer the following questions briefly:

> When a person uses "he" or "his" in a sentence, does it always mean it's a male? For example, if I say "In a large coeducational institution the average student will feel isolated in his introductory courses," does that mean that the student is a male? If your answer is no, then what does the "he" or "his" mean?

Results

Sex of Character in Story The results, tabulated as percentage of stories written about female characters, are shown in Figure 1. The data were analyzed using a four-way chi-square* (Sex of Subject × Sex of Character in Story × Pronoun × Grade). Following the recommendation of Everitt (1977) the first test carried out was for the mutual independence of all four variables (or equivalently, whether sex of subject, pronoun, and grade showed a three-way interaction in affecting the dependent variable, sex of character). The results were highly significant, $x^2(40, N = 310) = 95.36, p < .001$ [N = number

*[Chi-square is a statistical test.—Ed.]

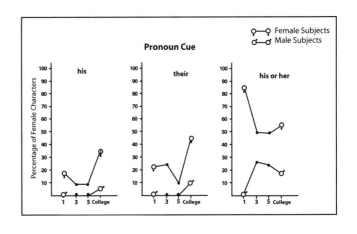

Figure 1 Percentage of stories about female characters written under the "his," "their," and "his or her" pronoun conditions, for male and female subjects at the three grade levels

of subjects; p = probability that results were not due to random chance]. Once this test was significant, other specific hypotheses of interest could be tested (Everitt, 1977). In particular, the main effect [that is, examining one variable at a time,] for sex of subject was significant, $x^2(1, N = 310) = 35.54, p < .001$, with males overall telling 8% of their stories about females and females telling 38% female stories. The main effect for pronoun was also significant, $x^2(2, N = 310) = 28.81, p < .001$. When the pronoun was "he" or "his," overall 12% of the stories were about females; when it was "they" or "their," 18% were female, and when the pronoun was "his" or "her" ("he" or "she"), 42% of the stories were about females. The main effect of grade level was not significant, $x^2(3, N = 310) = 5.34$, although it must be remembered that grade level interacted significantly with sex of subject and pronoun as noted above. The nature of this interaction can be seen in Figure 1. Note that not a single first-grade boy told a story about a female. Third-grade boys produced no female stories when the pronoun was "he" or "they," but nearly 30% of their stories were about females in response to "his" or "her."

Correct Sentences Overall, children (the correct-sentences task was not given to college students) judged most sentences to be correct (76%). Sentences with "he" inserted were judged wrong 19% of the time, whereas sentences with "she" were judged wrong 28% of the time. The children's judgments interacted with the sex typing of the sentence. For example, in the sentence about football, "he" was judged wrong 6% of the time, but "she" was judged wrong 39% of the time. This effect in turn showed age trends. "She" in the football sentence was judged wrong by 18% of the first graders and by 67% of the fifth graders....

Fill-In Sentences ... At all grade levels, the great majority of children supplied "he" or "his" in the sentences, with the exception of Sentence 2, in which "their" was correct, and was correctly supplied. In the remaining three singular sentences, the sex typing of the sentence was varied, "candy" being gender-neutral, "football" masculine, and "read" feminine. In fact, "he" was supplied so uniformly and frequently that the sex typing of the sentence had little impact. The most important sentence is the first, in which the cue is explicitly gender neutral (referring to candy), yet 72% of first graders, 88% of third graders, and 76% of fifth graders provided the pronoun "he" for the blank.

Rule Knowledge Knowledge of the rule that, in gender-neutral contexts, "he" refers to both males and females was tested by asking "When you use 'he' in a sentence, does it always mean it's a boy? For example, when I say "when a kid goes to school, he often feels excited on the first day, does that mean the kid is a boy?" If the subject responded "no" and indicated that it could be a boy or girl, the subject was scored as knowing the rule. Knowledge of the rule increased with age: 28% of first graders, 32% of third graders, 42% of fifth graders, and 84% of college students gave responses indicating they knew the rule. An additional 6% of college students gave "feminist" responses indicating that they knew the rule but disagreed with it—for example, "Yes, he refers to males, so one should use 'he or she' to be clear that everyone is included."...

Discussion

In general, the results from the college students in Experiment 1 replicate those of Moulton et al. (1978), although with even lower percentages of female stories (39% in Moulton et al.'s study vs. 30% in the present study). As Moulton et al. found, females are more likely to write stories about female characters than males are. The pronoun "his" yielded the lowest percentage of female stories, and "his or her" yielded the highest percentage. If "his" were gender neutral in a psychological sense, then approximately 50% of stories would be about females, yet college students created only 21% of their stories about females in response to "his." Thus the conclusion from the present data is the same as the conclusion of Moulton et al. (1978): "His" is not gender neutral in a psychological sense.

The data for the children are equally striking. The tendency for first, third, and fifth graders to create male characters when the pronoun is "he" is even stronger than it is for college students. Only 7% of elementary school children's stories were about females when the pronoun was "he." ...

The strong tendency for children to tell stories about male characters in response to the "he" cue becomes more understandable when one looks at the data on the children's knowledge of the grammatical rule. Few know the rule and the majority apparently believe that "he" always means the person is a male.

The data from the fill-in task indicate that elementary school children, and particularly third and fifth graders, have already learned to supply "he" in a singular, gender-neutral context, although the correct-sentences task indicates that they cannot articulate why they do so. The results of the fill-in task are quite similar to those of Martyna (1978) with college students completing sentences. . . .

Therefore, it seems reasonable to conclude that (a) the majority of elementary school children have learned to supply "he" in gender-neutral contexts, and (b) the majority of elementary school children do not know the rule that "he" in gender-neutral contents refers to both males and females, and have a strong tendency to think of males in creating stories from "he" cues. The chain of concepts for them, then, is that (a) the typical person is a "he"; and (b) "he" refers only to males. Logically then, might they not conclude (c) the typical person is a male?

We know that by first grade, girls have less self-confidence and lower expectations for success than do boys (Block, 1976; Crandall, 1969, 1978). A speculation as to one of the causes of that phenomenon arises from the present studies, namely that language may be a contributor. That is, if first graders routinely use "he" to refer to everyone without knowing the grammatical rule behind the use, might they not begin to attach greater status and normativeness to the male, and correspondingly devalue the female? If Bem (1981) is correct that self-concept is assimilated to the gender schema, could low self-confidence in females be related to aspects of the gender schema that have been shaped by sexist language? These are important questions deserving research. . . .

In summary, it is clear that the tendency for subjects to think of males when they hear "he" in a gender-neutral context (story-telling data) is present from first grade through the college years. . . . The contributions of language to sex role development are deserving of considerably more attention, both theoretical and empirically. We must find out how children think about sexist language and other gender-related features of language, and how these features influence the developing gender schema.

References

Bandura, A., & Walters, R. H. (1963). *Social learning and personality development*. New York: Holt, Rinehart & Winston.

Bem, S. L. (1981). Gender schema theory: A cognitive account of sex typing. *Psychological Review, 88,* 354–364.

Block, J. H. (1976). Issues, problems, and pitfalls in assessing sex differences: A critical review of *The Psychology of Sex Differences. Merrill-Palmer Quarterly, 22,* 283–308.

Crandall, V. C. (1969). Sex differences in expectancy of intellectual and academic reinforcement. In C. P. Smith (Ed.), *Achievement related motives in children.* New York: Russell Sage.

Crandall, V. C. (1978, August). *Expecting sex differences and sex differences in expectancies: A developmental analysis.* Paper presented at the meeting of the American Psychological Association, Toronto.

Everitt, B. S. (1977). *The analysis of contingency tables.* London: Chapman and Hall.

Kail, R. V., & Levine, L. E. (1976). Encoding processes and sex-role preferences. *Journal of Experimental Child Psychology, 21,* 256–263.

Kohlberg, L. (1966). A cognitive-developmental analysis of children's sex-role concepts and attitudes. In E. E. Maccoby (Ed.), *The development of sex differences* (pp. 82–172). Stanford, CA: Stanford University Press.

Liben, L. S., & Signorella, M. L. (1980). Gender-related schemata and constructive memory in children. *Child Development, 51,* 11–18.

Martin, C. L., & Halverson, C. F. (1981). A schematic processing model of sex-typing and stereotyping in children. *Child Development, 52,* 1119–1134.

Martin, C. L., & Halverson, C. F. (1983). The effects of sex-typing schemas on young children's memory. *Child Development, 54,* 563–574.

Martyna, W. (1978, Winter). What does "he" mean? Use of the generic masculine. *Journal of Communication, 28,* 131–138.

Martyna, W. (1980). Beyond the "he/man" approach: The case for nonsexist language. *Signs, 5,* 482–493.

Mischel, W. (1966). A social-learning view of sex differences in behavior. In E. E. Maccoby (Ed.), *The development of sex differences.* Stanford, CA: Stanford University Press.

Moulton, J., Robinson, G. M., & Elias, C. (1978). Psychology in action: Sex bias in language use: "Neutral" pronouns that aren't. *American Psychologist, 33,* 1032–1036.

Motivation

Selection 24
ABRAHAM H. MASLOW, from "A Theory of Human Motivation," Psychological Review

Selection 25
ALBERT BANDURA, from "Self-Efficacy: Toward a Unifying Theory of Behavioral Change," Psychological Review

Selection 26
EDWARD L. DECI, from "Work: Who Does Not Like It and Why," Psychology Today

A Theory of Human Motivation

Abraham H. Maslow (1943)

Motivation, a core concept in psychology, has been studied from a wide variety of perspectives. One intriguing perspective is Maslow's humanistic theory, which proposes that there is a hierarchy of needs that, when satisfied, leads to self-actualization, or the realization of one's potential.

Abraham H. Maslow (1908–1970), who first proposed the humanistic theory of motivation, earned his Ph.D. in experimental psychology from the University of Wisconsin in 1934. He taught at Brooklyn College and Brandeis University before going to The Laughlin Foundation in Menlo Park, California, in 1969. A leading proponent of the humanistic approach in psychology, Maslow wrote a number of books, including *Toward a Psychology of Being* (Van Nostrand Reinhold, 1962) and *Motivation and Personality* (Harper, 1954).

This selection is from "A theory of Human Motivation", which was published in *Psychological Review* in 1943. In it, Maslow presents his original thinking in developing his "positive" humanistic theory. He perceives human needs as composing a hierarchy, with self-actualization—becoming what one is capable of becoming—as the ultimate need. Maslow writes in a fairly straight forward style, but he deals with issues that are complex and that, in many ways, form the essence of being human. As you read this selection, consider what motivates you in your everyday life.

Key Concept: humanistic theory of motivation

APA Citation: Maslow, A. H. (1943). A theory of human motivation. *Psychological Review, 50*, 370–396.

*I*t is far easier to perceive and to criticize the aspects in motivation theory than to remedy them. Mostly this is because of the very serious lack of sound data in this area. I conceive this lack of sound facts to be due primarily to the absence of a valid theory of motivation. The present theory then must be considered to be a suggested program or framework for future research and must stand or fall, not so much on facts available or evidence presented, as upon researches yet to be done, researches suggested perhaps, by the questions raised in this paper.

The Basic Needs

The 'Physiological' Needs. The needs that are usually taken as the starting point for motivation theory are the so-called physiological drives. Two recent lines of research make it necessary to revise our customary notions about these needs, first, the development of the concept of homeostasis, and second, the finding that appetites (preferential choices among foods) are a fairly efficient indication of actual needs or lacks in the body.

Homeostasis refers to the body's automatic efforts to maintain a constant, normal state of the blood stream. Cannon[1] has described this process for (1) the water content of the blood, (2) salt content, (3) sugar content, (4) protein content, (5) fat content, (6) calcium content, (7) oxygen content, (8) constant hydrogen-ion level (acid-base balance) and (9) constant temperature of the blood. Obviously this list can be extended to include other minerals, the hormones, vitamins, etc.

Young in a recent article[3] has summarized the work on appetite in its relation to body needs. If the body lacks some chemical, the individual will tend to develop a specific appetite or partial hunger for that food element. Thus it seems impossible as well as useless to make any list of fundamental physiological needs for they can come to almost any number one might wish, depending on the degree of specificity of description. We can not identify all physiological needs as homeostatic. That sexual desire, sleepiness, sheer activity and maternal behavior in animals, are homeostatic, has not yet been demonstrated. Furthermore, this list would not include the various sensory pleasures (tastes, smells, tickling, stroking) which are probably physiological and which may become the goals of motivated behavior....

It should be pointed out again that any of the physiological needs and the consummatory behavior involved with them serve as channels for all sorts of other needs as well. That is to say, the person who thinks he is hungry may actually be seeking more for comfort, or dependence, than for vitamins or proteins. Conversely, it is possible to satisfy the hunger need in part by other activities such as drinking water or smoking cigarettes. In other words, relatively isolable as these physiological needs are, they are not completely so.

Undoubtedly these physiological needs are the most prepotent of all needs [they exceed all others in power]. What this means specifically is, that in the human being who is missing everything in life in an extreme fashion, it is most likely that the major motivation would be the physiological needs rather than any others. A person who is lacking food, safety, love, and esteem would most probably hunger for food more strongly than for anything else....

Obviously a good way to obscure the 'higher' motivations, and to get a lopsided view of human capacities and human nature, is to make the organism extremely and chronically hungry or thirsty. Anyone who attempts to make an emergency picture into a typical one, and who will measure all of man's goals and desires by his behavior during extreme physiological deprivation is certainly being blind to many things. It is quite true that man lives by bread alone—when there is no bread. But what happens to man's desires when there *is* plenty of bread and when his belly is chronically filled?

At once other (*and 'higher'*) *needs emerge* and these, rather than physiological hungers, dominate the organism. And when these in turn are satisfied, again new (and still 'higher') needs emerge and so on. This is what we mean by saying that the basic human needs are organized into a hierarchy of relative prepotency.

One main implication of this phrasing is that gratification becomes as important a concept as deprivation in motivation theory, for it releases the organism from the domination of a relatively more physiological need, permitting thereby the emergence of other more social goals. The physiological needs, along with their partial goals, when chronically gratified cease to exist as active determinants or organizers of behavior. They now exist only in a potential fashion in the sense that they may emerge again to dominate the organism if they are thwarted. But a want that is satisfied is no longer a want. The organism is dominated and its behavior organized only by unsatisfied needs. If hunger is satisfied, it becomes unimportant in the current dynamics of the individual....

The Safety Needs. If the physiological needs are relatively well gratified, there then emerges a new set of needs, which we may categorize roughly as the safety needs. All that has been said of the physiological needs is equally true, although in lesser degree, of these desires. The organism may equally well be wholly dominated by them. They may serve as the almost exclusive organizers of behavior, recruiting all the capacities of the organism in their service, and we may then fairly describe the whole organism as a safety-seeking mechanism. Again we may say of the receptors, the effectors, of the intellect and the other capacities that they are primarily safety-seeking tools. Again, as in the hungry man, we find that the dominating goal is a strong determinant not only of his current world-outlook and philosophy but also of his philosophy of the future. Practically everything looks less important than safety, (even sometimes the physiological needs which being satisfied, are now underestimated). A man, in this state, if it is extreme enough and chronic enough, may be characterized as living almost for safety alone.

Although in this paper we are interested primarily in the needs of the adult, we can approach an understanding of his safety needs perhaps more efficiently by observation of infants and children, in whom these needs are much more simple and obvious. One reason for the clearer appearance of the threat or danger reaction in infants, is that they do not inhibit this reaction at all, whereas adults in our society have been taught to inhibit it at all costs. Thus even when adults do feel their safety to be threatened we may not be able to see this on the surface. Infants will react in a total fashion and as if they were endangered, if they are disturbed or dropped suddenly, startled by loud noises, flashing light, or other unusual sensory stimulation, by rough handling, by general loss of support in the mother's arms, or by inadequate support....

From these and similar observations, we may generalize and say that the average child in our society generally prefers a safe, orderly, predictable, organized world, which he can count on, and in which unexpected, unmanageable or other dangerous things do not happen, and in which, in any case, he has all-powerful parents who protect and shield him from harm....

The healthy, normal, fortunate adult in our culture is largely satisfied in his safety needs. The peaceful, smoothly running, 'good' society ordinarily makes its members feel safe enough from wild animals, extremes of temperature, criminals, assault and murder, tyranny, etc. Therefore, in a very real sense, he no longer has any safety needs as active motivators. Just as a sated man no longer feels hungry, a safe man no longer feels endangered. If we wish to see these needs directly and clearly we must turn to neurotic or near-neurotic individuals, and to the economic and social underdogs. In between these extremes, we can perceive the expressions of safety needs only in such phenomena as, for instance, the common preference for a job with tenure and protection, the desire for a savings account, and for insurance of various kinds (medical, dental, unemployment, disability, old age).

Other broader aspects of the attempt to seek safety and stability in the world are seen in the very common preference for familiar rather than unfamiliar things, or for the known rather than the unknown. The tendency to have some religion or world-philosophy that organizes the universe and the men in it into some sort of satisfactorily coherent, meaningful whole is also in part motivated by safety-seeking. Here too we may list science and philosophy in general as partially motivated by the safety needs. . . .

The Love Needs. If both the physiological and the safety needs are fairly well gratified, then there will emerge the love and affection and belongingness needs, and the whole cycle already described will repeat itself with this new center. Now the person will feel keenly, as never before, the absence of friends, or a sweetheart, or a wife, or children. He will hunger for affectionate relations with people in general, namely, for a place in his group, and he will strive with great intensity to achieve this goal. He will want to attain such a place more than anything else in the world and may even forget that once, when he was hungry, he sneered at love. . . .

One thing that must be stressed at this point is that love is not synonymous with sex. Sex may be studied as a purely physiological need. Ordinarily sexual behavior is multi-determined, that is to say, determined not only by sexual but also by other needs, chief among which are the love and affection needs. Also not to be overlooked is the fact that the love needs involve both giving *and* receiving love.

The Esteem Needs. All people in our society (with a few pathological exceptions) have a need or desire for a stable, firmly based, (usually) high evaluation of themselves, for self-respect, or self-esteem, and for the esteem of others. By firmly based self-esteem, we mean that which is soundly based upon real capacity, achievement and respect from others. These needs may be classified into two subsidiary sets. These are, first, the desire for strength, for achievement, for adequacy, for confidence in the face of the world, and for independence and freedom. Secondly, we have what we may call the desire for reputation or prestige (defining it as respect or esteem from other people), recognition, attention, importance or appreciation. . . .

Satisfaction of the self-esteem need leads to feelings of self-confidence, worth, strength, capability and adequacy of being useful and necessary in the world. But thwarting of these needs produces feelings of inferiority, of weakness and of helplessness. These feelings in turn give rise to either basic discouragement or else compensatory or neurotic trends. An appreciation of the necessity of basic self-confidence and an understanding of how helpless people are without it, can be easily gained from a study of severe traumatic neurosis.[2]

The Need for Self-Actualization. Even if all these needs are satisfied, we may still often (if not always) expect that a new discontent and restlessness will soon develop, unless the individual is doing what he is fitted for. A musician must make music, an artist must paint, a poet must write, if he is to be ultimately happy. What a man *can* be, he *must* be. This need we may call self-actualization.

This term, first coined by Kurt Goldstein, is being used in this paper in a much more specific and limited fashion. It refers to the desire for selffulfillment, namely, to the tendency for him to become actualized in what he is potentially. This tendency might be phrased as the desire to become more and more what one is, to become everything that one is capable of becoming.

The specific form that these needs will take will of course vary greatly from person to person. In one individual it may take the form of the desire to be an ideal mother, in another it may be expressed athletically, and in still another it may be expressed in painting pictures or in inventions. It is not necessarily a creative urge although in people who have any capacities for creation it will take this form.

The clear emergence of these needs rests upon prior satisfaction of the physiological, safety, love and esteem needs. We shall call people who are satisfied in these needs, basically satisfied people, and it is from these that we may expect the fullest (and healthiest) creativeness. Since, in our society, basically satisfied people are the exception, we do not know much about self-actualization, either experimentally or clinically. It remains a challenging problem for research.

The Preconditions for the Basic Need Satisfactions. There are certain conditions which are immediate prerequisites for the basic need satisfactions. Danger to these is reacted to almost as if it were a direct danger to the basic needs themselves. Such conditions as freedom to speak, freedom to do what one wishes so long as no harm is done to others, freedom to express one's self, freedom to investigate and seek for information, freedom to defend one's self, justice, fairness, honesty, orderliness in the group are examples of such preconditions for basic need satisfactions. Thwarting in these freedoms will be reacted to with a threat or emergency response. These conditions are not ends in themselves but they are *almost* so since they are so closely related to the basic needs, which are apparently the only ends in themselves. These conditions are defended because without them the basic satisfactions are quite impossible, or at least, very severely endangered.

If we remember that the cognitive capacities (perceptual, intellectual, learning) are a set of adjustive tools, which have, among other functions, that of satisfaction of our basic needs, then it is clear that any danger to them, any deprivation or blocking of their free use, must also be indirectly threatening to the basic needs themselves. Such a statement is a partial solution of the general problems of curiosity, the search for knowledge, truth and wisdom, and the ever-persistent urge to solve the cosmic mysteries. . . .

The Desires to Know and to Understand. So far, we have mentioned the cognitive needs only in passing. Acquiring knowledge and systematizing the universe have been considered as, in part, techniques for the achievement of basic safety in the world, or, for the intelligent man, expressions of self-actualization. Also freedom of inquiry and expression have been discussed as preconditions of satisfactions of the basic needs. True though these formulations may be, they do not constitute definitive answers to the question as to the motivation role of curiosity, learning, philosophizing, experimenting, etc. They are, at best, no more than partial answers....

Further Characteristics of the Basic Needs

The Degree of Fixity of the Hierarchy of Basic Needs. We have spoken so far as if this hierarchy were a fixed order but actually it is not nearly as rigid as we may have implied. It is true that most of the people with whom we have worked have seemed to have these basic needs in about the order that has been indicated. However, there have been a number of exceptions....

Degrees of Relative Satisfaction. So far, our theoretical discussion may have given the impression that these five sets of needs are somehow in a stepwise, all-or-none relationship to each other. We have spoken in such terms as the following: "If one need is satisfied, then another emerges." This statement might give the false impression that a need must be satisfied 100 percent before the next need emerges. In actual fact, most members of our society who are normal, are partially satisfied in all their basic needs and partially unsatisfied in all their basic needs at the same time. A more realistic description of the hierarchy would be in terms of decreasing percentages of satisfaction as we go up the hierarchy of prepotency. For instance, if I may assign arbitrary figures for the sake of illustration, it is as if the average citizen is satisfied perhaps 85 percent in his physiological needs, 70 percent in his safety needs, 50 percent in his love needs, 40 percent in his self-esteem needs, and 10 percent in his self-actualization needs.

As for the concept of emergence of a new need after satisfaction of the prepotent need, this emergence is not a sudden saltatory phenomenon but rather a gradual emergence by slow degrees from nothingness. For instance, if prepotent need A is satisfied only 10 percent then need B may not be visible at all. However, as this need A becomes satisfied 25 percent, need B may emerge 5 percent, as need A becomes satisfied 75 percent need B may emerge 90 percent, and so on.

Unconscious Character of Needs. These needs are neither necessarily conscious nor unconscious. On the whole, however, in the average person, they are more often unconscious rather than conscious. It is not necessary at this point to overhaul the tremendous mass of evidence which indicates the crucial importance of unconscious motivation. It would by now be expected, on a priori grounds alone, that unconscious motivations would on the whole be rather more important than the conscious motivations. What we have called the basic needs are very often largely unconscious although they may, with suitable techniques, and with sophisticated people become conscious.

Cultural Specificity and Generality of Needs. This classification of basic needs makes some attempt to take account of the relative unity behind the superficial differences in specific desires from one culture to another. Certainly in any particular culture an individual's conscious motivational content will usually be extremely different from the conscious motivational content of an individual in another society. However, it is the common experience of anthropologists that people, even in different societies, are much more alike than we would think from our first contact with them, and that as we know them better we seem to find more and more of this commonness. We then recognize the most startling differences to be superficial rather than basic, *e.g.*, differences in style of hairdress, clothes, tastes in food, etc. Our classification of basic needs is in part an attempt to account for this unity behind the apparent diversity from culture to culture. No claim is made that it is ultimate or universal for all cultures. The claim is made only that it is relatively *more* ultimate, more universal, more basic, than the superficial conscious desires from culture to culture, and makes a somewhat closer approach to common-human characteristics. Basic needs are *more* common-human than superficial desires or behaviors.

Multiple Motivations of Behavior. These needs must be understood *not* to be *exclusive* or single determiners of certain kinds of behavior. An example may be found in any behavior that seems to be physiologically motivated, such as eating, or sexual play or the like. The clinical psychologists have long since found that any behavior may be a channel through which flow various determinants. Or to say it in another way, most behavior is multi-motivated. Within the sphere of motivational determinants any behavior tends to be determined by several or *all* of the basic needs simultaneously rather than by only one of them. The latter would be more an exception than the former. Eating may be partially for the sake of filling the stomach, and partially for the sake of comfort and amelioration of other needs. One may make love not only for pure sexual release, but also to convince one's self of one's masculinity, or to make a conquest, to feel powerful, or to win more basic affection. As an illustration, I may point out that it would be possible (theoretically if not practically) to analyze a single act of an individual and see in it the expression of his physiological needs, his safety needs, his love needs, his esteem needs and self-actualization. This contrasts sharply with the more naive brand of trait psychology in which one trait or one motive accounts for a certain kind of act, *i.e.*, an aggressive act is traced solely to a trait of aggressiveness....

Goals as Centering Principle in Motivation Theory. It will be observed that the basic principle in our classification has been neither the instigation nor the motivated behavior but rather the functions, effects, purposes, or goals of the behavior. It has been proven sufficiently by various people that this is the most suitable point for centering in any motivation theory.

References

1. Cannon, W. B. *Wisdom of the body.* New York: Norton, 1932.

2. Kardiner, A. *The traumatic neuroses of war.* New York: Hoeber, 1941.

3. Young, P. T. The experimental analysis of appetite. *Psychol. Bull.,* 1941, 38, 129–164.

Self-Efficacy: Toward a Unifying Theory of Behavioral Change

Albert Bandura (1977)

It is important to have a good understanding of ourselves, including our attitudes and abilities, asserts Albert Bandura. His concept of self-efficacy focuses on the belief that we can behave in a manner that produces successful outcomes. Bandura states that having the expectation that we can master a task has important implications for our self-concept and our ability to adjust to various situations.

Bandura (b. 1925) was born in Alberta, Canada in 1925. He earned his Ph.D. in clinical psychology from the University of Iowa in 1952. He then accepted a position at Stanford University, where he is currently a professor emeritus of psychology. Bandura served as president of the American Psychological Assocation in 1974. His research interests have focused on social cognitive theory, which assigns an important role to cognitive, vicarious, self-regulating, and self-reflective processes in human functioning. He has written numerous influential books, including *Social Foundations of Thought and Action: A Social Cognitive Theory* (Prentice Hall, 1986) and *Self-Efficacy: The Exercise of Control* (Freeman, 1997).

Bandura's theory of self-efficacy is described in this selection from "Self-Efficacy: Toward a Unifying Theory of Behavioral Change," which was published in *Psychological Review* in 1977. In this classic paper, he describes the factors that influence self-efficacy, including performance accomplishments, vicarious experience, verbal persuasion, and physiological arousal. In one part of the original article not included in this selection, Bandura reports that self-efficacy is important for successful behavioral change in therapy. As you read this selection, think about the variables that promote self-efficacy and how you could develop a program to help others improve their coping skills through enhanced self-understanding.

Key Concept: self-efficacy

APA Citation: Bandura, A. (1977). Self-efficacy: Toward a unifying theory of behavioral change. *Psychological Review, 84,* 191–215.

EFFICACY EXPECTATIONS AS A MECHANISM OF OPERATION

The present theory is based on the principal assumption that psychological procedures, whatever their form, serve as means of creating and strengthening expectations of personal efficacy. Within this analysis, efficacy expectations are distinguished from response–outcome expectancies. The difference is presented schematically in Figure 1.

An outcome expectancy is defined as a person's estimate that a given behavior will lead to certain outcomes. An efficacy expectation is the conviction that one can successfully execute the behavior required to produce the outcomes. Outcome and efficacy expectations are differentiated, because individuals can believe that a particular course of action will produce certain outcomes, but if they entertain serious doubts about whether they can perform the necessary activities such information does not influence their behavior.

In this conceptual system, expectations of personal mastery affect both initiation and persistence of coping behavior. The strength of people's convictions in their own effectiveness is likely to affect whether they will even try to cope with given situations. At this initial level, perceived self-efficacy influences choice of behavioral settings. People fear and tend to avoid threatening situations they believe exceed their coping skills, whereas they get involved in activities and behave assuredly when they judge themselves capable of handling situations that would otherwise be intimidating.

FIGURE 1

Diagrammatic Representation of the Difference Between Efficacy Expectations and Outcome Expectations

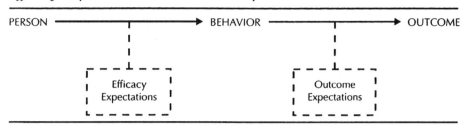

Not only can perceived self-efficacy have directive influence on choice of activities and settings, but, through expectations of eventual success, it can affect coping efforts once they are initiated. Efficacy expectations determine how much effort people will expend and how long they will persist in the face of obstacles and aversive experiences. The stronger the perceived self-efficacy, the more active the efforts. Those who persist in subjectively threatening activities that are in fact relatively safe will gain corrective experiences that reinforce their sense of efficacy, thereby eventually eliminating their defensive behavior. Those who cease their coping efforts prematurely will retain their self-debilitating expectations and fears for a long time.

The preceding analysis of how perceived self-efficacy influences performance is not meant to imply that expectation is the sole determinant of behavior. Expectations alone will not produce desired performance if the component capabilities are lacking. Moreover, there are many things that people can do with certainty of success that they do not perform because they have no incentives to do so. Given appropriate skills and adequate incentives, however, efficacy expectations are a major determinant of people's choice of activities, how much effort they will expend, and of how long they will sustain effort in dealing with stressful situations.

DIMENSIONS OF EFFICACY EXPECTATIONS

Empirical tests of the relationship between expectancy and performance of threatening activities have been hampered by inadequacy of the expectancy analysis. In most studies the measures of expectations are mainly concerned with people's hopes for favorable outcomes rather than with their sense of personal mastery. Moreover, expectations are usually assessed globally only at a single point in a change process as though they represent a static, unidimensional factor. Participants in experiments of this type are simply asked to judge how much they expect to benefit from a given procedure. When asked to make such estimates, participants assume, more often than not, that the benefits will be produced by the external ministrations rather than gained through the development of self-efficacy. Such global measures reflect a mixture of, among other things, hope, wishful thinking, belief in the potency of the procedures, and faith in the therapist. It therefore comes as no surprise that outcome expectations of this type have little relation to magnitude of behavioral change (Davison & Wilson, 1973; Lick & Bootzin, 1975).

Efficacy expectations vary on several dimensions that have important performance implications. They differ in *magnitude.* Thus when tasks are ordered in level of difficulty, the efficacy expectations of different individuals may be limited to the simpler tasks, extend to moderately difficult ones, or include even the most taxing performances. Efficacy expectations also differ in *generality.* Some experiences create circumscribed mastery expectations. Others instill a more generalized sense of efficacy that extends well beyond the specific treatment situation. In addition, expectancies vary in *strength.* Weak expectations are easily extinguishable by disconfirming experiences, whereas individuals who possess strong expectations of mastery will persevere in their coping efforts despite disconfirming experiences.

An adequate expectancy analysis, therefore, requires detailed assessment of the magnitude, generality, and strength of efficacy expectations commensurate with the precision with which behavioral processes are measured. Both efficacy expectations and performance should be assessed at significant junctures in the change process to clarify their reciprocal effects on each other. Mastery expectations influence performance and are, in turn, altered by the cumulative effects of one's efforts.

SOURCES OF EFFICACY EXPECTATIONS

In this social learning analysis, expectations of personal efficacy are based on four major sources of information: performance accomplishments, vicarious experience, verbal persuasion, and physiological states. Figure 2 presents the diverse influence procedures commonly used to reduce defensive behavior and presents the principal source through which each treatment operates to create

Work: Who Does Not Like It and Why

Edward L. Deci (1972)

Psychologists have always been interested in why people do what they do—in short, their motivation. Sometimes people do things for extrinsic or outside reasons (such as for money or for praise), and sometimes they do things for intrinsic or internal reasons (simply because they enjoy the activities). There are a number of situations, however, in which people are *expected* to work, such as in school or on the job. Teachers and employers are especially interested in work motivation. Edward L. Deci has spent much of his career trying to determine the influences on intrinsic and extrinsic motivation.

Deci (b. 1942) earned his Ph.D. in psychology from Carnegie-Mellon University in 1970. He is a professor of psychology at the University of Rochester, where he has been teaching since 1970. A leader in the study of intrinsic motivation, he has authored or co-authored a number of books, including *Intrinsic Motivation and Self-determination in Human Behavior* (Plenum, 1985), with Richard M. Ryan.

This selection, "Work: Who Does Not Like It and Why," published in *Psychology Today* in 1972, is an informal discussion of the influences on intrinsic motivation and work. In this selection, Deci provides some practical advice to anyone wanting to enjoy what he or she does. In his later research, Deci has found that self-determination is an important variable in intrinsic motivation. As you read this selection, notice how each experiment leads to the next one. Also, think about what you enjoy doing most and what motivates you to do it.

Key Concept: intrinsic motivation

APA Citation: Deci, E. L. (1972). Work: Who does not like it and why. *Psychology Today, 6*, 56-58; 92.

I am fascinated with a child's unflagging curiosity. He explores everything; for him objects exist to be touched, smelled, tasted, and where possible, eaten. He learns, and learning excites and delights him. Yet by the time he reaches seventh grade, he is likely to complain that he doesn't like school and having to "learn stuff." And when he is out of school he may give up reading books entirely.

The work I have done over the last three years may account for some of this loss of curiosity. I began with the distinction that psychologists make between intrinsic and extrinsic motivation. When a person does a thing solely for the pleasure of the activity, we say that he is intrinsically motivated: the activity is its own reward. (I once spent a solid 12 hours doing a jigsaw puzzle. No one forced me; no one even knew that I had done it. I was intrinsically motivated.) By contrast, when a person does something for an outside reward—money, a better job—or to avoid a punishment—loss of money, censure—we say that he is extrinsically motivated.

Joy

Many psychologists have documented such intrinsically motivated acts as exploration and curiosity. Harry Harlow reports that monkeys will spend hours working on a puzzle for no apparent reward; they seem to like to work on the puzzle, much as I do. Robert W. White has suggested that man strives to deal effectively with his environment: we are, he says, intrinsically motivated to be creative, spontaneous and curious. Daniel Berlyne and other researchers have written about play, another intrinsic activity. In all, it is clear that human beings do many things for the simple joy of the activity.

Now consider a person who is involved in an intrinsically interesting task for which he is also receiving extrinsic rewards. This situation marks the child's development: he is eager to learn, but the school soon controls his learning with grades, threats of failure, gold stars, and so on. One must wonder what happens—whether extrinsic reinforcements increase a person's intrinsic motivation, decrease it, or leave it unchanged.

Puzzle

In quest of answers, I have observed hundreds of college students at work on an intrinsically interesting task. I used a popular puzzle called Soma, which consists of seven three-dimensional pieces, all variously shaped. We asked students to use the pieces to reproduce several configurations that were outlined on paper. Our pilot tests showed clearly that the students thought the puzzle was intrinsically interesting.

The outline for our series of experiments was the same. We gave each student four configurations to solve, allowing him 10 minutes for each puzzle. If he could not solve a puzzle in the allotted time, we stopped him and showed him the solution. After completing the four puzzles, the student remained alone in the experimental room, free to do what he wished: read magazines, solve more puzzles, or whatever. We reasoned that the students were intrinsically motivated if they continued to work on puzzles when they were alone, since there were other things they could do in that situation. Thus the additional amount of time they spent with the Soma game was our measure of their intrinsic motivation for that activity.

Pay

Our first experiment looked at the effect of money. We told half of the 64 student subjects at the outset that they would receive one dollar for each correct solution; the most they could win, then, was four dollars (the average was over two dollars). The money reward was therefore contingent upon their performance. The other half of the students also worked on the four puzzles, but we did not pay them for the correct answer.

Money made a difference. Those students whom we had paid spent significantly less time with the puzzles when they were alone later than did those who had done the same puzzles for free. Once they got money for doing a fun game, their intrinsic motivation decreased; to an extent, they had become dependent on the external reward.

Buzzer

In a second experiment, Wayne Cascio and I sought to determine whether threats of punishment would have the same effect. We told half of the 32 students that if they were unable to solve a puzzle within 10 minutes a buzzer would sound, indicating that their time was up for that puzzle. We gave them a short sample blast of the noise, so they knew that it was truly obnoxious—to be avoided if at all possible. This group, then, worked on Soma partly to avoid a punishment, the buzzer. We found that these students, like those who had worked for money, were less intrinsically interested in the puzzle later than students who had not been threatened with the unpleasant sound. Actually, few students had to endure the punishment of the buzzer, since most were able to solve all the problems.

So it seems to have been the *threat* of punishment that was critical in decreasing their intrinsic motivation.

Locus

In our third variation, we paid each student two dollars for participating in the experiment regardless of performance, instead of paying for each solution. This time they showed no change in degree of intrinsic motivation.

We can explain these findings in terms of locus of causality. That is, when a person does a thing for no apparent reward, he explains his behavior in terms of internal causes: I *am doing this because I like to,* he seems to say. When we give him external reasons, however, he begins to attribute his behavior to other causes: I *am doing this for the money, or to avoid punishments.* When we paid our students for each solution the locus of causality for their behavior shifted from internal motives to external ones. They readily came to perceive of the money as the reason for their behavior. However, when we did not tie payments directly to their performance—when we gave the flat fee to everyone—the students were less likely to think that the money was the reason for working. Doing the puzzles was not instrumental in getting the money so they were less likely to think of the money as their reason for doing the puzzle.

A change in locus of causality is one of two processes that affect intrinsic motivation. The other concerns verbal feedback. We found, for instance, that if we rewarded a student for each correct solution with statements such as "good, that's very fast for that one," his intrinsic motivation increased markedly. The 48 students told us that they liked the puzzle more, and spent more free time working on it, than the 48 students whom we had not so praised.

Why did verbal rewards increase intrinsic motivation, while money rewards decreased it? The answer, we think, is that an intrinsically motivated activity is one that provides feelings of competence and self-determination for a person. I stayed with that 12-hour jigsaw partly out of furious resolve to beat the damned thing, and my success reinforced my feelings of competence. Verbal feedback does much the same thing: it reaffirms the individual's confidence in himself; it makes him feel competent and self-determining.

Pair

Thus external rewards have at least two functions: one is a controlling function that makes a person dependent on the reward; the other is a feedback function that affects his feelings of competence and self-determination. Money and threats are common controllers; we do not generally think of them as reassurance about our competence. Praise and compliments, however, make a person feel good. In this sense, verbal feedback from someone else may not differ phenomenologically from the feedback an individual gives himself; both help him feel that he is worthy and capable. Both, therefore, maintain one's intrinsic motivation.

Of course it is possible that a heavy dosage of verbal reward would make a person dependent on praise, just as he becomes dependent on money or threats; and it also is possible that this type of dependency too would decrease intrinsic motivation. So far, however, we can conclude that feedback rewards differ significantly from controlling rewards.

Offset

In our next experiment, we gave our subjects both money (one dollar per correct puzzle) and praise. Apparently, the two kinds of reward offset each other: this group showed the same level of intrinsic motivation that we found with students who received neither reward.

Finally, we wondered what would happen when feedback was negative. Cascio and I gave 32 students new puzzles that were much more difficult. They failed miserably at solving them; and later they were indeed less likely to spend time working on them than the 24 students who had worked on somewhat easier puzzles with higher success rates. The negative feelings associated with failure counteracted the positive feelings associated with the puzzle. Failure won: failing at a task, it seems, reduces our motive to stay with it. Similarly, Cascio and I found that negative verbal feedback also decreases intrinsic motivation.

Toy

Another area of social psychology that fits nicely with our research is that of insufficient justification. This line of theory suggests that when persons do not have sufficient external reasons to explain their actions, they develop internal reasons; attitudes change accordingly.

For example, Elliot Aronson and J. Merrill Carlsmith gave one group of children strong warnings against playing with a particular toy, and gave another group milder warnings. The first group had a clear, external reason for avoiding the attractive toy; hence they felt no need for internal justification for not playing with it. But the second group, those who were warned mildly, changed their attitudes toward the toy significantly: they decided that they really didn't want to play with the "dumb old thing" anyway. Since there were insufficient outside threats, they developed internal reasons. Jonathan Freedman reported similar findings. Children who developed internal reasons for not playing with the toy were less likely to play with the toy in a free situation even two months later. Intrinsic controls, it appears, have lasting effect.

Controls

When we apply the results of these experiments to the real world, we begin to see why curiosity and pleasure in learning decrease as the child grows up. When the child enters school he immediately becomes subject to numerous extrinsic controls. Teachers grade him, and warn him that he will fail if he does not do what he is told to do. Teachers determine what the child should learn, and at what pace he must learn it. Some parents compound the process by promising money or gifts for good marks. So the child begins to work for the grade, or the gift, or to avoid the consequences of failure. The result is a student who works only for external rewards.

John Holt has described this process beautifully. Children fail, he says, because they are afraid of punishment and bored by the dull and trivial tasks they must perform. The school provides little that is intrinsically interesting, and then teachers control the student's behavior in such a way that they destroy any intrinsic motivation that may sneak through.

Systems

Educators are not the only ones who want to know how to maintain intrinsic motivation. Organizations and businesses have become concerned. Managerial psychologists have begun to focus on factors that promote the worker's intrinsic motivation and ego-involvement with his job. They stress tilt of work that promote creativity and they argue that workers should participate in the decision-making processes of the company.

Yet others look more at reward systems that tie money and other benefits to performance—sales commissions and piece-rate payments are examples. My research indicates, however, that such pay systems will *decrease* the intrinsic motivation that is aroused by the interesting jobs and sharing of decision-making. (Straight salaries, however, which are not directly tied to workers' performances, run less risk of this.)

Chaos

There are many individuals who argue that if we remove external controls, people will flounder about in their new-found freedom and abuse it. Lift curfews, say the administrators, and students will carouse all night. Lift threats, says the employer, and employees will stop working. Lift grades, says the parent, and my child will not strive for college.

In fact, they are probably right. The external controls which they have used have co-opted internal control, so the initial response to the breakdown of external controls can be chaotic or destructive behavior. However, I think that the internal control can be reestablished. Forced to rely on his own resources, a person establishes internal controls and limits. This is especially so if the administrators, the employers, and the parents are supportive.

Intrinsic motivation and internal controls have the advantage of being operative when no one is looking. More importantly, they help to maintain a person's sense of self-esteem and personal worth. Abraham Maslow, in *Eupsychian Management,* argues that internal controls also produce less anxiety and are more conducive to strong mental health than external controls are.

Level

It is clear to me that if we want individuals to enjoy what they do, to derive joy and satisfaction from their work as well as their play, we must do two things. We must create more activities that are inherently interesting and gratifying; and we must not use extrinsic rewards in a way that will lower the interest level of those activities that are intrinsically motivated. We should learn to give verbal support to our friends, colleagues and children, and not rely on tendencies to reward or threaten. External controls may get others to act the way we want them to, but such controls absolve them of the feeling of responsibility for those acts. Controlling others seems to insure that others will not control themselves.

Emotion

THE JAMES-LANGE THEORY OF EMOTIONS : A CRITICAL EXAMINATION AND AN ALTERNATIVE THEORY

Walter B. Cannon (1927)

Emotion has always been at the core of human existence, but until the past century, researchers were not able to scientifically study it. Psychologists were interested in understanding emotion, and since William James first proposed a theory to explain it, there has been controversy, mainly because emotion is a personal subjective experience and therefore very difficult to study. Walter B. Cannon wanted to ensure that the study of emotion focused on the influence of the brain, and specifically the role of the thalamus. The definitive theory of emotion is yet to be found, and later research disputed some of Cannon's specific findings, but today's emphasis continues to be on physiological mechanisms.

Cannon (1871-1945) earned his M.D. in 1910 from Harvard University Medical School, where he was a professor of physiology until he retired in 1942. He published *Bodily Changes in Pain, Hunger, Fear, and Rage* in 1915. Cannon was a prolific researcher, and his accomplishments included studying the role of the adrenal glands on sympathetic nervous system, coining the term 'homeostasis', studying physiological influences on emotion and investigating hunger and the process of digestion.

This selection is from "The James-Lange Theory of Emotions: A Critical Examination and an Alternative Theory," which was published in *American Journal of Psychology* in 1927. In it, Cannon describes research indicating that when the thalamus is activated, bodily changes occur simultaneously with emotional experience. He refutes James's notion that emotional experience is due to the later processing of peripheral sensory information and behavior changes. As you read this selection, consider the variables that contribute to your emotional state. How much control do we have over the emotions we feel?

Key concept: theory of emotion

APA Citation: Cannon, W.B. (1927). The James-Lange theory of emotions: A critical examination and an alternative theory. *American Journal of Psychology, 39,* 106-124.

*I*n his introduction to the reprinting of the classic papers *by* James and Lange, Dunlap[1] declares that their theory of emotions as organic processes "has not only become so strongly entrenched in scientific thought that it is practically assumed today as the basis for the study of the emotional life, but has also led to the development of the hypothesis of reaction or response as the basis of all mental life." And Perry[2] has written, "This famous doctrine is so strongly fortified by proof and so repeatedly confirmed by experience that it cannot be denied substantial truth. In spite of elaborate refutation it shows no signs of obsolescence." With some trepidation, therefore, one ventures to criticize a view of the nature of emotions which has proved so satisfactory as a means of interpreting affective experience and which has commended itself so generally to psychologists. There are now at hand, however, pertinent physiological facts which were not available when James and Lange developed their ideas and which should be brought to bear on those ideas, and there are alternative explanations of affective experience which should be considered, before the James-Lange theory is granted basal claims in this realm of psychology.

James first presented his view in 1884, Lange's monograph appeared in Danish in 1885. The cardinal points in their respective ideas of the nature of emotions are so well known that for purposes of comment only brief references need be made to them. James theory may be summarized, in nearly his own terms, as follows. An object stimulates one or more sense organs; afferent impulses pass to the cortex and the object is perceived; thereupon currents run down to muscles and viscera and alter them in complex ways; afferent impulses from these disturbed organs course back to the cortex and when there perceived transform the "object-simply-apprehended" to the "object-emotionally-felt." In other words, "the feeling of the bodily changes as they occur is the emotion—the common sensational, associations and motor elements explain all."[3] The main evidence cited for the theory is that we are aware of the tensions, throbs, flushes, pangs, suffocations—we feel them, indeed, the moment they occur—and that if we should take away from the picture of a fancied emotion these bodily symptoms, nothing would be left.

According to Lange[4] stimulation of the vasomotor center is "the root of the causes of the affections, however else they may be constituted." "We owe all the emotional side of our mental life," he wrote, "our joys and sorrows, our happy and unhappy hours, to our vasomotor system. If the impressions which fall upon our senses did not possess the power of stimulating it, we would wander through life unsympathetic and passionless, all impressions of the outer world would only enrich our experience, increase our knowledge, but would arouse neither joy nor anger, would give us neither care nor fear." Since we are unable to differentiate subjectively between feelings of a central and peripheral origin, subjective evidence is unreliable. But because wine, certain mushrooms, hashish, opium, a cold shower, and other agencies cause physiological effects which are accompanied by altered states of feeling, and because abstraction of the bodily manifestations from a frightened individual leaves nothing of his fear, the emotion is only a perception of changes in the body. It is clear that Lange had the same conception as James, but elaborated it on a much narrower basis—on changes in the circulatory system alone.

A THEORY OF EMOTION BASED ON THALAMIC PROCESSES

The foregoing discussion has disclosed the fact that the neural arrangements for emotional expression reside in subcortical centers, and that these centers are ready for instant and vigorous discharge when they are released from cortical restraint and are properly stimulated. Furthermore, the evidence is clear that when these centers are released the processes aroused in them become a source of vivid affective experience. That this experience is felt on only one side in hemiplegic cases is a peculiarly happy circumstance, for in the same individual the influence of the same affective stimulus can be observed under normal conditions and compared with its influence when given free rein.

The neural organization for an emotion which is suggested by the foregoing observations is as follows. An external situation stimulates receptors and the consequent excitation starts impulses towards the cortex. Arrival of the impulses in the cortex is associated with conditioned processes which determine the direction of the response.

Either because the response is initiated in a certain mode or figure and the cortical neurones therefore stimulate the thalamic processes, or because on their centripetal course the impulses from the receptors excite thalamic processes, they are roused and ready for discharge. That the thalamic neurones act in a special combination in a given emotional expression is proved by the reaction patterns typical of the several affective states. These neurones do not require detailed innervation from above in order to be driven into action. Being *released* for action is a primary condition for their service to the body—they then discharge precipitately and intensely. Within and near the thalamus the neurones concerned in an emotional expression lie close to the relay in the sensory path from periphery to cortex. We may assume that when these neurones discharge in a particular combination, they not only innervate muscles and viscera but also excite afferent paths to the cortex by direct connection or by irradiation. The theory which naturally presents itself is that *the peculiar quality of the emotion is added to simple sensation when the thalamic processes are roused.*

The theory just suggested appears to fit all the known facts. Its service in explaining these facts may be briefly summarized.

When the thalamic discharge occurs, the bodily changes occur almost simultaneously with the emotional experience. This coincidence of disturbances in muscles and viscera with thrills, excitements or depressions was naturally misleading, for, with the role of the thalamus omitted from consideration, obvious inference was that the peculiar quality of the emotion arose from the peripheral changes. Indeed, that inference is the heart of the James-Lange theory. The evidence presented in the foregoing pages shows that the inference is ill-founded; the sensations from the peripheral changes, contrary to James' view, are "pale, colorless and destitute of emotional warmth," whereas the thalamic disturbances contribute glow and color to otherwise simply cognitive states. The theory now proposed explains how James and Lange could reasonably make the suggestion which they made. The lack of factual support for their suggestion requires another account of emotional origins. This is provided by the evidence that thalamic processes can add to sensation an aura of feeling.

One of the strongest arguments advanced for the James-Lange theory is that the assumption of an attitude does in fact help to establish the emotional state which the attitude expresses. "Sit all day in a moping posture, sigh, and reply to everything with a dismal voice, and your melancholy lingers." On the contrary, "smooth the brow, brighten the eye, contract the dorsal rather than the ventral aspect of the frame, and speak in a major key, pass the genial compliment, and your heart must be frigid indeed if you do not gradually thaw!" Persons who have tried this advice have testified to its soundness, and have been convinced, therefore, of the truth of the claim that the moods have followed the assumed attitudes. Not all agree, however, that mimicking the outward appearance of an emotion results in the emotion itself. James suggested that the explanation of the discrepancy lay in variations of involvement of the viscera in the artificial expression. As shown above, however, the visceral changes offer only unreliable support for that idea. Again the processes in the thalamus offer a reasonable and simple explanation. As the cases reported by Head have shown, emotions originating from memories and imagination affect more intensely the half-thalamus that has been released from motor control than they affect the normal half. This shows that cortical processes may start thalamic processes and thus arouse an affective return from that portion of the brain. And if in addition a typical emotional attitude is assumed the cortical inhibition of the thalamic neurones with reference to that attitude is abolished so that they have complete release. Under such circumstances the enacted emotion would have reality. On the other hand a purely cortical mimicry of emotional expression without thalamic involvement would be as cold and unaffective as some actors have declared it to be. Whether the emotion results or not, the thalamic theory of the source of feeling offers a more satisfactory explanation of the effects of assumed postures than does the James-Lange theory.

The cases of release thalamus from cortical control on one side, with accompanying ipsilateral intensification of emotional tone, present an insurmountable obstacle to the James-Lange theory. Neither the thoracic nor the abdominal viscera can function by halves, the vasomotor center is a unity, and the patients certainly do not engage in right- or left-sided laughter and weeping. The impulses sent back from the disturbed peripheral organs, therefore, must be bilaterally equal. For explanation of the unsymmetrical feeling we are driven to the organ which is functioning unsymmetrically—*i.e.* the thalamus. It is there that the suggested theory places the source of the emotions.

Another serious difficulty for the James-Lange theory is the evidence that the emotion increases in intensity although the expression is checked. Indeed, there are psychologists who maintain that the emotional state lasts only so long as there is inner conflict between the impulse to act and the hesitant or prudential check on that impulse. So long as the check prevails, however, the organic changes supposed to be the source of the feeling are suppressed. How then can there be felt-emotion? Two answers to this question may be found in James' argument. First he denies the objection. "Refuse to express a passion," he wrote, "and it dies." "Count ten before venting your anger, and its occasion seems ridiculous." On the other hand, he appears to admit that a pent emotion may operate disastrously. "If tears or anger are simply suppressed, whilst the object of grief or rage remains unchanged before the mind, the current which would have invaded the normal channels turns into others, for it must find some outlet of escape. It may then work different and worse effects later on. Thus vengeful brooding may re-

place a burst of indignation; a dry heat may consume the frame of one who fain would weep, or he may, as Dante says, turn to stone within." There is no intimation that vengeful brooding, being consumed by a dry heat, and turning to stone within are not emotional experiences. Instead of recognizing them as such, however, James stressed the importance of training for repression of emotional display. These rather equivocal and indecisive comments leave untouched the common testimony that intense fear, for example, may be felt, with a pathetic sense of helplessness, before any overt act occurs, and that scarcely does the appropriate behavior start than the inner tumult begins to subside and the bodily forces are directed vigorously and effectively to serviceable ends. The difficulties of the James-Lange theory in meeting this situation are obvious. If there is a double control of behavior, however, both the inner conflict with its keen emotional accompaniment and the later partial subsidence of feeling are readily explicable. The thalamic patterned processes are inherent in the nervous organization, they are like reflexes in being instantly ready to seize control of the motor responses, and when they do so they operate with great power. They can be controlled, however, by the processes in the cerebral cortex, by processes conditioned by all sorts of previous impressions. The cortex also can control all the peripheral machinery except the viscera. The inhibited processes in the thalamus cannot set the organism in action, except the parts not under voluntary control, but the turmoil there can produce emotions in the usual manner, and possibly with greater violence because of the inhibition. And when the cortical check is released, suddenly the conflict is resolved. The two controls formerly in opposition, are now cooperative. The thalamic neurones, so long as they continue energetically active, provide the condition for the emotion to persist, as James claimed it does, *during* the manifestation. The new theory, therefore, not only avoids the difficulty of the James-Lange theory, but accounts satisfactorily for the poignancy of feeling in the period of paralyzed inaction.

In relation to the double control of the response there is another point that may be emphasized. McDougall[5] has objected to the James-Lange theory on the ground that it is admittedly concerned with the *sensory* aspect of emotion; it pays little or no attention to the always present and sometimes overwhelming *impulsive* aspect of the experience. The localization of the reaction patterns for emotional expression in the thalamus—in a region which, like the spinal cord, works directly by simple automatisms unless held in check—not only accounts for the sensory side, the "felt emotion," but also for the impulsive side, the tendency of the thalamic neurones to discharge. These powerful impulses originating in a region of the brain not associated with cognitive consciousness and arousing therefore in an *obscure* and *unrelated* manner the strong feelings of emotional excitement, explain the sense of being seized, possessed, of being controlled by an outside force and made to act without weighing of the consequences.

Finally, the view that thalamic processes add feeling-tone to sensation meets satisfactorily a difficulty which the James-Lange theory encountered in explaining the "subtler emotions." James had to assume indefinite and hypothetical bodily reverberations in order to account for mild feelings of pleasure and satisfaction. If a warm test tube, however, is capable of yielding keen delight on the damaged side in a case of thalamic injury, it is clear that almost any object or situation which can rouse thalamic processes can add affective quality to sensation. And just as a stimulus can become conditioned for a certain motor or glandular response, so likewise a stimulus can be conditioned for the patterns of neurone action in the thalamus. When that stimulus recurs the emotion recurs because the pattern is activated. In such manner we may consider that richness and variety of our emotional life are elaborated.

Notes

1. W. James and C. G. Lange, *The Emotions*, 1922.
2. R. B. Perry, *General Theory of Value*, 1926, 295.
3. James, *op. cit.*, 123.
4. Lange, *op. cit.*, 73.
5. W. McDougall, *Outline of Psychology*, 1923, 328.

Pan-Cultural Elements in Facial Displays of Emotion

Paul Ekman, E. Richard Sorenson, and Wallace V. Friesen (1969)

During the few decades, researchers have discovered that facial expressions for a number of emotions are recognized—that is, people from a wide variety of cultures will attribute certain facial expressions to the same emotions. Psychologists have also reported that muscular actions associated with specific emotions (such as frowning, which indicates sadness) cause changes in physiological arousal as well as enhance feelings of the emotion associated with the muscular movements. Paul Ekman has been at the cutting edge of research on facial expression of emotion throughout his career.

Ekman (b. 1934) earned his Ph.D. from Adelphi University in 1958. He is currently a professor emeritus of psychology at the University of California at San Francisco and Director of the Human Interaction Laboratory. He has written a number of books, including *Telling Lies* 3rd ed. (W. W. Norton, 2002) and *Emotions Revealed.* (Times Books, 2003). Wallace V. Friesen (1933) received his Ph.D. in 1972 from the University of California in San Francisco. He was at Wayne State University and University of California San Francisco until he accepted his current position at the University of Kentucky. E. Richard Sorenson earned his PhD in anthropology. After serving as scientist at the Smithsonian Institution in Washington, D.C., he spent much of his time in Asia, studying culture and wildlife. He was with the Roonguthai Research Institute, Phuket, Thailand.

This selection, from "Pan-Cultural Elements in Facial Displays of Emotion," was published in *Science* in 1969. In it, the authors provide a glimpse at the beginning of a decades-long research program in facial displays of emotion. The question of the role of culture and heredity motivated the researchers to compare participants from literate and non-literate societies. As you read this selection, notice the care taken by the researchers to keep conditions in the study constant throughout the cultures. Does culture also contribute to facial displays of emotions?

Key Concept: emotion and culture

APA Citation: Ekman, P., Sorenson, E. R. & Friesen, W. V. (1969). Pan-cultural elements in facial displays of emotion. *Science, 164,* 86–88.

In studies in New Guinea, Borneo, the United States, Brazil, and Japan we found evidence of pan-cultural elements in facial displays of affect. Observers in these cultures recognize some of the same emotions when they are shown a standard set of facial photographs. This finding contradicts (i) the theory (1) that facial displays of emotion are socially learned and therefore culturally variable; and (ii) the findings from studies within a single culture that observers of the face alone do not achieve either accuracy or high agreement in recognizing different emotional states (2).

Bruner and Taguiri (3) said: "The best evidence available [from 30 years of research] seems to indicate that there is no invariable pattern (or at least no innate invari-

able pattern of expression) accompanying specific emotions." In contrast, our findings support Darwin's (4) suggestion that facial expressions of emotion are similar among humans, regardless of culture, because of their evolutionary origin.

Our study was based in part on Tomkins' (5) theory of personality, which emphasized the importance of affect and which postulated innate subcortical programs linking certain evokers to distinguishable, universal facial displays for each of the primary affects—interest, joy, surprise, fear, anger, distress, disgust-contempt, and shame. Ekman and Friesen (6) reasoned that past impressions of cultural differences in facial displays of affect may represent a failure to distinguish what is pan-cultural (the association of facial muscular movements with each primary affect) from what is culturally variable (learned affect evokers, behavioral consequences of an affect display, and the operation of display rules).

Display rules were defined as procedures learned early in life for the management of affect displays and include deintensifying, intensifying, neutralizing, or masking an affect display. These rules prescribe what to do about the display of each affect in different social settings; they vary with the social role and demographic characteristics, and should vary across cultures.

To uncover the pan-cultural elements in facial displays of affect, the investigator must obtain samples (photographs) of facial expression that are free of cultural differences because of learned evokers, display rules, and consequences. We attempted to select such photographs and to prove that observers from different cultures recognize the same affect from the same photograph. Because similarities in the recognition of emotion among literate cultures might be attributed to learning their own or each other's facial affect cues from a shared visual source (television, movies, or magazines), it was necessary to obtain data also from visually isolated cultures, preferably preliterate cultures.

Photographs were selected from over 3000 pictures to obtain those which showed only the pure display of a single affect. The selection was guided by a study in which Ekman, Friesen, and Tomkins (7) developed a procedure for scoring facial affects that was based on a compilation of lists of cues particular to each primary affect. The scoring procedure had not been completed when the photographs were selected for this cross-cultural study, but the partial lists provided the basis for choosing pictures which contained cues distinctive for happiness, surprise, fear, anger, disgust-contempt, and sadness. This list of affects includes all of Tomkins' primary affect categories except for interest and shame; it also includes almost all of the affect states, discriminable within any one culture.

The most common reasons for rejecting photographs were that they showed the influence of display rules or blends of the cues of one affect with those of one or more other affects rather than single-affect pictures. Thirty photographs met our criteria; they showed male and female Caucasians, adults and children, professional and amateur actors, and mental patients. The stimuli were reproduced as 35-mm slides and photographs (13 by 18 cm) cropped to include only the face and neck.

The observers' task was to select a word from a list of six affects for each picture. In the United States, Brazil, and Japan, slides were projected one at a time for 20 seconds each to groups of freshmen college students from whom the foreign-born had been eliminated. The photographic prints (13 by 18 cm) were shown one at a time to each observer in New Guinea and Borneo. The affect words were translated into the locally understood languages (Japanese, Portuguese, Neo-Melanesian Pidgin, Fore, and Bidayuh). There were no Neo-Melanesian Pidgin equivalents for disgust-contempt or surprise, and in

these cases a phrase was submitted (looking at something which stinks, looking at something new).

For our isolated, non-Western preliterate samples we attempted to find those least affected by the modern technological, commercial, and ideological currents. The New Guinea sample was the Fore linguistic-cultural group *(8)* who until 12 years ago were an isolated Neolithic material culture. We studied the Fore most influenced by contacts with Westerners (government, missionaries, and others) as well as those least influenced by these recent contacts who have preferred to remain in their isolated hamlets in the mountains.

We report in detail only on the most Westernized Fore; we summarize the results on the less Westernized Fore, whose unfamiliarity with certain tasks required development of specialized judgment procedures and conducting a number of additional experiments. There were two subsamples in the most Westernized Fore; one subsample performed the judgment task by using Pidgin translations of the affect terms, and the other subsample used the affect terms of their own Fore language.

The Borneo sample was the Sadong, a Bidayuh-speaking group of Hill Dyaks in southwest Sarawak. These people still lived in their traditional long houses and maintained their traditional agrarian way of life. Only one man spoke English, most men spoke some Malay, and many had seen a few movies in a commercial center located about a day's walk from their village.

The distribution of six responses to each category (affect) of photographs was tallied, and the most frequent judgment response for each affect category was converted into a percentage of the total responses to the stimuli which represented that category (Table 1). The data from the three literate samples support our contention of a pan-cultural element in facial affect display. Agreement and accuracy were far higher in each group than had been reported for recognition of emotions within cultures, and the same affect term was the most frequent response in the United States and Brazil for all of the stimuli and for 29 out of the 30 stimuli when Japan is compared. Three literate cultures are not a sufficient sample to proclaim universality; however, Izard *(9)*, who worked independently at the same time as we, but with his own set of facial photographs obtained results for eight other literate cultures that are substantially the same as ours.

When exposure to common visual input is controlled (to answer the argument that such similarities among literate cultures only reflect learned recognitions from mass media) the agreement and accuracy were lower in the preliterate cultures than in the literate ones. We believe that this is because of the enormous obstacles imposed by language barriers and task unfamiliarity in preliterate cultures (even with the more Westernized observers). Despite such handicaps, there were similar recognitions of happiness, anger, and fear in all samples, and for disgust, surprise, and sadness in two out of three samples (Table 1). An affect category was never misidentified by the majority of observers in more than one

Table 1.   Rates of recognition of six affects among samples from the United States, Brazil, Japan, New Guinea, and Borneo.

Affect category	United States	Brazil	Japan	New Guinea* Pidgin responses	New Guinea* Fore responses	Borneo*
Happy (H)	97 H	97 H	87 H	99 H	82 H	92 H
Fear (F)	88 F	77 F	71 F	46 F	54 F	40 F
			26 Su	31 A	25 A	33 Su
Disgust-contempt (D)	82 D	86 D	82 D	29 D	44 D	26 Sa
				23 A	30 A	23 H
Anger (A)	69 A	82 A	63 A	56 A	50 A	64 A
	29 D		14 D	22 F	25 F	
Surprise (SU)	91 Su	82 Su	87 Su	38 Su	45 F	36 Su
				30 F	19 A	23 F
Sadness (SA)	73 Sa	82 Sa	74 Sa	55 Sa	56 A	52 Sa
				23 A		
Number of observers						
	99	40	29	18	14	15
Number of stimuli for which most frequent response was predicted response						
	30/30	30/30	29/30	11/24	12/24	18/23
Number of stimuli for which 70 percent of the observers agreed						
	25/30	26/30	23/30	7/24	6/24	6/23
Chi-square†						
	10,393	3818	2347	532	261	427
Chi-square excluding happy stimuli†						
	5718	2119	1241	188	92	211

*A few photographs, mostly happy pictures, were eliminated in work with preliterate observers in order to make the task shorter. † All chi-squares were significant beyond P=.01

of the preliterate samples. Our studies of other much less Westernized Fore observers yielded similar results, with the exception of the sadness category, and we also obtained additional support in studies in progress on how these affects are expressed in the Fore. The possibility that the data on the preliterate samples might have been biased by the use of Caucasoid faces as stimuli was negated by additional studies in which Melanesian (South Fore) faces were shown to the South Fore observers and results similar to those reported here were obtained. The proposition that there are pan-cultural elements in human affect displays appears to be largely supported, both in the literate cultures that we and Izard have studied, and for the most part in the preliterate cultures that we have investigated.

References and Notes

1. For example, O. Klineberg, *Social Psychology* (Holt, New York, 1940); W. La Barre, *J. Personality* **16,** 49 (1947).

2. Although the semantic dimensions which may underlie the judgment of emotions are similar across cultures, it has not been demonstrated that the face displays the same emotion in the same way across cultures. H. Schlosberg, *Psychol. Rev.* 61, 81 (1954); C. E. Osgood, *Scand. J. Psychol.* **7,** 1 (1966); H. C. Triandis and W. W. Lamber, *J. Abnorm. Soc. Psychol.* 56, 321 (1958).

3. J. S. Bruner and R. Taguiri, "The perception of people," in *Handbook of Social Psychology*, G. Lindzey, Ed. (Addison-Wesley, Cambridge, Mass., 1954), vol. 2, pp. 634–654.

4. C. Darwin, *The Expression of the Emotions in Man and Animals* (Murray, London, 1872).

5. S. S. Tomkins, "The positive affects," *Affect, Imagery, Consciousness* (Springer, New York, 1962), vol. 1; "The negative affects," *Affect, Imagery, Consciousness* (Springer, New York, 1963), vol. 2; —— and R. McCarter, *Percept. Motor Skills* **18** (Monogr. Suppl. No. 1-V18), 119 (1964).

6. P. Ekman and W. V. Friesen, "Origins, usage and coding of nonverbal behavior, in *Communication Theory and Linguistic Models in the Social Sciences*, E. Vernon, Ed. (Di Telia, Buenos Aires, 1968); "The repertoire of nonverbal behavior," *Semiotica*, in press.

7. P. Ekman, W. V. Friesen, S. S. Tomkins, "*A* facial affect scoring technique; and initial validity study," in preparation.

8. D. C. Gajdusek, *Trans. Roy. Soc. Trop. Med. Hyg.* **57** (No. 3), 151 (1963); B. R. Sorenson and D. C. Gajdusek, *Pediatrics* **37** (No. 1), 149 (1966).

9. C. E. Izard, "The emotions and emotion constructs in personality and culture research," in *Handbook of Modern Personality Theory*, R. D. Cattell, Ed. (Aldine, Chicago, in press).

The Ingredients of Love

Robert J. Sternberg (1988)

Love is one of the most important human emotions. Although it has been the subject of countless poems and works of art, it has only recently become the focus of research by psychologists. Researchers recognize that there are different kinds of love, making it difficult to generalize the results of love studies. In an attempt to make such a generalization, Yale University psychologist Robert J. Sternberg has proposed a triangular theory of love in which love consists of intimacy, passion, and decision/commitment.

Sternberg (b. 1949) earned his Ph.D. from Stanford University in 1975. He has been very influential in psychology in the cognitive area of intelligence and in the emotional area of love. The American Psychological Association awarded him the Distinguished Scientific Award for Early Career Contribution to Psychology in 1981. Sternberg has written much about his research on love, including his book The Triangle of Love: Intimacy, Passion, and Commitment (Basic Books, 1988).

This selection is from chapter 2, "The ingredients of love," of Sternberg's *The Triangle of Love*. In it, Sternberg describes, in an informal, practical style, how the three ingredients intimacy, passion, and commitment combine to form eight possible kinds of love. He provides many examples, some of which should seem familiar to you. Sternberg's objective is to help you more fully understand the characteristics of love. As you read this selection, evaluate Sternberg's theory of love. Are there any other ingredients that he may have left out of his theory?

Key Concept: love

APA Citation: Sternberg, R. J. (1988). *The triangle of love.* New York: Basic Books.

A substantial body of evidence suggests that the components of intimacy, passion, and commitment play a key role in love over and above other attributes. Even before I collected the first bit of data to test my theory, I had several reasons for choosing these three components as the building blocks for it.

First, many of the other aspects of love prove, on close examination, to be either parts or manifestations of these three components. Communication, for example, is a building block of intimacy, as is caring or compassion. Were one to subdivide intimacy and passion and commitment into their own subparts, the theory would eventually contain so many elements as to become unwieldy. There is no one, solely correct fineness of division. But a division into three components works well in several ways. . . .

Second, my review of the literature on couples in the United States, as well as in other lands, suggested that, whereas some elements of love are fairly time-bound or culture-specific, the three I propose are general across time and place. The three components are not equally weighted in all cultures, but each component receives at least some weight in virtually any time or place. Third,

the three components do appear to be distinct, although, of course, they are related. You can have any one without either or both of the others. In contrast, other potential building blocks for a theory of love—for example, nurturance and caring—tend to be difficult to separate, logically as well as psychologically.

Fourth, . . . many other accounts of love seem to boil down to something similar to my own account, or a subset of it. If we take away differences in language and tone, the spirit of many other theories converges with mine.

Finally, and perhaps most important, the theory works. . . .

INTIMACY

In the context of the triangular theory, intimacy refers to those feelings in a relationship that promote closeness, bondedness, and connectedness. My research with Susan Grajek . . . indicates that intimacy includes at least ten elements:

1. *Desiring to promote the welfare of the loved one.* The lover looks out for the partner and seeks to pro-

mote his or her welfare. One may promote the other's welfare at the expense of one's own—but in the expectation that the other will reciprocate when the time comes.

2. *Experiencing happiness with the loved one.* The lover enjoys being with his or her partner. When they do things together, they have a good time and build a store of memories upon which they can draw in hard times. Furthermore, good times shared will spill over into the relationship and make it better.

3. *Holding the loved one in high regard.* The lover thinks highly of and respects his or her partner. Although the lover may recognize flaws in the partner, this recognition does not detract from the overall esteem in which the partner is held.

4. *Being able to count on the loved one in times of need.* The lover feels that the partner is there when needed. When the chips are down, the lover can call on the partner and expect that he or she will come through.

5. *Having mutual understanding with the loved one.* The lovers understand each other. They know each other's strengths and weaknesses and how to respond to each other in a way that shows genuine empathy for the loved one's emotional states. Each knows where the other is "coming from."

6. *Sharing oneself and one's possessions with the loved one.* One is willing to give of oneself and one's time, as well as one's things, to the loved one. Although all things need not be joint property, the lovers share their property as the need arises. And, most important, they share themselves.

7. *Receiving emotional support from the loved one.* The lover feels bolstered and even renewed by the loved one, especially in times of need.

8. *Giving emotional support to the loved one.* The lover supports the loved one by empathizing with, and emotionally supporting, him or her in times of need.

9. *Communicating intimately with the loved one.* The lover can communicate deeply and honestly with the loved one, sharing innermost feelings.

10. *Valuing the loved one.* The lover feels the great importance of the partner in the scheme of life.

These are only some of the possible feelings one can experience through the intimacy of love; moreover, it is not necessary to experience all of these feelings in order to experience intimacy. To the contrary, our research indicates that you experience intimacy when you sample a sufficient number of these feelings, with that number probably differing from one person and one situation to another. You do not usually experience the feelings independently, but often as one overall feeling. . . .

Intimacy probably starts in self-disclosure. To be intimate with someone, you need to break down the walls that separate one person from another. It is well known

that self-disclosure begets self-disclosure: if you want to get to know what someone else is like, let him or her learn about you. But self-disclosure is often easier in same-sex friendships than in loving relationships, probably because people see themselves as having more to lose by self-disclosure in a loving relationship. And odd as it may sound, there is actually evidence that spouses may be less symmetrical in self-disclosure than are strangers, again probably because the costs of self-disclosure can be so high in love. . . .

Intimacy, then, is a foundation of love, but a foundation that develops slowly, through fits and starts, and is difficult to achieve. Moreover, once it starts to be attained, it may, paradoxically, start to go away because of the threat it poses. It poses a threat in terms not only of the dangers of self-disclosure but of the danger one starts to feel to one's existence as a separate, autonomous being. Few people want to be "consumed" by a relationship, yet many people start to feel as if they are being consumed when they get too close to another human being. The result is a balancing act between intimacy and autonomy which goes on throughout the lives of most couples, a balancing act in which a completely stable equilibrium is often never achieved. But this in itself is not necessarily bad: the swinging back and forth of the intimacy pendulum provides some of the excitement that keeps many relationships alive.

PASSION

The passion component of love includes what Elaine Hatfield and William Walster refer to as a "state of intense longing *for union* with the other." Passion is largely the expression of desires and needs—such as for self-esteem, nurturance, affiliation, dominance, submission, and sexual fulfillment. The strengths of these various needs vary across persons, situations, and kinds of loving relationship. For example, sexual fulfillment is likely to be a strong need in romantic relationships but not in filial ones. These needs manifest themselves through psychological and physiological arousal, which are often inseparable from each other.

Passion in love tends to interact strongly with intimacy, and often they fuel each other. For example, intimacy in a relationship may be largely a function of the extent to which the relationship meets a person's need for passion. Conversely, passion may be aroused by intimacy. In some close relationships with members of the opposite sex, for example, the passion component develops almost immediately; and intimacy, only after a while. Passion may have drawn the individuals into the relationship in the first place, but intimacy helps sustain the closeness in the relationship. In other close relationships, however, passion, especially as it applies to physical attraction, develops only after intimacy. Two close friends of the opposite sex may find themselves eventually developing a physical attraction for each other once they have achieved a certain emotional intimacy. . . .

Most people, when they think of passion, view it as sexual. But any form of psychophysiological arousal can generate the experience of passion. For example, an individual with a high need for affiliation may experience passion toward an individual who provides him or her with a unique opportunity to affiliate. For example, Debbie grew up in a broken home, with no extended family to speak of, and two parents who were constantly at war with each other and eventually divorced when she was an adolescent. Debbie felt as though she never had a family, and when she met Arthur, her passion was kindled. What he had to offer was not great sex but a large, warm, closely knit family that welcomed Debbie with open arms. Arthur was Debbie's ticket to the sense of belongingness she had never experienced but had always craved, and his ability to bring belongingness into her life aroused her passion for him. . . .

For other people, the need for submission can be the ticket to passion. . . . Social workers are often frustrated when, after months spent getting a battered woman to leave her husband, the woman ultimately goes back to the batterer. To some observers, her return may seem incomprehensible; to others, it may seem like a financial decision. But often it is neither. Such a woman has had the misfortune to identify abuse with being loved and, in going back to the abuse, is returning to what is, for her, love as she has learned it.

These patterns of response have been established through years of observation and sometimes first-hand experience, which cannot be easily undone by a social worker or anyone else in a few months. Probably the strangest learning mechanism for the buildup of passionate response is the mechanism of *intermittent reinforcement,* the periodic, sometimes random rewarding of a particular response to a stimulus. If you try to accomplish something, and sometimes are rewarded for your efforts and sometimes not, you are being intermittently reinforced. Oddly enough, intermittent reinforcement is even more powerful at developing or sustaining a given pattern of behavior than is continuous reinforcement. You are more likely to lose interest in or desire for something, and to become bored, if you are always rewarded when you seek it than if you are sometimes rewarded, but sometimes not. Put another way, sometimes the fun is in wanting something rather than in getting it. And if you are never rewarded for a given pattern of behavior, you are likely to give up on it ("extinguish," as learning theorists would say), if only because of the total frustration you experience when you act in that particular way.

Passion thrives on the intermittent reinforcement that is intense at least in the early stages of a relationship. When you want someone, sometimes you feel as if you are getting closer to him or her, and sometimes you feel you are not—an alternation that keeps the passion aroused. . . .

DECISION AND COMMITMENT

The decision/commitment component of love consists of two aspects—one short-term and one long-term. The short-term aspect is the decision to love a certain other, whereas the long-term one is the commitment to maintain that love. These two aspects of the decision/commitment component of love do not necessarily occur together. The decision to love does not necessarily imply a commitment to that love. Oddly enough, the reverse is also possible, where there is a commitment to a relationship in which you did not make the decision, as in arranged marriages. Some people are committed to loving another without ever having admitted their love. Most often, however, a decision precedes the commitment both temporally and logically. Indeed, the institution of marriage represents a legalization of the commitment to a decision to love another throughout life.

While the decision/commitment component of love may lack the "heat" or "charge" of intimacy and passion, loving relationships almost inevitably have their ups and downs, and in the latter, the decision/commitment component is what keeps a relationship together. This component can be essential for getting through hard times and for returning to better ones. In ignoring it or separating it from love, you may be missing exactly that component of a loving relationship that enables you to get through the hard times as well as the easy ones. Sometimes, you may have to trust your commitment to carry you through to the better times you hope are ahead.

The decision/commitment component of love interacts with both intimacy and passion. For most people, it results from the combination of intimate involvement and passionate arousal; however, intimate involvement or passionate arousal can follow from commitment, as in certain arranged marriages or in close relationships in which you do not have a choice of partners. For example, you do not get to choose your mother, father, siblings, aunts, uncles, or cousins. In these close relationships, you may find that whatever intimacy or passion you experience results from your cognitive commitment to the relationship, rather than the other way around. Thus, love can start off as a decision.

The expert in the study of commitment is the UCLA psychologist Harold Kelley. . . . For Kelley, commitment is the extent to which a person is likely to stick with something or someone and see it (or him or her) through to the finish. A person who is committed to something is expected to persist until the goal underlying the commitment is achieved. A problem for contemporary relationships is that [the] two members of a couple may have different ideas about what it means to stick with someone to the end or to the realization of a goal. These differences, moreover, may never be articulated. One person, for example, may see the "end" as that point where the relationship is no longer working, whereas the other may see the end as the ending of one of the couple's lives. In a time of changing values and notions of commitment, it is becoming increasingly common for couples to find themselves in disagreement about the exact nature and duration of their commitment to each other. When marital commitments were always and automatically assumed to be for life, divorce was clearly frowned upon. Today, divorce is clearly more acceptable than it was even fifteen years ago, in part because many people have different ideas about how durable and lasting the marital commitment need be.

Difficulties in mismatches between notions of commitment cannot always be worked out by discussing mutual definitions of it, because these may change over time and differently for the two members of a couple. Both may intend a life-long commitment at the time of marriage, for example; but one of them may have a change of mind—or heart—over time. . . .

KINDS OF LOVING

How do people love, and what are some examples of ways in which they love? A summary of the various kinds of love captured by the triangular theory is shown in table 1.

Intimacy Alone: Liking

. . . Liking results when you experience only the intimacy component of love without passion or decision/commitment. The term *liking* is used here in a nontrivial sense, to describe not merely the feelings you have toward casual acquaintances and passers-by, but rather the set of feelings you experience in relationships that can truly be characterized as friendships. You feel closeness, bondedness, and warmth toward the other, without feelings of intense passion or long-term commitment. Stated another way, you feel emotionally close to the friend, but the friend does not arouse your passion or make you feel that you want to spend the rest of your life with him or her.

It is possible for friendships to have elements of passionate arousal or long-term commitment, but such friendships go beyond mere liking. You can use the absence test to distinguish mere liking from love that goes beyond liking. If a typical friend whom you like goes away, even for an extended period of time, you may miss him or her but do not tend to dwell on the loss. You can pick up the friendship some years later, often in a different form, without even having thought much about the friendship during the intervening years. When a close relationship goes beyond liking, however, you actively miss the other person and tend to dwell on or be preoccupied with his or her absence. The absence has a substantial and fairly long-term effect on your life. When the absence of the other arouses strong feelings of intimacy, passion, or commitment, the relationship has gone beyond liking.

TABLE 1

Taxonomy of Kinds of Love

Kind of Love	Intimacy	Passion	Decision/Commitment
Non-love	-	-	-
Liking	+	-	-
Infatuated love	-	+	-
Empty love	-	-	+
Romantic love	+	+	-
Companionate love	+	-	+
Fatuous love	-	+	+
Consummate love	+	+	+

Note: + = component present; - = component absent.

Passion Alone: Infatuated Love

Tom met Lisa at work. One look at her was enough to change his life: he fell madly in love with her. Instead of concentrating on his work, which he hated, he would think about Lisa. She was aware of this, but did not much care for Tom. When he tried to start a conversation with her, she moved on as quickly as possible. . . .

Tom's "love at first sight" is infatuated love or, simply, infatuation. It results from the experiencing of passionate arousal without the intimacy and decision/commitment components of love. Infatuation is usually obvious, although it tends to be somewhat easier for others to spot than for the person who is experiencing it. An infatuation can arise almost instantaneously and dissipate as quickly. Infatuations generally manifest a high degree of psychophysiological arousal and bodily symptoms such as increased heartbeat or even palpitations of the heart, increased hormonal secretions, and erection of genitals. . . .

Decision/Commitment Alone: Empty Love

John and Mary had been married for twenty years, for fifteen of which Mary had been thinking about getting a divorce, but could never get herself to go through with it. . . .

Mary's kind of love emanates from the decision that you love another and are committed to that love even without having the intimacy or the passion associated with some loves. It is the love sometimes found in stagnant relationships that have been going on for years but that have lost both their original mutual emotional involvement and physical attraction. Unless the commitment to the love is very strong, such love can be close to none at all. Although in our society we see empty love generally as the final or near-final stage of a long-term relationship, in other societies empty love may be the first stage of a long-term relationship. As I have said, in societies where marriages are arranged, the marital partners start with the commitment to love each other, or to try to do so, and not much more. Here, *empty* denotes a relationship that may come to be filled with passion and intimacy, and thus marks a beginning rather than an end.

Intimacy + Passion: Romantic Love

Susan and Ralph met in their junior year of college. Their relationship started off as a good friendship, but rapidly turned into a deeply involved romantic love affair. They spent as much time together as possible, and enjoyed practically every minute of it. But Susan and Ralph were not ready to commit themselves permanently to the relationship: both felt they were too young to make any long-term decisions, and that until they at least knew where they would go after college, it was impossible to tell even how much they could be together....

Ralph and Susan's relationship combines the intimacy and passion components of love. In essence, it is liking with an added element: namely, the arousal brought about by physical attraction. Therefore, in this type of love, the man and woman are not only drawn physically to each other but are also bonded emotionally. This is the view of romantic love found in classic works of literature, such as *Romeo and Juliet*. . . .

Intimacy + Commitment: Companionate Love

In their twenty years of marrige, Sam and Sara had been through some rough times. They had seen many of their friends through divorces, Sam through several jobs, and Sara through an illness that at one point had seemed as though it might be fatal. Both had friends, but there was no doubt in either of their minds that they were each other's best friend. When the going got rough, each of them knew he or she could count on the other. Neither Sam nor Sara felt any great passion in their relationship, but they had never sought out others. . . .

Sam and Sara's kind of love evolves from a combination of the intimacy and decision/commitment components of love. It is essentially a long-term, committed friendship, the kind that frequently occurs in marriages in which physical attraction (a major source of passion) has waned. . . .

Passion + Commitment: Fatuous Love

When Tim and Diana met at a resort in the Bahamas, they were each on the rebound. Tim's fiancé had abruptly broken off their engagement. . . . Diana was recently divorced, the victim of the "other woman." Each felt desperate for love, and when they met each other, they immediately saw themselves as a match made in heaven. . . . The manager of the resort, always on the lookout for vacation romances as good publicity, offered to marry them at the resort and to throw a lavish reception at no charge, other than cooperation in promotional materials. After thinking it over, Tim and Diana agreed. . . .

Fatuous love, as in the case of Tim and Diana, results from the combination of passion and decision/commitment without intimacy, which takes time to develop. It is the kind of love we sometimes associate with Hollywood, or with a whirlwind courtship, in which a couple meet one day, get engaged two weeks later, and marry the next month. This love is fatuous in the sense that the couple commit themselves to one another on the basis of passion without the stabilizing element of intimate involvement. Since passion can develop almost instantaneously, and intimacy cannot, relationships based on fatuous love are not likely to last.

Intimacy + Passion + Commitment: Consummate Love

Harry and Edith seemed to all their friends to be the perfect couple. And what made them distinctive from many such "perfect couples" is that they pretty much fulfilled the notion. They felt close to each other, they continued to have great sex after fifteen years, and they could not imagine themselves happy over the long term with anyone else. . . .

Consummate, or complete, love like Edith and Harry's results from the combination of the three components in equal measure. It is a love toward which many of us strive, especially in romantic relationships. Attaining consummate love is analogous, in at least one respect, to meeting your goal in a weight-reduction program: reaching your ideal weight is often easier than maintaining it. Attaining consummate love is no guarantee that it will last; indeed, one may become aware of the loss only after it is far gone. Consummate love, like other things of value, must be guarded carefully. . . .

The Absence of the Components: Non-Love

Jack saw his colleague Myra at work almost every day. They interacted well in their professional relationship, but neither was particularly fond of the other. Neither felt particularly comfortable talking to the other about personal matters; and after a few tries, they decided to limit their conversations to business. Non-love, as in the relationship of Jack and Myra, refers simply to the absence of all three components of love.

Non-love characterizes many personal relationships, which are simply casual interactions that do not partake of love or even liking.

Human Development

SELECTION 30

The Stages of the Intellectual Development of the Child

Jean Piaget (1962)

Psychologists have traditionally had difficulty studying cognitive development in children because young children cannot effectively communicate their thoughts to others. Swiss psychologist Jean Piaget, however, became interested in cognitive development in infants and children, and he spent nearly 60 years investigating the differences between the thought processes of children and those of adults.

Piaget (1896–1980) earned his Ph.D. in zoology from the University of Neuchâtel, Switzerland, in 1918. His educational training helped him in his studies on children's cognitive development because he learned how to make careful observations of noncommunicative organisms solving problems. He theorized that when children are unsuccessful at solving particular problems, they develop more complex mental structures to help them in the future. Piaget was the founder and director of the International Center of Genetic Epistemology in Geneva and a professor of psychology at the University of Geneva.

The selection that follows is from "The Stages of the Intellectual Development of the Child," which was published in *Bulletin of the Menninger Clinic* in 1962. Here Piaget describes the four periods of cognitive development through which people progress. These periods trace the development of intelligence from simple reflexes to complex reasoning. As you read this selection, note the ages at which Piaget suggests each stage begins. Consider the implications for understanding how infants and children think. Why is it important to realize that children think differently from how adults do?

Key Concept: cognitive development

APA Citation: Piaget, J. (1962). The stages of the intellectual development of the child. *Bulletin of the Menninger Clinic, 26,* 120–128.

A consideration of the stages of the development of intelligence should be preceded by asking the question, What is intelligence? Unfortunately, we find ourselves confronted by a great number of definitions. For [Swiss psychologist Edouard] Claparède, intelligence is an adaptation to new situations. When a situation is new, when there are no reflexes, when there are no habits to rely on, then the subject is obliged to search for something new. That is to say, Claparède defines intelligence as groping, as feeling one's way, trial-and-error behavior. We find this trial-and-error behavior in all levels of intelligence, even at the superior level, in the form of hypothesis testing. As far as I am concerned, this definition is too vague, because trial and error occurs in the formation of habits, and also in the earliest established reflexes: when a newborn baby learns to suck.

Karl Bühler defines intelligence as an act of immediate comprehension; that is to say, an insight. Bühler's definition is also very precise, but it seems to me too narrow. I know that when a mathematician solves a problem, he ends by having an insight, but up to that moment he feels, or gropes for, his way; and to say that the trial-and-error behavior is not intelligent and that intelligence starts only when he finds the solution to the problem, seems a very narrow definition. I would, therefore, propose to define intelligence not by a static criterion, as in previous definitions, but by the direction that intelligence follows in its evolution, and then I would define intelligence as a form of equilibration, or forms of equilibration, toward which all cognitive functions lead.

But I must first define equilibration. Equilibration in my vocabulary is not an exact and automatic balance, as it would be in Gestalt theory; I define equilibration principally as a compensation for an external disturbance.

When there is an external disturbance, the subject succeeds in compensating for this by an activity. The maximum equilibration is thus the maximum of the activity, and not a state of rest. It is a mobile equilibrium, and not an immobile one. So equilibration is defined as compensation; compensation is the annulling of a transformation by an inverse transformation. The compensation which intervenes in equilibration implies the fundamental idea of reversibility, and this reversibility is precisely what characterizes the operations of the intelligence. An operation is an internalized action, but it is also a reversible action. But an operation is never isolated; it is always subordinated to other operations; it is part of a more inclusive structure. Consequently, we define intelligence in terms of operations, coordination of operations.

Take, for example, an operation like addition: Addition is a material action, the action of reuniting. On the other hand, it is a reversible action, because addition may be compensated by subtraction. Yet addition leads to a structure of a whole. In the case of numbers, it will be the structure that the mathematicians call a "group." In the case of addition of classes which intervene in the logical structure it will be a more simple structure that we will call a grouping, and so on.

Consequently, the study of the stages of intelligence is first a study of the formation of operational structures. I shall define every stage by a structure of a whole, with the possibility of its integration into succeeding stages, just as it was prepared by preceding stages. Thus, I shall distinguish four great stages, or four great periods, in the development of intelligence: first, the sensori-motor period before the appearance of language; second, the period from about two to seven years of age, the preoperational period which precedes real operations; third, the period from seven to 12 years of age, a period of concrete operations (which refers to concrete objects); and finally after 12 years of age, the period of formal operations, or positional operations.

SENSORI-MOTOR STAGE

Before language develops, there is behavior that we can call intelligent. For example, when a baby of 12 months or more wants an object which is too far from him, but which rests on a carpet or blanket, and he pulls it to get to the object, this behavior is an act of intelligence. The child uses an intermediary, a means to get to his goal. Also, getting to an object by means of pulling a string when the object is tied to the string, or when the child uses a stick to get the object, are acts of intelligence. They demonstrate in the sensori-motor period a certain number of stages, which go from simple reflexes, from the formation of the first habits, up to the coordination of means and goals.

Remarkable in this sensori-motor stage of intelligence is that there are already structures. Sensori-motor intelli-

gence rests mainly on actions, on movements and perceptions without language, but these actions are coordinated in a relatively stable way. They are coordinated under what we may call schemata of action. These schemata can be generalized in actions and are applicable to new situations. For example, pulling a carpet to bring an object within reach constitutes a schema which can be generalized to other situations when another object rests on a support. In other words, a schema supposes an incorporation of new situations into the previous schemata, a sort of continuous assimilation of new objects or new situations to the actions already schematized. For example, I presented to one of my children an object completely new to him—a box of cigarettes, which is not a usual toy for a baby. The child took the object, looked at it, put it in his mouth, shook it, then took it with one hand and hit it with the other hand, then rubbed it on the edge of the crib, then shook it again, and gave the impression of trying to see if there were noise. This behavior is a way of exploring the object, of trying to understand it by assimilating it to schemata already known. The child behaves in this situation as he will later in Binet's famous vocabulary test, when he defines by usage, saying, for instance, that a spoon is for eating, and so on.

But in the presence of a new object, even without knowing how to talk, the child knows how to assimilate, to incorporate this new object into each of his already developed schemata which function as practical concepts. Here is a structuring of intelligence. Most important in this structuring is the base, the point of departure of all subsequent operational constructions. At the sensori-motor level, the child constructs the schema of the permanent object.

The knowledge of the permanent object starts at this point. The child is not convinced at the beginning that when an object disappears from view, he can find it again. One can verify by tests that object permanence is not yet developed at this stage. But there is there the beginning of a subsequent fundamental idea which starts being constructed at the sensori-motor level. This is also true of the construction of the ideas of space, of time, of causality. What is being done at the sensori-motor level concerning all the foregoing ideas will constitute the substructure of the subsequent, fully achieved ideas of permanent objects, of space, of time, of causality. . . .

PRE-OPERATIONAL STAGE

From one and one-half to two years of age, a fundamental transformation in the evolution of intelligence takes place in the appearance of symbolic functions. Every action of intelligence consists in manipulating significations (or meanings) and whenever (or wherever) there is significations, there are on the one hand the "significants" and on the other the "significates." This is true in the sensori-motor level, but the only significants that intervene there are perceptual signs or signals (as in conditioning) which are undifferentiated in regard to the significate; for example, a perceptual cue, like distance, which will be a cue for the size of the distant object, or the apparent size of an object, which will be the cue for the distance of the object. There, perhaps, both indices are different aspects of the same reality, but they are not yet differentiated significants. At the age of one and one-half to two years a new class of significants arises, and these significants are differentiated in regard to their significates. These differentiations can be called symbolic function. The appearance of symbols in a children's game is an example of the appearance of new significants. At the sensori-motor level the games are nothing but exercises; now they become symbolic play, a play of fiction; these games consist in representing something by means of something else. Another example is the beginning of delayed imitation, an imitation that takes place not in the presence of the original object but in its absence, and which consequently constitutes a kind of symbolization or mental image.

At the same time that symbols appear, the child acquires language; that is to say, there is the acquisition of another phase of differentiated significants, verbal signals, or collective signals. This symbolic function then brings great flexibility into the field of intelligence. Intelligence up to this point refers to the immediate space which surrounds the child and to the present perceptual situation; thanks to language, and to the symbolic functions, it becomes possible to invoke objects which are not present perceptually, to reconstruct the past, or to make projects, plans for the future, to think of objects not present but very distant in space—in short, to span spatio-temporal distances much greater than before.

But this new stage, the stage of representation of thought which is superimposed on the sensori-motor stage, is not a simple extension of what was referred to at the previous level. Before being able to prolong, one must in fact reconstruct, because behavior in words is a different thing from representing something in thought. When a child knows how to move around in his house or garden by following the different successive cues around him, it does not mean that he is capable of representing or reproducing the total configuration of his house or his garden. To be able to represent, to reproduce something, one must be capable of reconstructing this group of displacements, but at a new level, that of the representation of the thought.

I recently made an amusing test with Nel Szeminska. We took children of four to five years of age who went to school by themselves and came back home by themselves, and asked them if they could trace the way to school and back for us, not in design, which would be too difficult, but like a construction game, with concrete objects. We found that they were not capable of representation; there was a kind of motor-memory, but it was not yet a representation of a whole—the group of displacements had not yet been reconstructed on the plan of the representation of thought. In other words, the operations were not yet formed. There are representations which are

internalized actions, but actions still centered on the body itself, on the activity itself. These representations do not allow the objective combinations, the decentrated combinations that the operations would. The actions are centered on the body. I used to call this egocentrism; but it is better thought of as lack of reversibility of action.

At this level, the most certain sign of the absence of operations which appear at the next stage is the absence of the knowledge of conservation. In fact, an operation refers to the transformation of reality. The transformation is not of the whole, however; something constant is always untransformed. If you pour a liquid from one glass to another there is transformation; the liquid changes form, but its liquid property stays constant. So at the pre-operational level, it is significant from the point of view of the operations of intelligence that the child has not yet a knowledge of conservation. For example, in the case of liquid, when the child pours it from one bottle to the other, he thinks that the quantity of the liquid has changed. When the level of the liquid changes, the child thinks the quantity has changed—there is more or less in the second glass than in the first. And if you ask the child where the larger quantity came from, he does not answer this question. What is important for the child is that perceptually it is not the same thing any more. We find this absence of conservation in all object properties, in the length, surface, quantity, and weight of things. . . .

STAGE OF CONCRETE OPERATIONS

The first operations of the manipulation of objects, the concrete operations, deal with logical classes and with logical relations, or the number. But these operations do not deal yet with propositions, or hypotheses, which do not appear until the last stage.

Let me exemplify these concrete operations: the simplest operation is concerned with classifying objects according to their similarity and their difference. This is accomplished by including the subclasses within larger and more general classes, a process that implies inclusion. This classification, which seems very simple at first, is not acquired until around seven to eight years of age. Before that, at the pre-operational level, we do not find logical inclusion. For example, if you show a child at the pre-operational level a bouquet of flowers of which one half is daisies and the other half other flowers and you ask him if in this bouquet there are more flowers or more daisies, you are confronted with this answer, which seems extraordinary until it is analyzed: The child cannot tell you whether there are more flowers than daisies; either he reasons on the basis of the whole or of the part. He cannot understand that the part is complementary to the rest, and he says there are more daisies than flowers, or as many daisies as flowers, without understanding this inclusion of the subclass, the daisies, in the class of flowers.

It is only around seven to eight years of age that a child is capable of solving a problem of inclusion.

Another system of operation that appears around seven to eight years of age is the operation of serializing; that is, to arrange objects according to their size, or their progressive weight. It is also a structure of the whole, like the classification which rests on concrete operations, since it consists of manipulating concrete objects. At this level there is also the construction of numbers, which is, too, a synthesis of classification and seriation. In numbers, as in classes, we have inclusion, and also a serial order, as in serializing. These elementary operations constitute structures of wholes. There is no class without classification; there is no symmetric relation without serialization; there is not a number independent of the series of numbers. But the structures of these wholes are simple structures, groupings in the case of classes and relations, which are already groups in the case of numbers, but very elementary structures compared to subsequent structures.

STAGE OF FORMAL OPERATIONS

The last stage of development of intelligence is the stage of formal operations or propositional operations. At about eleven to twelve years of age we see great progress; the child becomes capable of reasoning not only on the basis of objects, but also on the basis of hypotheses, or of propositions.

An example which neatly shows the difference between reasoning on the basis of propositions and reasoning on the basis of concrete objects comes from Burt's tests. Burt asked children of different ages to compare the colors of the hair of three girls: Edith is fairer than Susan, Edith is darker than Lilly; who is the darkest of the three? In this question there is seriation, not of concrete objects, but of verbal statements which supposes a more complicated mental manipulation. This problem is rarely solved before the age of 12.

Here a new class of operations appears which is superimposed on the operations of logical class and number, and these operations are the propositional operations. Here, compared to the previous stage, are fundamental changes. It is not simply that these operations refer to language, and then to operations with concrete objects, but that these operations have much richer structures.

The first novelty is a combinative structure; like mathematical structures, it is a structure of a system which is superimposed on the structure of simple classifications or seriations which are not themselves systems, because they do not involve a combinative system. A combinative system permits the grouping in flexible combinations of each element of the system with any other element of that system. The logic of propositions supposes such a combinative system. If children of different ages are shown a number of colored disks and asked to combine each color with each other two by two, or three by three, we find these combinative operations are not accessible to the child at the stage of concrete operations. The child is capable of some combination, but not of all the possible combinations. After the age of 12, the child can find a method to make all the possible combinations. At the same time he acquires both the logic of mathematics and the logic of propositions, which also supposes a method of combining.

A second novelty in the operations of propositions is the appearance of a structure which constitutes a group of four transformations. Hitherto there were two reversibilities: reversibility by inversion, which consists of annulling, or canceling; and reversibility which we call reciprocity, leading not to cancellation, but to another combination. Reciprocity is what we find in the field of a relation. If A equals B, by reciprocity B equals A. If A is smaller than B, by reciprocity B is larger than A. At the level of propositional operations a new system envelops these two forms of reversibility. Here the structure combines inversion and reversibility in one single but larger and more complicated structure. It allows the acquisition of a series of fundamental operational schemata for the development of intelligence, which schemata are not possible before the constitution of this structure.

It is around the age of 12 that the child, for example, starts to understand in mathematics the knowledge of proportions, and becomes capable of reasoning by using two systems of reference at the same time. For example, if you advance the position of a board and a car moving in opposite directions, in order to understand the movement of the board in relation to the movement of the car and to other movement, you need a system of four transformations. The same is true in regard to proportions, to problems in mathematics or physics, or to other logical problems.

The four principal stages of the development of intelligence of the child progress from one stage to the other by the construction of new operational structures, and these structures constitute the fundamental instrument of the intelligence of the adult.

SELECTION **31**

Infant–Mother Attachment

Mary D. S. Ainsworth (1979)

How babies form attachments to their parents is of interest to a variety of people, from parents to educators to psychologists. Especially intriguing is the notion that there are different patterns of attachment behavior shown by infants. A major contribution to our knowledge in this area has been provided by psychologist Mary D. S. Ainsworth.

Ainsworth (1913–1999) was born in Glendale, Ohio, and spent most of her childhood in Toronto. She earned her Ph.D. in personality psychology in 1939 from the University of Toronto. She taught at Johns Hopkins University from 1956 to 1975, when she became a professor of psychology at the University of Virginia. Among her many publications in the area of development and attachment is her 1967 book *Infancy in Uganda: Infant Care and the Growth of Love* (Johns Hopkins University Press).

This selection is from "Infant–Mother Attachment" was published in *American Psychologist* in 1979. In it, Ainsworth describes her classic research on the development of attachment. Her "strange situation" is used to test the behavior patterns of infants, and it has shown at least three distinguishable attachment patterns. Ainsworth argues that the infant's crying is a key to determining how the infant–mother interaction will develop. As you read this selection, speculate about the long-term development of attachment patterns. How will the secure, anxious, and avoidant babies relate to other people when they become adults?

Key Concept: infant attachment

APA Citation: Ainsworth, M. D. S. (1979). Infant–mother attachment. *American Psychologist, 34,* 932–937.

Bowlby's (1969) ethological–evolutionary attachment theory implies that it is an essential part of the ground plan of the human species—as well as that of many other species—for an infant to become attached to a mother figure. This figure need not be the natural mother but can be anyone who plays the role of principal caregiver. This ground plan is fulfilled, except under extraordinary circumstances when the baby experiences too little interaction with any one caregiver to support the formation of an attachment. The literature on maternal deprivation describes some of these circumstances, but it cannot be reviewed here, except to note that research has not yet specified an acceptable minimum amount of interaction required for attachment formation.

However, there have been substantial recent advances in the areas of individual differences in the way attachment behavior becomes organized, differential experiences associated with the various attachment patterns, and the value of such patterns in forecasting subsequent development. These advances have been much aided by a standardized laboratory situation that was devised to supplement a naturalistic, longitudinal investigation of the development of infant–mother attachment in the first year of life. This *strange situation*, as we entitled it, has proved to be an excellent basis for the assessment of such attachment in 1-year-olds (Ainsworth, Blehar, Waters, & Wall, 1978).

The assessment procedure consists of classification according to the pattern of behavior shown in the strange situation, particularly in the episodes of reunion after separation. Eight patterns were identified, but I shall deal here only with the three main groups in which they fell—Groups A, B, and C. To summarize, Group B babies use their mothers as a secure base from which to explore in the preseparation episodes; their attachment behavior is greatly intensified by the separation episodes so that exploration diminishes and distress is likely; and in the reunion episodes they seek contact with, proximity to, or at least interaction with their mothers. Group C babies tend to show some signs of anxiety even in the preseparation episodes; they are intensely distressed by separation; and in the reunion episodes they are ambivalent with the mother, seeking close contact with her and yet resisting contact or interaction. Group A babies, in sharp contrast, rarely cry in the separation episodes and, in the reunion episodes, avoid the mother, either mingling proximity-seeking and avoidant behaviors or ignoring her altogether.

COMPARISON OF STRANGE-SITUATION BEHAVIOR AND BEHAVIOR ELSEWHERE

Groups A, B, and C in our longitudinal sample were compared in regard to their behavior at home during the first year. Stayton and Ainsworth (1973) had identified a security-anxiety dimension in a factor analysis of fourth-quarter infant behavior. Group B infants were identified as securely attached because they significantly more often displayed behaviors characteristic of the secure pole of this dimension, whereas both of the other groups were identified as anxious because their behaviors were characteristic of the anxious pole. A second dimension was clearly related to close bodily contact, and this was important in distinguishing Group A babies from those in the other two groups, in that Group A babies behaved less positively to being held and yet more negatively to being put down. The groups were also distinguished by two behaviors not included in the factor analysis—cooperativeness and anger. Group B babies were more cooperative and less angry than either A or C babies; Group A babies were even more angry than those in Group C. Clearly, something went awry in the physical-contact interaction Group A babies had with their mothers, and as I explain below, I believe it is this that makes them especially prone to anger.

Ainsworth et al. (1978) reviewed findings of other investigators who had compared A-B-C groups of 1-year-olds in terms of their behavior elsewhere. Their findings regarding socioemotional behavior support the summary just cited, and in addition three investigations using cognitive measures found an advantage in favor of the securely attached.

COMPARISON OF INFANT STRANGE-SITUATION BEHAVIOR WITH MATERNAL HOME BEHAVIOR

Mothers of the securely attached (Group B) babies were, throughout the first year, more sensitively responsive to infant signals than were the mothers of the two anxiously attached groups, in terms of a variety of measures spanning all of the most common contexts for mother–infant interaction (Ainsworth et al., 1978). Such responsiveness, I suggest, enables an infant to form expectations, primitive at first, that moderate his or her responses to events, both internal and environmental. Gradually, such an infant constructs an inner representation—or "working model" (Bowlby, 1969)—of his or her mother as generally accessible and responsive to him or her. Therein lies his or her security. In contrast, babies whose mothers have dis-

regarded their signals, or have responded to them belatedly or in a grossly inappropriate fashion, have no basis for believing the mother to be accessible and responsive; consequently they are anxious, not knowing what to expect of her.

In regard to interaction in close bodily contact, the most striking finding is that the mothers of avoidant (Group A) babies all evinced a deep-seated aversion to it, whereas none of the other mothers did. In addition they were more rejecting, more often angry, and yet more restricted in the expression of affect than were Group B or C mothers. Main (e.g., in press) and Ainsworth et al. (1978) have presented a theoretical account of the dynamics of interaction of avoidant babies and their rejecting mothers. This emphasizes the acute approach–avoidance conflict experienced by these infants when their attachment behavior is activated at high intensity—a conflict stemming from painful rebuff consequent upon seeking close bodily contact. Avoidance is viewed as a defensive maneuver, lessening the anxiety and anger experienced in the conflict situation and enabling the baby nevertheless to remain within a tolerable range of proximity to the mother.

Findings and interpretations such as these raise the issue of direction of effects. To what extent is the pattern of attachment of a baby attributable to the mother's behavior throughout the first year, and to what extent is it attributable to built-in differences in potential and temperament? I have considered this problem elsewhere (Ainsworth, 1979) and have concluded that in our sample of normal babies there is a strong case to be made for differences in attachment quality being attributable to maternal behavior. Two studies, however (Connell, 1976; Waters, Vaughn, & Egeland, in press), have suggested that Group C babies may as newborns be constitutionally "difficult." Particularly if the mother's personality or life situation makes it hard for her to be sensitively responsive to infant cues, such a baby seems indeed likely to form an attachment relationship of anxious quality.

Contexts of Mother-Infant Interaction

Of the various contexts in which mother–infant interaction commonly takes place, the face-to-face situation has been the focus of most recent research. By many (e.g., Walters & Parke, 1965), interaction mediated by distance receptors and behaviors has been judged especially important in the establishment of human relationships. Microanalytic studies, based on frame-by-frame analysis of film records, show clearly that maternal sensitivity to infant behavioral cues is essential for successful pacing of face-to-face interaction (e.g., Brazelton, Koslowski, & Main, 1974; Stern, 1974). Telling evidence of the role of vision, both in the infant's development of attachment to the mother and in the mother's responsiveness to the infant, comes from Fraiberg's (1977) longitudinal study of blind infants.

So persuasive have been the studies of interaction involving distance receptors that interaction involving close bodily contact has been largely ignored. The evolutionary perspective of attachment theory attributes focal importance to bodily contact. Other primate species rely on the maintenance of close mother–infant contact as crucial for infant survival. Societies of hunter-gatherers, living much as the earliest humans did, are conspicuous for very much more mother–infant contact than are western societies (e.g., Konner, 1976). Blurton Jones (1972) presented evidence suggesting that humans evolved as a species in which infants are carried by the mother and are fed at frequent intervals, rather than as a species in which infants are left for long periods, are cached in a safe place, and are fed but infrequently. Bowlby (1969) pointed out that when attachment behavior is intensely activated it is close bodily contact that is specifically required. Indeed, Bell and Ainsworth (1972) found that even with the white, middle-class mothers of their sample, the most frequent and the most effective response to an infant's crying throughout the first year was to pick up the baby. A recent analysis of our longitudinal findings (Blehar, Ainsworth, & Main, Note 1) suggests that mother–infant interaction relevant to close bodily contact is at least as important a context of interaction as face-to-face is, perhaps especially in the first few months of life. Within the limits represented by our sample, however, we found that it was *how* the mother holds her baby rather than *how much* she holds him or her that affects the way in which attachment develops.

In recent years the feeding situation has been neglected as a context for mother–infant interaction, except insofar as it is viewed as a setting for purely social, face-to-face interaction. Earlier, mother's gratification or frustration of infant interest to both psychoanalytically oriented and social-learning research, on the assumption that a mother's gratification or frustration of infant instinctual drives, or her role as a secondary reinforcer, determined the nature of the baby's tie to her. Such research yielded no evidence that methods of feeding significantly affected the course of infant development, although these negative findings seem almost certainly to reflect methodological deficiencies (Caldwell, 1964). In contrast, we have found that sensitive maternal responsiveness to infant signals relevant to feeding is closely related to the security or anxiety of attachment that eventually develops (Ainsworth & Bell, 1969). Indeed, this analysis seemed to redefine the meaning of "demand" feeding—letting infant behavioral cues determine not only when feeding is begun but also when it is terminated, how the pacing of feeding proceeds, and how new foods are introduced.

Our findings do not permit us to attribute overriding importance to any one context of mother–infant interaction. Whether the context is feeding, close bodily contact, face-to-face interaction, or indeed the situation defined by the infant's crying, mother–infant interaction provides the baby with opportunity to build up expectations of the mother and, eventually, a working model of her as more or less accessible and responsive. Indeed, our findings suggest that a mother who is sensitively responsive to signals in one context tends also to be responsive to signals in other contexts. . . .

Using the Mother as a Secure Base from Which to Explore

Attachment theory conceives of the behavioral system serving attachment as only one of several important systems, each with its own activators, terminators, predictable outcomes, and functions. During the prolonged period of human infancy, when the protective function of attachment is especially important, its interplay with exploratory behavior is noteworthy. The function of exploration is learning about the environment—which is particularly important in a species possessing much potential for adaptation to a wide range of environments. Attachment and exploration support each other. When attachment behavior is intensely activated, baby tends to seek proximity/contact rather than exploring; when attachment behavior is at low intensity a baby is free to respond to the pull of novelty. The presence of an attachment figure, particularly one who is believed to be accessible and responsive, leaves the baby open to stimulation that may activate exploration.

Nevertheless, it is often believed that somehow attachment may interfere with the development of independence. Our studies provide no support for such a belief. For example, Blehar et al.[1] found that babies who respond positively to close bodily contact with their mothers also tend to respond positively to being put down again and to move off into independent exploratory play. Fostering the growth of secure attachment facilitates rather than hampers the growth of healthy self-reliance (Bowlby, 1973).

Response to Separation from Attachment Figures

Schaffer (1971) suggested that the crucial criterion for whether a baby has become attached to a specific figure is that he or she does not consider this figure interchangeable with any other figure. Thus, for an infant to protest the mother's departure or continued absence is a dependable criterion for attachment (Schaffer & Callender, 1959). This does not imply that protest is an invariable response to separation from an attachment figure under all circumstances; the context of the separation influences the likelihood and intensity of protest. Thus there is ample evidence, which cannot be cited here, that protest is unlikely to occur, at least initially, in the case of voluntary separations, when the infant willingly leaves the mother in order to explore elsewhere. Protest is less likely to occur if the baby is left with another attachment figure than if he or she is left with an unfamiliar person or alone. Being left in an unfamiliar environment is more distressing than comparable separations in the familiar environment of the home—in which many infants are able to build up expectations that reassure them of mother's accessibility and responsiveness even though she may be absent. Changes attributable to developmental processes affect separation protest in complex ways. Further research will undoubtedly be able to account for these shifts in terms of progressive cognitive achievements. . . .

Other Attachment Figures

Many have interpreted Bowlby's attachment theory as claiming that an infant can become attached to only one person—the mother. This is a mistaken interpretation. There are, however, three implications of attachment theory relevant to the issue of "multiple" attachments. First, as reported by Ainsworth (1967) and Schaffer and Emerson (1964), infants are highly selective in their choices of attachment figures from among the various persons familiar to them. No infant has been observed to have many attachment figures. Second, not all social relationships may be identified as attachments. Harlow (1971) distinguished between the infant–mother and peer–peer affectional systems, although under certain circumstances peers may become attachment figures in the absence of anyone more appropriate (see, e.g., Freud & Dann, 1951; Harlow, 1963). Third, the fact that a baby may have several attachment figures does not imply that they are all equally important. Bowlby (1969) suggested that they are not—that there is a principal attachment figure, usually the principal caregiver, and one or more secondary figures. Thus a hierarchy is implied. A baby may both enjoy and derive security from all of his or her attachment figures, but under certain circumstances (e.g., illness, fatigue, stress), is likely to show a clear preference among them.

In recent years there has been a surge of interest in the father as an attachment figure, as reported elsewhere in this issue. Relatively lacking is research into attachments to caregivers other than parents. Do babies become attached to their regular baby-sitters or to caregivers in day-care centers? Studies by Fleener (1973), Farran and Ramey (1977), and Ricciuti (1974) have suggested that they may but that the preference is nevertheless for the mother figure. Fox (1977) compared the mother and the metapelet as providers of security to kibbutz-reared infants in a strange situation, but surely much more research is needed into the behavior of infants and young children toward caregivers as attachment figures in the substitute-care environment.

Consequences of Attachment

. . . In comparison with anxiously attached infants, those who are securely attached as 1-year-olds are later more cooperative with and affectively more positive as well as less aggressive and/or avoidant toward their mothers and other less familiar adults. Later on, they emerge as

more competent and more sympathetic in interaction with peers. In free-play situations they have longer bouts of exploration and display more intense exploratory interest, and in problem-solving situations they are more enthusiastic, more persistent, and better able to elicit and accept their mother's help. They are more curious, more self-directed, more ego-resilient—and they usually tend to achieve better scores on both developmental tests and measures of language development. Some studies also reported differences between the two groups of anxiously attached infants, with the avoidant ones (Group A) continuing to be more aggressive, noncompliant, and avoidant, and the ambivalent ones (Group C) emerging as more easily frustrated, less persistent, and generally less competent.

Conclusion

It is clear that the nature of an infant's attachment to his or her mother as a 1-year-old is related both to earlier interaction with the mother and to various aspects of later development. The implication is that the way in which the infant organizes his or her behavior toward the mother affects the way in which he or she organizes behavior toward other aspects of the environment, both animate and inanimate. This organization provides a core of continuity in development despite changes that come with developmental acquisitions, both cognitive and socioemotional.

NOTES

1. Blehar, M. C., Ainsworth, M. D. S., & Main, M. *Mother–infant interaction relevant to close bodily contact*. Monograph in preparation, 1979.

REFERENCES

Ainsworth, M. D. S. *Infancy in Uganda: Infant care and the growth of love.* Baltimore, Md.: Johns Hopkins Press, 1967.

Ainsworth, M. D. S. Attachment as related to mother–infant interaction. In J. S. Rosenblatt, R. A. Hinde, C. Beer, & M. Busnel (Eds.), *Advances in the study of behavior* (Vol. 9). New York: Academic Press, 1979.

Ainsworth, M. D. S., & Bell, S. M. Some contemporary patterns of mother-infant interaction in the feeding situation. In A. Ambrose (Ed.), *Stimulation in early infancy.* London: Academic Press, 1969.

Ainsworth, M. D. S., Blehar, M. C., Waters, E., & Wall, S. *Patterns of attachment: A psychological study of the strange situation.* Hillsdale, N.J.: Erlbaum, 1978.

Bell, S. M., & Ainsworth, M. D. S. Infant crying and maternal responsiveness. *Child Development*, 1972, *43*, 1171–1190.

Blurton Jones, N. G. Comparative aspects of mother–child contact. In N. G. Blurton Jones (Ed.), *Ethological studies of child behaviour.* London: Cambridge University Press, 1972.

Bowlby, J. *Attachment and loss: Vol. 1. Attachment.* New York: Basic Books, 1969.

Bowlby, J. *Attachment and loss: Vol. 2. Separation: Anxiety and anger.* New York: Basic Books, 1973.

Brazelton, T. B., Koslowski, B., & Main, M. The origins of reciprocity: The early mother–infant interaction. In M. Lewis & L. A. Rosenblum (Eds.), *The effect of the infant on its caregiver.* New York: Wiley, 1974.

Caldwell, B. M. The effects of infant care. In M. L. Hoffman & L. W. Hoffman (Eds.), *Review of child development research* (Vol. 1). New York: Russell Sage Foundation, 1964.

Connell, D. B. *Individual differences in attachment: An investigation into stability, implications, and relationships to the structure of early language development.* Unpublished doctoral dissertation, Syracuse University, 1976.

Farran, D. C., & Ramey, C. T. Infant day care and attachment behavior toward mother and teachers. *Child Development,* 1977, *48,* 112– 116.

Fleener, D. E. Experimental production of infant-maternal attachment behaviors. *Proceedings of the 81st Annual Convention of the American Psychological Association,* 1973, *8,* 57–58. (Summary)

Fox, N. Attachment of kibbutz infants to mother. *Child Development,* 1977, *48,* 1228–1239.

Fraiberg, S. *Insights from the blind.* New York: Basic Books, 1977.

Freud, A., & Dann, S. An experiment in group upbringing. *Psychoanalytic Study of the Child,* 1951, *6,* 127–168.

Harlow, H. F. The maternal affectional system. In B. M. Foss (Ed.), *Determinants of infant behavior* (Vol. 2). New York: Wiley, 1963.

Harlow, H. F. *Learning to love.* San Francisco: Albion, 1971.

Konner, M. J. Maternal care, infant behavior, and development among the !Kung. In R. B. Lee and I. DeVore (Eds.), *Kalahari hunter–gatherers.* Cambridge, Mass.: Harvard University Press, 1976.

Main, M. Avoidance in the service of proximity. In K. Immelmann, G. Barlow, M. Main, & L. Petrinovich (Eds.), *Behavioral development: The Bielefeld Interdisciplinary Project.* New York: Cambridge University Press, in press.

Ricciuti, H. N. Fear and the development of social attachments in the first year of life. In M. Lewis & L. A. Rosenblum (Eds.), *The origins of fear.* New York: Wiley, 1974.

Schaffer, H. R. *The growth of sociability.* London: Penguin Books, 1971.

Schaffer, H. R., & Callender, W. M. Psychological effects of hospitalization in infancy. *Pediatrics,* 1959, *25,* 528–539.

Schaffer, H. R., & Emerson, P. E. The development of social attachments in infancy. *Monographs of the Society for Research in Child Development,* 1964, *3* (Serial No. 94).

Stayton, D. J., & Ainsworth, M. D. S. Individual differences in infant responses to brief, everyday separations as related to other infant and maternal behaviors. *Developmental Psychology,* 1973, *9,* 226–235.

Stern, D. N. Mother and infant at play: The dyadic interaction involving facial, vocal, and gaze behaviors. In M. Lewis & L. A. Rosenblum (Eds.), *The effect of the infant on its caregiver.* New York: Wiley, 1974.

Walters, R. H., & Parke, R. D. The role of the distance receptors in the development of social responsiveness. In L. P. Lipsitt & C. C. Spiker (Eds.), *Advances in child development and behavior.* New York: Academic Press, 1965.

Waters, E., Vaughn, B. E., & Egeland, B. R. Individual differences in infant–mother attachment relationships at age one: Antecedents in neonatal behavior in an urban economically disadvantaged sample. *Child development,* in press.

Gender and Relationships: A Developmental Account

Eleanor E. Maccoby

Psychologists have shown increasing interest in gender differences during the past two decades. Much of the research that has been conducted has focused on individual differences, such as cognitive abilities, mathematical problem-solving skills, emotional expression, and verbal skills. Leading developmental psychologist Eleanor E. Mcacoby has argued that focusing on individual differences obscures important dimensions of gender differences in social relationships.

Maccoby (b. 1917) earned her Ph.D. in experimental psychology from the University of Michigan in 1950. She worked in the Laboratory of Human Development at Harvard University until 1958 and then moved to Stanford University, where she is currently a professor emeritus. Among her many publications are the classic book *The Psychology of Sex Differences* (Stanford University Press, 1974), coauthored by Carol Jacklin and the recent book *The Two Sexes: Growing Up Apart, Coming Together* (Belknap Press of Harvard University Press, 1998).

This selection is from "Gender and Realtionships: A Developmental Account," which was published in *American Psychologist* in 1990. In it, Maccoby argues that behavioral sex differences are minimal when children are tested individually but that they appear in social situations. One important finding is that children prefer same-sex partners and often segregate themselves in social settings. Note how the distinctive interactive styles that develop in same-sex groups are carried over into mixed-sex group interactions. How can better understanding of these gender differences help in everyday social interactions?

Key Concept: gender and social relations

APA Citation: Maccoby, E. E. (1990). Gender and relationships: A developmental account. *American Psychologist, 45,* 513–520.

*H*istorically, the way we psychologists think about the psychology of gender has grown out of our thinking about individual differences. We are accustomed to assessing a wide variety of attributes and skills and giving scores to individuals based on their standing relative to other individuals in a sample population. On most psychological attributes, we see wide variation among individuals, and a major focus of research has been the effort to identify correlates or sources of this variation. Commonly, what we have done is to classify individuals by some antecedent variable, such as age or some aspect of their environment, to determine how much of the variance among individuals in their performance on a given task can be accounted for by this so-called *antecedent* or *independent* variable. Despite the fact

that hermaphrodites exist, almost every individual is either clearly male or clearly female. What could be more natural for psychologists than to ask how much variance among individuals is accounted for by this beautifully binary factor?

Fifteen years ago, Carol Jacklin and I put out a book summarizing the work on sex differences that had come out of the individual differences perspective (Maccoby & Jacklin, 1974). We felt at that time that the yield was thin. That is, there were very few attributes on which the average values for the two sexes differed consistently. Furthermore, even when consistent differences were found, the amount of variance accounted for by sex was small, relative to the amount of variation within each sex. Our conclusions fitted in quite well with the feminist zeitgeist of the times, when most feminists were taking a minimalist position, urging that the two sexes were basically alike and that any differences were either illusions in the eye of the beholder or reversible outcomes of social shaping. Our conclusions were challenged as having both overstated the case for sex differences (Tieger, 1980) and for having understated it (Block, 1976).

In the last 15 years, work on sex differences has become more methodologically sophisticated, with greater use of meta analyses to reveal not only the direction of sex differences but quantitative estimates of their magnitude. In my judgment, the conclusions are still quite similar to those Jacklin and I arrived at in 1974: There are still some replicable sex differences, of moderate magnitude, in performance on tests of mathematical and spatial abilities, although sex differences in verbal abilities have faded. Other aspects of intellectual performance continue to show gender equality. When it comes to attributes in the personality-social domain, results are particularly sparse and inconsistent. Studies continue to find that men are more often agents of aggression than are women (Eagly, 1987; Huston, 1985; Maccoby & Jacklin, 1980). Eagly (1983, 1987) reported in addition that women are more easily influenced than men and that men are more altruistic in the sense that they are more likely to offer help to others. In general, however, personality traits measured as characteristics of individuals do not appear to differ systematically by sex (Huston, 1985). This no doubt reflects in part the fact that male and female persons really are much alike, and their lives are governed mainly by the attributes that all persons in a given culture have in common. Nevertheless, I believe that the null findings coming out of comparisons of male and female individuals on personality measures are partly illusory. That is, they are an artifact of our historical reliance on an individual differences perspective. Social behavior, as many have pointed out, is never a function of the individual alone. It is a function of the interaction between two or more persons. Individuals behave differently with different partners. There are certain important ways in which gender is implicated in social behavior—ways that may be obscured or missed altogether when behavior is summed across all categories of social partners.

An illustration is found in a study of social interaction between previously unacquainted pairs of young children (mean age, 33 months; Jacklin & Maccoby, 1978). In some pairs, the children had same-sex play partners; in othrs, the pair was made up of a boy and a girl. Observers recorded the social behavior of each child on a time-sampling basis. Each child received a score for total social behavior directed toward the partner. This score included both positive and negative behaviors (e.g., offering a toy and grabbing a toy; hugging and pushing; vocally greeting, inviting, protesting, or prohibiting). There was no overall sex difference in the amount of social behavior when this was evaluated without regard to sex of partner. But there was a powerful interaction between sex of the subject and that of partner: Children of each sex had much higher levels of social behavior when playing with a same-sex partner than when playing with a child of the other sex. This result is consistent with the findings of Wasserman and Stern (1978) that when asked to approach another child, children as young as age three stopped farther away when the other child was of the opposite sex, indicating awareness of gender similarity or difference, and wariness toward the other sex.

The number of time intervals during which a child was simply standing passively watching the partner play with the toys was also scored. There was no overall sex difference in the frequency of this behavior, but the behavior of girls was greatly affected by the sex of the partner. With other girls, passive behavior seldom occurred; indeed, in girl-girl pairs it occurred less often than it did in boy-boy pairs. However when paired with boys, girls frequently stood on the sidelines and let the boys monopolize the toys. Clearly, the little girls in this study were not more passive than the little boys in any overall, traitlike sense. Passivity in these girls could be understood only in relation to the characteristics of their interactive partners. It was a characteristics of girls in cross-sex dyads. This conclusion may not seem especially novel because for many years we have known that social behavior is situationally specific. However, the point here is that interactive behavior is not just situationally specific, but that it depends on the gender category membership of the participants. We can account for a good deal more of the behavior if we know the gender mix of dyads, and this probably holds true for larger groups as well.

An implication of our results was that if children at this early age found same-sex play partners more compatible, they ought to prefer same-sex partners when they entered group setting that included children of both sexes. There were already many indications in the literature that children do have same-sex playmate preferences, but there clearly was a need for more systematic attention to the degree of sex segregation that prevails in naturally occurring children's groups at different ages. As part of a longitudinal study of children from birth to age six, Jacklin and I did time-sampled behavioral observation of approximately 100 children on their preschool playgrounds, and again two years later when the children were playing during school recess periods (Maccoby & Jacklin, 1987). Same-sex playmate preference was clearly apparent in preschool when the children were approximately 4½. At this age, the children were spending nearly 3 times as much time with same-sex play partners as with children of the other sex. By age 6½, the preference had grown much stronger. At this time, the children were spending 11 times as much time with same-sex as with opposite-sex partners.

Elsewhere we have reviewed the literature on playmate choices (Maccoby, 1988; Maccoby & Jacklin, 1987), and here I will simply summarize what I believe the existing body of research shows:

1. Gender segregation is a widespread phenomenon. It is found in all the cultural settings in which children are in social groups large enough to permit choice.

2. The sex difference in the gender of preferred playmates is large in absolute magnitude, compared to sex differences found when children are observed or tested in nonsocial situations.

3. In a few instances, attempts have been made to break down children's preferences for interacting with other same-sex children. It has been found that the preferences are difficult to change.

4. Children choose same-sex playmates spontaneously in situations in which they are not under pressure from adults to do so. In modern coeducational schools, segregation is more marked in situations that have not been structured by adults than in those that have (e.g., Eisenhart & Holland, 1983). Segregation is situationally specific, and the two sexes can interact comfortably under certain conditions, for example, in an absorbing joint task, when structures and roles are set up by adults, or in nonpublic settings (Thorne, 1986).

5. Gender segregation is not closely linked to involvement in sex-typed activities. Preschool children spend a great deal of their time engaged in activities that are gender neutral, and segregation prevails in these activities as well as when they are playing with dolls or trucks.

6. Tendencies to prefer same-sex playmates can be seen among three-year-olds and at even earlier ages under some conditions. But the preferences increase in strength between preschool and school and are maintained at a high level between the ages of 6 and at least age 11.

7. The research base is thin, but so far it appears that a child's tendency to prefer same-sex playmates has little to do with that child's standing on measures of individual differences. In particular, it appears to be unrelated to measures of masculinity or femininity and also to measures of gender schematicity (Powlishta, 1989).

Why do we see such pronounced attraction to same-sex peers and avoidance of other-sex peers in childhood? Elsewhere I have summarized evidence pointing to two factors that seem to be important in the preschool years (Maccoby, 1988). The first is the rough-and-tumble play style characteristic of boys and their orientation toward issues of competition and dominance. These aspects of male-male interaction appear to be somewhat aversive to most girls. At least, girls are made wary by male play styles. The second factor of importance is that girls find it difficult to influence boys. Some important work by Serbin and colleagues (Serbin, Sprafkin, Elman, & Doyle, 1984) indicates that between the ages of 3½ and 5½, children greatly increase the frequency of their attempts to influence their play partners. This indicates that children are learning to integrate their activities with those of others so as to be able to carry out coordinated activities. Serbin and colleagues found that the increase in influence attempts by girls was almost entirely an increase in making polite suggestions to others, whereas among boys the increase took the form of more use of direct demands. Furthermore, during this formative two-year period just before school entry, boys were becoming less and less responsive to polite suggestions, so that the style being progressively adopted by girls was progressively less effective with boys. Girls' influence style was effective with each other and was well adapted to interaction with teachers and other adults.

These asymmetries in influence patterns were presaged in our study with 33-month-old children: We found then that boys were unresponsive to the vocal prohibitions of female partners (in that they did not withdraw), although they would respond when a vocal prohibition was issued by a male partner. Girls were responsive to one another and to a male partner's prohibitions. Fagot (1985) also reported that boys are "reinforced" by the reactions of male peers—in the sense that they modify their behavior following a male peer's reaction—but that their behavior appears not to be affected by a female's response.

My hypothesis is that girls find it aversive to try to interact with someone who is unresponsive and that they begin to avoid such partners. Students of power and bargaining have long been aware of the importance of reciprocity in human relations. Pruitt (1976) said, "Influence and power are omnipresent in human affairs. Indeed, groups cannot possibly function unless their members can influence one another" (p. 343). From this standpoint, it becomes clear why boys and girls have difficulty forming groups that include children of both sexes.

Why do little boys not accept influence from little girls? Psychologists almost automatically look to the nuclear family for the origins of behavior patterns seen in young children. It is plausible that boys may have been more reinforced for power assertive behavior by their parents, and girls more for politeness, although the evidence for such differential socialization pressure has proved difficult to come by. However, it is less easy to imagine how or why parents should reinforce boys for being unresponsive to *girls*. Perhaps it is a matter of observational learning: Children may have observed that between their two parents, their fathers are more influential than their mothers. I am skeptical about such an explanation. In the first place, mothers exercise a good deal of managerial authority within the households in which children live, and it is common for fathers to defer to their judgment in matters concerning the children. Or, parents form a coalition, and in the eyes of the children they become a joint authority, so that it makes little difference to them whether it is a mother or a father who is wielding authority at any given time. Furthermore, the asymmetry in children's cross-sex influence with their peers appears to have its origins at quite an early age—earlier, I would suggest, than children have a very clear idea about the connection between their own sex and that of the same-sex parent. In other words, it seems quite unlikely that little boys ignore girls' influence attempts because little girls remind them of their mothers. I think we simply do not know why girls' influence styles are ineffective with boys, but the fact that they are has important implications for a variety of social behaviors, not just for segregation.

Here are some examples from recent studies. Powlishta (1987) observed preschool-aged boy-girl pairs competing for a scarce resource. The children were brought to a playroom in the nursery school and were given an opportunity to watch cartoons through a movie-viewer that could only be accessed by one child at a time. Powlishta found that when the two children were alone together in the playroom, the boys got more than their share of access to the movie-viewer. When there was an adult present, however, this was no longer the case. The adult's presence appeared to inhibit the boys' more power-assertive techniques and resulted in girls having at least equal access.

This study points to a reason why girls may not only avoid playing with boys but may also stay nearer to a teacher or other adult. Following up on this possibility, Greeno (1989) brought four-child groups of kindergarten and first-grade children into a large playroom equipped with attractive toys. Some of the quartets were all-boy groups, some all-girl groups, and some were made up of two boys and two girls. A female adult sat at one end of the room, and halfway through the play session, moved to a seat at the other end of the room. The question posed for this study was: Would girls move closer to the teacher when boys were

present than when they were not? Would the sex composition of a play group make any difference to the locations taken up by the boys? The results were that in all-girl groups, girls actually took up locations *farther* from the adult than did boys in all-boy groups. When two boys were present, however, the two girls were significantly closer to the adult than were the boys, who tended to remain at intermediate distances. When the adult changed position halfway through the session, boys' locations did not change, and this was true whether there were girls present or not. Girls in all-girl groups tended to move in the opposite direction when the adult moved, maintaining distance between themselves and the adult; when boys were present, however, the girls tended to move *with* the adult, staying relatively close. It is worth noting, incidentally, that in all the mixed-sex groups except one, segregation was extreme; both boys and girls behaved as though there was only one playmate available to them, rather than three.

There are some fairly far-reaching implications of this study. Previous observational studies in preschools had indicated that girls are often found in locations closer to the teacher than are boys. These studies have been done in mixed-sex nursery school groups. Girls' proximity seeking toward adults has often been interpreted as a reflection of some general affiliative trait in girls and perhaps as a reflection of some aspect of early socialization that has bound them more closely to caregivers. We see in the Greeno study that proximity seeking toward adults was *not* a general trait in girls. It was a function of the gender composition of the group of other children present as potential interaction partners. The behavior of girls implied that they found the presence of boys to be less aversive when an adult was nearby. It was as though they realized that the rough, power-assertive behavior of boys was likely to be moderated in the presence of adults, and indeed, there is evidence that they were right.

We have been exploring some aspects of girls' avoidance of interaction with boys. Less is known about why boys avoid interaction with girls, but the fact is that they do. In fact, their cross-sex avoidance appears to be even stronger. Thus, during middle childhood both boys and girls spend considerable portions of their social play time in groups of their own sex. This might not matter much for future relationships were it not for the fact that fairly distinctive styles of interaction develop in all-boy and all-girl groups. Thus, the segregated play groups constitute powerful socialization environments in which children acquire distinctive interaction skills that are adapted to same-sex partners. Sex-typed modes of interaction become consolidated, and I wish to argue that the distinctive patterns developed by the two sexes at this time have implications for the same-sex and cross-sex relationships that individuals form as they enter adolescence and adulthood.

It behooves us, then, to examine in somewhat more detail the nature of the interactive milieus that prevail in all-boy and all-girl groups. Elsewhere I have reviewed some of the findings of studies in which these two kinds of groups have been observed (Maccoby, 1988). Here I will briefly summarize what we know.

The two sexes engage in fairly different kinds of activities and games (Huston, 1985). Boys play in somewhat larger groups, on the average, and their play is rougher (Humphreys & Smith, 1987) and takes up more space. Boys more often play in the streets and other public places; girls more often congregate in private homes or yards. Girls tend to form close, intimate friendships with one or two other girls, and these friendships are marked by the sharing of confidences (Kraft & Vraa, 1975). Boys' friendships, on the other hand, are more oriented around mutual interests in activities (Erwin, 1985). The breakup of girls' friendships is usually attended by more intense emotional reactions than is the case for boys.

For our present purposes, the most interesting thing about all-boy and all-girl groups is the divergence in the interactive styles that develop in them. In male groups, there is more concern with issues of dominance. Several psycholinguists have recorded the verbal exchanges that occur in these groups, and Maltz and Borker (1983) summarized the findings of several studies as follows: Boys in their groups are more likely than girls in all-girl groups to interrupt one another; use commands, threats, or boasts of authority; refuse to comply with another child's demand; give information; heckle a speaker; tell jokes or suspenseful stories; top someone else's story; or call another child names. Girls in all-groups, on the other hand, are more likely than boys to express agreement with what another speaker has just said, pause to give another girl a chance to speak, or when starting a speaking turn, acknowledge a point previously made by another speaker. This account indicates that among boys, speech serves largely egoistic functions and is used to establish and protect an individual's turf. Among girls, conversation is a more socially binding process.

In the past five years, analysts of discourse have done additional work on the kinds of interactive processes that are seen among girls, as compared with those among boys. The summary offered by Maltz and Borker has been both supported and extended. Sachs (1987) reported that girls soften their directives to partners, apparently attempting to keep them involved in a process of planning a play sequence, while boys are more likely simply to tell their partners what to do.

Leaper (1989) observed children aged five and seven and found that verbal exchanges among girls more often take the form of what he called "collaborative speech acts" that involve positive reciprocity, whereas among boys, speech acts are more controlling and include more negative reciprocity. Miller and colleagues (Miller, Danaher, & Forbes, 1986) found that there was more conflict in boys' groups, and given that conflict had occurred, girls were more likely to use "conflict mitigating strategies," whereas boys more often used threats and physical force. Sheldon (1989) reported that when girls talk, they seem to have a double agenda: to be "nice" and sustain social relationships, while at the same time working to achieve their own individual ends. For boys, the agenda is more often the single one of self-assertion. Sheldon (1989) has noted that in interactions among themselves, girls are *not* unassertive. Rather, girls do successfully pursue their own ends, but they do so while toning down coercion and dominance, trying to bring about agreement, and restoring or maintaining group functioning. It should be noted that boys' confrontational style does not necessarily impede effective group functioning, as evidenced by boys' ability to cooperate with teammates for sports. A second point is that although researchers' own gender has been found to influence to some degree the kinds of questions posed and the answers obtained, the summary provided here includes the work of both male and female researchers, and their findings are consistent with one another.

As children move into adolescence and adulthood, what happens to the interactive styles that they developed in their largely segregated childhood groups? A first point to note is that despite the powerful attraction to members of the opposite sex in adolescence, gender segregation by no means disappears. Young people continue to spend a good portion of their social time with same-sex partners. In adulthood, there is extensive gender segregation in workplaces (Reskin, 1984), and in some societies and some social-class or ethnic groups, leisure time also is largely spent with same-sex others even after marriage. The literature on the nature of the interactions that occur among same-sex partners in adolescence and adulthood is quite extensive and cannot be reviewed here. Suffice it to say in summary that there is now considerable evidence that the interactive patterns found in sex-homogeneous dyads or groups in adolescence and adulthood are very similar to those that prevailed in the gender-segregated groups of childhood (e.g., Aries, 1976; Carli, 1989; Cowan, Drinkard, & MacGavin, 1984; Savin-Williams, 1979).

How can we summarize what it is that boys and girls, or men and women, are doing in their respective groups that distinguishes these groups from one another? There have been a number of efforts to find the major dimensions that best describe variations in interactive styles. Falbo and Peplau (1980) have factor analyzed a battery of measures and have identified two dimensions: one called direct versus indirect, the other unilateral versus bilateral. Hauser et al. (1987) have distinguished what they called *enabling* interactive styles from *constricting* or *restrictive* ones, and I believe this distinction fits the styles of the two sexes especially well. A restrictive style is one that tends to derail the interaction—to inhibit the partner or cause the partner to withdraw, thus shortening the interaction or bringing it to an end. Examples are threatening a partner, directly contradicting or interrupting, topping the partner's story, boasting, or engaging in other forms of self-display. Enabling or facilitative styles are those, such as acknowledging another's comment or expressing agreement, that support whatever the partner is doing and tend to keep the interaction going. I want to suggest that it is because women and girls use more enabling styles that they are able to form more intimate and more integrated relationships. Also I think it likely that it is the male concern for turf and dominance—that is, with not showing weakness to other men and boys—that underlies their restrictive interaction style and their lack of self-disclosure.

References

Aries, E. (1976). Interaction patterns and themes of male, female, and mixed groups. *Small Group Behavior, 7*, 7–18.

Block, J. H. (1976). Debatable conclusions about sex differences. *Contemporary Psychology, 21*, 517–522.

Carli, L. L. (1989). Gender differences in interaction style and influence. *Journal of Personality and Social Psychology, 56*, 565–576.

Cowan, C., Drinkard, J., & MacGavin, L. (1984). The effects of target, age and gender on use of power strategies. *Journal of Personality and Social Psychology, 47*, 1391–1398.

Eagly, A. H. (1983). Gender and social influence. *American Psychologist, 38*, 971–981.

Eagly, A. H. (1987). *Sex differences in social behavior: A social role interpretation.* Hillsdale, NJ: Erlbaum.

Eisenhart, M. A., & Holland, D. C. (1983). Learning gender from peers: The role of peer group in the cultural transmission of gender. *Human Organization, 42*, 321–332.

Erwin, P. (1985). Similarity of attitudes and constructs in children's friendships. *Journal of Experimental Child Psychology, 40*, 470–485.

Fagot, B. I. (1985). Beyond the reinforcement principle: Another step toward understanding sex roles. *Developmental Psychology, 21*, 1097–1104.

Falbo, T., & Peplau, L. A. (1980). Power strategies in intimate relationships. *Journal of Personality and Social Psychology, 38*, 618–628.

Greeno, C. G. (1989). *Gender differences in children's proximity to adults.* Unpublished doctoral dissertation, Stanford University, Stanford, CA.

Hauser, S. T., Powers, S. I., Weiss-Perry, B., Follansbee, D. J., Rajapark, D., & Greene, W. M. (1987). *The constraining and enabling coding system manual.* Unpublished manuscript.

Humphreys, A. P., & Smith, P. K. (1987). Rough and tumble friendship and dominance in school children: Evidence for continuity and change with age in middle childhood. *Child Development, 58*, 201–212.

Huston, A. C. (1985). The development of sex-typing: Themes from recent research. *Developmental Review, 5*, 1–17.

Jacklin, C. N., & Maccoby, E. E. (1978). Social behavior at 33 months in same-sex and mixed-sex dyads. *Child Development, 49*, 557–569.

Kraft, L. W., & Vraa, C. W. (1975). Sex composition of groups and pattern of self-disclosure by high school females. *Psychological Reports, 37*, 733–734.

Leaper, C. (1989). *The sequencing of power and involvement in boys' and girls' talk.* Unpublished manuscript (under review), University of California, Santa Cruz.

Maccoby, E. E. (1988). Gender as a social category. *Developmental Psychology, 26*, 755–765.

Maccoby, E. E., & Jacklin, C. N. (1974). *The psychology of sex differences.* Standford, CA: Stanford University Press.

Maccoby, E. E., & Jacklin, C. N. (1980). Sex differences in aggression: A rejoinder and reprise. *Child Development, 51*, 964–980.

Maccoby, E. E., & Jacklin, C. N. (1987). Gender segregation in childhood. In H. W. Reese (Ed.), *Advances in child development and behavior* (Vol. 20, pp. 239–288). New York: Academic Press.

Maltz, D. N., & Borker, R. A. (1983). A cultural approach to male-female miscommunication. In John A. Gumperz (Ed.), *Language and social identity* (pp. 195–216). New York: Cambridge University Press.

Miller, P., Danaher, D., & Forbes, D. (1986). Sex-related strategies for coping with interpersonal conflict in children aged five and seven. *Developmental Psychology, 22*, 543–548.

Powlishta, K. K. (1987, April). *The social context of cross-sex interactions.* Paper presented at biennial meeting of the Society for Research in Child Development, Baltimore, MD.

Powlishta, K. K. (1989). *Salience of group membership: The case of gender.* Unpublished doctoral dissertation, Stanford University, Stanford, CA.

Pruitt, D. G. (1976). Power and bargaining. In B. Seidenberg & A. Snadowsky (Eds.), *Social psychology: An introduction* (pp. 343–375). New York: Free Press.

Reskin, B. F. (Ed.) (1984). *Sex segregation in the workplace: Trends, explanations and remedies.* Washington, DC: National Academy Press.

Sachs, J. (1987). Preschool boys' and girls' language use in pretend play. In S. U. Phillips, S. Steele, & C. Tanz & (Eds.), *Language, gender and sex in comparative perspective* (pp. 178–188). Cambridge, England: Cambridge University Press.

Savin-Williams, R. C. (1979). Dominance hierarchies in groups of early adolescents. *Child Development, 50*, 923–935.

Serbin, L. A., Sprafkin, C., Elman, M., & Doyle, A. (1984). The early development of sex differentiated patterns of social influence. *Canadian Journal of Social Science, 14,* 350–363.

Sheldon, A. (1989, April). *Conflict talk: Sociolinguistic challenges to self-assertion and how young girls meet them.* Paper presented at the biennial meeting of the Society for Research in Child Development, Kansas City.

Thorne, B. (1986). Girls and boys together, but mostly apart. In W. W. Hartup & L. Rubin (Eds.), *Relationships and development* (pp. 167–184). Hillsdale, NJ: Erlbaum.

Tieger, T. (1980). On the biological basis of sex differences in aggression. *Child Development, 51,* 943–963.

Wasserman, G. A., & Stern, D. N. (1978). An early manifestation of differential behavior toward children of the same and opposite sex. *Journal of Genetic Psychology, 133,* 129–137.

Personality

The Psychical Apparatus

Sigmund Freud (1940)

In many ways, personality is the sum total of who you are and what you do. There are many different approaches to personality; some researchers stress overt behavior, while others focus on internal processes. Sigmund Freud's psychoanalytic theory of personality, which is discussed in this selection, represents an early attempt to describe the unseen structures of personality.

Sigmund Freud (1856-1939), an Austrian neurologist, obtained his M.D. from the University of Vienna in 1881. Through his medical practice, he began to study patients' mental disorders by employing his theory of psychoanalysis. Freud thought of personality as an iceberg, with only the tip showing above water (i.e., revealed in outward behavior). Personality, he believed, is the result of the interaction of the three personality structures that he dubbed the id, ego, and superego.

This selection, from chapter 1, "The Psychical Apparatus", of Freud's *An Outline of Psycho-Analysis*, which was originally published in 1940 and which was intended to be a very concise summary of a very complicated theory. In this selection, Freud describes the characteristics of personality and briefly defines the id, ego, and superego. Notice that Freud begins by stating that we do not really know what the apparatus of personality is, but from observing people we can make a prediction. As you read this selection, think about how Freud's theory of personality could be tested.

Key Concept: psychoanalytic theory of personality

APA citation: Freud, S. (1940). *An outline of psycho-analysis.* New York: Norton.

*P*sycho-analysis makes a basic assumption, the discussion of which is reserved to philosophical thought but the justification for which lies in its results. We know two kinds of things about what we call our psyche (or mental life): firstly, its bodily organ and scene of action, the brain (or nervous system) and, on the other hand, our acts of consciousness, which are immediate data and cannot be further explained by any sort of description. Everything that lies between is unknown to us, and the data do not include any direct relation between these two terminal points of our knowledge. If it existed, it would at the most afford an exact localization of the processes of consciousness and would give us no help towards understanding them.

Our two hypotheses start out from these ends or beginnings of our knowledge. The first is concerned with localization. We assume that mental life is the function of an apparatus to which we ascribe the characteristics of being extended in space and of being made up of several portions—which we imagine, that is, as resembling a telescope or microscope or something of the kind. Notwithstanding some earlier attempts in the same direction, the consistent working-out of a conception such as this is a scientific novelty.

We have arrived at our knowledge of this psychical apparatus by studying the individual development of human beings. To the oldest of these psychical provinces or agencies we give the name of *id*. It contains everything that is inherited, that is present at birth, that is laid down in the constitution—above all, therefore, the instincts, which originate from the somatic organization and which find a first psychical expression here [in the id] in forms unknown to us.

Under the influence of the real external world around us, one portion of the id has undergone a special development. From what was originally a cortical layer, equipped with the organs for receiving stimuli and with arrangements for acting as a protective shield against stimuli, a special organization has arisen which henceforward acts as an intermediary between the id and the external world. To this region of our mind we have given the name of *ego*.

Here are the principal characteristics of the ego. In consequence of the pre-established connection between sense perception and muscular action, the ego has voluntary movement at its command. It has the task of self-preservation. As regards *external* events, it performs that task by becoming aware of stimuli, by storing up experiences about them (in the memory), by avoiding excessively strong stimuli (through flight), by dealing with moderate stimuli (through adaptation) and finally by learning to bring about expedient changes in the external world to its own advantage (through activity). As regards *internal* events, in relation to the id, it performs that task by gaining control over the demands of the instincts, by deciding whether they are to be allowed satisfaction, by postponing that satisfaction to times and circumstances favourable in the external world or by suppressing their excitations entirely. It is guided in its activity by consideration of the tensions produced by stimuli, whether these tensions are present in it or introduced into it. The raising of these tensions is in general felt as *unpleasure* and their lowering as *pleasure*. It is probable, however, that what is felt as pleasure or unpleasure is not the *absolute* height of this tension but something in the rhythm of the changes in them. The ego strives after pleasure and seeks to avoid unpleasure. An increase in unpleasure that is expected and foreseen is met by a *signal of anxiety,* the occasion of such an increase, whether it threatens from without or within, is known as a *danger.* From time to time the ego gives up its connection with the external world and withdraws into the state of sleep, in which it makes far-reaching changes in its organization. It is to be inferred from the state of sleep that this organization consists in a particular distribution of mental energy.

The long period of childhood, during which the growing human being lives in dependence on his parents, leaves behind it as a precipitate the formation in his ego of a special agency in which this parental influence is prolonged. It has received the name of *super-ego.* In so far as this super-ego is differentiated from the ego or is opposed to it, it constitutes a third power which the ego must take into account.

An action by the ego is as it should be if it satisfies simultaneously the demands of the id, of the super-ego and of reality—that is to say, if it is able to reconcile their demands with one another. The details of the relation between the ego and the superego become completely intelligible when they are traced back to the child's attitude to its parents. This parental influence of course includes in its operation not only the personalities of the actual parents but also the family, racial and national traditions handed on through them, as well as the demands of the immediate social *milieu* which they represent. In the same way, the super-ego, in the course of an individual's development, receives contributions from later successors and substitutes of his parents, such as teachers and models in public life of admired social ideals. It will be observed that, for all their fundamental difference, the id and the super-ego have one thing in common: they both represent the influences of the past—the id the influence of heredity, the super-ego the influence, essentially, of what is taken over from other people—whereas the ego is principally determined by the individual's own experience, that is by accidental and contemporary events.

This general schematic picture of a psychical apparatus may be supposed to apply as well to the higher animals which resemble man mentally. A superego must be presumed to be present wherever, as is the case with man, there is a long period of dependence in childhood. A distinction between ego and id is an unavoidable assumption. Animal psychology has not yet taken in hand the interesting problem which is here presented.

External Control and Internal Control

Julian B. Rotter (1971)

Psychologists do not agree on what determines personality, but many accept that reinforcement can shape behaviors that ultimately may influence personality. The social learning theory of personality suggests that behavior that is rewarded leads to the expectancy that the behavior will continue to produce rewards in the future. According to Julian B. Rotter's locus of control personality theory, which is based in the social learning theory, two personality types exist: People with an internal locus of control, who perceive that reinforcement is due to their own behavior; and people with an external locus of control, who perceive that reinforcement is independent of their behavior.

Rotter (b. 1916) earned his Ph.D. from Indiana University in 1941. He taught at several schools, including Ohio State University, before going to the University of Connecticut in 1963, where he is currently a professor of clinical psychology. Rotter's social learning theory (proposed in his 1954 book Social Learning and Clinical Psychology) has greatly influenced modern psychologists.

This selection is from "External control and internal control," which was published in *Psychology Today* in 1971. It contains a straightforward description of Rotter's theory of personality as well as some fascinating applications. Note the development of Rotter's thinking as he describes how the idea of locus of control came to him. As you read this selection, think about the implications for people who have an internal or external locus of control.

Key Concept: internal and external locus of control

APA Citation: Rotter, J. B. (1971). External control and internal control. Psychology Today, 5, 37–42; 58–59.

Some social scientists believe that the impetus behind campus unrest is youth's impatient conviction that they can control their own destinies, that they can change society for the better.

My research over the past 12 years has led me to suspect that much of the protest, outcry and agitation occurs for the opposite reason—because students feel they *cannot* change the world, that the system is too complicated and too much controlled by powerful others to be changed through the students' efforts. They feel more powerless and alienated today than they did 10 years ago, and rioting may be an expression of their hostility and resentment.

Dog

One of the most pervasive laws of animal learning is that a behavior followed by a reward tends to be repeated, and a behavior followed by a punishment tends not to be repeated. This seems to imply that reward and punishment act directly on behavior, but I think this formulation is too simplistic to account for many types of human behavior.

For example, if a dog lifts its leg at the exact moment that someone throws a bone over a fence, the dog may begin to lift its leg more often than usual when it is in the same situation—whether or not anyone is heaving a bone. Adult human beings are usually not so superstitious—a person who finds a dollar bill on the sidewalk immediately after stroking his hair is not likely to stroke his hair when he returns to the same spot.

It seemed to me that, at least with human beings who have begun to form concepts, the important factors in learning were not only the strength and frequency of rewards and punishments but also whether or not the person believed his behavior produced the reward or punishment.

According to the social-learning theory that I developed several years ago with my colleagues and students, rewarding a behavior strengthens an *expectancy* that the behavior will produce future rewards.

In animals, the expectation of reward is primarily a function of the strength and frequency of rewards. In human beings, there are other things that can influence the expectation of reward—the information others give us,

TABLE 1 Internal Control—External Control: A Sampler

Julian B. Rotter is the developer of a forced-choice 29-item scale for measuring an individual's degree of internal control and external control. This I-E test is widely used. The following are sample items taken from an earlier version of the test, but not, of course, in use in the final version. The reader can readily find for himself whether he is inclined toward internal control or toward external control, simply by adding up the choices he makes on each side.

I more strongly believe that:	OR
Promotions are earned through hard work and persistence.	Making a lot of money is largely a matter of getting the right breaks.
In my experience I have noticed that there is usually a direct connection between how hard I study and the grades I get.	Many times the reactions of teachers seem haphazard to me.
The number of divorces indicates that more and more people are not trying to make their marriages work.	Marriage is largely a gamble
When I am right I can convince others.	It is silly to think that one can really change another person's basic attitudes.
In our society a man's future earning power is dependent upon his ability.	Getting promoted is really a matter of being a little luckier than the next guy.
If one knows how to deal with people they are really quite easily led.	I have little influence over the way other people behave.
In my case the grades I make are the results of my own efforts; luck has little or nothing to do with it.	Sometimes I feel that I have little to do with the grades I get.
People like me can change the course of world affairs if we make ourselves heard.	It is only wishful thinking to believe that one can really influence what happens in society at large.
I am the master of my fate.	A great deal that happens to me is probably a matter of chance.
Getting along with people is a skill that must be practiced.	It is almost impossible to figure out how to please some people.

our knowledge generalized from a variety of experiences, and our perceptions of causality in the situation.

Consider the ancient shell game. Suppose I place a pea under one of three shells and quickly shuffle the shells around the table. A player watches my movements carefully and then, thinking that he is using his fine perceptual skills, he tells me which shell the pea is under. If his choice is correct, he will likely choose the same shell again the next time he sees me make those particular hand movements. It looks like a simple case of rewarding a response.

But suppose I ask the subject to turn his back while I shuffle the shells. This time, even if his choice is rewarded by being correct, he is not so likely to select the same shell again, because the outcome seems to be beyond his control—just a lucky guess.

Chips

In 1957, E. Jerry Phares tried to find out if these intuitive differences between chance-learning and skill-learning would hold up in the laboratory. Phares would give each subject a small gray-colored chip and ask him to select one of 10 standard chips that had exactly the same shade of gray. The standards were all different but so similar in value that discrimination among them was very difficult. Phares told half of his subjects that matching the shades required great skill and that some persons were very

good at it. He told the rest that the task was so difficult that success was a matter of luck. Before the experiment began, Phares arbitrarily decided which trials would be "right" and which would be "wrong"; the schedule was the same for everyone. He found that because of the difficulty of the task all subjects accepted his statements of right and wrong without question.

Phares gave each subject a stack of poker chips and asked him to bet on his accuracy before each trial as a measure of each subject's expectancy of success.

The subjects who thought that success depended on their own skills shifted and changed frequently—their bets would rise after success and drop after failure, just as reinforcement-learning theory would predict. But subjects who thought that a correct match was a matter of luck reacted differently. In fact, many of them raised their bets after failure and lowered them after success—the "gambler's fallacy." Thus, it appeared that traditional laws of learning could not explain some types of human behavior. . . .

I decided to study internal and external control (I-E), the beliefs that rewards come from one's own behavior or from external sources. The initial impetus to study internal-external control came both from an interest in individual differences and from an interest in explaining the way human beings learn complex social situations. There seemed to be a number of attitudes that would lead a person to feel that a reward was not contingent upon his own behavior, and we tried to build all of these attitudes into a measure of individual differences. A person might feel that luck or chance controlled what happened to him. He might feel that fate had preordained what would happen to him. He might feel that powerful others controlled what happened to him or he might feel that he simply could not predict the effects of this behavior because the world was too complex and confusing.

Scale

Phares first developed a test of internal-external control as part of his doctoral dissertation, and [William H.] James enlarged and improved on Phares' scale as part of his doctoral dissertation. Later scales were constructed with the important help of several of my colleagues including Liverant, Melvin Seeman and Crowne. In 1962 I developed a final 29-item version of the I-E scale and published it in *Psychological Monographs* in 1966. This is a forced-choice scale in which the subject reads a pair of statements and then indicates with which of the two statements he more strongly agrees. The scores range from zero (the consistent belief that individuals can influence the environment—that rewards come from *internal* forces) to 23 (the belief that all rewards come from *external* forces)....

Degree

One conclusion is clear from I-E studies: people differ in the tendency to attribute satisfactions and failures to themselves rather than to external causes, and these differences are relatively stable. For the sake of convenience most investigators divide their subjects into two groups—internals and externals—depending on which half of the distribution a subject's score falls into. This is not meant to imply that there are two personality types and that everyone can be classified as one or the other, but that there is a continuum, and that persons have varying degrees of internality or externality.

Many studies have investigated the differences between internals and externals. For example, it has been found that lower-class children tend to be external; children from richer, better-educated families tend to have more belief in their own potential to determine what happens to them. The scores do not seem to be related to intelligence, but young children tend to become more internal as they get older.

Esther Battle and I examined the attitudes of black and white children in an industrialized Ohio city. The scale we used consisted of five comic-strip cartoons; the subjects told us what they thought one of the children in the cartoon would say. We found that middle-class blacks were only slightly more external in their beliefs than middle-class whites but that among children from lower socioeconomic levels blacks were significantly more external than whites. Herbert Lefcourt and Gordon Lad-

wig also found that among young prisoners in a Federal reformatory, blacks were more external than whites.

Ute

It does not seem to be socioeconomic level alone that produces externality, however. Theodore Graves, working with Richard and Shirley L. Jessor, found that Ute Indians were more external than a group of Spanish-Americans, even though the Indians had higher average living standards than the Spanish-Americans. Since Ute tradition puts great emphasis on fate and unpredictable external forces, Graves concluded that internality and externality resulted from cultural training. A group of white subjects in the same community were more internal than either the Indians or the Spanish-Americans.

A measure of internal-external control was used in the well-known Coleman Report on Equality of Educational Opportunity. The experimenters found that among disadvantaged children in the sixth, ninth and 12th grades, the students with high scores on an achievement test had more internal attitudes than did children with low achievement scores.

One might expect that internals would make active attempts to learn about their life situations. To check on this, Seeman and John Evans gave the I-E scale to patients in a tuberculosis hospital. The internal patients knew more details about their medical conditions and they questioned doctors and nurses for medical feedback more often than did the external patients. The experimenters made sure that in their study there were no differences between the internals and externals in education, occupational status or ward placement....

Bet

Highly external persons feel that they are at the mercy of the environment, that they are being manipulated by outside forces. When they *are* manipulated, externals seem to take it in stride. Internals are not so docile. For example, Crowne and Liverant set up an experiment to see how readily their subjects would go along with a crowd. In a simple ... conformity experiment in which there is one true subject plus several stooges posing as subjects, Crowne and Liverant found that neither internals nor externals were more likely to yield to an incorrect majority judgment. But when the experimenters gave money to the subjects and allowed them to bet on their own judgments, the externals yielded to the majority much more often than did the internals. When externals did vote against the majority they weren't confident about their independence—they bet less money on being right than they did when they voted along with the crowd....

Suspicion

Some externals, who feel they are being manipulated by the outside world, may be highly suspicious of authorities. With Herbert Hamsher and Jesse Geller, I found that male subjects who believed that the Warren Commission Report was deliberately covering up a conspiracy were significantly more external than male subjects who accepted the report.

To some degree externality may be a defense against expected failure but internals also have their defenses. In investigating failure defenses, Jay Efran studied high-school students' memories for tasks they had completed or failed. He found that the tendency to forget failures was more common in internal subjects than in external ones. This suggests that external subjects have less need to repress past failures because they have already resigned themselves to the defensive position that failures are not their responsibility. Internals, however, are more likely to forget or repress their failures.

Today's activist student groups might lead one to assume that our universities are filled with internals—people with strong belief in their ability to improve conditions and to control their own destinies. But scores on the same I-E test involving large numbers of college students in many localities show that between 1962 and 1971 there was a large increase in externality on college campuses. Today the average score on the I-E scale is about 11. In 1962 about 80 per cent of college students had more internal scores than this. The increase in externality has been somewhat less in Midwest colleges than in universities on the coasts, but there is little doubt that, overall, college students feel more powerless to change the world and control their own destinies now than they did 10 years ago.

Clearly, we need continuing study of methods to reverse this trend. Our society has so many critical problems that it desperately needs as many active, participating internal-minded members as possible. If feelings of external control, alienation and powerlessness continue to grow, we may be heading for a society of dropouts—each person sitting back, watching the world go by.

Validation of the Five-Factor Model of Personality Across Instruments and Observers

Robert R. McCrae and Paul T. Costa, Jr. (1987)

Over the years, there have been numerous attempts to classify personality traits. Little agreement was reached among psychologists until the five-factor model became popular. The five-factor model of personality was originally proposed in the early 1960s, but it did not become popular among psychologists until the 1980s. The five factors of this model are extraversion (sociability), agreeableness (friendliness), conscientiousness (dependability), emotional stability (versus neuroticism), and openness (liberalism). Psychologists do not all agree on the specific labels, but there is some consensus on the five areas of personality. Robert R. McCrae and Paul T. Costa, Jr., are among the leaders in the quest to understand these factors and how they can explain personality.

McCrae earned his Ph.D. from Boston University in 1976. He has since been an associate of the Gerontology Research Center of the National Institute of Aging, National Institutes of Health. Costa (b. 1942) received his Ph.D. from the University of Chicago in 1970. He is also with the National Institute on Aging, National Institutes of Health.

This selection is from "Validation of the Five-Factor Model of Personality Across Instruments and Observers," which was published in the American Psychological Association's Journal of Personality and Social Psychology in 1987. In it, McCrae and Costa describe the history and interpretation of each of the five factors in this model. In one part of the original article not included here, the authors report an experiment in which they used self-reports, peer ratings, and questionnaire scales to measure the five factors. The results of this study validated the five-factor model. As you read this selection, note which characteristics best describe your personality. Can you think of any other major factors of personality that might be included in this model?

Key Concept: five-factor model of personality

APA Citation: McCrae, R. R., & Costa, P. T., Jr. (1987). Validation of the five-factor model of personality across instruments and observers. *Journal of Personality and Social Psychology, 52,* 81–90.

erhaps in response to critiques of trait models (Mischel, 1968) and to rebuttals that have called attention to common inadequacies in personality research (Block, 1977), personologists in recent years have devoted much of their attention to methodological issues. . . . As a body, these studies have simultaneously increased the level of methodological sophistication in personality research and restored confidence in the intelligent use of individual difference models of personality.

In contrast, there has been relatively little interest in the substance of personality—the systematic description of traits. The variables chosen as vehicles for tests of methodological hypotheses often appear arbitrary. . . . Indeed, Kenrick and Dantchik (1983) complained that "catalogs of convenience" have replaced meaningful taxonomies of personality traits among "most of the current generation of social/personality researchers" (p. 299).

This disregard of substance is unfortunate because substance and method are ultimately interdependent. Unless methodological studies are conducted on well-defined and meaningful traits their conclusions are dubious; unless the traits are selected from a comprehensive taxonomy, it is impossible to know how far or in what ways they can be generalized.

Fortunately, a few researchers have been concerned with the problem of structure and have recognized the need for a consensus on at least the general outlines of a trait taxonomy (H. J. Eysenck & Eysenck, 1984; Kline & Barrett, 1983; Wiggins, 1979). One particularly promising candidate has emerged. The five-factor model—comprising extraversion or surgency, agreeableness, conscientiousness, emotional stability versus neuroticism, and culture—of Tupes and Christal (1961) was replicated by Norman in 1963 and heralded by him as the basis for "an adequate taxonomy of personality." Although it was largely neglected for several years, variations on this model have recently begun to reemerge (Amelang & Borkenau, 1982; Bond, Nakazato, & Shiraishi, 1975; Conley, 1985; Digman & Takemoto-Chock, 1981; Goldberg, 1981, 1982; Hogan, 1983; Lorr & Manning, 1978; McCrae & Costa, 1985b). . . .

THE NATURE OF THE FIVE FACTORS

. . . A growing body of research has pointed to the five-factor model as a recurrent and more or less comprehensive taxonomy of personality traits. Theorists disagree, however, in precisely how to conceptualize the factors themselves. It seems useful at this point to review each of the factors and attempt to define the clear elements as well as disputed aspects. . . .

Neuroticism Versus Emotional Stability

There is perhaps least disagreement about neuroticism, defined here by such terms as worrying, insecure, self-conscious, and temperamental. Although adjectives describing neuroticism are relatively infrequent in English (Peabody, 1984), psychologists' concerns with psychopathology have led to the development of innumerable scales saturated with neuroticism. Indeed, neuroticism is so ubiquitous an element of personality scales that theorists sometimes take it for granted.

A provocative view of neuroticism is provided by Tellegen (in press), who views it as negative emotionality, the propensity to experience a variety of negative affects, such as anxiety, depression, anger, and embarrassment. Virtually all theorists would concur in the centrality of negative affect to neuroticism; the question is whether other features also define it. Tellegen himself (in press) pointed out that his construct of negative emotionality has behavioral and cognitive aspects. Guilford included personal relations and objectivity in his emotional health factor (Guilford, Zimmerman, & Guilford, 1976), suggesting that mistrust and self-reference form part of neuroticism. We have found that impulsive behaviors, such as tendencies to overeat, smoke, or drink excessively, form a facet of neuroticism (Costa & McCrae, 1980), and *impulse-*

ridden is a definer of the neuroticism factor in self-reports, although not in ratings. Others have linked neuroticism to irrational beliefs (Teasdale & Rachman, 1983; Vestre, 1984) or to poor coping efforts (McCrae & Costa, 1986).

What these behaviors seem to share is a common origin in negative affect. Individuals high in neuroticism have more difficulty than others in quitting smoking because the distress caused by abstinence is stronger for them. They may more frequently use inappropriate coping responses like hostile reactions and wishful thinking because they must deal more often with disruptive emotions. They may adopt irrational beliefs like self-blame because these beliefs are cognitively consistent with the negative feelings they experience. Neuroticism appears to include not only negative affect, but also the disturbed thoughts and behaviors that accompany emotional distress.

Extraversion or Surgency

Sociable, fun-loving, affectionate, friendly, and talkative are the highest loading variables on the extraversion factor. This is not Jungian extraversion (see Guilford, 1977), but it does correspond to the conception of H. J. Eysenck and most other contemporary researchers, who concur with popular speech in identifying extraversion with lively sociability.

However, disputes remain about which elements are central and which are peripheral to extraversion. Most writers would agree that sociability, cheerfulness, activity level, assertiveness, and sensation seeking all covary, however loosely. But the Eysencks have at times felt the need to distinguish between sociability and what they call impulsiveness (S. B. G. Eysenck & Eysenck, 1963; Revelle, Humphreys, Simon, & Gilliland, 1980). Hogan (1983) believed that the five-factor model was improved by dividing extraversion into sociability and assertiveness factors. In Goldberg's analyses, surgency (dominance and activity) were the primary definers of extraversion, and terms like warm–cold were assigned to the agreeableness–antagonism factor. Tellegen (in press) emphasized the complementary nature of neuroticism and extraversion by labeling his extraversion factor positive emotionality.

These distinctions do seem to merge at a high enough level of analysis (H. J. Eysenck & Eysenck, 1976; McCrae & Costa, 1983a), and sociability—the enjoyment of others' company—seems to be the core. What is essential to recall, however, is that liking people does not necessarily make one likable. Salesmen, those prototypic extraverts, are generally happier to see you than you are to see them.

Openness to Experience

The reinterpretation of Norman's culture as openness to experience was the focus of some of our previous articles (McCrae & Costa, 1985a, 1985b), and the replication of results in peer ratings was one of the purposes of the present article. According to adjective-factor results,

TABLE 1 80 Adjective Items from Peer Ratings

Adjectives	Adjectives
Neuroticism (N)	**Agreeableness vs. antagonism (A)**
Calm–worrying	Irritable–good natured
At ease–nervous	Ruthless–soft hearted
Relaxed–high-strung	Rude–courteous
Unemotional–emotional	Selfish–selfless
Even-tempered–temperamental	Uncooperative–helpful
Secure–insecure	Callous–sympathetic
Self-satisfied–self-pitying	Suspicious–trusting
Patient–impatient	Stingy–generous
Not envious–envious/jealous	Antagonistic–acquiescent
Comfortable–self-conscious	Critical–lenient
Not impulse ridden–impulse ridden	Vengeful–forgiving
Hardy–vulnerable	Narrow-minded–open-minded
Objective–subjective	Disagreeable–agreeable
	Stubborn–flexible
Extraversion (E)	Serious–cheerful
Retiring–sociable	Cynical–gullible
Sober–fun loving	Manipulative–straightforward
Reserved–affectionate	Proud–humble
Aloof–friendly	
Inhibited–spontaneous	**Conscientiousness vs. undirectedness (C)**
Quiet–talkative	Negligent–conscientious
Passive–active	Careless–careful
Loner–joiner	Undependable–reliable
Unfeeling–passionate	Lazy–hardworking
Cold–warm	Disorganized–well organized
Lonely–not lonely	Lax–scrupulous
Task oriented–person oriented	Weak willed–self-disciplined
Submissive–dominant	Sloppy–neat
Timid–bold	Late–punctual
	Impractical–practical
Openness (O)	Thoughtless–deliberate
Conventional–original	Aimless–ambitious
Down to earth–imaginative	Unstable–emotionally stable
Uncreative–creative	Helpless–self-reliant
Narrow interests–broad interests	Playful–businesslike
Simple–complex	Unenergetic–energetic
Uncurious–curious	Ignorant–knowledgeable
Unadventurous–daring	Quitting–persevering
Prefer routine–prefer variety	Stupid–intelligent
Conforming–independent	Unfair–fair
Unanalytical–analytical	Imperceptive–perceptive
Conservative–liberal	Uncultured–cultured
Traditional–untraditional	
Unartistic–artistic	

openness is best characterized by original, imaginative, broad interests, and daring. In the case of this dimension, however, questionnaires may be better than adjectives as a basis for interpretation and assessment. Many aspects of openness (e.g., openness to feelings) are not easily expressed in single adjectives, and the relative poverty of the English-language vocabulary of openness and closedness may have contributed to confusions about this domain (McCrae & Costa, 1985a). We know from questionnaire studies that openness can be manifest in fantasy, aesthetics, feelings, actions, ideas, and values (Costa & McCrae, 1978, 1980), but only ideas and values are well represented in the adjective factor. Interestingly, questionnaire measures of openness give higher validity coefficients than do adjective-factor measures. . . .

Perhaps the most important distinction to be made here is between openness and intelligence. Open individuals tend to be seen by themselves and others as somewhat more intelligent. . . . However, joint factor analyses using Army Alpha intelligence subtests and either adjectives (McCrae & Costa, 1985b) or NEO Inventory scales (McCrae & Costa, 1985a) show that intelligence scales define a factor clearly separate from openness. Intelligence may in some degree predispose the individual to openness, or openness may help develop intelligence, but the two seem best construed as separate dimensions of individual differences.

Agreeableness Versus Antagonism

As a broad dimension, agreeableness–antagonism is less familiar than extraversion or neuroticism, but some of its component traits, like trust (Stark, 1978) and Machiavellianism (Christie & Geis, 1970), have been widely researched. The essential nature of agreeableness–antagonism is perhaps best seen by examining the disagreeable pole, which we have labeled antagonism. . . . [A]ntagonistic people seem always to set themselves against others. Cognitively they are mistrustful and skeptical; affectively they are callous and unsympathetic; behaviorally they are uncooperative, stubborn, and rude. It would appear that their sense of attachment or bonding with their fellow human beings is defective, and in extreme cases antagonism may resemble sociopathy (cf. H. J. Eysenck & Eysenck's, 1975, psychoticism).

An insightful description of antagonism in its neurotic form is provided by Horney's account of the tendency to move against people (1945, 1950). She theorized that a struggle for mastery is the root cause of this tendency and that variations may occur, including narcissistic, perfectionistic, and arrogant vindictive types. Whereas some antagonistic persons are overtly aggressive, others may be polished manipulators. The drive for mastery and the overt or inhibited hostility of antagonistic individuals suggests a resemblance to some formulations of Type A personality (Dembroski & MacDougall, 1983), and systematic studies of the relations between agreeableness–

antagonism and measures of coronary-prone behavior should be undertaken.

Unappealing as antagonism may be, it is necessary to recognize that extreme scores on the agreeable pole may also be maladaptive. The person high in agreeableness may be dependent and fawning, and agreeableness has its neurotic manifestation in Horney's self-effacing solution of moving toward people.

Antagonism is most easily confused with dominance. Amelang and Borkenau (1982), working in German and apparently unaware of the Norman taxonomy, found a factor they called *dominance*. Among its key definers, however, were Hartnäckigkeit (*stubbornness*) and Erregbarkeit (*irritability*); scales that measure agreeableness and cooperation defined the opposite pole in their questionnaire factor. Clearly, this factor corresponds to antagonism. In self-reports (McCrae & Costa, 1985b), submissive–dominant is a weak definer of extraversion; from the peers' point of view, it is a definer of antagonism. The close etymological relationship of *dominant* and *domineering* shows the basis of the confusion.

Agreeableness–antagonism and conscientiousness–undirectedness are sometimes omitted from personality systems because they may seem too value laden. Indeed, the judgment of character is made largely along these two dimensions: Is the individual well or ill intentioned? Is he or she strong or weak in carrying out those intentions? Agreeableness–antagonism, in particular, has often been assumed to be an evaluative factor of others' perceptions rather than a veridical component of personality (e.g., A. Tellegen, personal communication, March 28, 1984).

However, the fact that a trait may be judged from a moral point of view does not mean that it is not a substantive aspect of personality. The consensual validation seen among peers and between peer-reports and self-reports demonstrates that there are some observable consistencies of behavior that underlie attributions of agreeableness and conscientiousness. They may be evaluated traits, but they are not mere evaluations.

Conscientiousness Versus Undirectedness

Conscientious may mean either governed by conscience or careful and thorough (Morris, 1976), and psychologists seem to be divided about which of these meanings best characterizes the last major dimension of personality. Amelang and Borkenau (1982) labeled their factor self-control versus impulsivity, and Conley (1985) spoke of impulse control. This terminology connotes an inhibiting agent, as Cattell (Cattell, Eber, & Tatsuoka, 1970) recognized when he named his Factor G superego strength. A conscientious person in this sense should be dutiful, scrupulous, and perhaps moralistic.

A different picture, however, is obtained by examining the adjectives that define this factor. In addition to conscientious and scrupulous, there are a number of adjectives that suggest a more proactive stance: hardworking, ambitious, energetic, persevering. Digman and Takemoto-Chock (1981) labeled this factor *will to achieve,* and it is notable that one of the items in the questionnaire measure of conscientiousness, "He strives for excellence in all he does," comes close to the classic definition of need for achievement (McClelland, Atkinson, Clark, & Lowell, 1953).

At one time, the purposefulness and adherence to plans, schedules, and requirements suggested the word *direction* as a label for this factor, and we have retained that implication in calling the opposite pole of conscientiousness *undirectedness.* In our view, the individual low in conscientiousness is not so much uncontrolled as undirected, not so much impulse ridden as simply lazy.

It seems probable that these two meanings may be related. Certainly individuals who are well organized, habitually careful, and capable of self-discipline are more likely to be able to adhere scrupulously to a moral code if they choose to—although there is no guarantee that they will be so inclined. An undirected individual may have a demanding conscience and a pervasive sense of guilt but be unable to live up to his or her own standards for lack of self-discipline and energy. In any case, it is clear that this is a dimension worthy of a good deal more empirical attention than it has yet received. Important real-life outcomes such as alcoholism (Conley & Angelides, 1984) and academic achievement (Digman & Takemoto-Chock, 1981) are among its correlates, and a further specification of the dimension is sure to be fruitful.

Some personality theorists might object that trait ratings, in whatever form and from whatever source, need not provide the best foundation for understanding individual differences. Experimental analysis of the psychophysiological basis of personality (H. J. Eysenck & Eysenck, 1984), examination of protypic acts and act frequencies (Buss & Craik, 1983), psychodynamic formulations (Horney, 1945), or behavioral genetics (Plomin, DeFries, & McClearn, 1980) provide important alternatives. But psychophysiological, behavioral, psychodynamic, and genetic explanations must eventually be related to the traits that are universally used to describe personality, and the five-factor model can provide a framework within which these relations can be systematically examined. The minor conceptual divergences noted in this article suggest the need for additional empirical work to fine-tune the model, but the broad outlines are clear in self-reports, spouse ratings, and peer ratings; in questionnaires and adjective factors; and in English and in German (Amelang & Borkenau, 1982; John, Goldberg, & Angleitner, 1984). Deeper causal analyses may seek to account for the structure of personality, but the structure that must be explained is, for now, best represented by the five-factor model.

REFERENCES

Amelang, M., & Borkenau, P. (1982). Über die faktorielle Struktur und externe Validitäteiniger Fragebogen-Skalen zur Erfassung von Dimensionen der Extraversion und emotionalen Labilität [On the factor structure and external validity of some questionnaire scales measuring dimensions of extraversion and neuroticism]. *Zeitschrift für Differentielle und Diagnostische Psychologie, 3,* 119–146.

Block J. (1977). Advancing the psychology of personality: Paradigmatic shift or improving the quality of research? In D. Magnusson & N. S. Endler (Eds.), *Personality at the crossroads: Current issues in interactional psychology* (pp. 37–63), Hillsdale, NJ: Erlbaum.

Bond, M. H., Nakazato, H., & Shiraishi, D. (1975). Universality and distinctiveness in dimensions of Japanese person perception. *Journal of Cross-Cultural Psychology, 6,* 346–357.

Buss, D. M., & Craik, K. H. (1983). The act frequency approach to personality. *Psychological Review, 90,* 105–126.

Cattell, R. B., Eber, H.W., & Tatsuoka, M. M. (1970). *The handbook for the Sixteen Personality Factor Questionnaire.* Champaign, IL: Institute for Personality and Ability Testing.

Christie, R., & Geis, R. L. (Eds.). (1970). *Studies in Machiavellianism.* New York: Academic Press.

Conley, J. J. (1985). Longitudinal stability of personality traits: A multitrait–multimethod–multioccasion analysis. *Journal of Personality and Social Psychology, 49,* 1266–1282.

Conley, J. J., & Angelides, M. (1984). *Personality antecedents of emotional disorders and alcohol abuse in men: Results of a forty-five year prospective study.* Manuscript submitted for publication.

Costa, P. T., Jr., & McCrae, R. R. (1978). Objective personality assessment. In M. Storandt, I. C. Siegler, & M. F. Elias (Eds.), *The clinical psychology of aging* (pp. 119–143). New York: Plenum Press.

Costa, P. T., Jr., & McCrae, R. R. (1980). Still stable after all these years: Personality as a key to some issues in adulthood and old age. In P. B. Baltes & O. G. Brim, Jr. (Eds.), *Life span development and behavior* (Vol. 3, pp. 65–102). New York: Academic Press.

Dembroski, T. M., & MacDougall, J. M. (1983). Behavioral and psychophysiological perspectives on coronary-prone behavior. In T. M. Dembroski, T. H. Schmidt, & G. Blumchen (Eds.), *Biobehavioral bases of coronary heart disease* (pp. 106–129). New York: Karger.

Digman, J. M., & Takemoto-Chock, N. K. (1981). Factors in the natural language of personality: Re-analysis, comparison, and interpretation of six major studies. *Multivariate Behavioral Research, 16,* 149–170.

Eysenck, H. J., & Eysenck, M. (1984). *Personality and individual differences.* London: Plenum Press.

Eysenck, H. J., & Eysenck, S. B. G. (1967). On the unitary nature of extraversion. *Acta Psychologica, 26,* 383–390.

Eysenck, H. J., & Eysenck, S. B. G. (1975). *Manual of the Eysenck Personality Questionnaire.* San Diego, CA: EdITS.

Eysenck, S. B. G., & Eysenck, H. J. (1963). On the dual nature of extraversion. *British Journal of Social and Clinical Psychology, 2,* 46–55.

Goldberg, L. R. (1981). Language and individual differences: The search for universals in personality lexicons. In L. Wheeler (Ed.), *Review of personality and social psychology* (Vol. 2, pp. 141–165). Beverly Hills, CA: Sage.

Goldberg, L. R. (1982). From ace to zombie: Some explorations in the language of personality. In C. D. Spielberger & J. N. Butcher (Eds.), *Advances in personality assessment* (Vol. 1, pp. 203–234). Hillsdale, NJ: Erlbaum.

Guilford, J. P. (1977).Will the real factor of extraversion–introversion please stand up? A reply to Eysenck. *Psychological Bulletin, 84,* 412–416.

Guilford, J. S., Zimmerman, W. S., & Guilford, J. P. (1976). *The Guilford–Zimmerman Temperament Survey handbook: Twenty-five years of research and application.* San Diego, CA: EdITS.

Hogan, R. (1983). Socioanalytic theory of personality. In M. M. Page (Ed.), *1982 Nebraska Symposium on Motivation: Personality—current theory and research* (pp. 55–89). Lincoln: University of Nebraska Press.

Horney, K. (1945). *Our inner conflicts.* New York: Norton.

Horney, K. (1950). *Neurosis and human growth.* New York: Norton.

John, O. P., Goldberg, L. R., & Angleitner, A. (1984). Better than the alphabet: Taxonomies of personality-descriptive terms in English, Dutch, and German. In H. J. C. Bonarius, G. L. M. van Heck, & N. G. Smid (Eds.), *Personality psychology in Europe: Theoretical and empirical developments.* Lisse, Switzerland: Swets & Zeitlinger.

Kenrick, D. T., & Dantchik, A. (1983). Interactionism, idiographics, and the social psychological invasion of personality. *Journal of Personality, 51,* 286–307.

Kline, P., & Barrett, P. (1983). The factors in personality questionnaires among normal subjects. *Advances in Behaviour Research and Therapy, 5,* 141–202.

Lorr, M., & Manning, T. T. (1978). Higher-order personality factors of the ISI. *Multivariate Behavioral Research, 13,* 3–7.

McClelland, D. C., Atkinson, J. W., Clark, R. A., & Lowell, E. L. (1953). *The achievement motive.* New York: Appleton-Century-Crofts.

McCrae, R. R., & Costa, P. T., Jr. (1983a). Joint factors in self-reports and ratings: Neuroticism, extraversion, and openness to experience. *Personality and Individual Differences, 4,* 245–255.

McCrae, R. R., & Costa, P. T., Jr. (1985a). Openness to experience. In R. Hogan & W. H. Jones (Eds.), *Perspectives in personality: Theory, measurement, and interpersonal dynamics* (Vol. 1). Greenwich, CT: JAI Press.

McCrae, R. R., & Costa, P. T., Jr. (1985b). Updating Norman's "adequate taxonomy": Intelligence and personality dimensions in natural language and in questionnaires. *Journal of Personality and Social Psychology, 49,* 710–721.

McCrae, R. R., & Costa, P. T., Jr. (1986). Personality, coping, and coping effectiveness in an adult sample. *Journal of Personality, 54,* 385–405.

Mischel, W. (1968). *Personality and assessment.* New York: Wiley.

Morris, W. (Ed.). (1976). *The American Heritage dictionary of the English language.* Boston: Houghton Mifflin.

Peabody, D. (1984). Personality dimensions through trait inferences. *Journal of Personality and Social Psychology, 46,* 384–403.

Plomin, R., DeFries, J. C., & McClearn, G. E. (1980). *Behavior genetics: A primer.* San Francisco: Freeman.

Revelle, W., Humphreys, M. S., Simon, L., & Gilliland, K. (1980). The interactive effect of personality, time of day, and caffeine: A test of the arousal model. *Journal of Experimental Psychology: General, 109,* 1–31.

Stark, L., (1978). Trust. In H. London & J. E. Exner, Jr. (Eds.), *Dimensions of personality* (pp. 561–599). New York: Wiley.

Teasdale, J. D., & Rachman, S. (Eds.). (1983). Cognitions and mood: Clinical aspects and applications [Special issue]. *Advances in Behaviour Research and Therapy, 5,* 1–88.

Tellegen, A. (in press). Structures of mood and personality and their relevance to assessing anxiety, with an emphasis on self-report. In A. H. Tuma & J. D. Maser (Eds.), *Anxiety and the anxiety disorders.* Hillsdale, NJ: Erlbaum.

Tupes, E. C., & Christal, R. E. (1961). Recurrent personality factors based on trait ratings. *USAF ASD Technical Report* (No. 61–97).

Vestre, N. D. (1984). Irrational beliefs and self-reported depressed mood. *Journal of Abnormal Psychology, 93,* 239–241.

Wiggins, J. S. (1979). A psychological taxonomy of trait-descriptive terms: The interpersonal domain. *Journal of Personality and Social Psychology, 37,* 395–412.

SELECTION 36

Culture and the Self: Implications for Cognition, Emotion, and Motivation

Hazel Rose Markus and Shinobu Kitayama (1991)

During the past decade, psychologists have been increasingly aware of the importance of culture in determining how people define themselves. Although much knowledge has been gained through studying people in Western cultures, such as the United States, there is a great deal that we now know differs in the personality and social behavior of individuals in Eastern cultures, such as Japan. Hazel Rose Markus and Shinobu Kitayama have begun to explore some of the differences in the concept of self in individuals from different cultures.

Markus earned her Ph.D. in social psychology from the University of Michigan in 1975. She was with the University of Michigan's Research Center for Group Dynamics unil 1994, when she accepted her current position at Stanford University. Kitayama (b. 1957) received his Ph.D. in 1987 in social psychology from the University of Michigan. Kitayama taught at the University of Oregon prior to accepting a position in 1992 at Kyoto University in Japan.

The following selection is from "Culture and the Self: Implications for Cognition, Emotion, and Motivation," which was published in *Psychological Review* in 1991. In it, the authors describe the independent and interdependent viewpoints of the self. The American concept of the self tends to emphasize the individual's uniqueness and independence from others. The Japanese concept of the self emphasizes interrelatedness and group harmony. In a part of the original article not included in this selection, the authors discuss the implications of the differences in the self on the individual's thinking, emotion, and motivation.

Key Concept: culture and the concept of the self

APA Citation: Markus, H. R., & Kitayama, S. (1991). Culture and the self: Implications for cognition, emotion, and motivation. *Psychological Review, 98,* 224–253.

*I*n America, "the squeaky wheel gets the grease." In Japan, "the nail that stands out gets pounded down." American parents who are trying to induce their children to eat their suppers are fond of saying "think of the starving kids in Ethiopia, and appreciate how lucky you are to be different from them." Japanese parents are likely to say "Think about the farmer who worked so hard to produce this rice for you; if you don't eat it, he will feel bad, for his efforts will have been in vain" (H. Yamada, February 16, 1989). A small Texas corporation seeking to elevate productivity told its employees to look in the mirror and say "I am beautiful" 100 times before coming to work each day. Employees of a Japanese supermarket that was recently opened in New Jersey were instructed to begin the day by holding hands and telling each other that "he" or "she is beautiful" ("A Japanese Supermarket," 1989).

Such anecdotes suggest that people in Japan and America may hold strikingly divergent construals of the self, others, and the interdependence of the two. The American examples stress attending to the self, the appreciation of one's difference from others, and the importance of asserting the self. The Japanese examples emphasize attending to and fitting in with others and the importance of harmonious interdependence with them. These construals of the self and others are tied to the implicit, normative tasks that various cultures hold for what people should be doing in their lives (cf. Cantor & Kihlstrom, 1987; Erikson, 1950; Veroff, 1983). . . .

Despite the growing body of psychological and anthropological evidence that people hold divergent views about the self, most of what psychologists currently know about human nature is based on one particular view—the so-called Western view of the individual as an independent, self-contained, autonomous entity who (a) comprises a unique configuration of internal attributes (e.g., traits, abilities, motives, and values) and (b) behaves primarily as a consequence of these internal attributes (Geertz, 1975; Sampson, 1988, 1989; Shweder & LeVine, 1984). As a result of this monocultural approach to the self (see Kennedy, Scheier, & Rogers, 1984), psychologists' understanding of those phenomena that are linked in one way or another to the self may be unnecessarily restricted (for some important exceptions, see Bond, 1986, 1988; Cousins, 1989; Fiske, in press; Maehr & Nicholls, 1980; Stevenson, Azuma, & Hakuta, 1986; Triandis, 1989; Triandis, Bontempo, Villareal, Asai, & Lucca, 1988). In this article, we suggest that construals of the self, of others, and of the relationship between the self and others may be even more powerful than previously suggested and that their influence is clearly reflected in differences among cultures. In particular, we compare an *independent* view of the self with one other, very different view, an *interdependent* view. The independent view is most clearly exemplified in some sizable segment of American culture, as well as in many Western European cultures. The interdependent view is exemplified in Japanese culture as well as in other Asian cultures. But it is also characteristic of African cultures, Latin-American cultures, and many southern European cultures. . . .

Universal Aspects of the Self

In exploring the possibility of different types of self-construals, we begin with Hallowell's (1955) notion that people everywhere are likely to develop an understanding of themselves as physically distinct and separable from others. Head (1920), for example, claimed the existence of a universal schema of the body that provided one with an anchor in time and space. Similarly, Allport (1937) suggested that there must exist an aspect of personality that allows one, when awakening each morning, to be sure that he or she is the same person who went to sleep the night before. Most recently, Neisser (1988) referred to this aspect of self as the *ecological self*, which he defined as "the self as perceived with respect to the physical environment: 'I' am the person here in this place, engaged in this particular activity" (p. 3). Beyond a physical or ecological sense of self, each person probably has some awareness of internal activity, such as dreams, and of the continuous flow of thoughts and feelings, which are private to the extent that they cannot be directly known by others. The awareness of this unshared experience will lead the person to some sense of an inner, private self.

Divergent Aspects of the Self

Some understanding and some representation of the private, inner aspects of the self may well be universal, but many other aspects of the self may be quite specific to particular cultures. People are capable of believing an astonishing variety of things about themselves (cf. Heelas & Lock, 1981; Marsella et al., 1985; Shweder & LeVine, 1984; Triandis, 1989). The self can be construed, framed, or conceptually represented in multiple ways. A cross-cultural survey of the self lends support to Durkheim's (1912/1968) early notion that the category of the self is primarily the product of social factors, and to Mauss's (1938/1985) claim that as a social category, the self is a "delicate" one, subject to quite substantial, if not infinite, variation.

The exact content and structure of the inner self may differ considerably by culture. Furthermore, the nature of the outer or public self that derives from one's relations with other people and social institutions may also vary markedly by culture. And, as suggested by Triandis (1989), the significance assigned to the private, inner aspects versus the public, relational aspects in regulating behavior will vary accordingly. In fact, it may not be unreasonable to suppose, as did numerous earlier anthropologists (see Allen, 1985), that in some cultures, on certain occasions, the *individual,* in the sense of a set of significant inner attributes of the person, may cease to be the primary unit of consciousness. Instead, the sense of belongingness to a social relation may become so strong that it makes better sense to think of the *relationship* as the functional unit of conscious reflection.

The current analysis focuses on just one variation in what people in different cultures can come to believe about themselves. This one variation concerns what they believe about the relationship between the self and *others* and, especially, the degree to which they see themselves as *separate* from others or as *connected* with others. We suggest that the significance and the exact functional role that the person assigns to the other when defining the self depend on the culturally shared assumptions about the separation or connectedness between the self and others.

TWO CONSTRUALS OF THE SELF: INDEPENDENT AND INTERDEPENDENT

The Independent Construal

In many Western cultures, there is a faith in the inherent separateness of distinct persons. The normative imperative of this culture is to become independent from others and to discover and express one's unique attributes (Johnson, 1985; Marsella et al., 1985; J. G. Miller, 1988;

FIGURE 1

Conceptual Representations of the Self.
(A: Independent Construal. B: Interdependent Construal.)

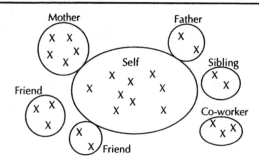

A. Independent View of Self

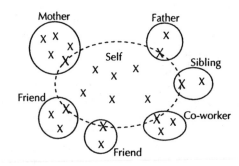

B. Interdependent View of Self

Shweder & Bourne, 1984). Achieving the cultural goal of independence requires construing oneself as an individual whose behavior is organized and made meaningful primarily by reference to one's own internal repertoire of thoughts, feelings, and action, rather than by reference to the thoughts, feelings, and actions of others. According to this construal of self, to borrow Geertz's (1975) often quoted phrase, the person is viewed as "a bounded, unique, more or less integrated motivational and cognitive universe, a dynamic center of awareness, emotion, judgment, and action organized into a distinctive whole and set contrastively both against other such wholes and against a social and natural background" (p. 48).

This view of the self derives from a belief in the wholeness and uniqueness of each person's configuration of internal attributes (Johnson, 1985; Sampson, 1985, 1988, 1989; Waterman, 1981). It gives rise to processes like "self-factualization," "realizing oneself," "expressing one's unique configuration of needs, rights, and capacities," or "developing one's distinct potential." The essential aspect of this view involves a conception of the self as an autonomous, independent person; we thus refer to it as the *independent construal of the self.* Other similar labels include *individualist, egocentric, separate, autonomous, idiocentric,* and *self-contained.* We assume that, on average, relatively more individuals in Western cultures will hold

this view than will individuals in non-Western cultures. Within a given culture, however, individuals will vary in the extent to which they are good cultural representatives and construe the self in the mandated way.

The independent self must, of course, be responsive to the social environment (Fiske, in press). This responsiveness, however, is fostered not so much for the sake of the responsiveness itself. Rather, social responsiveness often, if not always, derives from the need to strategically determine the best way to express or assert the internal attributes of the self. Others, or the social situation in general, are important, but primarily as standards of reflected appraisal, or as sources that can verify and affirm the inner core of the self.

The Western, independent view of the self is illustrated in Figure 1. The large circle represents the self, and the smaller circles represent specific others. The Xs are representations of the various aspects of the self or the others. In some cases, the larger circle and the small circle intersect, and there is an X in the intersection. This refers to a representation of the self-in-relation-to-others or to a particular social relation (e.g., "I am very polite in front of my professor"). An X within the self circle but outside of the intersection represents an aspect of the self perceived to be relatively independent of specific others and, thus, invariant over time and context. These self-representations usually have as their referent some individual desire, preference, attribute, or ability (e.g., "I am creative"). For those with independent construals of the self, it is these inner attributes that are most significant in regulating behavior and that are assumed, both by the actor and by the observer alike, to be diagnostic of the actor. Such representations of the inner self are thus the most elaborated in memory and the most accessible when thinking of the self (as indicated by Xs in Figure 1A). They can be called *core conceptions, salient identities,* or *self-schemata* (e.g., Gergen, 1968; Markus, 1977; Stryker, 1986).

The Interdependent Construal

In contrast, many non-Western cultures insist, in Kondo's (1982) terms, on the fundamental *connectedness* of human beings to each other. A normative imperative of these cultures is to maintain this interdependence among individuals (De Vos, 1985; Hsu, 1985; Miller, 1988; Shweder & Bourne, 1984). Experiencing interdependence entails seeing oneself as part of an encompassing social relationship and recognizing that one's behavior is determined, contingent on, and, to a large extent organized by what the actor perceives to be the thoughts, feelings, and actions of *others* in the relationship. The Japanese experience of the self, therefore, includes a sense of interdependence and of one's status as a participant in a larger social unit (Sampson, 1988). Within such a construal, the self becomes most meaningful and complete when it is cast in the appropriate social relationship. According to Lebra (1976) the Japanese are most fully human in the context of others.

This view of the self and the relationship between the self and others features the person not as separate from the social context but as more connected and less differentiated from others. People are motivated to find a way to fit in with relevant others, to fulfill and create obligation, and in general to become part of various interpersonal relationships. Unlike the independent self, the significant features of the self according to this construal are to be found in the interdependent and thus, in the more public components of the self. We therefore call this view the *interdependent construal of the self.* The same notion has been variously referred to, with somewhat different connotations, as *sociocentric, holistic, collective, allocentric, ensembled, constitutive, contextualist, connected,* and *relational.* As with the independent self, others are critical for social comparison and self-validation, yet in an interdependent formulation of the self, these others become an integral part of the setting, situation, or context to which the self is connected, fitted, and assimilated. The exact manner in which one achieves the task of connection, therefore, depends crucially on the nature of the context, particularly the others present in the context. Others thus participate actively and continuously in the definition of the interdependent self.

The interdependent self also possesses and expresses a set of internal attributes, such as abilities, opinions, judg-

ments, and personality characteristics. However, these internal attributes are understood as situation specific, and thus as sometimes elusive and unreliable. And, as such, they are unlikely to assume a powerful role in regulating overt behavior, especially if this behavior implicates significant others. In many domains of social life, one's opinions, abilities, and characteristics are assigned only secondary roles—they must instead be constantly controlled and regulated to come to terms with the primary task of interdependence. Such voluntary control of the inner attributes constitutes the core of the cultural ideal of becoming mature. The understanding of one's autonomy as secondary to, and constrained by, the primary task of interdependence distinguishes interdependent selves from independent selves, for whom autonomy and its expression is often afforded primary significance. An independent behavior (e.g., asserting an opinion) exhibited by a person in an interdependent culture is likely to be based on the premise of underlying interdependence and thus may have a somewhat different significance than it has for a person from an independent culture.

The interdependent self is illustrated in Figure 1B. For those with interdependent selves, the significant self-representations (the Xs) are those in relationship to specific others. Interdependent selves certainly include representations of invariant personal attributes and abilities, and these representations can become phenomenologically quite salient, but in many circumstances they are less important in regulating observable behavior and are not assumed to be particularly diagnostic of the self. Instead, the self-knowledge that guides behavior is of the self-in-relation to specific others in particular contexts. The fundamental units of the self-system, the core conceptions, or self-schemata are thus predicated on significant interpersonal relationships.

An interdependent self cannot be properly characterized as a bounded whole, for it changes structure with the nature of the particular social context. Within each particular social situation, the self can be differently instantiated. The uniqueness of such a self derives from the specific configuration of relationships that each person has developed. What is focal and objectified in an interdependent self, then, is not the inner self, but the *relationships* of the person to other actors (Hamaguchi, 1985).

The notion of an interdependent self is linked with a monistic philosophical tradition in which the person is thought to be of the same substance as the rest of nature (see Bond, 1986; Phillips, 1976; Roland, 1988; Sass, 1988). As a consequence, the relationship between the self and other, or between subject and object, is assumed to be much closer. Thus, many non-Western cultures insist on the inseparability of basic elements (Galtung, 1981), including self and other, and person and situation. In Chinese culture, for instance, there is an emphasis on synthesizing the constituent parts of any problem or situation into an integrated or harmonious whole (Moore, 1967; Northrop, 1946). Thus, persons are only parts that when separated from the larger social whole cannot be fully understood (Phillips, 1976; Shweder, 1984). Such a holistic view is in opposition to the Cartesian, dualistic tradition that characterizes Western thinking and in which the self is separated from the object and from the natural world. . . .

The role of the other in the interdependent self. In an interdependent view, in contrast to an independent view, others will be assigned much more importance, will carry more weight, and will be relatively focal in one's own behavior. There are several direct consequences of an interdependent construal of the self. First, relationships, rather than being means for realizing various individual goals, will often be ends in and of themselves. Although people everywhere must maintain some relatedness with others, an appreciation and a need for people will be more important for those with an interdependent self than for those with an independent self. Second, maintaining a connection to others will mean being constantly aware of others and focusing on their needs, desires, and goals. In some cases, the goals of others may become so focal in consciousness that the goals of others may be experienced as personal goals. In other cases, fulfilling one's own goals may be quite distinct from those of others, but meeting another's goals, needs, and desires will be a necessary requirement for satisfying one's own goals, needs, and desires. The assumption is that while promoting the goals of others, one's own goals will be attended to by the person with whom one is interdependent. Hence, people may actively work to fulfill the others' goals while passively monitoring the reciprocal contributions from these others for one's own goal-fulfillment. Yamagishi (1988), in fact, suggested that the Japanese feel extremely uncomfortable, much more so than Americans, when the opportunity for such passive monitoring of others' actions is denied.

From the standpoint of an independent, "self-ish" self, one might be led to romanticize the interdependent self, who is ever attuned to the concerns of others. Yet in many cases, responsive and cooperative actions are exercised only when there is a reasonable assurance of the "good-intentions" of others, namely their commitment to continue to engage in reciprocal interaction and mutual support. Clearly, interdependent selves do not attend to the needs, desires, and goals of *all* others. Attention to others is not indiscriminate; it is highly selective and will be most characteristic of relationships with "in-group" members. These are others with whom one shares a common fate, such as family members or members of the same lasting social group, such as the work group. Out-group members are typically treated quite differently and are unlikely to experience either the advantages or disadvantages of interdependence. Independent selves are also selective in their association with others but not to the extent of interdependent selves because much less of their behavior is directly contingent on the actions of others. Given the importance of others in constructing reality and regulating behavior, the in-group–out-group distinction is a vital one for interdependent selves, and the sub-jective boundary of one's "in-group" may tend to be narrower for the interdependent selves than for the independent selves (Triandis, 1989).

To illustrate the reciprocal nature of interaction among those with interdependent views, imagine that one has a friend over for lunch and has decided to make a sandwich for him. The conversation might be: "Hey, Tom, what do you want in your sandwich? I have turkey, salami, and cheese." Tom responds, "Oh, I like turkey." Note that the friend is given a choice because the host assumes that friend has a right, if not a duty, to make a choice reflecting his inner attributes, such as preferences or desires. And the friend makes his choice exactly because of the belief in the same assumption. This script is "natural," however, only within the independent view of self. What would happen if the friend were a visitor from Japan? A likely response to the question "Hey, Tomio, what do you want?" would be a little moment of bewilderment and then a noncommittal utterance like "I don't know." This happens because under the assumptions of an interdependent self, it is the responsibility of the host to be able to "read" the mind of the friend and offer what the host perceives to be the best for the friend. And the duty of the guest, on the other hand, is to receive the favor with grace and to be prepared to return the favor in the near future, if not right at the next moment. A likely interdependent script for the same situation would be: "Hey, Tomio, I made you a turkey sandwich because I remember that last week you said you like turkey more than beef." And Tomio will respond, "Oh, thank you, I really like turkey."

The reciprocal interdependence with others that is the sign of the interdependent self seems to require constant engagement of what Mead (1934) meant by taking the role of the other. It involves the willingness and ability to feel and think what others are feeling and thinking, to absorb this information without being told, and then to help others satisfy their wishes and realize their goals. Maintaining connection requires inhibiting the "I" perspective and processing instead from the "thou" perspective (Hsu, 1981). The requirement is to "read" the other's mind and thus to know what the other is thinking or feeling. In contrast, with an independent self, it is the individual's responsibility to "say what's on one's mind" if one expects to be attended to or understood.

REFERENCES

Allen, N. J. (1985). The category of the person: A reading of Mauss's last essay. In M. Carrithers, S. Collins, & S. Lukes (Eds.), *The category of the person: Anthropology, philosophy, history* (pp. 26–35). Cambridge, England: Cambridge University Press.

Allport, G. W. (1937). *Personality: A psychological interpretation.* New York: Holt.

Bond, M. H. (1986). *The psychology of the Chinese people.* New York: Oxford University Press.

Bond, M. H. (Eds.), (1988). *The cross-cultural challenge to social psychology.* Beverly Hills, CA: Sage.

Cantor, N., & Kihlstrom, J. (1987). *Personality and social intelligence.* Englewood Cliffs, NJ: Prentice-Hall.

Cousins, S. (1989). Culture and selfhood in Japan and the U.S. *Journal of Personality and Social Psychology, 56,* 124–131.

De Vos, G. (1985). Dimensions of the self in Japanese culture. In A. Marsella, G. De Vos, & F. L. K. Hsu (Eds.), *Culture and self* (pp. 149–184). London: Tavistock.

Durkheim, E. (1968). *Les formes elementaires de la vie religieuse* [Basic forms of religious belief] (6th ed.). Paris: Presses Universitarires de France. (Original work published 1912)

Erikson, E. (1950). Identification as the basis for a theory of motivation. *American Psychological Review, 26,* 14–21.

Fiske, A. P. (in press). *Making up society: The four elementary relational structures.* New York: Free Press.

Galtung, J. (1981). Structure, culture, and intellectual style: An essay comparing Saxonic, Teutonic, Gallic and Nipponic approaches. *Social Science Information, 20,* 817–856.

Geertz, C. (1975). On the nature of anthropological understanding. *American Scientist, 63,* 47–53.

Gergen, K. J. (1968). Personal consistency and the presentation of self. In C. Gordon & K. J. Gergen (Eds.), *The self in social interaction: Classic and contemporary perspectives* (Vol. 1, pp. 299–308). New York: Wiley.

Hallowell, A. I. (1955). *Culture and experience.* Philadelphia: University of Pennsylvania Press.

Hamaguchi, E. (1985). A contextual model of the Japanese: Toward a methodological innovation in Japan studies. *Journal of Japanese Studies, 11,* 289–321.

Head, H. (1920). *Studies in neurology.* London: Oxford University Press.

Heelas, P. L. F., & Lock, A. J. (Eds.). (1981). *Indigenous psychologies: The anthropology of the self.* London: Academic Press.

Hsu, F. L. K. (1981). *American and Chinese: Passage to differences.* Honolulu: University of Hawaii Press.

Hsu, F. L. K. (1985). The self in cross-cultural perspective. In A. J. Marsella, G. De Vos, & F. L. K. Hsu (Eds.), *Culture and self* (pp. 24–55). London: Tavistock.

Johnson, F. (1985). The Western concept of self. In A. Marsella, G. De Vos, & F. L. K. Hsu (Eds.), *Culture and self.* London: Tavistock.

Kennedy, S., Scheier, J., & Rogers, A. (1984). The price of success: Our monocultural science. *American Psychologist, 39,* 996–997.

Kondo, D. (1982). *Work, family and the self: A cultural analysis of Japanese family enterprise.* Unpublished doctoral dissertation, Harvard University.

Lebra, T. S. (1976). *Japanese patterns of behavior.* Honolulu: University of Hawaii Press.

Maehr, M., & Nicholls, J. (1980). Culture and achievement motivation: A second look. In N. Warren (Ed.), *Studies in cross-cultural psychology* (Vol. 2, pp. 221–267). New York: Academic Press.

Markus, H. (1977). Self-schemas and processing information about the self. *Journal of Personality and Social Psychology, 35,* 63–78.

Marsella, A., De Vos, G., & Hsu, F. L. K. (Eds.). (1985). *Culture and self.* London: Tavistock.

Mauss, M. (1985). A category of the human mind: The notion of person; the notion of self (W. D. Halls, Trans.). In M. Carrithers, S. Collins, & S. Lukes (Eds.), *The category of the person: Anthropology, philosophy, history* (pp. 1–25). Cambridge, England: Cambridge University Press. (Original work published 1938)

Mead, G. H. (1934). *Mind, self and society.* Chicago: University of Chicago Press.

Miller, J. G. (1988). Bridging the content-structure dichotomy: Culture and the self. In M. H. Bond (Ed.), *The cross-cultural challenge to social psychology* (pp. 266–281). Beverly Hills, CA: Sage.

Moore, C. A. (Ed.). (1967). Introduction: The humanistic Chinese mind. In *The Chinese mind: Essentials of Chinese philosophy and culture* (pp. 1–10). Honolulu: University of Hawaii Press.

Neisser, U. (1988). Five kinds of self-knowledge. *Philosophical Psychology, 1,* 35–59.

Northrop, F. S. C. (1946). *The meeting of East and West.* New York: Macmillan.

Phillips, D. C. (1976). *Holistic thought in social science.* Stanford, CA: Stanford University Press.

Roland, A. (1988). *In search of self in India and Japan: Toward a cross-cultural psychology.* Princeton, NJ: Princeton University Press.

Sampson, E. E. (1985). The decentralization of identity: Toward a revised concept of personal and social order. *American Psychologist, 40,* 1203–1211.

Sampson, E. E. (1988). The debate on individualism: Indigenous psychologies of the individual and their role in personal and societal functioning. *American Psychologist, 43,* 15–22.

Sampson, E. E. (1989). The challenge of social change for psychology: Globalization and psychology's theory of the person. *American Psychologist, 44,* 914–921.

Sass, L. A. (1988). The self and its vicissitudes: An "archaeological" study of the psychoanalytic avant-garde. *Social Research, 55,* 551–607.

Shweder, R. A. (1984). Preview: A colloquy of culture theorists. In R. A. Shweder & R. A. LeVine (Eds.), *Culture theory: Essays on mind, self, and emotion* (pp. 1–24). Cambridge, England: Cambridge University Press.

Shweder, R. A., & Bourne, E. J. (1984). Does the concept of the person vary cross-culturally? In R. A. Shweder & R. A. LeVine (Eds.), *Culture theory: Essays on mind, self, and emotion* (pp. 158–199). Cambridge, England: Cambridge University Press.

Shweder, R. A., & LeVine, R. A. (Eds.). (1984). *Culture theory: Essays on mind, self, and emotion.* Cambridge, England: Cambridge University Press.

Stevenson, H., Azuma, H., & Hakuta, K. (1986). *Child development and education in Japan.* New York: Freeman.

Stryker, S. (1986). Identity theory: Developments and extensions. In K. Yardley & T. Honess (Eds.), *Self and identity* (pp. 89–104). New York: Wiley.

Triandis, H. C. (1989). The self and social behavior in differing cultural contexts. *Psychological Review, 96,* 506–520.

Triandis, H. C., Bontempo, R., Villareal, MJ., Asai, M., & Lucca, N. (1988). Individualism and collectivism: Cross-cultural perspectives on self-ingroup relationships. *Journal of Personality and Social Psychology, 54,* 323–338.

Veroff, J. (1983). Contextual determinants of personality. *Personality and Social Psychology Bulletin, 9,* 331–344.

Waterman, A. S. (1981). Individualism and interdependence. *American Psychologist, 36,* 762–773.

Yamagishi, T. (1988). Exit from the group as an individualistic solution to the free-rider problem in the United States and Japan. *Journal of Experimental Social Psychology, 24,* 530–542.

Stress and Adjustment

Selection 37
HANS SELYE, from "The Evolution of the Stress Concept," American Scientist

Selection 38
RICHARD S. LAZARUS, from "Puzzles in the Study of Daily Hassles," Journal of Behavioral Medicine

The Evolution of the Stress Concept

Hans Selye (1973)

Only in the past couple of decades have psychologists become convinced that psychological as well as physiological variables can produce stress. However, as far back as the 1930s, Canadian physiologist Hans Selye was studying stress through the general adaptation syndrome (GAS). The general adaptation syndrome, first identified by Selye, is a consistent series of bodily reactions to stress that can be divided into three stages: the alarm reaction stage, the stage of resistance, and the stage of exhaustion. The GAS serves as a model for investigating the long-term effects of stress on the body.

Selye (1907–1982) received his D.Sc. from McGill University in 1942 and later earned a Ph.D. and an M.D. He spent most of his professional career at the Institute of Experimental Medicine and Surgery at the University of Montreal. As an endocrinologist, he dedicated his life to understanding the hormonal reactions in the stress syndrome. Selye wrote over 30 books on stress, including *The Stress of Life* (1956) and Stress without Distress (1974).

This selection is from "The Evolution of the Stress Concept," which was published in American Scientist in 1973. In it, Selye provides the history behind his famous general adaptation syndrome model of stress. Note how Selye's discoveries occurred in steps as he encountered different situations.

As you read this selection, consider the definition of stress and how you measure the effects of stress in your life.

Key Concept: stress and the general adaptation syndrome

APA Citation: Selye, H. (1973). The evolution of the stress concept. *American Scientist, 61,* 692–699.

$\mathcal{E}$verybody knows what stress is and nobody knows what it is. The word *stress*, like *success, failure,* or *happiness,* means different things to different people and, except for a few specialized scientists, no one has really tried to define it although it has become part of our daily vocabulary. . . .

Yet, how are we to cope with the stress of life if we cannot even define it? The businessman who is under constant pressure from his clients and employees alike, the air traffic controller who knows that a moment of distraction may mean death to hundreds of people, the athlete who desperately wants to win a race, and the husband who helplessly watches his wife slowly and painfully die of cancer—all suffer from stress. The problems they face are totally different, but medical research has shown that in many respects their bodies respond in a stereotyped manner with identical biochemical changes, meant fundamentally to cope with any type of increased demand upon the human machinery. The stress-producing factors—technically called *stressors*—are different, and yet they all produce essentially the same biologic stress response. This distinction between stressor and stress was perhaps the first important step in the scientific analysis of that most common biologic phenomenon that we all know only too well from personal experience.

But if we want to use what the laboratory has taught us about stress in formulating our own philosophy of life, if we want to avoid its bad effects and yet be able to enjoy the pleasures of accomplishment, we have to learn more about the nature and mechanism of stress. To succeed in this, we must concentrate on the fundamental technical data which the laboratory has given us as a basis for a scientific philosophy of conduct. Examination of the data seems to be the only way of finding purpose in life without having to fall back upon traditional beliefs whose acceptance depends primarily on indoctrination (1).

WHAT IS STRESS?

Stress is the nonspecific response of the body to any demand made upon it. In order to understand this definition we must first comprehend what is meant by "nonspecific." Each demand made upon our body is in a sense unique, that is, specific. When exposed to cold we shiver to produce more heat, and the blood vessels in our skin contract to diminish loss of heat from the body surface. When exposed to heat we sweat, because evaporation of perspiration from the surface of our skin has a cooling effect. When we eat so much sugar that the blood-sugar level rises above normal, we excrete some of it and try to activate chemical reactions which will enable us to store or burn up the rest so that the blood sugar may return to normal. A great muscular effort, such as running up many flights of stairs at full speed, makes increased demands upon our musculature and cardiovascular system: the muscles will need more energy to perform this unusual work; hence, the heart will beat more rapidly and strongly, and the blood pressure will rise to accelerate delivery of blood to the musculature.

Each drug and hormone has such specific actions: diuretics increase urine production; adrenalin augments the pulse rate and blood pressure, simultaneously increasing blood sugar, whereas insulin decreases blood sugar. Yet, no matter what kind of derangement is produced, all these agents have one thing in common: they also make an increased demand upon the body to readjust itself. This demand is nonspecific; it requires adaptation to a problem, regardless of what that problem may be. That is to say, in addition to their specific actions, all agents to which we are exposed produce a nonspecific increase in the need to perform certain adaptive functions and then to reestablish normalcy, which is independent of the specific activity that caused the rise in requirements. This nonspecific demand for activity as such is the essence of stress.

From the point of view of its stress-producing, or stressor, activity, it is even immaterial whether the agent or situation we face is pleasant or unpleasant; all that counts is the intensity of the demand for readjustment or adaptation. The mother who is suddenly told that her only son died in battle suffers a terrible mental shock; if years later it turns out that the news was false, and the son unexpectedly walks into her room alive and well, she experiences extreme joy. The *specific* results of the two events, sorrow and joy, are completely different, in fact, opposite to each other; yet their stressor effect—the *nonspecific* demand to readjust to an entirely new situation—may be the same.

It is difficult to see how such essentially different things as cold, heat, drugs, hormones, sorrow, and joy could provoke an identical biochemical reaction in the organism. Yet this is the case; it can now be demonstrated by highly objective quantitative biochemical determinations that certain reactions of the body are totally nonspecific and common to all types of exposure....

WHAT STRESS IS NOT

Since the term stress has been used quite loosely, many confusing and often contradictory definitions have been formulated; hence, it will be useful to add a few remarks stating clearly what it is *not*. Stress is not simply nervous tension; stress reactions do occur in lower animals, which have no nervous system, and even in plants. Stress is not the nonspecific result of damage. We have seen that it is immaterial whether an agent is pleasant or unpleasant; its stressor effect depends merely on the intensity of the demand made upon the adaptive work of the body. As I have explained elsewhere (2), "normal activities—a game of tennis or even a passionate kiss—can produce considerable stress without causing conspicuous damage."

Stress is not something to be avoided. In fact, it is evident from the definition given earlier that it cannot be avoided; no matter what you do or what happens to you, there arises a demand to provide the necessary energy to perform the tasks required to maintain life and to resist and adapt to the changing external influences. Even while fully relaxed and asleep, you are under some stress: your heart must continue to pump blood, your intestines to digest last night's dinner, your muscles to move your chest to permit respiration; even your brain is not at complete rest while you are dreaming.

Complete freedom from stress is death. Contrary to public opinion, we must not—and indeed cannot—avoid stress, but we can meet it efficiently and enjoy it by learning more about its mechanism and adjusting our philosophy of life accordingly (1).

HISTORIC DEVELOPMENT

The concept of stress is very old; it must have occurred even to prehistoric man that the loss of vigor and feeling of exhaustion that overcame him after hard labor, prolonged exposure to cold or heat, loss of blood, agonizing fear, or any kind of disease had something in common. He may not have been consciously aware of this similarity in his response to anything that was just too much for him, but when the feeling came he must have realized that he had exceeded the limits of what he could reasonably handle, in other words that "he had had it."

Man soon must have discovered also that whenever faced with a prolonged and unaccustomed strenuous task—be it swimming in cold water, lifting rocks, or going without food—he passes through three stages: at first the experience is a hardship, then one gets used to it, and finally one cannot stand it any longer. . . .

How could different agents produce the same result? Is there a nonspecific adaptive reaction to change as such? In 1926, as a second-year medical student, I first came across this problem of a stereotyped response to any exacting task. I began to wonder why patients suffering from the most diverse diseases have so many signs and symptoms in common. Whether a man suffers from severe loss of blood, an infectious disease, or advanced cancer, he loses his appetite, his muscular strength, and his ambition to accomplish anything; usually the patient also loses weight, and even his facial expression betrays that he is ill. What is the scientific basis of what I thought of at the time as the "syndrome of just being sick"? Could the mechanism of this syndrome be analyzed by modern scientific techniques? Could it be reduced to its elements and expressed in the precise terms of biochemistry, biophysics, and morphology? Could this reaction be subject to scientific analysis?

It was not until 1936 that the problem presented itself again, now under conditions more suited to analysis. At that time, I was working in the biochemistry department of McGill University, trying to find a new hormone in extracts of cattle ovaries. I injected the extracts into rats to see if their organs would show unpredictable changes that could not be attributed to any known hormone. Much to my satisfaction, the first and most impure extracts changed the rats in three ways: (1) the adrenal cortex became enlarged, (2) the thymus, spleen, lymph nodes, and all other lymphatic structures shrank, and (3) deep, bleeding ulcers appeared in the stomach and in the upper gut. Because the three types of change were closely interdependent they formed a definite syndrome. The changes varied from slight to pronounced, depending on the amount of extract I injected.

At first, I ascribed all these changes to a new sex hormone in the extract. But soon I found that all toxic substances—extracts of kidney, spleen, or even a toxin not derived from living tissue—produced the same syndrome. Gradually, my classroom concept of the "syndrome of just being sick" came back to me. I realized that the reaction I had produced with my impure extracts and toxic drugs was an experimental replica of this syndrome. Adrenal enlargement, gastrointestinal ulcers, and thymicolymphatic shrinkage were the omnipresent signs of damage to the body when under disease attack. The three changes thus became the objective indexes of stress and the basis for the development of the entire stress concept.

The reaction was first described in *Nature* (4 July 1936) as "A Syndrome Produced by Various Nocuous Agents" and, subsequently, it became known as the General Adaptation Syndrome (GAS) or biologic stress syndrome. In the same paper I also suggested the name *alarm reaction* for the initial response, arguing that it probably represents the somatic expression of a generalized "call to arms" of the body's defensive forces.

THE GENERAL ADAPTATION SYNDROME

The alarm reaction, however, was evidently not the entire response. Upon continued exposure to any noxious agent capable of eliciting this reaction, a stage of adaptation or resistance ensues. In other words, no organism can be maintained continuously in a state of alarm. If the agent is so drastic that continued exposure becomes incompatible with life, the animal dies during the alarm reaction within the first hours or days. If it can survive, this initial reaction is necessarily followed by the "stage of resistance." The manifestations of this second phase are quite different from—in many instances, the exact opposite of—those which characterize the alarm reaction. For example, during the alarm reaction, the cells of the adrenal cortex discharge their secretory granules into the bloodstream and thus become depleted of corticoid-containing lipid storage material; in the stage of resistance, on the other hand, the cortex becomes particularly rich in secretory granules. Whereas in the alarm reaction, there is hemoconcentration, hypochloremia, and general tissue catabolism, during the stage of resistance, there is hemodilution, hyperchloremia, and anabolism, with a return toward normal body weight.

Curiously, after still more exposure to the noxious agent, the acquired adaptation is lost again. The animal enters into a third phase, the "stage of exhaustion," which inexorably follows as long as the stressor is severe enough and applied for a sufficient length of time. Because of its great practical importance, it should be pointed out that the triphasic nature of the GAS gave us the first indication that the body's adaptability, or "adaptation energy," is finite since, under constant stress, exhaustion eventually ensues. We still do not know precisely what is lost, except that it is not merely caloric energy, since food intake is normal during the stage of resistance. Hence, one would think that once adaptation has occurred and ample energy is available, resistance should go on indefinitely. But just as any inanimate machine gradually wears out, so does the human machine sooner or later become the victim of constant wear and tear.

REFERENCES

1. H. Selye. In preparation. *Stress without Distress*. New York, Philadelphia: Lippincott.
2. H. Selye. 1956. *The Stress of Life*. New York: McGraw-Hill.

Puzzles in the Study of Daily Hassles

Richard S. Lazarus (1984)

There is no doubt that stress is harmful to mental and physical health. It has only been the past few decades that scientists have discovered how stress impacts on the body. The common belief that major life change events cause the most severe stress was challenged by Richard S. Lazarus, who emphasized the concept of daily hassles. Lazarus has demonstrated how the little hassles we all experience in everyday life can have major effects on our ability to successfully adjust.

Lazarus (1922–2002) earned his Ph.D. in experimental psychology from the University of Pittsburgh in 1948. He taught at Johns Hopkins University and Clark University before going to the University of California at Berkeley in 1959, where he remained until his death in 2002. Much of his professional career focused on emotions and stress, as evidenced by his book *Emotion and Adaptation* (Oxford University Press, 1991).

In this selection, from "Puzzles in the Study of Daily Hassles," which was published in *Journal of Behavioral Medicine* in 1984, Lazarus describes hassles as the irritating or frustrating little incidents that happen every day, like spilling a drink, losing your car keys, having an argument, or being caught in a long line. He states that these hassles are appraised by people as being harmful or threatening to their well-being. As you read this selection, note that he also discusses the pleasant daily uplifts that can occur. How do you generally respond to hassles in your life?

Key Concept: hassles and stress

APA Citation: Lazarus, R. S. (1984). Puzzles in the study of daily hassles. *Journal of Behavioral Medicine, 7,* 375-389.

Introduction

Theory and research in psychological stress have shifted from an earlier perspective of environmental inputs or outputs to a relational one. Stress is now treated as harms, threats, and challenges, the quality and intensity of which depend on personal agendas, resources and vulnerabilities of the person, and environmental conditions. This implies a knowing person who construes or appraises the significance of what is happening for his or her well-being. Such a "paradigm shift" requires a different approach to stress measurement, one that takes into account the cognitive activity evaluating the personal significance of transactions and examines the multiple specific variables of person and environment that influence the appraisal process. The need for a different approach to stress measurement has generated research by the Berkeley Stress and Coping Project on what we have called daily hassles and uplifts. . . .

What are Hassles and Uplifts?

When the members of the Berkeley Stress and Coping Project constructed the Hassles Scale for a field study be-

gun in 1977, we had not thought through all of the implications of format and wording. Our aim had been to cover the broad ground of relatively minor psychological difficulties of living as sensed by the person rather than to create pure and objective stimulus and response categories. Mixed together are references, implicit or explicit, to environmental inputs, appraisals, and emotional reactions, all brought within the same scale and usually within the same item. Therefore, the scale includes a mixture of items depicting (1) *environmental events* such as "an inconsiderate smoker" and "unexpected company," (2) disappointing or worrisome *chronic environmental conditions* such as "rising prices of common goods" and "neighborhood deterioration, " (3) *ongoing worries or concerns* such as "troubling thoughts about your future" and "job dissatisfactions, " and (4) *distressed emotional reactions* such as "being lonely" and "fear of rejection."

How should daily hassles and uplifts be defined? *Our approach, is that daily* hassles are *experiences and conditions of daily living that have been appraised as salient and harmful or threatening to the endorser's well-being.* This is a definition that emphasizes the individual psychological or subjectively experienced situation in the Lewinian sense and treats hassles as proximal phenomena rather than distal (cf. Jessor, 1981). Even when hassles reflect actual, objectively harmful or threatening events that have occurred, their meanings to the individual lead them to be remembered (because they are salient) and viewed as distressing. As we have argued alsewhere, what makes them harmful or threatening is that they involve demands that tax or exceed the person's resources. Daily uplifts, in contrast, consist of *experiences and conditions of daily living that have been appraised as salient and positive or favorable to the endorser's well-being.* For this reason they give people a lift, so to speak, and make them feel good—a good night's rest, making a friend, receiving a compliment, and so on.

Occurrences that to some are hassles can be experienced as uplifts by others, and vice versa. Thus, writing a paper can be a distressing chore to some and an exhilarating experience to others. Assessing uplifts as well as hassles seemed to us to offer a fuller picture of the affective bases of daily living, both positive and negative, than was possible by studying hassles alone. Our findings thus far with uplifts, however, have seemed less fruitful than those with hassles, and I emphasize the latter more in this presentation.

Hassles, Uplifts, and Health

The feature of our research that has gained the most attention is the relationships we have demonstrated between hassles and uplifts and health-related variables such as morale, psychological symptoms, and somatic health. We found that hassles frequency and intensity, averaged for 9 months of separate assessment on the same people, were capable of explaining psychological and somatic health better than life events could, the bivariate relationship to health being quite robust. Hassles and life events were only modestly correlated, and hassles scores added their own unique variance to the relationship, whereas life-events scores did not. Thus, some of the explained health variance reflected the overlap between life events and hassles, which we interpreted as evidence that life events alter the day-to-day routines of living and hence its daily hassles; however, many hassles were independent of life events, deriving alternatively from the individual's usual ways of living. It seemed to us that we had found a way to measure stress that supplemented life events measures importantly and was, besides, a more effective predictor of health outcomes.

Given the self-report nature of both hassles and health measurement, there is always the possibility that the obtained relationships are artifactual. This is of greater concern with psychological symptoms and morale, the outcome variables of the study by Kanner *et al.* (1981), than with somatic health, the outcome variable of the study by DeLongis *et al* (1982). It is noteworthy, too, that our basic claim about the relationships between hassles and psychological symptoms has already been supported in independent research conducted elsewhere (cf. Monroe, 1983); however, in that study, too, there is some danger of tautology between and antecedent and the outcome measures, though I do not think that this is the whole story. The methodological problems inherent in this research are substantial, and a degree of wariness is appropriate.

It is tempting to argue that hassles, as a subjective measure of daily stress, explain health variance because stress impairs health, an assumption that also has fueled extensive research with life events. We presented our original findings with this assumption in mind, though with the usual disclaimers that the obtained correlations—cross sectional rather than longitudinal—are subject to uncertainty about causal implication. In this regard, we had found hassles frequency scores quite stable over 9 months, and our strategy of analysis made them even more stable for purposes of explaining health by aggregating 9 months of hassles frequency scores for each subject (cf. Epstein, 1984). Because health status, too, was quite stable over the nearly 1 year of its assessment, we had not shown, therefore, that ups and downs in hassles covaried with ups and downs in health status within individuals, but only that people with overall high hassles scores had a poorer health status than people with overall low hassles scores. To demonstrate the functional significance of this relationship, it would also be important to show that ups and downs in hassles or uplifts are associated with ups and downs in health within the same persons (cf. Lazarus, 1978).

Some of our current research efforts are designed to examine the above possibility about within-individual covariation between daily stress and health. However, it is quite likely that some kinds of health outcomes are neither very variable nor responsive to stress, whereas others are both. Thus, although blood pressure in nonhypertensives may well bounce up and down with stress-related encounters and their cessation, in well-consolidated hypertensives blood pressure probably is consistently high regardless of circumstances, presumably because of irreversible somatic changes in kidney function that are part of the disorder (Kaplan, 1979). Similarly, disorders such as arthritis, atherosclerosis, Alzheimer's disease, etc., are probably not particularly subject to variation from day to day or week to week. On the other hand, many of the classic so-called psychosomatic disorders such as ulcers, intestinal colitis, allergy, asthma, etc., could be extremely subject to change with stress. And still others, such as bacterial and viral infections, which depend on variations in immune functioning, might also show a strong relationship with stress (e.g., Meyer and Haggerty, 1962), since there is substantial evidence of stress-related effects on immune competency (Ader, 1981). This means that to test the intraindividual covariation between stress and health requires that the global variable of health status be differentiated into the many states and conditions that comprise it, distinguishing thereby those subject to stress effect from those not (cf. Luborsky *et al.*, 1973). . . .

What are some of the promising candidates among the factors contributing to individual differences in the hassles and uplifts that people experience or that are salient enough for them to note and remember? The theory of primary and secondary cognitive appraisal processes in stress and emotion directs us toward some of the obvious possibilities.

Primary appraisal concerns mainly the discrimination between transactions in which there is some personal investment and those that are irrelevant for the person's well-being. The core psychological issue involved in such appraisal is whether there is something *at stake* in an encounter and whether this stake is considered to be in jeopardy. A traffic jam will be far more distressing when a person must get to an important appointment and there is just enough time than when there is plenty of time or when nothing important will be lost by a delay. If the sense of time urgency is high, for whatever reason, and if being late will endanger an important goal or violate strong internal standards, the person can be said to be vulnerable to stress and distress with respect to being on time. The quality and strength of the emotional reaction to even so common and relatively insignificant an event can inform us, after the fact, about *patterns of commitment* or about idiosyncratic personality characteristics that make the person especially vulnerable. Before the fact, person characteristics may permit prediction of threat appraisals in some people in contexts in which others might not be threatened.

Secondary appraisal concerns *resources and options for coping* with stressful demands and constraints. When the person faces stressful demands, negative beliefs about resources for coping effectively will enhance threat appraisals, and positive beliefs about such resources will dampen them. For some persons, the traffic jam mobilizes efforts—sometimes frantic—to locate alternative routes if they are available, which when successful eliminate the threat. Although any thought or act can serve multiple coping functions, we have spoken of the latter process as *problem-focused coping* (Folkman and Lazarus, 1980; Lazarus and Folkman, 1984). This sort of coping can also be anticipatory, as in the case of arranging to leave extra time in case a traffic jam or some other impediment materializes on the way to an important appointment.

Even when nothing can be done to alter the realities of the situation, *emotion-focused coping* can also dampen or short-circuit threat. For example, thinking that one can successfully counter the bad impression of being late, realizing that there are later airplane flights, or otherwise depreciating the significance of being late can neutralize or markedly reduce the stress and distress that would otherwise be entailed. Avoidance of thinking about the distressing possibilities can also help to regulate the emotions that might be generated. The above examples illustrate the role of secondary appraisal and emotion-focused coping as determinants of the experience of hassles. They are also relevant to uplifts because emotion-focused cop-

ing can result in thinking positively about bad experiences. In consequence of these cognitive coping processes, the person may not even think of the experience as stressful or will give a much reduced estimate of their severity when later asked about hassles. Therefore, what will be endorsed as a hassle or uplift by one person will not be by another.

Notice what has been done here analytically. I started with hassles as *antecedents* of appraisal and coping but noted the inadequacies of this stimulus-centered perspective. This led me to view hassles—and uplifts—as *consequences* of appraisal, and these processes are in turn dependent on personal agendas, resources for coping, and coping thoughts and acts. Thus, the causal question has been turned around so that the processes that underlie individual patterns of hassles and uplifts come into focus as the central issue. Such patterns can inform us not only about what is important to the person and hence threatening or challenging, but also about the arenas of human activity in which any given individual or group is vulnerable to stress. A transactional formulation in which all processes are interdependent, each capable of affecting the other in the ordinary flow of experience, can help turn attention toward hassles and uplifts patterns as diagnostic of individual strengths, liabilities, and hence vulnerabilities.

Consider, for example, the person who experiences frequent hassles in dealing with others, as in handling encounters with a supervisor at work. A stimulus or environmental formulation of such stress would implicate only the behavior of the other person. The other person could be hostile, demanding, and assaultive and might provoke nearly anyone, including the person in question. The same facts of stress could be explained, on the other hand, by tendencies in this person to overreact to hostility or even to imagine assaults; one might draw on hypotheses about sibling rivalries, an overcritical parent, or perhaps a rigid, compulsive style of defending, as sources of vulnerability. Both viewpoints are, in a sense, productive but incomplete. A transactionalist would assume that usually two sets of antecedent variables—one environmental, the other within the person—are operating.

One clue about such vulnerabilities in any given individual is the *quality and intensity of the emotion* generated. A second is the *recurrent or chronic nature of the hassle.* If we study the person's hassles over time we may find, for example, that the same type of hassles keep recurring, a sign either that the environment is fairly constant as a source of stressful demands and/or that the person is bringing to this environment special vulnerabilities. The two possibilities, of environmental or person causation, can probably never be fully disentangled. Still, recurrent hassles should be good candidates for special study to evaluate to what extent the problem lies in the person, to what extent in the environment, and in what respects. Only an in-depth examination of the pattern and experience of hassles can provide insight into the provocations, personal agendas, appraisal characteristics, and coping patterns contributing to recurrent hassles. . . .

References

Ader, R. (1981). *Psychoneuroimmunology*, Academic Press, New York.

DeLongis, A., and Lazarus, R. S. (1982). Hassles, uplifts and health in aging adults: A paradox examined. Paper presented at meetings of American Psychological Association, Washington, D.C.

Epstein, S. (1984). Aggregation and beyond: some basic issues on the prediction of behavior. *J. Personal.* (in press).

Folkman, S., & Lazarus, R. S. (1980). An analysis of coping in a middle-aged community sample. *Journal of Health and Social Behavior, 21*, 219–239.

Jessor, R. (1981). The perceived environment in psychological theory and research. In Magnusson, D. (ed.), *Toward a Psychology of Situations: An Interactional Perspective*, Erlbaum, Hillsdale, N.J., pp. 297–317.

Kanner, A. D., Coyne, J. C., Schaefer, C., and Lazarus, R. S. (1981). Comparison of two modes of stress measurement: Daily hassles and uplifts versus major life events. *J. Behav. Med.* 4: 1–39.

Kaplan, N. M. (1979). The Goldblatt Memorial Lecture. The role of the kidney in hypertension. *Hypertension* 1: 456–461.

Lazarus, R. S. (1978). A strategy for research on psychological and social factors in hypertension. *J. Hum. Stress* 4: 35–40.

Lazarus, R. S., and Folkman, S. (1984). Coping and adaptation. In Gentry, W. D. (ed.), *The Handbook of Behavioral Medicine*, Guilford, New York, pp. 282–325.

Luborsky, L., Doeherty, J. P., and Penick, S. (1973). Onset conditions for psychosomatic symptoms: A comparative review of immediate observation with retrospective research. *Psychosom. Med.* 35: 187–204.

Meyer, R. J., and Haggerty, R. J. (1962). Streptococcal infections in families. *Pediatrics* April: 539–549.

Monroe, S. M. (1983). Major and minor life events as predictors of psychological distress: Further issues and findings. *J. Behav. Med.* 6: 189–205.

Abnormal Behavior

On Being Sane in Insane Places

David L. Rosenhan (1973)

Mental health workers have devised various classification schemes to help them diagnose abnormal behaviors. Although this may be beneficial in the vast majority of cases, some psychologists worry that misdiagnosis can result in inappropriate treatments or stigmatization and that mental health workers therefore need to be extremely careful about labeling mental patients. David L. Rosenhan is a leading critic of the method in which patients are labeled in mental hospitals.

Rosenhan (b. 1929) earned his Ph.D. from Columbia University in 1958. He is currently a professor emeritus of psychology at Stanford University. Among his books is Abnormal Psychology, coauthored with Martin Seligman (W. W. Norton, 1995).

This selection is from "On being sane in insane places," which was published in *Science* in 1973. In it, Rosenhan describes his and others' experiences as pseudopatients (healthy people who secretly gained admission to mental hospitals as patients), and he discusses the implications of labeling mental patients as insane or as mentally ill. Rosenhan's article encouraged debate among mental health providers on diagnosis in clinical psychology that is still going on today. A readable article, it provides a good inside look at mental institutions as well as the labeling process. Although Rosenhan's research successfully persuaded psychologists to discuss the problems that come with diagnosing mental patients, some people have criticized the study as unethical. As you read this selection, consider what it must be like for mental patients to live in an institution.

Key Concept: labeling and the diagnosis of abnormal behavior

APA Citation: Rosenhan, D. L. (1973). On being sane in insane places. *Science, 179,* 250–258.

*I*f sanity and insanity exist, how shall we know them?

The question is neither capricious nor itself insane. However much we may be personally convinced that we can tell the normal from the abnormal, the evidence is simply not compelling. It is commonplace, for example, to read about murder trials wherein eminent psychiatrists for the defense are contradicted by equally eminent psychiatrists for the prosecution on the matter of the defendant's sanity. More generally, there are a great deal of conflicting data on the reliability, utility, and meaning of such terms as "sanity," "insanity," "mental illness," and "schizophrenia." Finally, as early as 1934, Benedict suggested that normality and abnormality are not universal (1). What is viewed as normal in one culture may be seen as quite aberrant in another. Thus, notions of normality and abnormality may not be quite as accurate as people believe they are.

To raise questions regarding normality and abnormality is in no way to question the fact that some behaviors are deviant or odd. Murder is deviant. So, too, are hallucinations. Nor does raising such questions deny the existence of the personal anguish that is often associated with "mental illness." Anxiety and depression exist. Psychological suffering exists. But normality and abnormality, sanity and insanity, and the diagnoses that flow from them may be less substantive than many believe them to be.

At its heart, the question of whether the sane can be distinguished from the insane (and whether degrees of insanity can be distinguished from each other) is a simple matter: do the salient characteristics that lead to diagnoses reside in the patients themselves or in the environments and contexts in which observers find them? . . . [T]he belief has been strong that patients present symptoms, that those symptoms can be categorized, and, implicitly, that the sane are distinguishable from the insane. More recently, however, this belief has been questioned. Based in part on theoretical and anthropological considerations, but also on philosophical, legal, and therapeutic ones, the view has grown that psychological categorization of mental illness is useless at best and downright harmful, misleading, and pejorative at worst. Psychiatric diagnoses, in this view, are in the minds of the observers and are not valid summaries of characteristics displayed by the observed.

Gains can be made in deciding which of these is more nearly accurate by getting normal people (that is, people who do not have, and have never suffered, symptoms of serious psychiatric disorders) admitted to psychiatric hospitals and then determining whether they were discovered to be sane and, if so, how. If the sanity of such pseudopatients were always detected, there would be prima facie evidence that a sane individual can be distinguished from the insane context in which he is found. Normality (and presumably abnormality) is distinct enough that it can be recognized wherever it occurs, for it is carried within the person. If, on the other hand, the sanity of the pseudopatients were never discovered, serious difficulties would arise for those who support traditional modes of psychiatric diagnosis. Given that the hospital staff was not incompetent, that the pseudopatient had been behaving as sanely as he had been outside of the hospital, and that it had never been previously suggested that he belonged in a psychiatric hospital, such an unlikely outcome would support the view that psychiatric diagnosis betrays little about the patient but much about the environment in which an observer finds him.

This article describes such an experiment. Eight sane people gained secret admission to 12 different hospitals. Their diagnostic experiences constitute the data of the first part of this article; the remainder is devoted to a description of their experiences in psychiatric institutions. Too few psychiatrists and psychologists, even those who have worked in such hospitals, know what the experience is like. They rarely talk about it with former patients, perhaps because they distrust information coming from the previously insane. Those who have worked in psychiatric hospitals are likely to have adapted so thoroughly to the settings that they are insensitive to the impact of the experience. And while there have been occasional reports of researchers who submitted themselves to psychiatric hospitalization (3), these researchers have commonly remained in the hospitals for short periods of time, often with the knowledge of the hospital staff. It is difficult to know the extent to which they were treated like patients or like research colleagues. Nevertheless, their reports about the inside of the psychiatric hospital have been valuable. This article extends those efforts.

PSEUDOPATIENTS AND THEIR SETTINGS

The eight pseudopatients were a varied group. One was a psychology graduate student in his 20's. The remaining seven were older and "established." Among them were three psychologists, a pediatrician, a psychiatrist, a painter, and a housewife. Three pseudopatients were women, five were men. All of them employed pseudonyms, lest their alleged diagnoses embarrass them later.

Those who were in mental health professions alleged another occupation in order to avoid the special attentions that might be accorded by staff, as a matter of courtesy or caution, to ailing colleagues. With the exception of myself (I was the first pseudopatient and my presence was known to the hospital administrator and chief psychologist and, so far as I can tell, to them alone), the presence of pseudopatients and the nature of the research program was not known to the hospital staffs.

The settings were similarly varied. In order to generalize the findings, admission into a variety of hospitals was sought. The 12 hospitals in the sample are located in five different states on the East and West coasts. Some were old and shabby, some were quite new. Some were research-oriented, others not. Some had good staff-patient ratios, others were quite understaffed. Only one was a strictly private hospital. All the others were supported by state or federal funds or, in one instance, by university funds.

After calling the hospital for an appointment, the pseudopatient arrived at the admissions office complaining that he had been hearing voices. Asked what the voices said, he replied that they were often unclear, but as far as he could tell they said "empty," "hollow," and "thud." The voices were unfamiliar and were of the same sex as the pseudopatient. The choice of these symptoms was occasioned by their apparent similarity to existential symptoms. Such symptoms were alleged to arise from painful concerns about the perceived meaninglessness of one's life. It is as if the hallucinating person were saying, "My life is empty and hollow." The choice of these symptoms was also determined by the *absence* of a single report of existential psychoses in the literature.

Beyond alleging the symptoms and falsifying name, vocation, and employment, no further alterations of person, history, or circumstances were made. The significant events of the pseudopatient's life history were presented as they had actually occurred. Relationships with parents and siblings, with spouse and children, with people at work and in school, consistent with the aforementioned exceptions, were described as they were or had been. Frustrations and upsets were described along with joys and satisfactions. These facts are important to remember. If anything, they strongly biased the subsequent results in favor of detecting sanity, since none of their histories or current behaviors were seriously pathological in any way.

Immediately upon admission to the psychiatric ward, the pseudopatient ceased simulating *any* symptoms of abnormality. In some cases, there was a brief period of mild nervousness and anxiety, since none of the pseudopatients really believed that they would be admitted so easily. Indeed their shared fear was that they would be immediately exposed as frauds and greatly embarrassed. Moreover, many of them had never visited a psychiatric ward; even those who had, nevertheless, had some genuine fears about what might happen to them. Their nervousness, then, was quite appropriate to the novelty of the hospital setting, and it abated rapidly.

Apart from that short-lived nervousness, the pseudo-patient behaved on the ward as he "normally" behaved. The pseudopatient spoke to patients and staff as he might ordinarily. Because there is uncommonly little to do on a psychiatric ward, he attempted to engage others in conversation. When asked by staff how he was feeling, he indicated that he was fine, that he no longer experienced symptoms. He responded to instructions from attendants, to calls for medication (which was not swallowed), and to dining-hall instructions. Beyond such activities as were available to him on the admissions ward, he spent his time writing down his observations about the ward, its patients, and the staff. Initially these notes were written "secretly," but as it soon became clear that no one much cared, they were subsequently written on standard tablets of paper in such public places as the dayroom. No secret was made of these activities.

The pseudopatient, very much as a true psychiatric patient, entered a hospital with no foreknowledge of when he would be discharged. Each was told that he would have to get out by his own devices, essentially by convincing the staff that he was sane. The psychological stresses associated with hospitalization were considerable, and all but one of the pseudopatients desired to be discharged almost immediately after being admitted. They were, therefore, motivated not only to behave sanely, but to be paragons of cooperation. That their behavior was in no way disruptive is confirmed by nursing reports, which have been obtained on most of the patients. These reports uniformly indicate that the patients were "friendly," "cooperative," and "exhibited no abnormal indications."

THE NORMAL ARE NOT DETECTABLY SANE

Despite their public "show" of sanity, the pseudopatients were never detected. Admitted, except in one case, with a diagnosis of schizophrenia, each was discharged with a diagnosis of schizophrenia "in remission." The label "in remission" should in no way be dismissed as a formality, for at no time during any hospitalization had any question been raised about any pseudopatient's simulation. Nor are there any indications in the hospital records that the pseudopatient's status was suspect. Rather, the evidence is strong that, once labeled schizophrenic, the pseudopatient was stuck with that label. If the pseudopatient was to be discharged, he must naturally be "in remission"; but he was not sane, nor, in the institution's view, had he ever been sane.

The uniform failure to recognize sanity cannot be attributed to the quality of the hospitals, for, although there were considerable variations among them, several are considered excellent. Nor can it be alleged that there was simply not enough time to observe the pseudopatients. Length of hospitalization ranged from 7 to 52 days, with

an average of 19 days. The pseudopatients were not, in fact, carefully observed, but this failure clearly speaks more to traditions within psychiatric hospitals than to lack of opportunity.

Finally, it cannot be said that the failure to recognize the pseudopatients' sanity was due to the fact that they were not behaving sanely. While there was clearly some tension present in all of them, their daily visitors could detect no serious behavioral consequences—nor, indeed, could other patients. It was quite common for the patients to "detect" the pseudopatients' sanity. During the first three hospitalizations, when accurate counts were kept, 35 of a total of 118 patients on the admissions ward voiced their suspicions, some vigorously. "You're not crazy. You're a journalist, or a professor [referring to the continual note-taking]. You're checking up on the hospital." While most of the patients were reassured by the pseudopatient's insistence that he had been sick before he came in but was fine now, some continued to believe that the pseudopatient was sane throughout his hospitalization. The fact that the patients often recognized normality when staff did not raises important questions.

Failure to detect sanity during the course of hospitalization may be due to the fact that physicians operate with a strong bias toward what statisticians call the type 2 error (2). This is to say that physicians are more inclined to call a healthy person sick (a false positive, type 2) than a sick person healthy (a false negative, type 1). The reasons for this are not hard to find: it is clearly more dangerous to misdiagnose illness than health. Better to err on the side of caution, to suspect illness even among the healthy.

But what holds for medicine does not hold equally well for psychiatry. Medical illnesses, while unfortunate, are not commonly pejorative. Psychiatric diagnoses, on the contrary, carry with them personal, legal, and social stigmas (4). . . .

THE STICKINESS OF PSYCHODIAGNOSTIC LABELS

Beyond the tendency to call the healthy sick—a tendency that accounts better for diagnostic behavior on admission than it does for such behavior after a lengthy period of exposure—the data speak to the massive role of labeling in psychiatric assessment. Having once been labeled schizophrenic, there is nothing the pseudopatient can do to overcome this tag. The tag profoundly colors others' perceptions of him and his behavior. . . .

Once a person is designated abnormal, all of his other behaviors and characteristics are colored by that label. Indeed, that label is so powerful that many of the pseudopatients' normal behaviors were overlooked entirely or profoundly misinterpreted. . . .

All pseudopatients took extensive notes publicly. Under ordinary circumstances, such behavior would have raised questions in the minds of observers, as, in fact, it did among patients. Indeed, it seemed so certain that the notes would elicit suspicion that elaborate precautions were taken to remove them from the ward each day. But the precautions proved needless. The closest any staff member came to questioning these notes occurred when one pseudopatient asked his physician what kind of medication he was receiving and began to write down the response. "You needn't write it," he was told gently. "If you have trouble remembering, just ask me again."

If no questions were asked of the pseudopatients, how was their writing interpreted? Nursing records for three patients indicate that the writing was seen as an aspect of their pathological behavior. "Patient engages in writing behavior" was the daily nursing comment on one of the pseudopatients who was never questioned about his writing. Given that the patient is in the hospital, he must be psychologically disturbed. And given that he is disturbed, continuous writing must be a behavioral manifestation of that disturbance, perhaps a subset of the compulsive behaviors that are sometimes correlated with schizophrenia. . . .

A psychiatric label has a life and an influence of its own. Once the impression has been formed that the patient is schizophrenic, the expectation is that he will continue to be schizophrenic. When a sufficient amount of time has passed, during which the patient has done nothing bizarre, he is considered to be in remission and available for discharge. But the label endures beyond discharge, with the unconfirmed expectation that he will behave as a schizophrenic again. Such labels, conferred by mental health professionals, are as influential on the patient as they are on his relatives and friends, and it should not surprise anyone that the diagnosis acts on all of them as a self-fulfilling prophecy. Eventually, the patient himself accepts the diagnosis, with all of its surplus meanings and expectations, and behaves accordingly (5). . . . If it makes no sense to label ourselves permanently depressed on the basis of an occasional depression, then it takes better evidence than is presently available to label all patients insane or schizophrenic on the basis of bizarre behaviors or cognitions. It seems more useful, as Mischel (5) has pointed out, to limit our discussions to *behaviors*, the stimuli that provoke them, and their correlates. . . . I may hallucinate because I am sleeping, or I may hallucinate because I have ingested a peculiar drug. These are termed sleep-induced hallucinations, or dreams, and drug-induced hallucinations, respectively. But when the stimuli to my hallucinations are unknown, that is called craziness, or schizophrenia—as if that inference were somehow as illuminating as the others. . . .

SUMMARY AND CONCLUSIONS

It is clear that we cannot distinguish the sane from the insane in psychiatric hospitals. The hospital itself imposes a special environment in which the meanings of behavior can easily be misunderstood. The consequences to patients hospitalized in such an environment—the powerlessness, depersonalization, segregation, mortification, and self-labeling—seem undoubtedly countertherapeutic.

I do not, even now, understand this problem well enough to perceive solutions. But two matters seem to have some promise. The first concerns the proliferation of community mental health facilities, of crisis intervention centers, of the human potential movement, and of behavior therapies that, for all of their own problems, tend to avoid psychiatric labels, to focus on specific problems and behaviors, and to retain the individual in a relatively nonpejorative environment. Clearly, to the extent that we refrain from sending the distressed to insane places, our impressions of them are less likely to be distorted. (The risk of distorted perceptions, it seems to me, is always present, since we are much more sensitive to an individual's behaviors and verbalizations than we are to the subtle contextual stimuli that often promote them. At issue here is a matter of magnitude. And, as I have shown, the magnitude of distortion is exceedingly high in the extreme context that is a psychiatric hospital).

The second matter that might prove promising speaks to the need to increase the sensitivity of mental health workers and researchers to the *Catch 22* position of psychiatric patients. Simply reading materials in this area will be of help to some such workers and researchers. For others, directly experiencing the impact of psychiatric hospitalization will be of enormous use. Clearly, further research into the social psychology of such total institutions will both facilitate treatment and deepen understanding.

NOTES

1. R. Benedict, *J. Gen. Psychol.* **10,** 59 (1934).
2. T. J. Scheff, *Being Mentally Ill: A Sociological Theory* (Aldine, Chicago, 1966).
3. A. Barry, *Bellevue Is a State of Mind* (Harcourt Brace Jovanovich, New York, 1971); . . .
4. J. Cumming and E. Cumming, *Community Ment. Health* **1,** 135 (1965); . . .
5. W. Mischel, *Personality and Assessment* (Wiley, New York, 1968).

Inhibitions, Symptoms and Anxiety

Sigmund Freud (1926)

Anxiety is a part of everyone's life. Much of what psychologists know about anxiety has been shaped by the views of Sigmund Freud. Freud developed the psychoanalytic approach to psychological disorders, and anxiety was one of his cornerstones.

Freud (1856–1939), an Austrian neurologist, obtained his M.D. in 1881 from the University of Vienna. Through his medical practice, he began to study patients' mental disorders. In doing so, he employed his theory of psychoanalysis, which emphasizes past experiences and unconscious motivations as the determinants of personality.

This selection is from chapter 7 of Freud's book *Inhibitions, Symptoms and Anxiety* (W. W. Norton, 1926). In it, Freud describes the symptoms of anxiety and discusses the functions of anxiety. He argues that anxiety is a reaction to danger and occurs whenever one perceives danger. Notice how he focuses on early experiences (e.g., birth) to explain the origins of anxiety. As you read this selection, think about what causes anxiety in your life. What do you think the function of anxiety might be?

Key Concept: anxiety disorders

APA Citation: Freud, S. (1926). *Inhibitions, symptoms, and anxiety.* New York: Norton.

*A*nxiety . . . is in the first place something that is felt. We call it an affective state, although we are also ignorant of what an affect is. As a feeling, anxiety has a very marked character of unpleasure. But that is not the whole of its quality. Not every unpleasure can be called anxiety, for there are other feelings, such as tension, pain or mourning, which have the character of unpleasure. Thus anxiety must have other distinctive features besides this quality of unpleasure. Can we succeed in understanding the differences between these various unpleasurable affects?

We can at any rate note one or two things about the feeling of anxiety. Its unpleasurable character seems to have a note of its own—something not very obvious, whose presence is difficult to prove yet which is in all likelihood there. But besides having this special feature which is difficult to isolate, we notice that anxiety is accompanied by fairly definite physical sensations which can be referred to particular organs of the body. As we are not concerned here with the physiology of anxiety, we shall content ourselves with mentioning a few representatives of these sensations. The clearest and most frequent ones are those connected with the respiratory organs and with the heart. They provide evidence that motor innervations—that is, processes of discharge—play a part in the general phenomenon of anxiety.

Analysis of anxiety-states therefore reveals the existence of (1) a specific character of unpleasure, (2) acts of discharge and (3) perceptions of those acts. The two last points indicate at once a difference between states of anxiety and other similar states, like those of mourning and pain. The latter do not have any motor manifestation; or if they have, the manifestation is not an integral part of the whole state but is distinct from it as being a result of it or a reaction to it. Anxiety, then, is a special state of unpleasure with acts of discharge along particular paths. In accordance with our general views we should be inclined to think that anxiety is based upon an increase of excitation which on the one hand produces the character of unpleasure and on the other finds relief through the acts of discharge already mentioned. But a purely physiological account of this sort will scarcely satisfy us. We are tempted to assume the presence of a historical factor which binds the sensations of anxiety and its innervations firmly together. We assume, in other words, that an anxiety-state is the reproduction of some experience which contained the necessary conditions for such an increase of excitation and a discharge along particular paths, and that from this circumstance the unpleasure of anxiety receives its specific character. In man, birth provides a prototypic experience of this kind, and we are therefore inclined to regard anxiety-states as a reproduction of the trauma of birth.

This does not imply that anxiety occupies an exceptional position among the affective states. In my opinion the other affects are also reproductions of very early, perhaps even pre-individual, experiences of vital importance; and I should be inclined to regard them as universal, typical and innate hysterical attacks, as compared to the recently and individually acquired attacks which occur in hysterical neuroses and whose origin and significance as mnemic symbols have been revealed by analysis. It would be very desirable, of course, to be able to demonstrate the truth of this view in a number of such affects—a thing which is still very far from being the case.

The view that anxiety goes back to the event of birth raises immediate objections which have to be met. It may be argued that anxiety is a reaction which, in all probability, is common to every organism, certainly every organism of a higher order, whereas birth is only experienced by the mammals; and it is doubtful whether in all of them, even, birth has the significance of a trauma. Therefore there can be anxiety without the prototype of birth. But this objection takes us beyond the barrier that divides psychology from biology. It may be that, precisely because anxiety has an indispensable biological function to fulfil as a reaction to a state of danger, it is differently contrived in different organisms. We do not know, besides, whether anxiety involves the same sensations and innervations in organisms far removed from man as it does in man himself. Thus there is no good argument here against the view that, in man, anxiety is modelled upon the process of birth.

If the structure and origin of anxiety are as described, the next question is: what is the function of anxiety and on what occasions is it reproduced? The answer seems to be obvious and convincing: anxiety arose originally as a reaction to a state of *danger* and it is reproduced whenever a state of that kind recurs.

This answer, however, raises further considerations. The innervations involved in the original state of anxiety probably had a meaning and purpose, in just the same way as the muscular movements which accompany a first hysterical attack. In order to understand a hysterical attack, all one has to do is to look for the situation in which the movements in question formed part of an appropriate and expedient action. Thus at birth it is probable that the innervation, in being directed to the respiratory organs, is preparing the way for the activity of the lungs, and, in accelerating the heartbeat, is helping to keep the blood free from toxic substances. Naturally, when the anxiety-state is reproduced later as an affect it will be lacking in any such expediency, just as are the repetitions of a hysterical attack. When the individual is placed in a new situation of danger it may well be quite inexpedient for him to respond with an anxiety-state (which is a reaction to an earlier danger) instead of initiating a reaction appropriate to the current danger. But his behavior may become expedi-

ent once more if the danger-situation is recognized as it approaches and is signalled by an outbreak of anxiety. In that case he can at once get rid of his anxiety by having recourse to more suitable measures. Thus we see that there are two ways in which anxiety can emerge: in an inexpedient way, when a new situation of danger has occurred, or in an expedient way in order to give a signal and prevent such a situation from occurring.

But what is a 'danger'? In the act of birth there is a real danger to life. We know what this means objectively; but in a psychological sense it says nothing at all to us. The danger of birth has as yet no psychical content. We cannot possibly suppose that the foetus has any sort of knowledge that there is a possibility of its life being destroyed. It can only be aware of some vast disturbance in the economy of its narcissistic libido. Large sums of excitation crowd in upon it, giving rise to new kinds of feelings of unpleasure, and some organs acquire an increased cathexis, thus foreshadowing the object-cathexis which will soon set in. What elements in all this will be made use of as the sign of a 'danger-situation'?

Unfortunately far too little is known about the mental make-up of a newborn baby to make a direct answer possible. I cannot even vouch for the validity of the description I have just given. It is easy to say that the baby will repeat its affect of anxiety in every situation which recalls the event of birth. The important thing to know is what recalls the event and what it is that is recalled.

All we can do is to examine the occasions on which infants in arms or somewhat older children show readiness to produce anxiety. In his book on the trauma of birth, Rank (1924) has made a determined attempt to establish a relationship between the earliest phobias of children and the impressions made on them by the event of birth. But I do not think he has been successful. His theory is open to two objections. In the first place, he assumes that the infant has received certain sensory impressions, in particular of a visual kind, at the time of birth, the renewal of which can recall to its memory the trauma of birth and thus evoke a reaction of anxiety. This assumption is quite unfounded and extremely improbable. It is not credible that a child should retain any but tactile and general sensations relating to the process of birth. If, later on, children show fear of small animals that disappear into holes or emerge from them, this reaction, according to Rank, is due to their perceiving an analogy. But it is an analogy of which they cannot be aware. In the second place, in considering these later anxiety-situations Rank dwells, as suits him best, now on the child's recollection of its happy intra-uterine existence, now on its recollection of the traumatic disturbance which interrupted that existence—which leaves the door wide open for arbitrary interpretation. There are, moreover, certain examples of childhood anxiety which directly traverse his theory. When, for instance, a child is left alone in the dark one would expect it, according to his view, to welcome the re-establishment of the intra-uterine situation; yet it is precisely on such occasions that the child reacts with anxiety. And if this is explained by saying that the child is being reminded of the interruption which the event of birth made in its intra-uterine happiness, it becomes impossible to shut one's eyes any longer to the far-fetched character of such explanations.

I am driven to the conclusion that the earliest phobias of infancy cannot be directly traced back to impressions of the act of birth and that so far they have not been explained. A certain preparedness for anxiety is undoubtedly present in the infant in arms. But this preparedness for anxiety, instead of being at its maximum immediately after birth and then slowly decreasing, does not emerge till later, as mental development proceeds, and lasts over a certain period of childhood. If these early phobias persist beyond that period one is inclined to suspect the presence of a neurotic disturbance, although it is not at all clear what their relation is to the undoubted neuroses that appear later on in childhood.

Only a few of the manifestations of anxiety in children are comprehensible to us, and we must confine our attention to them. They occur, for instance, when a child is alone, or in the dark, or when it finds itself with an unknown person instead of one to whom it is used—such as its mother. These three instances can be reduced to a single condition—namely, that of missing someone who is loved and longed for. But here, I think, we have the key to an understanding of anxiety and to a reconciliation of the contradictions that seem to beset it.

The child's mnemic image of the person longed for is no doubt intensely cathected, probably in a hallucinatory way at first. But this has no effect; and now it seems as though the longing turns into anxiety. This anxiety has all the appearance of being an expression of the child's feeling at its wits' end, as though in its still very undeveloped state it did not know how better to cope with its cathexis of longing. Here anxiety appears as a reaction to the felt loss of the object; and we are at once reminded of the fact that castration anxiety, too, is a fear of being separated from a highly valued object, and that the earliest anxiety of all—the 'primal anxiety' of birth—is brought about on the occasion of a separation from the mother.

But a moment's reflection takes us beyond this question of loss of object. The reason why the infant in arms wants to perceive the presence of its mother is only because it already knows by experience that she satisfies all its needs without delay. The situation, then, which it regards as a 'danger' and against which it wants to be safeguarded is that of non-satisfaction, of a *growing tension due to need,* against which it is helpless. I think that if we adopt this view all the facts fall into place. The situation of non-satisfaction in which the amounts of stimulation rise to an unpleasurable height without its being possible for them to be mastered psychically or discharged must for the infant be analogous to the experience of being born—must be a repetition of the situation of danger. What both situations have in common is the economic disturbance caused by an accumulation of amounts of stimulation which require to be disposed of. It is this factor, then, which is the real essence of the 'danger'. In both cases the reaction of anxiety sets in. (This reaction is still an expedient one in the infant in arms, for the discharge, being directed into the respiratory and vocal muscular apparatus, now calls its mother to it, just as it activated the lungs of the newborn baby to get rid of the internal stimuli.) It is unnecessary to suppose that the child carries anything more with it from the time of its birth than this way of indicating the presence of danger.

When the infant has found out by experience that an external, perceptible object can put an end to the dangerous situation which is reminiscent of birth, the content of the danger it fears is displaced from the economic situation on to the condition which determined that situation, viz., the loss of object. It is the absence of the mother that is now the danger; and as soon as that danger arises the infant gives the signal of anxiety, before the dreaded economic situation has set in. This change constitutes a first great step forward in the provision made by the infant for its self-preservation, and at the same time represents a transition from the automatic and involuntary fresh appearance of anxiety to the intentional reproduction of anxiety as a signal of danger.

Fall into Helplessness

Martin E. P. Seligman (1973)

Depression is a very serious mental disorder, and a number of different theoretical explanations of depression have been proposed. In the 1970s, Martin E. P. Seligman proposed the learned helplessness model of depression. This theory suggests that when people come to believe that they have no control over a situation, they feel helpless and tend to give up; they passively accept adverse stimuli. This helplessness can lead to depression.

Seligman (b. 1942) received his Ph.D. in psychology in 1967 from the University of Pennsylvania. He taught at Stanford University before returning to University of Pennsylvania in 1972, where he is currently professor of psychology. In addition to learned helplessness, Seligman has also had an impact in psychology in the areas of learning theory, phobias, and personality and adjustment. Currently his interests lie in positive psychology and helping people become more optimistic about their lives. He served as president of the American Psychological Association in 1998. His book *Helplessness: On Depression, Development, and Death* (W. H. Freeman, 1975), remains a classic today.

This selection, from "Fall into helplessness," was published in *Psychology Today* in 1973. In it, Seligman presents a readable description of the causes of, consequences of, and treatments for learned helplessness, and relates it to depression. As you read this selection, note the emphasis Seligman places on common, everyday occurrences and their role in helplessness. How can we help prevent learned helplessness in people today?

Key Concept: helplessness and depression

APA Citation: Seligman, M.E. (1973). Fall into helplessness. *Psychology Today, 7*, 43–46; 48.

There are considerable parallels between the behaviors that define learned helplessness and the major symptoms of depression. In addition, the types of events that set off depression parallel the events that set off learned helplessness. I believe that cure for depression occurs when the individual comes to believe that he is not helpless and that an individual's susceptibility to depression depends or the success of failure of his previous experience with controlling his environment.

So the focus of my theory is that if the symptoms of learned helplessness and depression are equivalent, then what we have learned experimentally about the cause, cure and prevention of learned helplessness can be applied to depression.

Inescapable Shock. A few years ago, Steven F. Maier, J. Bruce Overmier and I stumbled onto the behavioral phenomenon of learned helplessness while we were using dogs and traumatic shock to test a particular learning theory. We had strapped dogs into a Pavlovian harness and given them electric shock—traumatic, but not physically damaging.

Later the dogs were put into a two-compartment shuttlebox where they were supposed to learn to escape shock by jumping across the barrier separating the compartments.

A nonshocked, experimentally naive dog, when placed in a shuttlebox, typically behaves in the following way: at the onset of the first electric shock, the dog defecates, urinates, howls, and runs around frantically until it accidentally scrambles over the barrier and escapes the shock. On the next trial, the dog, running and howling, crosses the barrier more quickly. This pattern continues until the dog learns to avoid shock altogether.

But our dogs were not naive. While in a harness from which they could not escape, they had already experienced shock over which they had no control. That is, nothing they did or did not do affected their receipt of shock. When placed in the shuttlebox, these dogs reacted at first in much the same manner as a naive dog, but not for long. The dogs soon stopped running and howling, settled down and took the shock, whining quietly. Typically, the dog did not cross the barrier and escape. Instead, it seemed to give up. On succeeding trials, the dog made virtually no attempts to get away. It passively took as much shock as was given.

After testing alternative hypotheses, we developed the theory that it was not trauma per se (electric shock) that interfered with the dog's adaptive responding. Rather, it was the experience of having *no control* over the trauma. We have found that if animals can control shock by any response—be it an active or a passive one—they do not later become helpless. Only those animals who receive uncontrollable shock will later give up. The experience in the harness had taught the dog that its responses did not pay, that his actions did not matter. We concluded that the dogs in our experiments had learned that they were helpless.

Our learned-helplessness hypothesis has been tested and confirmed in many ways with both animal and human subjects. Tests with human beings revealed dramatic parallels between the behavior of subjects who have learned helplessness and the major symptoms exhibited by depressed individuals. . . .

Goodies From the Sky. Many clinicians have reported an increasing pervasiveness of depression among college students. Since this is a generation that has been raised with more reinforcers—more and more intellectual stimulation, more buying power, more cars, more music, etc. than any previous generation, why should they be depressed? Yet the occurrence of reinforcers in our affluent society is so independent of the actions of the children who receive them, the goodies might as well have fallen from the sky. And perhaps that is our answer. Rewards as well as punishments that come independently of one's own effort can be depressing.

We can mention "success" depression in this context. When an individual finally reaches a goal after years of striving, such as getting a Ph.D. or becoming company president, depression often ensues. Even the disciplined astronaut, hero of his nation and the world, can become depressed after he has returned from walking on the Moon.

From a learned-helplessness viewpoint, success depression may occur because reinforcers are no longer contingent on present responding. After years of goal-directed activity, a person now gets his reinforcers because of who he *is* rather than because of what he is *doing*. Perhaps this explains the number of beautiful women who become depressed and attempt suicide. They receive abundant positive reinforcers not for what they do but for how they look.

Symptoms in Common. Consider the parallels between depression and learned helplessness: the most prominent symptom of depression, passivity, is also the central symptom of learned helplessness. . . .

Experiments in learned helplessness have produced passivity in many kinds of animals, even the lowly cockroach, and in human subjects. Donald Hiroto subjected

college students to loud noise. He used three groups: group one could not escape hearing the loud noise, group two heard the loud noise but could turn it off by pressing a button, group three heard no noise.

In the second part of the experiment, Hiroto presented the students with a finger shuttlebox. Moving one's fingers back and forth across the shuttlebox turned off the loud noise. The students in group two, who had previously learned to silence the noise by pushing a button, and those in group three, who had no experience with the loud noise, readily learned to move their fingers across the shuttlebox to control the noise. But the students in group one, whose previous attempts to turn off the noise had been futile, now merely sat with their hands in the shuttlebox, passively accepting the loud noise. They had learned that they were helpless.

Hiroto also found out that "externals" [see "External Control and Internal Control," by Julian B. Rotter, PT, June 1971] were more susceptible to learned helplessness than "internals." Externals are persons who believe that reinforcement comes from outside themselves, they believe in luck. Internals believe that their own actions control reinforcement.

Born Losers. Depressed patients not only make fewer responses, but they are "set" to interpret their own responses, when they do make them, as failures or as doomed to failure. Each of them bears an invisible tattoo: "I'm a Born Loser." [Aaron] Beck considers this negative cognitive set to be the primary characteristic of depression:

"…The depressed patient is peculiarly sensitive to any impediments to his goal-directed activity. An obstacle is regarded as an impossible barrier, difficulty in dealing with a problem is interpreted as total failure. His cognitive response to a problem of difficulty is likely to be an idea such as 'I'm licked,' 'I'll never be able to do this,' or 'I'm blocked no matter what I do'…"

This cognitive set crops up repeatedly in experiments with depressives. Alfred S. Friedman observed that although a patient was performing adequately during a test, the patient would occasionally reiterate his original protest of "I can't do it," "I don't know how," etc. this is also our experience in testing depressed patients.

Negative cognitive set crops up in both depression and learned helplessness. When testing students, William Miller, David Klein and I found that depression and learned helplessness produced the same difficulty in seeing that responding is successful. We found that depressed individuals view their skilled actions very much as if they were in a chance situation. Their depression is not a general form of pessimism about the world, but pessimism that is specific to their own actions. In animal behavior this is demonstrated by associative retardation: animals don't catch on even though they make a response that turns off shock; they have difficulty in learning what responses produce relief.

Maier and I found in separate experiments, that normal aggressiveness and competitiveness become deficient in the subjects who have succumbed to learned helplessness. In competition, these animals lose out to animals who have learned that they control the effects of their responses. Further, they do not fight back when attacked.

Depressed individuals, similarly, are usually less aggressive and competitive than nondepressed individuals. The behavior of depressed patients is depleted of hostility and even their dreams are less hostile. This symptom forms the basis for the Freudian view of depression. Freud claimed that the hostility of depressed people was directed inward toward themselves rather than outward. Be this as it may, the *symptom* corresponds to the depleted aggression and competitiveness of helpless dogs and rats.

The Balm of Time. Depression also often dissipates with time. When a man's wife dies he may be depressed for several days, several months, or even several years. But time usually heals. One of the most tragic aspects of suicide is that if the person could have waited for a few weeks, the depression might well have lifted.

Time is also an important variable in learned helplessness. Overmier and I found that the day after they received one session of inescapable shock, dogs behaved helplessly in the shuttlebox. However, if two days elapsed between the inescapable shock and testing, the dogs were not helpless, their helplessness, like the widower's depression, had run its course. Unfortunately, helplessness does not always respond so well to the elixir of time. We found that multiple sessions of inescapable shock made the animals' learned helplessness virtually irreversible. We also found that animals that had been reared from birth in our laboratories with a limited history of controlling reinforcers also failed to recover from learned helplessness over time.

Often when we are depressed we lose our appetites and our zest for life. Jay M. Weiss, Neal E. Miller and their colleagues at Rockefeller University found that rats that had received inescapable shock lost weight and ate less than rats who had been able to escape from shock. In addition, the brains of the rats subjected to inescapable shock are depleted of norepinephrine, an important transmitter substance in the central nervous system. Joseph J. Schildkraut and Seymour S. Kety have suggested that the cause of depression may be a deficiency of norephinephrine at receptor sites in the brain. This is because reserpine, a drug that depletes norephinephrine, among other things, produces depression in man. Moreover, antidepressant drugs increase the brain's supply of norephinephrine. Therefore, there may be a chemical similarity between depression and learned helplessness. . . .

The Chances for Cure. As arrayed above, there are considerable parallels between the behaviors which define learned helplessness and the major symptoms of depression. We have also seen that the cause of learned helplessness and reactive depression is similar; both occur when important events are out of control. Let me now speculate about the possibility of curing both.

In our animal experiments, we knew that only when the dog learned to escape the shock, only when it learned that it could control its environment, would a cure for its learned helplessness be found.

At first, we could not persuade the dog to move to the other side of the box. Not even by dropping meat there when the dog was hungry. As a last resort, we forcibly dragged the dog across the barrier on a leash. After much dragging, the dog caught on and eventually was able to escape the shock on its own. Recovery from helplessness was complete and lasting for each animal. We can say with confidence that so far only "directive theraphy"—forcing the animal to see that it can succeed by responding—works reliably in curing learned helplessness. However, T.R. Dorworth has recently found that electroconvulsive shock breaks up helplessness in dogs. Electroconvulsive shock is often used as a therapy for depression and it seems to be effective about 60 percent of the time.

Although we do not know how to cure depression, there are therapies that alleviate it, and they are consonant with the learned helplessness approach. Successful therapy occurs when the patient believes that his responses produce gratification, that he is an effective human being.

Against the Grain. In an Alabama hospital, for instance, E.S. Taulbee and H.W. Wright have created an "antidepression room." They seat a severely depressed patient in the room and then abuse him in a simple manner. He is told to sand a block of wood, then is reprimanded because he is sanding against the grain of the wood. After he switches to sanding *with* the grain, he is reprimanded for sanding with the grain. The abuse continues until the depressed patient gets angry. He is then promptly led out of the room with apologies. His outburst, and its immediate effect on the person abusing him, breaks up his depression. From the helplessness viewpoint, the patient is forced to vent his anger, one of the most powerful responses people have for controlling others. When anger is dragged out of him, he is powerfully reinforced.

Other methods reported to be effective against depression involve the patient's relearning that he controls reinforcers.

Expressing strong emotions is a therapy that seems to help depressed patients, as self-assertion does. In assertive training, the patient rehearses asserting himself and then puts into practice the responses he has learned that bring him social reinforcers. . . .

The Lift of Success. Other forms of graded-task assignments also have been effective. Elaine P. Burgess first had her patients perform some simple task, such as making a telephone call. As the task requirements increased, the patient was reinforced by the therapist for successfully completing each task. Burgess emphasized how crucial it is in the graded-task treatment that the patient succeed.

Using a similar form of graded-task assignment, Aaron Beck, Dean Schuyler, Peter Brill and I began by asking patients to read a short paragraph aloud. Finally, we could get severely depressed patients to give extemporaneous speeches, with a noticeable lifting of their depression. What one patient said was illuminating: "You know, I used to be a debater in high school and I had forgotten how good I was."

Finally, there is the age-old strategy adopted by individuals to dispel their own minor depressions: doing work that is difficult but gratifying. There is no better way to see that one's responses are still effective. It is crucial to succeed. Merely starting and giving up only makes things worse.

Dramatic successes in medicine have come more frequently from prevention than from treatment, and I would hazard a guess that inoculation and immunization have saved more lives than cure. Surprisingly, psychotherapy is almost exclusively limited to curative procedures, and preventive procedures rarely play an explicit role.

In studies of dogs and rats we have found that behavioral immunization prevents learned helplessness. Dogs that first receive experience in mastering shock do not become helpless after experiencing subsequent inescapable shock. Dogs that are deprived of natural opportunities to control their own rewards in their development are more vulnerable to helplessness than naturally immunized dogs.

The Masterful Life. Even less is known about the prevention of depression than about its cure. We can only speculate on this, but the data on immunization against learned helplessness guide our speculations. The life histories of those individuals who are particularly resistant to depression or who are resilient from depression may have been filled with mastery. Persons who have had extensive experience in controlling and manipulating the sources of reinforcement in their lives may see the future optimistically. A life without mastery may produce vulnerability to depression. Adults who lost their parents when they were children are unusually susceptible to depression and suicide.

A word of caution is in order. While it may be possible to immunize people against debilitating depression by giving them a history of control over reinforcers, it may be possible to immunize people against debilitating depression by giving them a history of control over reinforcers, it may be possible to get too much of a good thing. The person who has met only success may be highly susceptible to depression when he faces a loss. One is reminded, for example, of the stock market crash of 1929: it was not the low-income people who jumped to their deaths, but those who had been "super-successful" and suddenly faced gross defeat.

One can also look at successful therapy as preventative. After all, therapy usually does not focus just on undoing past problems. It also should arm the patient against future depressions. Perhaps therapy for depression would be more successful if it explicitly aimed at providing the patient with a wide repertoire of coping responses. He could use these responses in future situations where he finds his usual reactions do not control his reinforcements. Finally, we can speculate about child rearing. What kind of experiences can best protect our children against the debilitating effects of helplessness and depression? A tentative answer follows from the learned helplessness view of depression: to see oneself as an effective human being may require a childhood filled with powerful synchronies between responding and its consequences.

Therapy

Some Hypotheses Regarding the Facilitation of Personal Growth

Carl R. Rogers (1961)

Insight therapy is designed to help people gain an understanding of who they are and why they feel the way they do. One popular type of insight therapy is person-centered therapy (formerly called "client-centered therapy"), which was founded by Carl R. Rogers. The main assumption of person-centered therapy is that everyone has the capacity to be psychologically healthy. The therapist's role is to provide a warm, nondirective atmosphere, to draw out the client's thoughts and feelings, and to help the client accept his or her true self.

Rogers (1902–1987), who helped develop the humanistic approach to psychology, earned his Ph.D. in clinical psychology from Columbia University in 1931. He taught at Ohio State University, the University of Chicago, and the University of Wisconsin before establishing the Center for Studies of the Person in La Jolla, California. Rogers wrote numerous books, including *Client-Centered Therapy* (Houghton Mifflin, 1951) and *A Way of Being* (Houghton Mifflin, 1980).

This selection is from chapter 2 "Some Hypotheses Regarding the Facilitation of Personal Growth," of *On Becoming a Person: A Therapist's View of Psychotherapy* (Houghton Mifflin, 1961). In this chapter, which is based on a talk he gave at Oberlin College in Ohio in 1954, Rogers presents the core characteristics of the person-centered approach to therapy and he tries to present his approach in an understandable fashion. As you read this selection, consider how the core characteristics of the person-centered relationship might be used to help foster personal growth in normal individuals.

Key Concept: person-centered therapy

APA Citation: Rogers, C. R. (1961). *On becoming a person: a therapist's view of psychotherapy.* Boston: Houghton Mifflin.

To be faced by a troubled, conflicted person who is seeking and expecting help, has always constituted a great challenge to me. Do I have the knowledge, the resources, the psychological strength, the skill—do I have whatever it takes to be of help to such an individual?

For more than twenty-five years I have been trying to meet this kind of challenge. It has caused me to draw upon every element of my professional background: the rigorous methods of personality measurement which I first learned at Teachers' College, Columbia; the Freudian psychoanalytic insights and methods of the Institute for Child Guidance where I worked as interne; the continuing developments in the field of clinical psychology, with which I have been closely associated; the briefer exposure to the work of Otto Rank, to the methods of psychiatric social work, and other resources too numerous to mention. But most of all it has meant a continual learning from

my own experience and that of my colleagues at the Counseling Center as we have endeavored to discover for ourselves effective means of working with people in distress. Gradually I have developed a way of working which grows out of that experience, and which can be tested, refined, and reshaped by further experience and by research.

A GENERAL HYPOTHESIS

One brief way of describing the change which has taken place in me is to say that in my early professional years I was asking the question, How can I treat, or cure, or change this person? Now I would phrase the question in this way: How can I provide a relationship which this person may use for his own personal growth?

It is as I have come to put the question in this second way that I realize that whatever I have learned is applicable to all of my human relationships, not just to working with clients with problems. It is for this reason that I feel it is possible that the learnings which have had meaning for me in my experience may have some meaning for you in your experience, since all of us are involved in human relationships.

Perhaps I should start with a negative learning. It has gradually been driven home to me that I cannot be of help to this troubled person by means of any intellectual or training procedure. No approach which relies upon knowledge upon training, upon the acceptance of something that is *taught*, is of any use. These approaches seem so tempting and direct that I have, in the past, tried a great many of them. It is possible to explain a person to himself, to prescribe steps which should lead him forward, to train him in knowledge about a more satisfying mode of life. But such methods are, in my experience, futile and inconsequential. The most they can accomplish is some temporary change, which soon disappears, leaving the individual more than ever convinced of his inadequacy.

The failure of any such approach through the intellect has forced me to recognize that change appears to come about through experience in a relationship. So I am going to try to state very briefly and informally, some of the essential hypotheses regarding a helping relationship which have seemed to gain increasing confirmation both from experience and research.

I can state the overall hypothesis in one sentence, as follows. If I can provide a certain type of relationship, the other person will discover within himself the capacity to use that relationship for growth, and change and personal development will occur.

THE RELATIONSHIP

But what meaning do these terms have? Let me take separately the three major phrases in this sentence and indicate something of the meaning they have for me. What is this certain type of relationship I would like to provide?

I have found that the more that I can be genuine in the relationship, the more helpful it will be. This means that I need to be aware of my own feelings, in so far as possible, rather than presenting an outward facade of one attitude, while actually holding another attitude at a deeper or unconscious level. Being genuine also involves the willingness to be and to express, in my words and my behavior, the various feelings and attitudes which exist in me. It is only in this way that the relationship can have *reality,* and reality seems deeply important as a first condition. It is only by providing the genuine reality which is in me, that the other person can successfully seek for the reality in him. I have found this to be true even when the attitudes I feel are not attitudes with which I am pleased, or attitudes which seem conducive to a good relationship. It seems extremely important to be *real.*

As a second condition, I find that the more acceptance and liking I feel toward this individual, the more I will be creating a relationship which he can use. By acceptance I mean a warm regard for him as a person of unconditional self-worth—of value no matter what his condition, his behavior, or his feelings. It means a respect and liking for him as a separate person, a willingness for him to possess his own feelings in his own way. It means an acceptance of and regard for his attitudes of the moment, no matter how negative or positive, no matter how much they may contradict other attitudes he has held in the past. This acceptance of each fluctuating aspect of this other person makes it for him a relationship of warmth and safety, and the safety of being liked and prized as a person seems a highly important element in a helping relationship.

I also find that the relationship is significant to the extent that I feel a continuing desire to understand—a sensitive empathy with each of the client's feelings and communications as they seem to him at that moment. Acceptance does not mean much until it involves understanding. It is only as I *understand* the feelings and thoughts which seem so horrible to you, or so weak, or so sentimental, or so bizarre—it is only as I see them as you see them, and accept them and you, that you feel really free to explore all the hidden nooks and frightening crannies of your inner and often buried experience. This *freedom* is an important condition of the relationship. There is implied here a freedom to explore oneself at both conscious and unconscious levels, as rapidly as one can dare to embark on this dangerous quest. There is also a complete freedom from any type of moral or diagnostic evaluation, since all such evaluations are, I believe, always threatening.

Thus the relationship which I have found helpful is characterized by a sort of transparency on my part, in which my real feelings are evident; by an acceptance of this other person as a separate person with value in his own right; and by a deep empathic understanding which enables me to see his private world through his eyes. When these conditions are achieved, I become a companion to my client, accompanying him in the frightening search for himself, which he now feels free to undertake.

I am by no means always able to achieve this kind of relationship with another, and sometimes, even when I feel I have achieved it in myself, he may be too frightened to perceive what is being offered to him. But I would say that when I hold in myself the kind of attitudes I have described, and when the other person can to some degree experience these attitudes, then I believe that change and constructive personal development will *invariably* occur—and I include the word "invariably" only after long and careful consideration.

THE MOTIVATION FOR CHANGE

So much for the relationship. The second phrase in my overall hypothesis was that the individual will discover within himself the capacity to use this relationship for growth. I will try to indicate something of the meaning which that phrase has for me. Gradually my experience has forced me to conclude that the individual has within himself the capacity and the tendency, latent if not evident, to move forward toward maturity. In a suitable psychological climate this tendency is released, and becomes actual rather than potential. It is evident in the capacity of the individual to understand those aspects of his life and of himself which are causing him pain and dissatisfaction, an understanding which probes beneath his conscious knowledge of himself into those experiences which he has hidden from himself because of their threatening nature. It shows itself in the tendency to reorganize his personality and his relationship to life in ways which are regarded as more mature. Whether one calls it a growth tendency, a drive toward self-actualization, or a forward-moving directional tendency, it is the mainspring of life, and is, in the last analysis, the tendency upon which all psychotherapy depends. It is the urge which is evident in all organic and human life—to expand, extend, become autonomous, develop, mature—the tendency to express and activate all the capacities of the organism, to the extent that such activation enhances the organism or the self. This tendency may become deeply buried under layer after layer of encrusted psychological defenses; it may be hidden behind elaborate facades which deny its existence; but it is my belief that it exists in every individual, and awaits only the proper conditions to be released and expressed.

THE OUTCOMES

I have attempted to describe the relationship which is basic to constructive personality change. I have tried to put into words the type of capacity which the individual brings to such a relationship. The third phrase of my general statement was that change and personal development would occur. It is my hypothesis that in such a

relationship the individual will reorganize himself at both the conscious and deeper levels of his personality in such a manner as to cope with life more constructively, more intelligently, and in a more socialized as well as a more satisfying way.

Here I can depart from speculation and bring in the steadily increasing body of solid research knowledge which is accumulating. We know now that individuals who live in such a relationship even for a relatively limited number of hours show profound and significant changes in personality, attitudes, and behavior, changes that do not occur in matched control groups. In such a relationship the individual becomes more integrated, more effective. He shows fewer of the characteristics which are usually termed neurotic or psychotic, and more of the characteristics of the healthy, well-functioning person. He changes his perception of himself, becoming more realistic in his views of self. He becomes more like the person he wishes to be. He values himself more highly. He is more self-confident and self-directing. He has a better understanding of himself, becomes more open to his experience, denies or represses less of his experience. He becomes more accepting in his attitudes toward others, seeing others as more similar to himself.

In his behavior he shows similar changes. He is less frustrated by stress, and recovers from stress more quickly. He becomes more mature in his everyday behavior as this is observed by friends. He is less defensive, more adaptive, more able to meet situations creatively.

These are some of the changes which we now know come about in individuals who have completed a series of counseling interviews in which the psychological atmosphere approximates the relationship I described. Each of the statements made is based upon objective evidence. Much more research needs to be done, but there can no longer be any doubt as to the effectiveness of such a relationship in producing personality change.

Cognitive Therapy: Nature and Relation to Behavior Therapy

Aaron T. Beck (1970)

Aaron T. Beck developed cognitive therapy to help people with negative, self-defeating thoughts and feelings. Cognitive therapists attempt to restructure these negative thoughts and modify the way people view the world. Beck originally developed cognitive therapy to treat depression, but has also extended it to the treatment of anxiety disorders. Since its introduction by Beck, cognitive therapy has become a major method of treating a variety of psychological disorders.

Beck (b. 1921) earned his M.D. from the Yale University School of Medicine in 1946. He is currently a professor emeritus of psychiatry at the University of Pennsylvania, where he has been since 1954. Beck's theories of depression and cognitive therapy have had a significant impact on clinical psychology. His *Beck Depression Inventory* is widely used to diagnose depression. He has written many books in this area, including *Depression: Clinical, Experimental, and Theoretical Aspects* (University of Pennsylvania Press, 1970), and *Cognitive Therapy and the Emotional Disorders* (International Universities Press, 1976).

This selection, from "Cognitive Therapy: Nature and Relation to Behavior Therapy," was published in *Behavior Therapy* in 1970. In it, Beck presents the basic concepts of cognitive therapy, and he provides examples of how therapists apply these concepts in treating patients. As you read this selection, notice how he compares cognitive therapy with behavior therapy and explains why cognitive therapy is necessary to help treat mental problems. Note that cognitive therapy is designed for those who can think and reason about their problems. Can the principles be applied to everyday problems as well as to more serious psychological disorders?

Key Concept: cognitive therapy

APA Citation: Beck, A. T. (1970). Cognitive therapy: Nature and relation to behavior therapy. *Behavior Therapy*, 1, 184-200.

Two systems of psychotherapy that have recently gained prominence have been the subject of a rapidly increasing number of clinical and experimental studies. Cognitive therapy, the more recent entry into the field of psychotherapy, and behavior therapy already show signs of becoming institutionalized.

Although behavior therapy has been publicized in a large number of articles and monographs, cognitive therapy has received much less recognition. Despite the fact that behavior therapy is based primarily on learning theory whereas cognitive therapy is rooted more in cognitive theory, the two systems of psychotherapy have much in common.

First, in both systems of psychotherapy the therapeutic interview is more overtly structured and the therapist more active than in other psychotherapies. After the preliminary diagnostic interviews in which a systematic and highly detailed description of the patient's problems is obtained, both the cognitive and the behavior therapists formulate the patient's presenting symptoms (in cognitive or behavioral terms, respectively) and design specific sets of operations for the particular problem areas.

After mapping out the areas for therapeutic work, the therapist explicitly coaches the patient regarding the kinds of responses and behaviors that are useful with this particular form of therapy. Detailed instructions are presented to the patient, for example, to stimulate pictorial fantasies (systematic desensitization) or to facilitate his awareness and recognition of his cognitions (cognitive therapy). The goals of these therapies are circumscribed, in contrast to the evocative therapies whose goals are open ended (Frank, 1961).

Second, both the cognitive and behavior therapists aim their therapeutic techniques at the overt symptom or behavior problem, such as a particular phobia, obsession, or hysterical symptom. However, the target differs somewhat. The cognitive therapist focuses more on the ideational content involved in the symptom, viz., the irrational inferences and premises. The behavior therapist focuses more on the overt behavior, e.g., the maladaptive avoidance responses. Both psychotherapeutic systems conceptualize symptom formation in terms of constructs that are accessible either to behavioral observation or to introspection, in contrast to psychoanalysis, which views most symptoms as the disguised derivatives of unconscious conflicts.

Third, in further contrast to psychoanalytic therapy, neither cognitive therapy nor behavior therapy draws substantially on recollections or reconstructions of the patient's childhood experiences and early family relationships. The emphasis on correlating present problems with developmental events, furthermore, is much less prominent than in psychoanalytic psychotherapy.

A fourth point in common between these two systems is that their theoretical paradigms exclude many traditional psychoanalytic assumptions such as infantile sexuality, fixations, the unconscious, and mechanisms of defense. The behavior and cognitive therapists may devise their therapeutic strategies on the basis of introspective data provided by the patient; however, they generally take the patients' self-reports at face value and do not make the kind of high-level abstractions characteristic of psychoanalytic formulations.

Finally, a major assumption of both cognitive therapy and behavior therapy is that the patient has acquired maladaptive reaction patterns that can be "unlearned" without the absolute requirement that he obtain insight into the origin of the symptom. . . .

There are obvious differences in the techniques used in behavior therapy and cognitive therapy. In systematic desensitization, for example, the behavior therapist induces a predetermined sequence of pictorial images alternating with periods of relaxation. The cognitive therapist, on the other hand, relies more on the patient's spontaneously experienced and reported thoughts. These cognitions, whether in pictorial or verbal form, are the target for therapeutic work. The technical distinctions between the two systems of psychotherapy are often blurred, however. For example, the cognitive therapist uses induced images to clarify problems (Beck, 1967; 1970), and the behavior therapist uses verbal techniques such as "thought-stoppage" (Wolpe & Lazarus, 1966).

The most striking theoretical difference between cognitive and behavior therapy lies in the concepts used to explain the dissolution of maladaptive responses through therapy. Wolpe, for example, utilizes behavioral or neurophysiological explanations such as counterconditioning or reciprocal inhibition; the cognitivists postulate the modification of conceptual systems, i.e., changes in attitudes or modes of thinking. As will be discussed later, many behavior therapists implicitly or explicitly recognize the importance of cognitive factors in therapy, although they do not expand on these in detail (Davison, 1968; Lazarus, 1968). . . .

TECHNIQUES OF COGNITIVE THERAPY

Cognitive therapy may be defined in two ways: In a broad sense, any technique whose major mode of action is the modification of faulty patterns of thinking can be regarded as cognitive therapy. This definition embraces all therapeutic operations that *indirectly* affect the cognitive patterns, as well as those that directly affect them (Frank, 1961). An individual's distorted views of himself and his world, for example, may be corrected through insight into the historical antecedents of his misinterpretations (as in dynamic psychotherapy), through greater congruence between the concept of the self and the ideal (as in Rogerian therapy), and through increasingly sharp recognition of the unreality of fears (as in systematic desensitization). . . .

However, cognitive therapy may be defined more narrowly as a set of operations focused on a patient's cognitions (verbal or pictorial) and on the premises, assumptions, and attitudes underlying these cognitions. This section will describe the specific techniques of cognitive therapy.

Recognizing Idiosyncratic Cognitions

One of the main cognitive techniques consists of training the patient to recognize his idiosyncratic cognitions or "automatic thoughts" (Beck, 1963). Ellis (1962) refers to these cognitions as "internalized statements" or "self-statements," and explains them to the patient as "things that you tell yourself." These cognitions are termed idiosyncratic because they reflect a faulty appraisal, ranging from a mild distortion to a complete misinterpretation, and because they fall into a pattern that is peculiar to a given individual or to a particular psychopathological state.

In the acutely disturbed patient, the distorted ideation is frequently in the center of the patient's phenomenal field. In such cases, the patient is very much aware of these idiosyncratic thoughts and can easily describe them. The acutely paranoid patient, for instance, is bombarded with thoughts relevant to his being persecuted, abused, or discriminated against by other people. In the mild or moderate neurotic, the distorted ideas are generally at the periphery of awareness. It is therefore necessary to motivate and to train the patient to attend to these thoughts.

Many patients reporting unpleasant affects describe a sequence consisting of a specific event (external stimulus) leading to an unpleasant affect. For instance, the patient may outline the sequence of (a) seeing an old friend and then (b) experiencing a feeling of sadness. Oftentimes, the sadness is inexplicable to the patient. Another person (a) hears about somebody having been killed in an automobile accident and (b) feels anxiety. However, he cannot make a direct connection between these two phenomena; e.g., there is a missing link in the sequence.

In these instances of a particular event leading to an unpleasant affect, it is possible to discern an intervening variable, namely, a cognition, which forms the bridge between the external stimulus and the subjective feeling. Seeing an old friend stimulates cognitions such as "It won't be like old times," or "He won't accept me as he used to." The cognition then generates the sadness. The report of an automobile accident stimulates a pictorial image in which the patient himself is the victim of an automobile accident. The image then leads to the anxiety.

This paradigm can be further illustrated by a number of examples. A patient treated by the writer complained that he experienced anxiety whenever he saw a dog. He was puzzled by the fact that he experienced anxiety even when the dog was chained or caged or else was obviously harmless. The patient was instructed: "Notice what thoughts go through our mind the next time you see a dog—any dog." At the next interview, he patient reported that during numerous encounters with dogs between appointments, he had recognized a phenomenon that he had not noticed previously; namely, that each time he saw the dog he had a thought such as "It's going to bite me."

By being able to detect the intervening cognitions, the patient was able to understand why he felt anxious, namely, he indiscriminately regarded every dog as dangerous. He stated, "I even got that thought when I saw a small poodle. Then I realized how ridiculous it was to think that a poodle would hurt me." He also recognized that when he saw a big dog on a leash, the thought of the most deleterious consequences: "The dog will jump up and bite out one of my eyes," or "It will jump up and bite my jugular vein and kill me." Within 2 or 3 weeks, the patient was able to overcome completely his long-standing dog phobia simply by recognizing his cognitions when exposed to a dog.

Another example was provided by a college student who experienced explicable anxiety in a social situation. After being trained to examine and write down his cognitions, he reported that in social situations he would have thoughts such as, "They think I look pathetic," or "Nobody will want to talk to me," or "I'm just a misfit." These thoughts were followed by anxiety.

A patient complained that he was chronically angry at practically everybody whom he saw, but could not account for his angry response to these people. After some training at recognizing his cognitions, he reported having such thoughts as "He's pushing me around," "He thinks I'm a pushover," "He's trying to take advantage of me." Immediately after experiencing these thoughts, he would feel angry at the individual towards whom they were directed. He also realized that there was no realistic basis for his appraising people in this negative way.

Sometimes, the cognition may take a pictorial form instead of, or in addition to, the verbal form (Beck, 1970). A woman who experienced spurts of anxiety when riding across a bridge was able to recognize that the anxiety was preceded by a pictorial image of her car breaking through the guard rail and falling off the bridge. Another woman, with a fear of walking alone, found that her spells of anxiety followed images of her having a heart attack and being left helpless and dying on the street. A college student discovered that his anxiety at leaving his dormitory at night was triggered by visual fantasies of being attacked.

The idiosyncratic cognitions (whether pictorial or verbal) are very rapid and often may contain an elaborate idea compressed into a very short period of time, even into a split second. These cognitions are experienced as though they are automatic; i.e., they seem to arise as if by reflex rather than through reasoning or deliberation. They also seem to have an *involuntary* quality. A severely anxious or depressed or paranoid person, for example, may continually experience the idiosyncratic cognitions, even though he may try to ward them off. Furthermore, these cognitions tend to appear completely *plausible* to the patient

Distancing

Even after a patient has learned to identify his idiosyncratic ideas, he may have difficulty in examining these ideas objectively. The thought often has the same kind of salience as the perception of an external stimulus. "Distancing" refers to the process of gaining objectivity towards these cognitions. Since the individual with a neurosis tends to accept the validity of his idiosyncratic thoughts without subjecting them to any kind of critical evaluation, it is essential to train him to make a distinction between thought and external reality, between hypothesis and fact. Patients are often surprised to discover that they have been equating an inference with reality and that they have attached a high degree of truth-value to their distorted concepts.

The therapeutic dictum communicated to the patient is as follows: Simply because he *thinks* something does not necessarily mean that it is true. While such a dictum may seem to be a platitude, the writer has found with surprising regularity that patients have benefited from the repeated reminder that thoughts are not equivalent to external reality.

Once the patient is able to "objectify" his thoughts, he is ready for the later stages of reality testing: applying rules of evidence and logic and considering alternative explanations.

Correcting Cognitive Distortions and Deficiencies

The writer has already indicated that patients show faulty or disordered thinking in certain circumscribed areas of experience. In these particular sectors, they have a reduced ability to make fine discriminations and tend to make global, undifferentiated judgments. Part of the task of cognitive therapy is to help the patient to recognize faulty thinking and to make appropriate corrections. It is often very useful for the patient to specify the kind of fallacious thinking involved in his cognitive responses.

Arbitrary inference refers to the process of drawing a conclusion when evidence is lacking or is actually contrary to the conclusion. This type of deviant thinking usually takes the form of personalization (or self-reference). A depressed patient, who saw a frown on the face of a passerby, thought, "He is disgusted with me." A phobic girl of 21, reading about a woman who had had a heart attack, got the thought, "I probably have heart disease." A depressed woman, who was kept waiting for a few minutes by the therapist, thought, "He has deliberately left in order to avoid seeing me."

Overgeneralization refers to the process of making an unjustified generalization on the basis of a single incident. This may take the form that was described in the case of the man with the dog phobia, who generalized from a particular dog that might attack him to all dogs. Another example is a patient who thinks, "I never succeed at anything" when he has a single isolated failure.

Magnification refers to the propensity to exaggerate the meaning or significance of a particular event. A person with a fear of dying, for instance, interpreted every unpleasant sensation or pain in his body as a sign of some fatal disease such as cancer, heart attack, or cerebral hemorrhage. Ellis (1962) applied the label "castrophizing" to this kind of reaction.

As noted above, it is often helpful for the patient to label the particular aberration involved in his maladaptive cognition. Once the patient has firmly established that a particular type of cognition, such as "That dog is going to bite me," is invalid, he will be equipped to correct this cognition on subsequent occasions. For example, his planned, rational response to the stimulus of a toy poodle would be, "Actually, it is just a harmless poodle and there is only a remote chance that it would bite me. And even if it did, it could not really injure me."

Cognitive deficiency refers to the disregard for an important aspect of a life situation. Patients with this defect ignore, fail to integrate, or do not utilize information derived from experience. Such a patient, consequently, behaves as though he has a defect in his system of expectations: He consistently engages in behavior which he realizes, in retrospect, is self-defeating. This class of patients includes those who "act out," e.g., psychopaths, as well as those whose overt behavior sabotages important personal goals. These individuals sacrifice long-range satisfaction or expose themselves to later pain or danger in favor of immediate satisfactions. This category includes problems such as alcoholism, obesity, drug addition, sexual deviation, and compulsion gambling.

The deficient-anticipation patients show two major characteristics: First, when they yield to their wishes to engage in self-defeating, dangerous, or antisocial activities, they are oblivious of the probable consequences of their actions. At these times, they avoid thinking about the consequences by concentrating only on the present activity. They may fortify this *modus operandi* through an elaborate system of self-deceptions, such as "It can't do any harm to cut loose, now." Secondly, irrespective of how often the individual is "burned" as a result of his maladaptive actions, he does not seem to integrate knowledge of the cause-and-effect relationships into his behavior.

Therapy of such cases consists of training the patient to think of the consequences as soon as his self-defeating wish arises. Consideration of the long-range loss must be forced into the interval between impulse and action. A patient, for instance, who continually operated his car beyond the speed limit or drove through stoplights was surprised each time he was stopped by a traffic officer. On interview, it was discovered that the patient was generally absorbed in a fantasy while driving—he imaged himself as a famous racing-car driver engaged in a race. Therapy at first consisted of trying to get him to watch the odometer—but without success. The next approach consisted of inducing fantasies of speeding, getting caught, and receiving punishment. At first, the patient had great difficulty in visualizing getting caught even though, in general, he could fantasize almost everything. However, after several sessions of induced fantasies, he was able to incorporate a negative outcome into his fantasy. Subsequently, he stopped daydreaming while driving and was able to observe traffic regulations. . . .

CONCLUSIONS

A question could be legitimately raised whether introducing another system of psychotherapy is warranted. The justification is twofold. First, the theoretical framework of cognitive therapy is broader than that of behavior therapy and of some of the more traditional psychotherapies. This theoretical framework is congruent with many of the assumptions of behavior therapy, but provides a greater range of concepts for explaining psychopathology as well as the mode of action of therapy. Moreover, the theoretical structure of cognitive therapy yields hypotheses that can be (and have been) readily tested through the experimental techniques currently available.

Secondly, the cognitive theories provide a framework for the development of a number of therapeutic strategies that are not derivable from the predominantly extrinsic concepts of the conditioning model. Since these cognitive techniques, as well as the behavior techniques, are easily defined and have demonstrated some preliminary evidence of their efficacy in clinical practice, further exposition seems warranted.

Ultimately, the strategies of psychological modification may be usefully regrouped into the cognition-oriented techniques and the behavior-oriented techniques.

The cognitive techniques would include the methods making direct use of ideational material such as systematic desensitization and other forms of induced imagery and in the direct attempts to modify idiosyncratic cognitions. The behavioral techniques would include those operations of a nonintrospective nature, such as in operant conditioning, exposure therapy, graded task assignments, roleplaying, and assertive training.

REFERENCES

BECK, A. T. Thinking and depression; 1. Idiosyncratic content and cognitive distortions. *Archives of General Psychiatry,* 1963, **9,** 324-333.

BECK, A. T. *Depression: Clinical, experimental, and theoretical aspects.* New York: Hoeber, 1967.

BECK, A. T. Role of fantasies in psychotherapy and psychopathology. *Journal of Nervous and Mental Disease,* 1970. **150,** 3-17.

DAVISON, G. C. Systematic desensitization as a counter-conditioning process. *Journal of Abnormal Psychology,* 1968, **73,** 91-99.

ELLIS, A. *Reason and emotion in psychotherapy.* New York: Lyle Stuart, 1962.

FRANK, J. D. *Persuasion and healing.* Baltimore: Johns Hopkins Press, 1961.

LAZARUS, A. Variations in desensitization therapy. *Psychotherapy: Theory, research and practice,* 1968, **5,** 50-52.

WOLPE, J., LAZARUS, A. A. *Behavior therapy techniques: A guide to the treatment of neuroses.* New York: Pergamon Press, 1966.

SELECTION 44

The Effectiveness of Psychotherapy: The Consumer Reports Study

Martin E. P. Seligman (1995)

The evaluation of the effectiveness of psychotherapy is a major concern of psychologists. Obviously if one approach to therapy is vastly superior, it would be the preferred treatment. An even more basic concern is the degree to which any type of psychotherapy is effective. Martin E. P. Seligman served as a consultant to a study by *Consumer Reports* that measured the effectiveness of various types of psychotherapy.

Seligman was born in Albany, New York in 1942. He attended Princeton University as an undergraduate and received his Ph.D. in psychology from the University of Pennsylvania in 1967, where he is currently a professor of psychology. He served as president of the American Psychological Association in 1998. Seligman has written many books, including *Learned Optimism* (Knopf, 1991) and *What You Can Change and What You Can't* (Knopf, 1993).

The following selection is from "The Effectiveness of Psychotherapy: The Consumer Reports Study," which was published in *American Psychologist* in 1995. In it, Seligman reviews survey results that indicate that psychotherapy is indeed effective. As you read this selection, note the distinction between efficacy studies and effectiveness studies. It is important to remember that the information was obtained through survey results.

Key Concept: evaluation of psychotherapy

APA Citation: Seligman, M. E. P. (1995). The effectiveness of therapy: The Consumer Reports study. *American Psychologist, 50,* 965–974.

*C*onsumer Reports (1995, November) published an article which concluded that patients benefited very substantially from psychotherapy, that long-term treatment did considerably better than short-term treatment, and that psychotherapy alone did not differ in effectiveness from medication plus psychotherapy. Furthermore, no specific modality of psychotherapy did better than any other for any disorder; psychologists, psychiatrists, and social workers did not differ in their effectiveness as treaters; and all did better than marriage counselors and long-term family doctoring. Patients whose length of therapy or choice of therapist was limited by insurance or managed care did worse. The methodological virtues and drawbacks of this large-scale survey are examined and contrasted with the more traditional efficacy study, in which patients are randomized into a manualized, fixed duration treatment or into control groups. I conclude that the *Consumer Reports* survey complements the efficacy method, and that the best features

of these two methods can be combined into a more ideal method that will best provide empirical validation of psychotherapy.

How do we find out whether psychotherapy works? To answer this, two methods have arisen: the *efficacy study* and the *effectiveness study*. An efficacy study is the more popular method. It contrasts some kind of therapy to a comparison group under well-controlled conditions. But there is much more to an efficacy study than just a control group, and such studies have become a highparadigm endeavor with sophisticated methodology. In the ideal efficacy study, all of the following niceties are found:

1. The patients are randomly assigned to treatment and control conditions.

2. The controls are rigorous: Not only are patients included who receive no treatment at all, but placebos containing potentially therapeutic ingredients credi-

ble to both the patient and the therapist are used in order to control for such influences as rapport, expectation of gain, and sympathetic attention (dubbed *nonspecifics*).

3. The treatments are manualized, with highly detailed scripting of therapy made explicit. Fidelity to the manual is assessed using videotaped sessions, and wayward implementers are corrected.

4. Patients are seen for a fixed number of sessions.

5. The target outcomes are well operationalized (e.g., clinician-diagnosed DSM–IV disorder, number of reported orgasms, self-reports of panic attacks, percentage of fluent utterances).

6. Raters and diagnosticians are blind to which group the patient comes from. (Contrary to the "double-blind" method of drug studies, efficacy studies of psychotherapy can be at most "single-blind," since the patient and therapist both know what the treatment is. Whenever you hear someone demanding the double-blind study of psychotherapy, hold onto your wallet.)

7. The patients meet criteria for a single diagnosed disorder, and patients with multiple disorders are typically excluded.

8. The patients are followed for a fixed period after termination of treatment with a thorough assessment battery.

So when an efficacy study demonstrates a difference between a form of psychotherapy and controls, academic clinicians and researchers take this modality seriously indeed. In spite of how expensive and time-consuming they are, hundreds of efficacy studies of both psychotherapy and drugs now exist—many of them well done. These studies show, among many other things, that cognitive therapy, interpersonal therapy, and medications all provide moderate relief from unipolar depressive disorder; that exposure and clomipramine both relieve the symptoms of obsessive–compulsive disorder moderately well but that exposure has more lasting benefits; that cognitive therapy works very well in panic disorder; that systematic desensitization relieves specific phobias; that "applied tension" virtually cures blood and injury phobia; that transcendental meditation relieves anxiety; that aversion therapy produces only marginal improvement with sexual offenders; that disulfram (Antabuse) does not provide lasting relief from alcoholism; that flooding plus medication does better in the treatment of agoraphobia than either alone; and that cognitive therapy provides significant relief of bulimia, outperforming medications alone (see Seligman, 1991, for a review).

The high praise "empirically validated" is now virtually synonymous with positive results in efficacy studies, and many investigators have come to think that an efficacy study is the "gold standard" for measuring whether a treatment works.

I also had come to that opinion when I wrote *What You Can Change & What You Can't* (Seligman, 1994). In trying to summarize what was known about the effects of the panoply of drugs and psychotherapies for each major disorder, I read hundreds of efficacy studies and came to appreciate the genre. At minimum I was convinced that an efficacy study may be the best scientific instrument for telling us whether a novel treatment is *likely* to work on a given disorder when the treatment is exported from controlled conditions into the field. Because treatment in efficacy studies is delivered under tightly controlled conditions to carefully screened patients, sensitivity is maximized and efficacy studies are very useful for deciding whether one treatment is better than another treatment for a given disorder.

But my belief has changed about what counts as a "gold standard." And it was a study by *Consumer Reports* (1995, November) that singlehandedly shook my belief. I came to see that deciding whether one treatment, under highly controlled conditions, works better than another treatment or a control group is a different question from deciding what works in the field (Muñoz, Hollon, McGrath, Rehm, & VandenBos, 1994). I no longer believe that efficacy studies are the only, or even the best, way of finding out what treatments actually work in the field. I have come to believe that the "effectiveness" study of how patients fare under the actual conditions of treatment in the field, can yield useful and credible "empirical validation" of psychotherapy and medication. This is the method that *Consumer Reports* pioneered.

WHAT EFFICACY STUDIES LEAVE OUT

It is easy to assume that, if some form of treatment is not listed among the many which have been "empirically validated," the treatment must be inert, rather than just "untested" given the existing method of validation. I will dub this the *inertness assumption*. The inertness assumption is a challenge to practitioners, since long-term dynamic treatment, family therapy, and more generally, eclectic psychotherapy, are not on the list of treatments empirically validated by efficacy studies, and these modalities probably make up most of what is actually practiced. I want to look closely at the inertness assumption, since the effectiveness strategy of empirical validation follows from what is wrong with the assumption.

The usual argument against the inertness assumption is that long-term dynamic therapy, family therapy, and eclectic therapy cannot be tested in efficacy studies, and thus we have no hard evidence one way or another. They cannot be tested because they are too cumbersome for the efficacy study paradigm. Imagine, for example, what a decent efficacy study of long-term dynamic therapy would require: control groups receiving no treatment for several years; an equally credible comparison treatment of the same duration that has the same "nonspecifics"—rapport, attention, and expectation of gain—but is actually inert; a step-by-step manual covering hundreds of sessions; and the random assignment of patients to treatments which last a year or more. The ethical and scientific problems of such research are daunting, to say nothing of how much such a study would cost.

While this argument cannot be gainsaid, it still leaves the average psychotherapist in an uncomfortable position, with a substantial body of literature validating a panoply of short-term therapies the psychotherapist does not perform, and with the long-term, eclectic therapy he or she does perform unproven.

But there is a much better argument against the inertness assumption: *The efficacy study is the wrong method for empirically validating psychotherapy as it is actually done, because it omits too many crucial elements of what is done in the field.*

The five properties that follow characterize psychotherapy as it is done in the field. Each of these properties are absent from an efficacy study done under controlled conditions. If these properties are important to patients' getting better, efficacy studies will underestimate or even miss altogether the value of psychotherapy done in the field.

1. Psychotherapy (like other health treatments) in the field is *not of fixed duration*. It usually keeps going until the patient is markedly improved or until he or she quits. In contrast, the intervention in efficacy studies stops after a limited number of sessions—usually about 12—regardless of how well or how poorly the patient is doing.
2. Psychotherapy (again, like other health treatments) in the field is *self-correcting*. If one technique is not working, another technique—or even another modality—is usually tried. In contrast, the intervention in efficacy studies is confined to a small number of techniques, all within one modality and manualized to be delivered in a fixed order.
3. Patients in psychotherapy in the field often get there by *active* shopping, entering a kind of treatment they actively sought with a therapist they screened and chose. This is especially true of patients who work with independent practitioners, and somewhat less so of patients who go to outpatient clinics or have managed care. In contrast, patients enter efficacy studies by the *passive* process of random assignment to treatment and acquiescence with who and what happens to be offered in the study (Howard, Orlinsky, & Lueger, 1994).
4. Patients in psychotherapy in the field usually have *multiple problems*, and psychotherapy is geared to relieving parallel and interacting difficulties. Patients in efficacy studies are selected to have but one diagnosis (except when two conditions are highly comorbid) by a long set of exclusion and inclusion criteria.
5. Psychotherapy in the field is almost always concerned with *improvement in the general functioning* of patients, as well as amelioration of a disorder and relief of specific, presenting symptoms. Efficacy studies usually focus only on specific symptom reduction and whether the disorder ends.

It is hard to imagine how one could ever do a scientifically compelling efficacy study of a treatment which had variable duration and self-correcting improvisations and was aimed at improved quality of life as well as symptom relief, with patients who were not randomly assigned and had multiple problems. But this does not mean that the effectiveness of treatment so delivered cannot be empirically validated. Indeed it can, but it requires a different method: a survey of large numbers of people who have gone through such treatments. So let us explore the virtues and drawbacks of a well-done effectiveness study, the *Consumer Reports* (1995) one, in contrast to an efficacy study.

Consumer Reports Survey

Consumer Reports (CR) included a supplementary survey about psychotherapy and drugs in one version of its 1994 annual questionnaire, along with its customary inquiries about appliances and services. CR's 180,000 readers received this version, which included approximately 100 questions about automobiles and about mental health. CR asked readers to fill out the mental health section "if at any time over the past three years you experienced stress or other emotional problems for which you sought help from any of the following: friends, relatives, or a member of the clergy; a mental health professional like a psychologist or a psychiatrist; your family doctor; or a support group." Twenty-two thousand readers responded. Of these, approximately 7,000 subscribers responded to the mental health questions. Of these 7,000, about 3,000 had just talked to friends, relatives, or clergy, and 4,100 went to some combination of mental health professionals, family doctors, and support groups. Of these 4,100, 2,900 saw a mental health professional: Psychologists (37%) were the most frequently seen mental health professional, followed by psychiatrists (22%), social workers (14%), and marriage counselors (9%). Other mental health professionals made up 18%. In addition, 1,300 joined self-help groups, and about 1,000 saw family physicians. The respondents as a whole were highly educated, predominantly middle class; about half were women, and the median age was 46.

Twenty-six questions were asked about mental health professionals, and parallel but less detailed questions were asked about physicians, medications, and self-help groups:

- What kind of therapist
- What presenting problem (e.g., general anxiety, panic, phobia, depression, low mood, alcohol or drugs, grief, weight, eating disorders, marital or sexual problems, children or family, work, stress)
- Emotional state at outset (from *very poor* to *very good*)
- Emotional state now (from *very poor* to *very good*)
- Group versus individual therapy
- Duration and frequency of therapy

- Modality (psychodynamic, behavioral, cognitive, feminist)
- Cost
- Health care plan and limitations on coverage
- Therapist competence
- How much therapy helped (from *made things a lot better* to *made things a lot worse*) and in what areas (specific problem that led to therapy, relations to others, productivity, coping with stress, enjoying life more, growth and insight, self-esteem and confidence, raising low mood)
- Satisfaction with therapy
- Reasons for termination (problems resolved or more manageable, felt further treatment wouldn't help, therapist recommended termination, a new therapist, concerns about therapist's competence, cost, and problems with insurance coverage)

The data set is thus a rich one, probably uniquely rich, and the data analysis was sophisticated. Because I was privileged to be a consultant to this study and thus privy to the entire data set, much of what I now present will be new to you—even if you have read the *CR* article carefully. *CR*'s analysts decided that no single measure of therapy effectiveness would do and so created a multivariate measure. This composite had three subscales, consisting of:

1. Specific improvement ("How much did treatment help with the specific problem that led you to therapy?" *made no difference; made things somewhat worse; made things a lot worse; not sure*);
2. Satisfaction ("Overall how satisfied were you with this therapist's treatment of your problems?" *completely satisfied; very satisfied; fairly well satisfied; somewhat satisfied; very dissatisfied; completely dissatisfied*); and
3. Global improvement (how respondents described their "overall emotional state" at the time of the survey compared with the start of treatment: "*very poor:* I barely managed to deal with things; *fairly poor:* Life was usually pretty tough for me; *so-so:* I had my ups and downs; *quite good:* I had no serious complaints; *very good:* Life was much the way I liked it to be").

Each of the three subscales was transformed and weighted equally on a 0–100 scale, resulting in a 0–300 scale for effectiveness. The statistical analysis was largely multiple regression, with initial severity and duration of treatment (the two biggest effects) partialed out. Stringent levels of statistical significance were used.

There were a number of clear-cut results, among them:

- Treatment by a mental health professional usually worked. Most respondents got a lot better. Averaged over all mental health professionals, of the 426 people who were feeling *very poor* when they began therapy, 87% were feeling *very good, good,* or at least *so-so* by the time of the survey. Of the 786 people who were feeling *fairly poor* at the outset, 92% were

feeling *very good, good,* or at least *so-so* by the time of the survey. These findings converge with meta-analyses of efficacy (Lipsey & Wilson, 1993; Shapiro & Shapiro, 1982; Smith, Miller, & Glass, 1980).

- Long-term therapy produced more improvement than short-term therapy. This result was very robust, and held up over all statistical models.... This "dose–response curve" held for patients in both psychotherapy alone and in psychotherapy plus medication (see Howard, Kopta, Krause, & Orlinsky, 1986, for parallel dose–response findings for psychotherapy).
- There was no difference between psychotherapy alone and psychotherapy plus medication for any disorder (very few respondents reported that they had medication with no psychotherapy at all).
- While all mental health professionals appeared to help their patients, psychologists, psychiatrists, and social workers did equally well and better than marriage counselors. Their patients' overall improvement scores (0–300 scale) were 220, 226, 225 (not significantly different from each other), and 208 (significantly worse than the first three), respectively.
- Family doctors did just as well as mental health professionals in the short term, but worse in the long term. Some patients saw both family doctors and mental health professionals, and those who saw both had more severe problems. For patients who relied solely on family doctors, their overall improvement scores when treated for up to six months was 213, and it remained at that level (212) for those treated longer than six months. In contrast, the overall improvement scores for patients of mental health professionals was 211 up to six months, but climbed to 232 when treatment went on for more than six months. The advantages of long-term treatment by a mental health professional held not only for the specific problems that led to treatment, but for a variety of general functioning scores as well: ability to relate to others, coping with everyday stress, enjoying life more, personal growth and understanding, self-esteem and confidence.
- Alcoholics Anonymous (AA) did especially well, with an average improvement score of 251, significantly bettering mental health professionals. People who went to non-AA groups had less severe problems and did not do as well as those who went to AA (average score = 215).
- Active shoppers and active clients did better in treatment than passive recipients (determined by responses to "Was it mostly your idea to seek therapy? When choosing this therapist, did you discuss qualifications, therapist's experience, discuss frequency, duration, and cost, speak to someone who was treated by this therapist, check out other therapists? During therapy, did you try to be as open as possible, ask for explanation of diagnosis and un-

clear terms, do homework, not cancel sessions often, discuss negative feelings toward therapist?").

- No specific modality of psychotherapy did any better than any other for any problem. These results confirm the "dodo bird" hypothesis, that all forms of psychotherapies do about equally well (Luborsky, Singer, & Luborsky, 1975). They come as a rude shock to efficacy researchers, since the main theme of efficacy studies has been the demonstration of the usefulness of specific techniques for specific disorders.

- Respondents whose choice of therapist or duration of care was limited by their insurance coverage did worse . . . (determined by responses to "Did limitations on your insurance coverage affect any of the following choices you made? Type of therapist I chose; How often I met with my therapist; How long I stayed in therapy"). . . .

The Ideal Study

The *CR* study, then, is to be taken seriously—not only for its results and its credible source, but for its method. It is large-scale; it samples treatment as it is actually delivered in the field; it samples without obvious bias those who seek out treatment; it measures multiple outcomes including specific improvement and more global gains such as growth, insight, productivity, mood, enjoyment of life, and interpersonal relations; it is statistically stringent and finds clinically meaningful results. Furthermore, it is highly cost-effective.

Its major advantage over the efficacy method for studying the effectiveness of psychotherapy and medications is that it captures how and to whom treatment is actually delivered and toward what end. At the very least, the *CR* study and its underlying survey method provides a powerful addition to what we know about the effectiveness of psychotherapy and a pioneering way of finding out more.

The study is not without flaws, the chief one being the limited meaning of its answer to the question "Can psychotherapy help?" This question has three possible kinds of answers. The first is that psychotherapy does better than something else, such as talking to friends, going to church, or doing nothing at all. Because it lacks comparison groups, the *CR* study only answers this question indirectly. The second possible answer is that psychotherapy returns people to normality or more liberally to within, say, two standard deviations of the average. The *CR* study, lacking an untroubled group and lacking measures of how people were before they became troubled, does not answer this question. The third answer is "Do people have fewer symptoms and a better life after therapy than they did before?" This is the question that the *CR* study answers with a clear "yes."

The *CR* study can be improved upon, allowing it to speak to all three senses of "psychotherapy works." These improvements would combine several of the best features of efficacy studies with the realism of the survey method. First, the survey could be done prospectively: A large sample of those who seek treatment could be given an assessment battery before and after treatment, while still preserving progress-contingent treatment duration, self-correction, multiple problems, and self-selection of treatment. Second, the assessment battery could include well-normed questionnaires as well as detailed, behavioral information in addition to more global improvement information, thus increasing its sensitivity and allowing it to answer the return-to-normal question. Third, blind diagnostic workups could be included, adding multiple perspectives to self-report.

At any rate, *Consumer Reports* has provided empirical validation of the effectiveness of psychotherapy. Prospective and diagnostically sophisticated surveys, combined with the well-normed and detailed assessment used in efficacy studies, would bolster this pioneering study. They would be expensive, but, in my opinion, very much worth doing.

REFERENCES

Consumer Reports. (1995, November). Mental health: Does therapy help? pp. 734–739.

Howard, K., Kopta, S., Krause, M., & Orlinsky, D. (1986). The dose-effect relationship in psychotherapy. *American Psychologist, 41,* 159–164.

Howard, K., Orlinsky, D., & Lueger, R. (1994). Clinically relevant outcome research in individual psychotherapy. *British Journal of Psychiatry, 165,* 4–8.

Lipsey, M., & Wilson, D. (1993). The efficacy of psychological, educational, and behavioral treatment: Confirmation from meta-analysis. *American Psychologist, 48,* 1181–1209.

Luborsky, L., Singer, B., & Luborsky, L. (1975). Comparative studies of psychotherapies. *Archives of General Psychiatry, 32,* 995–1008.

Muñoz, R., Hollon, S., McGrath, E., Rehm, L., & VandenBos, G. (1994). On the AHCPR guidelines: Further considerations for practitioners. *American Psychologist, 49,* 42–61.

Seligman, M. (1991). *Learned optimism.* New York: Knopf.

Seligman, M. (1994). *What you can change & what you can't.* New York: Knopf.

Shapiro, D., & Shapiro, D. (1982). Meta-analysis of comparative therapy outcome studies: A replication and refinement. *Psychological Bulletin, 92,* 581–604.

Smith, M., Glass, G., & Miller, T. (1980). *The benefit of psychotherapy.* Baltimore: Johns Hopkins University Press.

Social Psychology

Selection 45
STANLEY MILGRAM, from "Behavioral Study of Obedience," Journal of Abnormal and Social Psychology

Selection 46
JOHN M. DARLEY and BIBB LATANÉ, from "When Will People Help in a Crisis?," Psychology Today

Selection 47
MUZAFER SHERIF, from "Superordinate Goals in the Reduction of Intergroup Conflict," The American Journal of Sociology

Selection 48
ALBERT BANDURA, DORTHEA ROSS, and SHEILA ROSS, from "Imitation of Film-Mediated Aggressive Models" Journal of Abnormal and Social Psychology

Behavioral Study of Obedience

Stanley Milgram (1963)

Obedience is a type of social influence in which an individual exhibits the behavior required by a command from someone else. We are taught as children to obey parents and teachers, and as we grow up we learn to obey employers, law enforcement officers, and a variety of other authority figures. One of the best-known studies on obedience was performed by Stanley Milgram at Yale University.

Milgram (1933–1984) studied under social psychologist Solomon E. Asch and earned his Ph.D. from Harvard University in 1960. He taught at Yale University and Harvard University before accepting a position at the Graduate Center of the City University of New York in 1967. Milgram, a very creative social psychologist, studied social communication, prejudice, interpersonal relationships, and obedience. Milgram wrote a more extensive account of his obedience research in his book *Obedience to Authority: An Experimental View* (Harper & Row, 1974).

This selection from "Behavioral Study of Obedience," was published in the *Journal of Abnormal and Social Psychology* in 1963. It presents the results of the first in a series of Milgram's obedience experiments in which a large percentage of his participants delivered what they believed to be the maximum level of electric shocks to "learners" (Milgram's confederate), despite the learners' screaming protests, because an authority figure told them to do so. This study has been a subject of controversy during the past four decades because of its ethical considerations as well as its social implications. As you read this selection, consider the extent to which you obey in today's society.

Key Concept: obedience

APA Citation: Milgram, S. (1963). Behavioral study of obedience. *Journal of Abnormal and Social Psychology, 67,* 371–378.

Obedience is as basic an element in the structure of social life as one can point to. Some system of authority is a requirement of all communal living, and it is only the man dwelling in isolation who is not forced to respond, through defiance or submission, to the commands of others. Obedience, as a determinant of behavior, is of particular relevance to our time. It has been reliably established that from 1933–45 millions of innocent persons were systematically slaughtered on command. Gas chambers were built, death camps were guarded, daily quotas of corpses were produced with the same efficiency as the manufacture of appliances. These inhumane policies may have originated in the mind of a single person, but they could only be carried out on a massive scale if a very large number of persons obeyed orders. . . .

General Procedure

A procedure was devised which seems useful as a tool for studying obedience (Milgram, 1961). It consists of ordering a naive subject to administer electric shock to a victim.

A simulated shock generator is used, with 30 clearly marked voltage levels that range from 15 to 450 volts. The instrument bears verbal designations that range from Slight Shock to Danger: Severe Shock. The responses of the victim, who is a trained confederate of the experimenter, are standardized. The orders to administer shocks are given to the naive subject in the context of a "learning experiment" ostensibly set up to study the effects of punishment on memory. As the experiment proceeds the naive subject is commanded to administer increasingly more intense shocks to the victim, even to a point of reaching the level marked Danger: Severe Shock. Internal resistances become stronger, and at a certain point the subject refuses to go on with the experiment. Behavior prior to this rupture is considered "obedience," in that the subject complies with the commands of the experimenter. The point of rupture is the act of disobedience. A quantitative value is assigned to the subject's performance based on the maximum intensity shock he is willing to administer before he refuses to participate further. Thus for any particular subject and for any particular experimental condition the degree of obedience may be specified with a numerical value. The crux of the study is to systematically vary the factors believed to alter the degree of obedience to the experimental commands. . . .

Method

Subjects

The subjects were 40 males between the ages of 20 and 50, drawn from New Haven and surrounding communities. Subjects were obtained by a newspaper advertisement and direct mail solicitation. Those who responded to the appeal believed they were to participate in a study of memory and learning at Yale University. A wide range of occupations is represented in the sample. Typical subjects were postal clerks, high school teachers, salesmen, engineers, and laborers. Subjects ranged in educational level from one who had not finished elementary school, to those who had doctorate and other professional degrees. They were paid $4.50 for their participation in the experiment. However, subjects were told that payment was simply for coming to the laboratory, and that the money was theirs no matter what happened after they arrived. . . .

Personnel and Locale

The experiment was conducted on the grounds of Yale University in the elegant interaction laboratory. (This detail is relevant to the perceived legitimacy of the experiment. In further variations, the experiment was dissociated from the university, with consequences for performance.) The role of experimenter was played by a 31-year-old high school teacher of biology. His manner was impassive, and his appearance somewhat stern throughout the experiment. He was dressed in a gray technician's coat. The victim was played by a 47-year-old accountant, trained for the role; he was of Irish-American stock, whom most observers found mild-mannered and likeable.

Procedure

One naive subject and one victim (an accomplice) performed in each experiment. A pretext had to be devised that would justify the administration of electric shock by the naive subject. This was effectively accomplished by the cover story. After a general introduction on the presumed relation between punishment and learning, subjects were told:

> But actually, we know *very little* about the effect of punishment on learning, because almost no truly scientific studies have been made of it in human beings.
>
> For instance, we don't know how *much* punishment is best for learning—and we don't know how much differ-

ence it makes as to who is giving the punishment, whether an adult learns best from a younger or an older person than himself—or many things of that sort.

> So in this study we are bringing together a number of adults of different occupations and ages. And we're asking some of them to be teachers and some of them to be learners.
>
> We want to find out just what effect different people have on each other as teachers and learners, and also what effect *punishment* will have on learning in this situation.
>
> Therefore, I'm going to ask one of you to be the teacher here tonight and the other one to be the learner.
>
> Does either of you have a preference?

Subjects then drew slips of paper from a hat to determine who would be the teacher and who would be the learner in the experiment. The drawing was rigged so that the naive subject was always the teacher and the accomplice always the learner. (Both slips contained the word "Teacher.") Immediately after the drawing, the teacher and learner were taken to an adjacent room and the learner was strapped into an "electric chair" apparatus.

The experimenter explained that the straps were to prevent excessive movement while the learner was being shocked. The effect was to make it impossible for him to escape from the situation. An electrode was attached to the learner's wrist, and electrode paste was applied "to avoid blisters and burns." Subjects were told that the electrode was attached to the shock generator in the adjoining room.

In order to improve credibility the experimenter declared, in response to a question by the learner: "Although the shocks can be extremely painful, they cause no permanent tissue damage."

Learning task. The lesson administered by the subject was a paired-associate learning task. The subject read a series of word pairs to the learner, and then read the first word of the pair along with four terms. The learner was to indicate which of the four terms had originally been paired with the first word. He communicated his answer by pressing one of four switches in front of him, which in turn lit up one of four numbered quadrants in a answer-box located atop the shock generator.

Shock generator. The instrument panel consists of 30 lever switches set in a horizontal line. Each switch is clearly labeled with a voltage designation that ranges from 15 to 450 volts. There is a 15-volt increment from one switch to the next going from left to right. In addition, the following verbal designations are clearly indicated for groups of four switches going from left to right: Slight Shock, Moderate Shock, Strong Shock, Intense Shock, Extremely Intense Shock, Danger: Severe Shock. (Two switches after this last designation are simply marked XXX.)

Upon depressing a switch: a pilot light corresponding to each switch is illuminated in bright red; an electric buzzing is heard; an electric blue light, labeled "voltage energizer," flashes; the dial on the voltage meter swings to the right; various relay clicks are sounded.

The upper left-hand corner of the generator is labeled Shock generator, Type ZLB, Dyson Instrument Company, Waltham, Mass. Output 15 Volts–450 Volts.

Details of the instrument were carefully handled to insure an appearance of authenticity. The panel was engraved by precision industrial engravers, and all components were of high quality. No subject in the experiment suspected that the instrument was merely a simulated shock generator.

Sample shock. Each naive subject is given a sample shock on the shock generator, prior to beginning his run as teacher. This shock is always 45 volts, and is applied by pressing the third switch of the generator. The shock is applied to the wrist of the naive subject, and has its source in a 45-volt battery wired into the generator. This further convinces the subject of the authenticity of the generator.

Shock instructions. The subject is told to administer a shock to the learner each time he gives a wrong response. Moreover—and this is the key command—the subject is instructed to "move one level higher on the shock generator each time the learner flashes a wrong answer." He is also instructed to announce the voltage level before administering a shock. This serves to continually remind subjects of the increasing intensity of shocks administered to the learner.

Preliminary and regular run. Pretests revealed that the procedure of reading words and administering shocks requires some practice before it can be handled smoothly. Therefore, immediately preceding the regular run, the teacher is given a preliminary series of 10 words to read to the learner. There are 3 neutral words in the practice series (i.e., words that the learner answers correctly), so that shocks are administered for 7 of the words, with the maximum shock of 105 volts (moderate shock). Almost all subjects master the procedure by the time the preliminary run is over.

Subjects are then presented with a second list, and are told that the procedure is the same as for the first list; the experimenter adds however:

When you get to the bottom of the list, repeat it over again, and continue giving shocks, until the learner has learned all the pairs correctly.

The experimenter instructs the subject to,

start from 15 volts and increase the shock level one step each time the learner gives a wrong answer.

Feedback from the victim. In all conditions the learner gives a predetermined set of responses to the word pair test, based on a schedule of approximately three wrong answers to one correct answer. In the present experimental condition no vocal response or other sign of protest is heard from the learner until Shock Level 300 is reached. When the 300-volt shock is administered, the learner pounds on the wall of the room in which he is bound to the electric chair. The pounding can be heard by the subject. From this point on, the learner's answers no longer appear on the four-way panel.

At this juncture, subjects ordinarily turn to the experimenter for guidance. The experimenter instructs the subject to treat absence of a response as a wrong answer, and to shock the subject according to the usual schedule. He advises the subjects to allow 5–10 seconds before considering no response as a wrong answer, and to increase the shock level one step each time the learner fails to respond correctly. The learner's pounding is repeated after the 315-volt shock is administered; afterwards he is not heard from, nor do his answers reappear on the four-way signal box.

Experimenter feedback. At various points in the experiment the subject may turn to the experimenter for advice on whether he should continue to administer shocks. Or he may indicate that he does not wish to go on. It was important to standardize the experimenter's responses to these inquiries and reactions.

If the subject indicated his unwillingness to go on, the experimenter responded with a sequence of "prods," using as many as necessary to bring the subject into line.

Prod 1: Please continue. *or* Please go on.

Prod 2: The experiment requires that you continue.

Prod 3: It is absolutely essential that you continue.

Prod 4: You have no other choice, you *must* go on.

The prods were always made in sequence: Only if Prod 1 had been unsuccessful, could Prod 2 be used. If the subject still refused to obey the experimenter after Prod 4, the experiment was terminated. The experimenter's tone of voice was at all times firm, but not impolite. The sequence was begun anew on each occasion that the subject balked or showed reluctance to follow orders.

Special prods. If the subject asked if the learner was liable to suffer permanent physical injury, the experimenter said:

Although the shocks may be painful, there is no permanent tissue damage, so please go on. [Followed by Prods 2, 3, and 4 if necessary.]

If the subject said that the learner did not want to go on, the experimenter replied:

Whether the learner likes it or not, you must go on until he has learned all the word pairs correctly. So please go on. [Followed by Prods 2, 3, and 4 if necessary.]

Dependent Measures

The primary dependent measure for any subject is the maximum shock he administers before he refuses to go any further. In principle this may vary from 0 (for a subject who refuses to administer even the first shock) to 30 (for a subject who administers the highest shock on the generator). A subject who breaks off the experiment at any point prior to administering the thirtieth shock level is termed a *defiant subject*. One who complies with experimental command fully, and proceeds to administer all shock levels commanded, is termed an *obedient* subject. ...

Interview and dehoax. Following the experiment, subjects were interviewed; open-ended questions, projective measures, and attitude scales were employed. After the interview, procedures were undertaken to assure that the subject would leave the laboratory in a state of well being. A friendly reconciliation was arranged between the subject and the victim, and an effort was made to reduce any tensions that arose as a result of the experiment.

Results

Preliminary Notions

Before giving an account of the experimental results, it is instructive to consider how persons predict others will perform when commanded to administer powerful shocks to another person. Fourteen Yale seniors, all psychology majors, were provided with a detailed description of the experimental situation. They were asked to reflect carefully on it, and to predict the behavior of 100 hypothetical subjects. More specifically, they were instructed to plot the distribution of obedience of "100 Americans of diverse occupations, and ranging in age from 20 to 50 years," who were placed in the experimental situation.

There was considerable agreement among the respondents on the expected behavior of hypothetical subjects. All respondents predicted that only an insignificant minority would go through to the end of the shock series. (The estimates ranged from 0 to 3%; i.e, the most "pessimistic" member of the class predicted that of 100 persons, 3 would continue through to the most potent shock available on the shock generator—450 volts.) The class mean was 1.2%. The question was also posed informally to colleagues of the author, and the most general feeling was that few if any subjects would go beyond the designation Very Strong Shock.

Result of Experiment I

Subjects accept situation. With few exceptions subjects were convinced of the reality of the experimental situation, that they were administering shocks to another person, and the most potent shocks were extremely painful. In the post-experimental interview subjects were asked: "How painful to the learner were the last few shocks that you administered to him?" Subjects were instructed to indicate their answers on a printed 14-point scale ranging from "Not at all painful" to "Extremely painful." The

modal response was 14 (Extremely painful) with the mean at 13.42.

Signs of extreme tension. Many subjects showed signs of nervousness in the experimental situation, and especially upon administering the more powerful shocks. In a large number of cases the degree of tension reached extremes that are rarely seen in sociopsychological laboratory studies. Subjects were observed to sweat, tremble, stutter, bite their lips, groan, and dig their fingernails into their flesh. These were characteristic rather than exceptional responses to the experiment.

One sign of tension was the regular occurrence of nervous laughing fits. Fourteen of the 40 subjects showed definite signs of nervous laughter and smiling. The laughter seemed entirely out of place, even bizarre. Full-blown, uncontrollable seizures were observed for 3 subjects. On one occasion we observed a seizure so violently convulsive that it was necessary to call a halt to the experiment. The subject, a 46-year-old encyclopedia salesman, was seriously embarrassed by his untoward and uncontrollable behavior. In the post-experimental interviews subjects took such pains to point out that they were not sadistic types, and that the laughter did not mean they enjoyed shocking the victim.

Distribution of scores. It had been conjectured that persons would not, in general, agree to administer shocks beyond the level designated Very Strong Shock. The distribution of maximum shocks for this experiment is shown in Table 1. The obtained distribution of scores deviates radically from the prediction.

Upon command of the experimenter, each of the 40 subjects went beyond the expected breakoff point. No subject stopped prior to administering Shock Level 20. (At this level—300 volts—the victim kicks on the wall and no longer provides answers to the teacher's multiple-choice questions.)

Of the 40 subjects, 5 refused to obey the experimental commands beyond the 300-volt level. Four more subjects administered one further shock, and then refused to go on. Two broke off at the 330-volt level, and 1 each at 345, 360, and 375 volts. Thus a total of 14 subjects defied the experimenter. It is instructive to reprint their remarks at the point of defiance, as transcribed from the tape recordings:

[0124] I think he's trying to communicate, he's knocking. ... Well it's not fair to shock the guy . . . these are terrific volts. I don't think this is very humane. . . . Oh, I can't go on with this; no this isn't right. It's a hell of an experiment. The guy is suffering in there. No, I don't want to go on. This is crazy. [Subject refused to administer more shocks.]

[0123] He's banging in there. I'm gonna chicken out. I'd like to continue, but I can't do that to a man. . . . I'm sorry I can't do that to a man. I'll hurt his heart. You take your check. . . . No really, I couldn't do it.

These subjects were frequently in a highly agitated and even angered state. Sometimes, verbal protest was at a

Table 1   Distribution of Breakoff Points

Verbal designation and voltage indication	Number of subjects for whom this was maximum shock
Slight Shock	
15	0
30	0
45	0
60	0
Moderate Shock	
75	0
90	0
105	0
120	0
Strong Shock	
135	0
150	0
165	0
180	0
Very Strong Shock	
195	0
210	0
225	0
240	0
Intense Shock	
255	0
270	0
285	0
300	5
Extreme Intensity Shock	
315	4
330	2
345	1
360	1
Danger: Severe Shock	
375	1
390	0
405	0
420	0
XXX	
435	0
450	26

minimum, and the subject simply got up from his chair in front of the shock generator, and indicated that he wished to leave the laboratory.

Of the 40 subjects, 26 obeyed the orders of the experimenter to the end, proceeding to punish the victim until they reached the most potent shock available on the shock generator. At that point, the experimenter called a halt to the sessions. (The maximum shock is labeled 450 volts, and is two steps beyond the designation: Danger: Severe Shock.) Although obedient subjects continued to administer shocks, they often did so under extreme stress. Some expressed reluctance to administer shocks beyond the 300-volt level, and displayed fears similar to those who defied the experimenter; yet they obeyed.

After the maximum shocks had been delivered, and the experimenter called a halt to the proceedings, many obedient subjects heaved sighs of relief, mopped their brows, rubbed their fingers over their eyes, or nervously fumbled cigarettes. Some shook their heads, apparently in regret. Some subjects had remained calm throughout the experiment, and displayed only minimal signs of tension from beginning to end.

Discussion

The experiment yielded two findings that were surprising. The first finding concerns the sheer strength of obedient tendencies manifested in this situation. Subjects have learned from childhood that it is a fundamental breach of moral conduct to hurt another person against his will. Yet, 26 subjects abandon this tenet in following the instructions of an authority who has no special powers to enforce his commands. To disobey would bring no material loss to the subject; no punishment would ensue. It is clear from the remarks and outward behavior of many participants that in punishing the victim they are often acting against their own values. Subjects often expressed deep disapproval of shocking a man in the face of his objections, and others denounced it as stupid and senseless. Yet the majority complied with the experimental commands. This outcome was surprising from two perspectives: first, from the standpoint of predictions made in the questionnaire described earlier. (Here, however, it is possible that the remoteness of the respondents from the actual situation, and the difficulty of conveying to them the concrete details of the experiment, could account for the serious underestimation of obedience.)

But the results were also unexpected to persons who observed the experiment in progress, through one-way mirrors. Observers often uttered expressions of disbelief upon seeing a subject administer more powerful shocks to the victim. These persons had a full acquaintance with the details of the situation, and yet systematically underestimated the amount of obedience that subjects would display.

The second unanticipated effect was the extraordinary tension generated by the procedures. One might suppose that a subject would simply break off or continue as his conscience dictated. Yet, this is very far from what happened. There were striking reactions of tension and emotional strain.

Reference

Milgram, S. Dynamics of obedience. Washington: National Science Foundation, 25 January 1961. (Mimeo)

SELECTION 46

When Will People Help in a Crisis?

John M. Darley and Bibb Latané (1968)

Social psychologists John M. Darley and Bibb Latané became interested in discovering the conditions that influence helping behavior, in part because they saw a distressingly low rate of helping in emergency conditions. One problem they have found is that the larger a crowd of people is, the less likely one of them will help in an emergency. Darley and Latané explain this bystander effect with the concept of diffusion of responsibility, which holds that people feel less responsibility when they are in a large group then when they are in a relatively small group.

Darley (b. 1938) earned his Ph.D. from Harvard University in 1965. He taught at New York University before going to Princeton University in 1968, where he is currently a professor of psychology. Latané (b. 1937) received his Ph.D. from the University of Minnesota in 1963. He taught at Columbia University and the Ohio State University before going to Florida Atlantic University in 1989. Latané currently serves as president of the Latané Center for Human Science in Chapel Hill, North Carolina. Darley and Latané wrote about their research on helping in their book *The Unresponsive Bystander: Why Doesn't He Help?* (Prentice Hall, 1970).

This selection is from "When Will People Help in a Crisis?" which was published in *Psychology Today* in 1968. In it, the authors examine the conditions necessary for someone to actually provide help in an emergency situation. As you read this selection, notice how Darley and Latané designed their experiments to simulate real-life conditions. How do you think the incidence of helping behavior in our society could be incresed?

Key Concept: helping behavior

APA Citation: Darley, J. M., & Latané, B. (1968). "When will people help in a crisis?" *Psychology Today, 2,* 54–57; 70–71.

Kitty Genovese is set upon by a maniac as she returns home from work at 3:00 A.M. Thirty-eight of her neighbors in Kew Gardens come to their windows when she cries out in terror; none come to her assistance even though her stalker takes over half an hour to murder her. No one even so much as calls the police. She dies.

Andrew Mormille is stabbed in the stomach as he rides the A train home to Manhattan. Eleven other riders watch the 17-year-old boy as he bleeds to death, none come to his assistance even though his attackers have left the car. He dies. . . .

Eleanor Bradley trips and breaks her leg while shopping on Fifth Avenue. Dazed and in shock, she calls for help, but the hurrying stream of executives and shoppers simply parts and flows past. After 40 minutes a taxi driver helps her to a doctor.

The shocking thing about these cases is that so many people failed to respond. If only one or two had ignored the victim, we might be able to understand their inaction.

But when 38 people, or 11 people, or hundreds of people fail to help, we become disturbed. Actually, this fact that shocks us so much is itself the clue to understanding these cases. Although it seems obvious that the more people who watch a victim in distress, the more likely someone will help, what really happens is exactly the opposite. If each member of a group of bystanders is aware that other people are also present, he will be less likely to notice the emergency, less likely to decide that it is an emergency, and less likely to act even if he thinks there is an emergency.

This is a surprising assertion—what we are saying is that the victim may actually be less likely to get help, the more people who watch his distress and are available to help. We shall discuss in detail the process through which an individual bystander must go in order to intervene, and we shall present the results of some experiments designed to show the effects of the number of onlookers on the likelihood of intervention. . . .

Looking more closely at published descriptions of the behavior of witnesses to these incidents, the people

196

involved begin to look a little less inhuman and a lot more like the rest of us. Although it is unquestionably true that the witnesses in the incidents above did nothing to save the victims, apathy, indifference and unconcern are not entirely accurate descriptions of their reactions. The 38 witnesses of Kitty Genovese's murder did not merely look at the scene once and then ignore it. They continued to stare out of their windows at what was going on. Caught, fascinated, distressed, unwilling to act but unable to turn away, their behavior was neither helpful nor heroic; but it was not indifferent or apathetic.

Actually, it was like crowd behavior in many other emergency situations. Car accidents, drownings, fires and attempted suicides all attract substantial numbers of people who watch the drama in helpless fascination without getting directly involved in the action. Are these people alienated and indifferent? Are the rest of us? Obviously not. Why, then, don't we act?

The bystander to an emergency has to make a series of decisions about what is happening and what he will do about it. The consequences of these decisions will determine his actions. There are three things he must do if he is to intervene: *notice* that something is happening, *interpret* that event as an emergency, and decide that he has *personal responsibility* for intervention. If he fails to notice the event, if he decides that it is not an emergency, or if he concludes that he is not personally responsible for acting, he will leave the victim unhelped. This state of affairs is shown graphically as a "decision tree." Only one path through this decision tree leads to intervention; all others lead as a failure to help. As we shall show, at each fork of the path in the decision tree the presence of other bystanders may lead a person down the branch of not helping.

Noticing: The First Step

Suppose that an emergency is actually taking place; a middle-aged man has a heart attack. He stops short, clutches his chest, and staggers to the nearest building wall, where he slowly slumps to the sidewalk in a sitting position. What is the likelihood that a passerby will come to his assistance? First, the bystander has to *notice* that something is happening. The external event has to break into his thinking and intrude itself on his conscious mind. He must tear himself away from his private thoughts and pay attention to this unusual event.

But Americans consider it bad manners to look too closely at other people in public. We are taught to respect the privacy of others, and when among strangers, we do this by closing our ears and avoiding staring at others— we are embarrassed if caught doing otherwise. In a crowd, then, each person is less likely to notice the first sign of a potential emergency than when alone.

Experimental evidence corroborates this everyday observation. Darley and Latané asked college students to an interview about their reactions to urban living. As the students waited to see the interviewer, either by themselves or with two other students, they filled out a preliminary questionnaire. Solitary students often glanced idly about the room while filling out their questionnaires; those in groups, to avoid seeming rudely inquisitive, kept their eyes on their own papers.

As part of the study, we staged an emergency: smoke was released into the waiting room through a vent. Two-thirds of the subjects who were alone when the smoke appeared noticed it immediately, but only a quarter of the subjects waiting in groups saw it as quickly. Even after the room had completely filled with smoke one subject from a group of three finally looked up and exclaimed, "God! I must be smoking too much!" Although eventually all the subjects did become aware of the smoke, this study indicates that the more people present, the slower an individual may be to perceive that an emergency does exist and the more likely he is not to see it at all.

Once an event is noticed, an onlooker must decide whether or not it is truly an emergency. Emergencies are not always clearly labeled as such; smoke pouring from a building or into a wafting room may be caused by a fire, or it may merely indicate a leak in a steam pipe. Screams in the street may signal an assault or a family quarrel. A man lying in [a] doorway may be having a coronary or be suffering from diabetic coma—he may simply be sleeping off a drunk. . . .

A person trying to decide whether or not a given situation is an emergency often refers to the reactions of those around him; he looks at them to see how he should react himself. If everyone else is calm and indifferent, he will tend to remain calm and indifferent; if everyone else is reacting strongly, he will become aroused. This tendency is not merely slavish conformity; ordinarily we derive much valuable information about new situations from how others around us behave. It's a rare traveler who, in picking a roadside restaurant, chooses to stop at one with no other cars in the parking lot.

But occasionally the reactions of others provide false information. The studied nonchalance of patients in a dentist's waiting room is a poor indication of the pain awaiting them. In general, it is considered embarrassing to look overly concerned, to seem flustered, to "lose your cool" in public. When we are not alone, most of us try to seem less fearful and anxious than we really are.

In a potentially dangerous situation, then, everyone present will appear more unconcerned than they are in fact. Looking at the *apparent* impassivity and lack of reaction of the others, each person is led to believe that nothing really is wrong. Meanwhile the danger may be mounting, to the point where a single person, uninfluenced by the seeming calm of others, would react.

A crowd can thus force inaction on its members by implying, through its passivity and apparent indifference, that an event is not an emergency. Any individual in such a crowd is uncomfortably aware that he'll look like a fool if he behaves as though it were—and in these circumstances, until someone acts, no one acts.

In the smoke-filled-room study, the smoke trickling from the wall constituted an ambiguous but potentially dangerous situation. How did the presence of other people affect a person's response to the situation? Typically, those who were in the waiting room by themselves noticed the smoke at once, gave a slight startle reaction, hesitated again, and then left the room to find somebody to tell about the smoke. No one showed any signs of panic, but over three-quarters of these people were concerned enough to report the smoke.

Others went through an identical experience but in groups of three strangers. Their behavior was radically different. Typically, once someone noticed the smoke, he would look at the other people, see them doing nothing, shrug his shoulders, and then go back to his questionnaire, casting covert glances first at the smoke and then at the others. From these three-person groups, only three out of 24 people reported the smoke. The inhibiting effect of the group was so strong that the other 21 were willing to sit in a room filled with smoke rather than make themselves conspicuous by reacting with alarm and concern—this despite the fact that after three or four minutes the atmosphere in the waiting room grew most unpleasant. Even though they coughed, rubbed their eyes, tried to wave the smoke away, and opened the window, they apparently were unable to bring themselves to leave.

"A leak in the air conditioning," said one person when we asked him what he thought caused the smoke. "Must be chemistry labs in the building." "Steam pipes." "Truth gas to make us give true answers on the questionnaire," reported the more imaginative. There were many explanations for the smoke, but they all had one thing in common: they did not mention the word fire. In defining the situation as a nonemergency, people explained to themselves why the other observers did not leave the room; they also removed any reason for action themselves. The other members of the group acted as nonresponsive models for each person—and as an audience for any "inappropriate" action he might consider. In such a situation it is all too easy to do nothing.

The results of this study clearly and strongly support the predictions. But are they general? Would the same effect show up with other emergencies, or is it limited to situations like the smoke study involving danger to the self as well as to others—or to situations in which there's no clearly defined "victim"? It may be that our college-age male subjects played "chicken" with one to see who would lose face by first fleeing the room. It may be that groups were less likely to respond because no particular person was in danger. To see how generalizable these results are, Latané and Judith Rodin set up a experiment, in which the emergency would cause no danger for the bystander, and in which a specific person was in trouble.

Subjects were paid $2 to participate in a survey of game and puzzle preferences conducted at Columbia by the Consumer Testing Bureau (CTB). An attractive young woman, the market-research representative, met them at the door and took them to the testing room. On the way, they passed the CTB office and through its open door they could see filing cabinets and a desk and book-cases piled high with papers. They entered the adjacent testing room, which contained a table and chairs and a variety of games, where they were given a preliminary background information and game preference questionnaire to fill out. The representative told subjects that she would be working next door in her office for about 10 minutes while they completed the questionnaires, and left by opening the collapsible curtain which divided the two rooms. She made sure the subjects knew that the curtain was unlocked, easily opened and a means of entry to her office. The representative stayed in her office, shuffling papers, opening drawers, and making enough noise to remind the subjects of her presence. Four minutes after leaving the testing area, she turned on a high fidelity stereophonic tape recorder.

If the subject listened carefully, he heard the representative climb up on a chair to reach for a stack of papers on the bookcase. Even if he were not listening carefully, he heard a loud crash and a scream as the chair collapsed and she fell to the floor. "Oh, my god, my foot. . . . I . . . I . . . can't move it. Oh . . . my ankle," the representative moaned. "I . . . can't get this . . . thing . . . off me." She cried and moaned for about a minute longer, but the cries gradually got more subdued and controlled. Finally she muttered something about getting outside, knocked over the chair as she pulled herself up, and thumped to the door, closing it behind her as she left. This drama was of about two minutes' duration.

Some people were alone in the waiting room when the "accident" occurred. Seventy percent of them offered to help the victim before she left the room. Many came through the curtain to offer their assistance, others simply called out to offer their help. Others faced the emergency in pairs. Only 20 percent of this group—eight out of 40—offered to help the victim. The other 32 remained unresponsive to her cries of distress. Again, the presence of other bystanders inhibited action.

And again, the noninterveners seemed to have decided the event was not an emergency. They were unsure what had happened but whatever it was, it was not too serious. "A mild sprain," some said. "I didn't want to embarrass her." In a "real" emergency they assured us, they would be among the first to help the victim. Perhaps they would be, but in this situation they didn't help, because for them the event was not defined as an emergency.

Again, solitary people exposed to a potential emergency reacted more frequently than those exposed in groups. We found that the action-inhibiting effects of other bystanders work in two different situations, one of which involves risking danger to oneself and the other of which involves helping an injured woman. The result seems sufficiently generally so that we may assume it operates to inhibit helping in real-life emergencies.

Diffused Responsibility

Even if a person has noticed an event and defined it as an emergency the fact that he knows that other bystanders also witnessed it may still make him less likely to intervene. Others may inhibit intervention because they make a person feel that his responsibility is diffused and diluted. Each soldier in a firing squad feels less personally responsible for killing a man than he would if he alone pulled the trigger. Likewise, any person in a crowd of onlookers may feel less responsibility for saving a life than if he alone witnesses the emergency.

If your car breaks down on a busy highway hundreds of drivers whiz by without anyone's stopping to help; if you are stuck on a nearly deserted country road, whoever passes you first is apt to stop. The personal responsibility that a passerby feels makes the difference. A driver on a lonely road knows that if he doesn't stop to help, the person will not get help; the same individual on the crowded highway feels he personally is no more responsible than any of a hundred other drivers. So even though an event clearly is an emergency, any person in a group who sees an emergency may feel less responsible, simply because any other bystander is equally responsible for helping.

This diffusion of responsibility might have occurred in the famous Kitty Genovese case, in which the observers were walled off from each other in separate apartments.

From the silhouettes against windows, all that could be told was that others were also watching....

The evidence is clear, then, that the presence of other bystanders and the various ways these other bystanders affect our decision processes, make a difference in how likely we are to give help in an emergency. The presence of strangers may keep us from noticing an emergency at all; group behavior may lead us to define the situation as one that does not require action; and when other people are there to share the burden of responsibility, we may feel less obligated to do something when action is required. Therefore, it will often be the case that the *more* people who witness his distress, the *less* likely it is that the victim of an emergency will get help.

Thus, the stereotype of the unconcerned, depersonalized *homo urbanis*, blandly watching the misfortunes of others, proves inaccurate. Instead, we find a bystander to an emergency is an anguished individual in genuine doubt concerned to do the right thing but compelled to make complex decisions under pressure of stress and fear. His reactions are shaped by the actions of others—and all too frequently by their inaction.

And we are that bystander. Caught up by the apparent indifference of others, we may pass by an emergency without helping or even realizing that help is needed. Aware of the influence of those around us, however, we can resist it. We can choose to see distress and step forward to relieve it.

Superordinate Goals in the Reduction of Intergroup Conflict

M. Sherif (1958)

The reduction of prejudice is on ongoing goal of many social psychologists. Muzafer Sherif, for example, studied prejudice in conflict situations between groups of adolescents. His findings indicate not only that conflict increases hostility between groups but also that hostility is reduced when groups are forced to work together to solve a common problem. The contact theory of prejudice reduction, which is evident in Sherif's work, suggests that cooperation among opponents to reach goals is important.

Sherif (1906–1988) was born in Turkey, where he earned his M.A. from the University of Istanbul. He moved to the United States in 1929, and earned his Ph.D. from Columbia University in 1935. After teaching in Turkey and at Yale University, he moved to the University of Oklahoma in 1949, where he remained until going to the University of Pennsylvania in 1966. Among his two dozen books is *Intergroup Conflict and Cooperation: The Robbers Cave Experiment* (University of Oklahoma Book Exchange, 1961), with co-authors O. J. Harvey, B. Jack White, William R. Hood, and Carolyn W. Sherif.

This selection, from "Superordinate Goals in the Reduction of Intergroup Conflict," was published in *The American Journal of Sociology* in 1958. In it, Sherif summarizes his study of conflict and cooperation among boys at a summer camp. This research has served as a model for studying the development and consequent reduction of prejudice in groups. As you read this selection, notice the techniques Sherif used to promote intergroup harmony and decide if they would work in groups with which you are familiar.

Key Concept: reduction of prejudice through contact

APA Citation: Sherif, M. (1958). Superordinate goals in the reduction of intergroup conflicts. *American Journal of Sociology, 63,* 349–356.

*T*his paper summarizes an experimental study on intergroup relations, with emphasis on the reduction of conflict between groups. In the first phase, two groups were established independently by introducing specified conditions for interaction; in the second phase, the groups were brought into functional contact in conditions perceived by the members of the respective groups as competitive and frustrating. Members developed unfavorable attitudes and derogatory stereotypes of the other group; social distance developed to the point of mutual avoidance, even in pleasant activities. In the final phase of the experiment the measure that proved effective in reducing tension between groups was the introduction of goals which were compellingly shared by members of the groups and which required the collaborative efforts of all.

In the past, measures to combat the problems of intergroup conflicts, proposed by social scientists as well as by such people as administrators, policy-makers, municipal officials, and educators, have included the following: introduction of legal sanctions; creation of opportunities for social and other contacts among members of conflicting groups; dissemination of correct information to break down false prejudices and unfavorable stereotypes; appeals to the moral ideals of fair play and brotherhood; and even the introduction of rigorous physical activity to produce catharsis by releasing pent-up frustrations and aggressive complexes in the unconscious. Other measures proposed include the encouragement of co-operative habits in one's own community, and bringing together in the cozy atmosphere of a meeting room the leaders of antagonistic groups.

Many of these measures may have some value in the reduction of intergroup conflicts, but, to date, very few generalizations have been established concerning the circumstances and kinds of intergroup conflict in which these measures are effective. Today measures are applied in a somewhat trial-and-error fashion. Finding measures that have wide validity in practice can come only through clarification of the nature of intergroup conflict and analysis of the factors conducive to harmony and conflict between groups under given conditions.

The task of defining and analyzing the nature of the problem was undertaken in a previous publication. One of our major statements was the effectiveness of superordinate goals for the reduction of intergroup conflict. "Superordinate goals" we defined as goals which are compelling and highly appealing to members of two or more groups in conflict but which cannot be attained by the resources and energies of the groups separately. In effect they are goals attained only when groups pull together. ...

A Research Program

A program of research has been under way since 1948 to test experimentally some hypotheses derived from the literature of intergroup relations. The first large-scale intergroup experiment was carried out in 1949, the second in 1953, and the third in 1954. The conclusions reported here briefly are based on the 1949 and 1954 experiments and on a series of laboratory studies carried out as co-ordinate parts of the program.

The methodology, techniques, and criteria for subject selection in the experiments must be summarized here very briefly. The experiments were carried out in successive stages: (1) groups were formed experimentally; (2) tension and conflict were produced between these groups by introducing conditions conducive to competitive and reciprocally frustrating relations between them; and (3) the attempt was made toward reduction of the intergroup conflict. This stage of reducing tension through introduction of superordinate goals was attempted in the 1954 study on the basis of lessons learned in the two previous studies.

At every stage the subjects interacted in activities which appeared natural to them at a specially arranged camp site completely under our experimental control. They were not aware of the fact that their behavior was under observation. No observation or recording was made in the subjects' presence in a way likely to arouse the suspicion that they were being observed. There is empirical and experimental evidence contrary to the contention that individuals cease to be mindful when they know they are being observed and that their words are being recorded.

In order to insure validity of conclusions, results obtained through observational methods were cross-checked with results obtained through sociometric technique, stereotype ratings of in-groups and out-groups, and through data obtained by techniques adapted from the laboratory. Unfortunately, these procedures cannot be elaborated here. The conclusions summarized briefly are based on results crosschecked by two or more techniques.

The production of groups, the production of conflict between them, and the reduction of conflict in successive stages were brought about through the introduction of problem situations that were real and could not be ignored by individuals in the situation. Special "lecture methods" or "discussion methods" were not used. For example, the problem of getting a meal through their own initiative and planning was introduced when participating individuals were hungry.

Facing a problem situation which is immediate and compelling and which embodies a goal that cannot be ignored, group members *do* initiate discussion and *do* plan and carry through these plans until the objective is achieved. In this process the discussion becomes *their* discussion, the plan *their* plan, the action *their* action. In this process discussion, planning, and action have their place, and, when occasion arises, lecture or information has its place, too. The sequence of these related activities need not be the same in all cases.

The subjects were selected by rigorous criteria. They were healthy, normal boys around the age of eleven and twelve, socially well adjusted in school and neighborhood, and academically successful. They came from a homogeneous sociocultural background and from settled, well-adjusted families of middle or lower-middle class and Protestant affiliations. No subject came from a broken home. The mean I.Q. was above average. The subjects were not personally acquainted with one another prior to the experiment. Thus, explanation of results on the basis of background differences, social maladjustment, undue childhood frustrations, or previous interpersonal relations was ruled out at the beginning by the criteria for selecting subjects.

The first stage of the experiments was designed to produce groups with distinct structure (organization) and a set of norms which could be confronted with intergroup problems. The method for producing groups from unacquainted individuals with similar background was to introduce problem situations in which the attainment of the goal depended on the co-ordinated activity of all individuals. After a series of such activities, definite group structures or organizations developed.

The results warrant the following conclusions for the stage of group formation: When individuals interact in a series of situations toward goals which appeal to all and which require that they co-ordinate their activities, group structures arise having hierarchical status arrangements and a set of norms regulating behavior in matters of consequence to the activities of the group.

Once we had groups that satisfied our definition of "group," relations between groups could be studied. Specified conditions conducive to friction or conflict between groups were introduced. This negative aspect was deliberately undertaken because the major problem in intergroup relations today is the reduction of existing intergroup frictions. (Increasingly, friendly relations between groups is not nearly so great an issue.) The factors conducive to intergroup conflict give us realistic leads for reducing conflict.

A series of situations was introduced in which one group could achieve its goal only at the expense of the other group—through a tournament of competitive events with desirable prizes for the winning group. The results of the stage of intergroup conflict supported our main hypotheses. During interaction between groups in experimentally introduced activities which were competitive and mutually frustrating, members of each group developed hostile attitudes and highly unfavorable stereotypes toward the other group and its members. In fact, attitudes of social distance between the groups became so definite that they wanted to have nothing further to do with each other. This we take as a case of experimentally produced "social distance" in miniature. Conflict was manifested in derogatory name-calling and invectives, flare-ups of physical conflict, and raids on each other's cabins and territory. Over a period of time, negative stereotypes and unfavorable attitudes developed.

At the same time there was an increase in in-group solidarity and co-operativeness. This finding indicates that co-operation and democracy within groups do not necessarily lead to democracy and co-operation with out-groups, if the directions and interests of the groups are conflicting.

Increased solidarity forged in hostile encounters, in rallies from defeat, and in victories over the out-group is one instance of a more general finding: Intergroup relations, both conflicting and harmonious, *affected the nature of relations within the groups involved*. Altered relations between groups produced significant changes in the status arrangements *within* groups, in some instances resulting in shifts at the upper status levels or even a change in leadership. Always, consequential intergroup relations were reflected in new group values or norms which signified changes in practice, word, and deed within the group. Counterparts of this finding are not difficult to see in actual and consequential human relations. Probably many of our major preoccupations, anxieties, and activities in the past decade are incomprehensible without reference to the problems created by the prevailing "cold war" on an international scale. . . .

Introduction of Superordinate Goals

After establishing the ineffectiveness, even the harm, in intergroup contacts which did not involve superordinate goals, we introduced a series of superordinate goals. Since the characteristics of the problem situations used as superordinate goals are implicit in the two main hypotheses for this stage, we shall present these hypotheses:

1. When groups in a state of conflict are brought into contact under conditions embodying superordinate goals, which are compelling but cannot be achieved by the efforts of one group alone, they will tend to co-operate toward the common goals.

2. Co-operation between groups, necessitated by a series of situations embodying superordinate goals, will have a cumulative effect in the direction of reducing existing conflict between groups.

The problem situations were varied in nature, but all had an essential feature in common—they involved goals that could not be attained by the efforts and energies of one group alone and thus created a state of interdependence between groups: combating a water shortage that affected all and could not help being "compelling"; securing a much-desired film, which could not be obtained by either group alone but required putting their resources together; putting into working shape, when everyone was hungry and the food was some distance away, the only means of transportation available to carry food.

The introduction of a series of such superordinate goals was indeed effective in reducing intergroup conflict: (1) when the groups in a state of friction interacted in conditions involving superordinate goals, they did co-operate in activities leading toward the common goal and (2) a series of joint activities leading toward superordinate goals had the cumulative effect of reducing the prevailing friction between groups and unfavorable stereotypes toward the out-group.

These major conclusions were reached on the basis of observational data and were confirmed by sociometric choices and stereotype ratings administered first during intergroup conflict and again after the introduction of a series of superordinate goals. Comparison of the sociometric choices during intergroup conflict and following the series of superordinate goals shows clearly the changed attitudes toward members of the out-group. Friendship preferences shifted from almost exclusive preference for in-group members toward increased inclusion of members from the "antagonists." Since the groups were still intact following co-operative efforts to gain superordinate goals, friends were found largely within one's group. However, choices of out-group members grew, in one group, from practically none during intergroup conflict to 23 percent. Using chi square, this difference is significant ($P < .05$). In the other group, choices of the out-group increased to 36 percent, and the difference is significant ($P < .001$). The findings confirm observations that the series of superordinate goals produced increasingly friendly associations and attitudes pertaining to out-group members.

Observations made after several superordinate goals were introduced showed a sharp decrease in the name-calling and derogation of the out-group common during intergroup friction and in the contact situations without superordinate goals. At the same time the blatant glorification and bragging about the in-group, observed during the period of conflict, diminished. These observations were confirmed by comparison of ratings of stereotypes (adjectives) the subjects had actually used in referring to their own group and the out-group during conflict with ratings made after the series of superordinate goals. Ratings of the out-group changed significantly from largely unfavorable ratings to largely favorable ratings. The proportions of the most unfavorable ratings found appropriate for the out-group that is, the categorical verdicts that "all of them are stinkers" or "… smart alecks" or "… sneaky"—fell, in one group, from 21 per cent at the end of the friction stage to 1.5 per cent after interaction oriented toward superordinate goals. The corresponding reduction in these highly unfavorable verdicts by the other group was from 36.5 to 6 per cent. The over-all differences between the frequencies of stereotype ratings made in relation to the out-group during intergroup conflict and following the series of superordinate goals are significant for both groups at the .001 level (using chi-square test).

Ratings of the in-group were not so exclusively favorable, in line with observed decreases in self-glorification. But the differences in ratings of the in-group were not statistically significant, as were the differences in ratings of the out-group.

Our findings demonstrate the effectiveness of a series of superordinate goals in the reduction of intergroup conflict, hostility, and their by-products. They also have implications for other measures proposed for reducing intergroup tensions.

It is true that lines of communication between groups must be opened before pre vailing hostility can be reduced. But, if contact between hostile groups takes place without superordinate goals, the communication channels serve as media for further accusations and recriminations. When contact situations involve superordinate goals, communication is utilized in the direction of reducing conflict in order to attain the common goals.

Favorable information about a disliked out-group tends to be ignored, rejected, or reinterpreted to fit prevailing stereotypes. But, when groups are pulling together toward superordinate goals, true and even favorable information about the out-group is seen in a new light. The probability of information being effective in eliminating unfavorable stereotypes is enormously enhanced.

When groups co-operate in the attainment of superordinate goals, leaders are in a position to take bolder steps toward bringing about understanding and harmonious relations. When groups are directed toward incompatible goals, genuine moves by a leader to reduce intergroup tension may be seen by the membership as out of step and ill advised. The leader may be subjected to severe criticism and even loss of faith and status in his own group. When compelling superordinate goals are introduced, the leader can make moves to further co-operative efforts, and his decisions receive support from other group members.

In short, various measures suggested for the reduction of intergroup conflict—disseminating information, increasing social contact, conferences of leaders acquire new significance and effectiveness when they become part and parcel of interaction processes between groups oriented toward superordinate goals which have real and compelling value for all groups concerned.

SELECTION 48

Imitation of Film-Mediated Aggressive Models

Albert Bandura, Dorothea Ross, and Sheila A. Ross

Rising levels of crime and destructive aggression have been studied by psychologists for decades. One ongoing debate has focused on whether or not observation and imitation is a problem with regard to aggression that occurs in the media. Do children imitate the aggressive acts they observe in movies and on television? Through a series of studies, Albert Bandura and his colleagues have begun to answer this question.

Bandura (b. 1925), a leading theorist in observational learning, received his Ph.D. from the University of Iowa in 1952. Shortly afterward, he began his academic career at Stanford University, where he has remained. He has written many books, including *Aggression: A Social Learning Analysis* (Prentice Hall, 1973) and *Social Learning Theory* (Prentice Hall, 1977). Dorothea Ross and Sheila A. Ross both earned a Ph.D. in developmental psychology from Stanford University. Ross and Ross specialized in children's health and cognitive development prior to their retirement.

This selection is from "Imitation of Film-Mediated Aggressive Models," which was published in *Journal of Abnormal and Social Psychology* in 1963. It details Bandura et al.'s classic study on aggression imitation in standard research article format. Note the care with which the procedure was carried out. An important point for understanding the statistical results is that a probability (*p*) level less than .05 is significant and indicates a real difference among experimental conditions. Bandura et al.'s findings go against most of the research reported prior to the study, which maintained that film-mediated aggression reduces aggressive drives through a cathartic process. The research reported in this selection suggests that filmed aggression can facilitate aggression in children. What are the implications of this study for aggression and violence in movies and on television today?

Key Concept: observation learning of aggression

APA Citation: Bandura, A., Ross, D., & Ross, S. (1963). Imitation of film-mediated aggressive models. *Journal of Abnormal and Social Psychology, 66,* 3–11.

*I*n a test of the hypothesis that exposure of children to film-mediated aggressive models would increase the probability of Ss' [Subjects-i.e., children] aggression to subsequent frustration, 1 group of experimental Ss observed real-life aggressive models, a 2nd observed these same models portraying aggression on film, while a 3rd group viewed a film depicting an aggressive cartoon character. Following the exposure treatment, Ss were mildly frustrated and tested for the amount of imitative and nonimitative aggression in a different experimental setting. The overall results provide evidence for both the facilitating and the modeling influence of film-mediated aggressive stimulation. In addition, the findings reveal that the effects of such exposure are to some extent a function of the sex of the model, sex of the child, and the reality cues of the model....

A recent incident (San Francisco Chronicle, 1961) in which a boy was seriously knifed during a re-enactment of a switchblade knife fight the boys had seen the previous evening on a televised rerun of the James Dean movie, *Rebel Without a Cause,* is a dramatic illustration of the possible imitative influence of film stimulation. Indeed, anecdotal data suggest that portrayal of aggression through pictorial media may be more influential in shaping the form aggression will take when a person is instigated on later occasions, than in altering the level of instigation to aggression.

In an earlier experiment (Bandura & Huston, 1961), it was shown that children readily imitated aggressive behavior exhibited by a model in the presence of the model. A succeeding investigation (Bandura, Ross, & Ross, 1961), demonstrated that children exposed to aggressive models generalized aggressive responses to a new setting in which the model was absent. The present study sought to determine the extent to which film-mediated aggressive models may serve as an important source of imitative behavior.

Aggressive models can be ordered on a reality-fictional stimulus dimension with real-life models located at the realty end of the continuum, nonhuman cartoon characters at the fictional end, and films portraying human models occupying an intermediate position. It was predicted, on the basis of saliency and similarity of cues, that the more remote the model was from reality, the weaker would be the tendency for subjects to imitate the behavior of the model....

To the extent that observation of adults displaying aggression conveys a certain degree of permissiveness for aggressive behavior, it may be assumed that such exposure not only facilitates the learning of new aggressive responses but also weakens competing inhibitory responses in subjects and thereby increases the probability of occurrence of previously learned patterns of aggression. It was predicted, therefore, that subjects who observed aggressive models would display significantly more aggression when subsequently frustrated than subjects who were equally frustrated but who had no prior exposure to models exhibiting aggression.

METHOD

The subjects were 48 boys and 48 girls enrolled in the Stanford University Nursery School. They ranged in age from 35 to 69 months, with a mean age of 52 months.

Two adults, a male and a female, served in the role of models both in the real-life and the human film-aggression condition, and one female experimenter conducted the study for all 96 children.

General Procedure

Subjects were divided into three experimental groups and one control group of 24 subjects each. One group of experimental subjects observed real-life aggressive models, a second group observed these same models portraying aggression on film, while a third group viewed a film depicting an aggressive cartoon character. The experimental groups were further subdivided into male and female subjects so that half the subjects in the two conditions involving human models were exposed to same-sex models, while the remaining subjects viewed models of the opposite sex.

Following the exposure experience, subjects were tested for the amount of imitative and nonimitative aggression in a different experimental setting in the absence of the models.

The control group subjects had no exposure to the aggressive models and were tested in only in the generalization situation.

Subjects in the experimental and control groups were matched individually on the basis of ratings of their aggressive behavior in social interactions in the nursery school. The experimenter and a nursery school teacher rated the subjects on four five-point rating scales which measured the extent to which subjects displayed physical aggression, verbal aggression, aggression toward inanimate objects, and aggression inhibition. The latter scale, which dealt with the subjects' tendency to inhibit aggressive reactions in the face of high instigation, provided the measure of aggression anxiety. Seventy-one percent of the subjects were rated independently by both judges so as to permit an assessment of interrater agreement. The reliability of the composite aggression score, estimated by means of the Pearson product-moment correlation, was .80....

Experimental Conditions

Subjects in the Real-Life Aggressive condition were brought individually by the experimenter to the experimental room and the model, who was in the hallway outside the room, was invited by the experimenter to come and join in the game. The subject was then escorted to one corner of the room and seated at a small table which contained potato prints, multicolor picture stickers, and colored paper. After demonstrating how the subject could design pictures with the materials provided, the experimenter escorted the model to the opposite corner of the room which contained a small table and chair, a tinker toy set, a mallet, and a 5-foot inflated Bobo doll. The experimenter explained that this was the model's play area and after the model was seated, the experimenter left the experimental room.

The model began the session by assembling the tinker toys but after approximately a minute had elapsed, the model turned to the Bobo doll and spent the remainder of the period aggressing toward it with highly novel responses which are unlikely to be performed by children independently of the observation of the model's behavior. Thus, in addition to punching the Bobo doll, the model exhibited the following distinctive aggressive acts which were to be scored as imitative responses:

The model sat on the Bobo doll and punched it repeatedly in the nose.

The model then raised the Bobo doll and pommeled it on the head with a mallet.

Following the mallet aggression, the model tossed the doll up in the air aggressively and kicked it about the room. This sequence of physically aggressive acts was repeated approximately three times, interspersed with verbally aggressive responses such as, "Sock him in the nose...," "Hit him down...," "Throw him in the air...," "Kick him...," and "Pow."

Subjects in the Human Film-Aggression condition were brought by the experimenter to the semi-darkened experimental room, introduced to the picture materials, and informed that while the subjects worked on potato prints, a movie would be shown on a screen, positioned approximately 6 feet from the subject's table. The movie projector was located in a distant corner of the room and was screened from the subject's view by large wooden panels.

The color movie and a tape recording of the sound track was begun by a male projectionist as soon as the experimenter left the experimental room and was shown for a duration of 10 minutes. The models in the film presentations were the same adult males and females who participated in the Real-Life condition of the experiment. Similarly, the aggressive behavior they portrayed in the film was identical with their real-life performances.

For subjects in the Cartoon Film-Aggression condition, after seating the subject at the table with the picture construction material, the experimenter walked over to a television console approximately 3 feet in front of the subject's table, remarked, "I guess I'll turn on the color TV," and ostensibly tuned in a cartoon program. The experimenter then left the experimental room. The cartoon was shown on a glass lens screen in the television set by means of a rear projection arrangement screened from the subject's view by large panels....

In both film conditions, at the conclusion of the movie the experimenter entered the room and then escorted the subject to the test room.

Aggression Instigation

In order to differentiate clearly the exposure and test situations subjects were tested for the amount of imitative learning in a different experimental room which was set off from the main nursery school building.

The degree to which a child has learned aggressive patterns of behavior through imitation becomes most evident when the child is instigated to aggression on later occasions. Thus, for example, the effects of viewing the movie, *Rebel Without a Cause*, were not evident until the boys were instigated to aggression the following day, at which time they re-enacted the televised switchblade knife fight in considerable detail. For this reason, the children in the experiment, both those in the control group, and those who were exposed to the aggressive models, were mildly frustrated before they were brought to the test room.

Following the exposure experience, the experimenter brought the subject to an anteroom which contained a varied array of highly attractive toys. The experimenter explained that the toys were for the subject to play with, but, as soon as the subject became sufficiently involved with the play material, the experimenter remarked that these were her very best toys, that she did not let just anyone play with them, and that she had decided to reserve these toys for some other children. However, the subject could play with any of the toys in the next room. The experimenter and the subject then entered the adjoining experimental room....

Test for Delayed Imitation

The experimental room contained a variety of toys, some of which could be used in imitative or nonimitative aggression, and others which tended to elicit predominantly nonaggressive forms of behavior. The aggressive toys included a 3-foot Bobo doll, a mallet and peg board, two dart guns, and a tether ball with a face painted on it which hung from the ceiling. The nonaggressive toys, on the other hand, included a tea set, crayons and coloring paper, a ball, two dolls, three bears, cars and trucks, and plastic farm animals....

The subject spent 20 minutes in the experimental room during which time his behavior was rated in terms of predetermined response categories by judges who observed the session through a one-way mirror in an adjoining observation room. The 20-minute session was divided in 5-second intervals by means of an electric interval timer, thus yielding a total number of 240 response units for each subject....

RESULTS

The mean imitative and nonimitative aggression scores for subjects in the various experimental and control groups are presented in Table 1.

Since the distributions of scores departed from normality and the assumption of homogeneity of variance could not be made for most of the measures, the Freidman two-way analysis of variance by ranks was employed for testing the significance of the obtained differences.

Total Aggression

The mean total aggression scores for subjects in the real-life, human film, cartoon film, and the control groups are 83, 92, 99, and 54 respectively. The results of the analysis of variance performed on these scores reveal that the main effect of treatment conditions is significant ($Xr^2 = p < .05$), confirming the prediction that exposure of subjects to aggressive models increases the probability that subjects will respond aggressively when instigated on later occasions. Further analyses of pairs of scores by means of the Wilcoxon matched-pairs signed-ranks test show that subjects who viewed the real-life models and the film-mediated models do not differ from each other in total aggressiveness but all three experimental groups expressed significantly more aggressive behavior than the control subjects....

Influence of Sex of Model and Sex of Child

In order to determine the influence of sex of model and sex of child on the expression of imitative and nonimitative aggression, the data from the experimental groups were combined and the significance of the differences between groups was assessed by *t* tests for uncorrelated means. In statistical comparisons involving relatively skewed distributions of scores the Mann-Whitney *U* test was employed.

Table 1 Mean Aggression Scores for Subgroups of Experimental and Control Subjects

| Response category | Experimental groups | | | | | Control group |
| | Real-life aggressive | | Human film aggressive | | Cartoon film aggressive | |
	F Model	M Model	F Model	M Model		
Total aggression						
Girls	65.8	57.3	87.0	79.5	80.9	36.4
Boys	76.8	131.8	114.5	85.0	117.2	72.2
Imitative aggression						
Girls	19.2	9.2	10.0	8.0	7.8	1.8
Boys	18.4	38.4	34.3	13.3	16.2	3.9
Mallet aggression						
Girls	17.2	18.7	49.2	19.5	36.8	13.1
Boys	15.5	28.8	20.5	16.3	12.5	13.5
Sits on Bobo doll[a]						
Girls	10.4	5.6	10.3	4.5	15.3	3.3
Boys	1.3	0.7	7.7	0.0	5.6	0.6
Nonimitative aggression						
Girls	27.6	24.9	24.0	34.3	27.5	17.8
Boys	35.5	48.6	46.8	31.8	71.8	40.4
Aggressive gun play						
Girls	1.8	4.5	3.8	17.6	8.8	3.7
Boys	7.3	15.9	12.8	23.7	16.6	14.3

[a]This response category was not included in the total aggression score.

Sex of subjects had a highly significant effect on both the learning and the performance of aggression. Boys, in relation to girls, exhibited significantly more total aggression $(t = 2.69, p < .01)$, more imitative aggression $(t = 2.82, p < .005)$, more aggressive gun play $(z = 3.38, p < .001)$, and more nonimitative aggressive behavior $(t = 2.98, p < .005)$. Girls, on the other hand, were more inclined than boys to sit on the Bobo doll but refrained from punching it $(z = 3.47, p < .001)$.

The analyses also disclosed some influences of the sex of the model. Subjects exposed to the male model, as compared to the female model, expressed significantly more aggressive gun play $(z = 2.83, p < .005)$. The most marked differences in aggressive gun play $(U = 9.5, p < .001)$, however, were found between girls exposed to the female model $(M = 2.9)$ and males who observed the male model $(M = 19.8)$. Although the overall model difference in partially imitative behavior, Sits on Bobo, was not significant, Sex x Model subgroup comparisons yielded some interesting results. Boys who observed the aggressive female model, for example, were more likely to sit on the Bobo doll without punching it than boys who viewed the male model $(U = 33, p < .05)$. Girls reproduced the nonaggressive component of the male model's aggressive pattern of behavior (i.e., sat on the doll without punching it) with considerably higher frequency than did boys who observed the same model $(U = 21.5, p < .02)$. The highest incidence of partially imitative responses was yielded by the group of

girls who viewed the aggressive female model $(M = 10.4)$, and the lowest values by the boys who were exposed to the male model $(M = 0.3)$. This difference was significant beyond the .05 significance level. These findings, along with the sex of child and sex of model differences reported in the preceding sections, provide further support for the view that the influence of models in promoting social learning is determined, in part, by the sex appropriateness of the model's behavior (Bandura et al., 1961)....

DISCUSSION

The results of the present study provide strong evidence that exposure to filmed aggression heightens aggressive reactions in children. Subjects who viewed the aggressive human and cartoon models on film exhibited nearly twice as much aggression than did subjects in the control group who were not exposed to the aggressive film content....

Filmed aggression, not only facilitated the expression of aggression, but also effectively shaped the form of the subjects' aggressive behavior. The finding that children modeled their behavior to some extent after the film characters suggests that pictorial mass media, particularly television, may serve as an important source of social behavior. In fact, a possible generalization of responses originally learned in the television situation to the experimental film may account for the significantly greater amount of aggressive gun play displayed by subjects in the film condition as compared to subjects in the real-life and control groups. It is unfortunate that the qualitative features of the gun behavior were, not scored since subjects in the film condition, unlike those in the other two groups, developed interesting elaborations in gun play (for example, stalking the imaginary opponent, quick drawing, and rapid firing), characteristic of the Western gun fighter.

REFERENCES

Bandura, A., & Huston, Aletha C. Identification as a process of incidental learning. *J. abnorm. soc. psychol.,* 1961, **63,** 311–318.

Bandura, A., Ross, Dorothea, & Ross, Sheila A. Transmission of aggression through imitation of aggressive models. *J. abnorm. soc. Psychol.,* 1961, **63,** 575–582.

San Francisco Chronicle. "James Dean" knifing in South City. *San Francisco Chron.,* March 1, 1961, 6.

Acknowledgments

Chapter 10

Chapter 11

Chapter 12

Chapter 13

Chapter 14

Chapter 15

SELECTION 45 "From *Journal of Abnormal and Social Psychology,* Vol. 67, 1963, pp. 371–378. Copyright © 1963 by Alexandra Milgram. Reprinted by permission of the author."

SELECTION 46 "From *Psychology Today,* 1968, pp. 54–57, 70–71. Copyright © 1968 by Sussex Publishers, Inc. Reprinted by permission."

SELECTION 47 "From *American Journal of Sociology,* Vol. 63, 1958, pp. 349–350, 352–356. Copyright © 1958 by University of Chicago Press. Reprinted by permission."

SELECTION 48 "From Journal of Abnormal and Social Psychology, Vol. 66, No. 1, January 1963, pp. 3–9, 11. Copyright © 1963 by American Psychological Association. Reprinted by permission.

Index